EMPLOYER'S GUIDE TO

Workplace Torts

EMPLOYER'S GUIDE TO
Workplace Torts

Negligent Hiring, Fraud, Defamation, and Other Emerging Areas of Employer Liability

Ronald M. Green
Richard J. Reibstein

The Bureau of National Affairs, Inc., Washington, D.C.

Copyright © 1992
The Bureau of National Affairs, Inc.

Library of Congress Cataloging-in-Publication Data

Green, Ronald Michael, 1943–
   Employer's guide to workplace torts / Ronald M. Green, Richard J. Reibstein.
     p.   cm.
     Includes index.
     ISBN 0-87179-746-1
     1. Employers' liability—United States.   2. Torts—United States.
I. Reibstein, Richard J.   II. Title.
KF1316.G74   1992
346.7303'1—dc20
[347.30631]
                                                                                                      92-25680
                                                                                                            CIP

Authorization to photocopy items for internal or personal use, or the internal or personal use of specific clients, is granted by BNA Books for libraries and other users registered with the Copyright Clearance Center (CCC) Transactional Reporting Service, provided that $0.50 per page is paid directly to CCC, 27 Congress St., Salem, MA 01970. 0-87179-746-1/92/$0 + .50.

Published by BNA Books, 1250 23rd St., N.W.
Washington, D.C. 20037
Printed in the United States of America
International Standard Book Number 0-87179-746-1

Preface

Despite the emergence of workplace tort claims in the 1980s, relatively little has been written on the topic. This book, which is designed for attorneys and human resource professionals, contains a thorough review of each of the workplace torts that employers have begun to face in the area of employment litigation. It also provides employers with practical guidance to avoid or minimize their exposure to workplace tort liability and to successfully defend employment tort claims.[1]

Although the book is not intended to be an exhaustive legal compendium of all cases decided in the area of workplace torts, it nonetheless summarizes over 175 cases. These cases illustrate the general legal principles of each workplace tort and demonstrate how workplace torts can arise in common employment scenarios, from recruitment and hiring to postemployment references. Many of the cases provide the basis for some of the 200 practical suggestions contained in the book for minimizing or avoiding exposure to workplace tort liability.[2]

Employer's Guide to Workplace Torts includes material from the BNA Special Report prepared by the authors in 1987 entitled "Negligent Hiring, Fraud, Defamation, and Other Emerging Areas of Employer Liability." This book not only updates the cases reported in that Special Report, but, in addition, summarizes over 80 new cases decided since the Special Report was published in 1988. This book also includes over 100 additional practical suggestions and contains a comprehensive treatment of the subject of workplace tort litigation.[3]

It is our hope that lawyers and human resource professionals will find the information and guidance contained in this book to be both useful and practical.

Notes

1. This book is designed to provide accurate, authoritative, and practical information with regard to the subject of workplace torts. It is not intended to serve as, or

substitute for, legal advice. Further, the reader should be aware that the law of workplace torts not only varies from state to state but also is constantly evolving. In publishing this book, neither the authors nor publisher is engaged in rendering legal or other professional services. If legal advice or other expert assistance is required, the services of a competent professional should be sought.
2. The book summarizes both reported and unreported cases, as reflected in pleadings, judicial decisions, and reports on jury verdicts and case settlements. In a number of instances, information was provided by one or more of the attorneys involved in the actual cases. The reader should be alerted that some of the facts referred to in the case summaries reflect allegations only, and some of the cases summarized may be the subject of subsequent appellate decisions. All of the cases, however, and all of the materials in the Appendices, have been checked as of January 1992.
3. This book does not address the subject of tort claims brought by employers *against their employees,* such as actions for defamation, misappropriation of company funds and property, and malicious prosecution and abuse of process. It is instead devoted to the treatment of workplace tort claims *against employers.*

Acknowledgments

Special appreciation is extended to Peter S. Gray, Esq., for his valuable editing of Chapters 1–12 and his preparation of the appendices to this book.

Special appreciation is also extended to William Kandel, Esq., for his valuable review of Chapter 13, "Litigating Workplace Tort Actions."

The authors are grateful to Marla K. Feinman, a student at University of Pennsylvania School of Law, for her substantial contributions as the sole legal research assistant for this book.

Finally, the authors wish to thank Carolyn Toth Nicol for her consummate cite-checking and Sean M. Breheney for his exceptional proofreading and copyediting.

Contents

Preface v
Acknowledgments vii
Introduction xix
    A. The Emergence of Workplace Torts xix
    B. Employer Liability for Workplace Torts xx
    C. Workplace Torts Based on Intentional
        or Reckless Conduct xx
    D. Workplace Torts Based on Negligence
        or Carelessness xxi
    E. The Scope of Workplace Torts xxii
    F. The Challenge of Workplace Torts xxiii
    G. Responding to the Challenge xxiv
    H. The Need for Preventive Measures xxv
    I. Overview xxv

Part One. Emerging Theories of Employer Tort Liability

**1. Negligent Hiring and Other Forms of Employer
        Negligence** 3
    A. Overview 3
    B. Trends in the Law 3
    C. General Principles of Law 4
        1. Negligent Hiring, Retention, and Supervision 4
        2. Other Forms of Employer Negligence 6
    D. Illustrative Cases 7
        1. Negligent Hiring 8
            a. Incompetent Employees 8
            b. Unsafe Employees 9
            c. Dangerous Employees 11
            d. Untrustworthy Employees 18
        2. Negligent Retention 19
            a. Unsafe Employees 19

        b. Supervisors Who Sexually Harass Subordinates ... 19
        c. Dangerous Employees 21
        d. Untrustworthy Employees 23
     3. Negligent Supervision 24
        a. Unsafe Employees 24
        b. Dangerous Employees 25
        c. Supervisors Who Sexually Harass Subordinates ... 26
     4. Negligent Failure to Warn 28
     5. Negligent Performance Evaluation 29
     6. Negligent Failure to Provide
        a Smoke-Free Workplace 31
     7. Negligent Polygraph Administration 32
     8. Negligent Furnishing of Alcohol
        to Intoxicated Employees 34
     9. Negligent Failure to Provide
        Alternative Transportation Home 35

2. **Fraud and Misrepresentation** 38
   A. Overview 38
   B. General Principles of Law 39
   C. Trend in the Law: Negligent Misrepresentation 40
   D. Illustrative Cases 41
     1. Fraudulent Recruitment and Hiring 42
        a. Misrepresentations of Employer's Business
           or Profitability 42
        b. Misrepresentations of Terms or Conditions
           of Employment 45
     2. Fraudulent Retention of Employees 51
     3. Misrepresentations Regarding Employee Benefits ... 53
     4. Fraudulent Employee Assignments 56
     5. Fraudulent Employee Investigations 57
     6. Fraudulent Inducement of Employee
        Resignations 59
     7. Fraudulent Concealment of Workplace Illnesses ... 60

3. **Defamation** 63
   A. Overview 63
   B. General Principles of Law 63
   C. Trend in the Law: Compelled Self-Publication 65
   D. Illustrative Cases 65
     1. Defamation in Workplace Investigations
        of Employee Misconduct 67

	a. Illegal Drug Use and Sales	67
	b. Theft and Fraudulent Conduct	69
	c. Sexual Harassment	70
2.	Defamatory Evaluations and Warnings	71
3.	Defamatory Statements Regarding Employees With AIDS	72
4.	Defamation in Group Employee Meetings	73
5.	Defamation in Internal Memos	75
6.	Defamation in Company Newsletters	77
7.	Unprivileged Defamatory Statements	79
8.	Defamatory Postemployment References	81
9.	Defamation by Compelled Self-Publication	86
10.	Defamatory Statements in Post-Termination Proceedings	88

4. Infliction of Emotional Distress ... 92
- A. Overview ... 92
- B. General Principles of Law ... 92
- C. Trend in the Law: Negligent Infliction of Emotional Distress ... 93
- D. Illustrative Cases ... 94
  1. Demotions, Negative Job Evaluations, and Undesirable Work Assignments ... 95
  2. Sexual Harassment ... 101
  3. Other Forms of Workplace Harassment ... 102
  4. Abusive Investigations of Employee Misconduct ... 105
     a. Unwarranted Threats of Criminal Prosecution ... 105
     b. Improper Use of Polygraph Examinations ... 106
  5. Unreasonable Drug Testing Techniques ... 108
  6. Improper Use of Employee Assistance Programs ... 109
  7. Workplace Injuries and Illnesses ... 110
  8. Smoking in the Workplace ... 111
  9. Abusive, Reckless, Discriminatory, and Negligent Methods of Termination ... 112

5. Invasion of Privacy ... 118
- A. Overview ... 118
- B. General Principles of Law ... 118
- C. Illustrative Cases ... 120
  1. Disclosure of Employees' Medical or Mental Condition ... 121
  2. Disclosure of Personal Matters About Employees ... 124

3. Inquiries Into Employees' Private Affairs 126
   4. Searches of Employees' Lockers and Mail 129
   5. False Light Publicity 131

6. **Assault and Battery** 135
   A. Overview 135
   B. General Principles of Law 135
   C. Illustrative Cases 136
      1. Sexual Harassment Battery 137
      2. Drug Testing Battery 142
      3. Polygraph Battery 142
      4. Assault and Battery During Investigations
         of Workplace Misconduct 144
      5. Battery by Exposure to Toxic Substances 145
      6. Other Workplace Assaults and Batteries 146

7. **Interference With Contractual Relations** 149
   A. Overview 149
   B. General Principles of Law 149
   C. Illustrative Cases 151
      1. Interference by Causing Termination
         of Employees 152
         a. At the Behest of an Employee's Supervisor 152
         b. At the Behest of a Former Employer 154
         c. At the Behest of a Prospective Employer 157
         d. As a Result of an Unsuccessful
            Takeover Attempt 159
      2. Interference With Job Performance 160
      3. Interference by Improper Work Assignments 161
      4. Negative Job References 162
      5. Unreasonable Enforcement
         of Noncompete Agreements 164

8. **False Imprisonment** 167
   A. Overview 167
   B. General Principles of Law 167
   C. Illustrative Cases 168
      1. Unreasonable Detention of Employees
         During Workplace Investigations 169
         a. Actual and Apparent Detentions 169
         b. Blocking an Employee's Egress From an Office
            or Work Site 173

2. Polygraph Examinations 174
　　3. Other Forms of False Imprisonment 175

9. Malicious Prosecution and Abuse of Process 178
　A. Overview 178
　B. General Principles of Law 178
　C. Illustrative Cases 179

10. RICO 187
　A. Overview 187
　B. General Principles of Law 188
　C. Illustrative Cases 188
　　1. Opposition to or Disclosure of Illegal Activities 188
　　2. Refusal to Participate in an Illegal Scheme 190
　　3. Physical Coercion of Employees 192

Part Two. A Practical Guide to Workplace Torts

**11. How Different Workplace Torts Arise
　　in Common Employment Contexts** 197
　A. Applicant Screening and Hiring of New Employees ... 198
　　1. Negligent Hiring 198
　　2. Fraud and Misrepresentation 200
　B. Workplace Environments 201
　　1. Sexual Harassment 201
　　　a. Negligent Retention 201
　　　b. Negligent Failure to Supervise
　　　　 and Train Managers 201
　　　c. Defamation 202
　　　d. Infliction of Emotional Distress 202
　　　e. Invasion of Privacy 203
　　　f. Assault and Battery 203
　　　g. Malicious Prosecution 203
　　2. Other Forms of Workplace Harassment 204
　　　a. Intentional Infliction of Emotional Distress 204
　　　b. Negligent Infliction of Emotional Distress 205
　　　c. Invasion of Privacy 205
　　　d. Battery 206
　　　e. RICO 206
　　3. Smoking in the Workplace 206
　　4. Exposure to Toxins and Other Workplace
　　　 Dangers 207

        a. Assault and Battery 207
        b. Fraud and Misrepresentation 208
        c. Negligent Failure to Warn 208
  C. Employee Disabilities 209
    1. Drug and Alcohol Abuse 209
        a. Negligent Retention and Other Negligence
           Theories of Tort Recovery 209
        b. Defamation 210
        c. Invasion of Privacy 210
    2. AIDS 211
        a. Negligent Hiring 212
        b. Defamation 212
        c. Invasion of Privacy 212
    3. Other Illnesses 213
        a. Invasion of Privacy 213
        b. Infliction of Emotional Distress 214
    4. Employee Assistance Programs 214
        a. Infliction of Emotional Distress 215
        b. Invasion of Privacy 215
        c. False Imprisonment 215
  D. Work Assignments, Performance Evaluations,
      Disciplinary Action, and Demotions 216
    1. Negligent Performance Evaluations 216
    2. Fraud and Misrepresentation 217
    3. Defamation 217
    4. Infliction of Emotional Distress 218
    5. Interference With Contractual Relations 218
  E. Investigating Workplace Misconduct 219
    1. Employee Theft 219
        a. Negligent Polygraph Administration 220
        b. Fraud and Misrepresentation 220
        c. Defamation 220
        d. Infliction of Emotional Distress 221
        e. Invasion of Privacy 221
        f. Assault and Battery 222
        g. False Imprisonment 222
        h. Malicious Prosecution 223
    2. Drug and Alcohol Abuse 223
        a. Defamation 223
        b. Infliction of Emotional Distress 224
        c. Invasion of Privacy 224
    3. Sexual Harassment 224

F. Termination and Retention of Employees 225
   1. Termination of Employment 225
      a. Fraud and Misrepresentation 226
      b. Defamation 227
      c. Infliction of Emotional Distress 228
      d. Invasion of Privacy 229
      e. Interference With Contractual Relations 229
      f. False Imprisonment 230
      g. RICO 231
   2. Retention of Employees 231
      a. Negligent Retention 231
      b. Fraud and Misrepresentation 232
G. Postemployment Matters 233
   1. Postemployment References 233
      a. Defamation 234
      b. Interference With Contractual Relations 235
   2. Criminal and Civil Proceedings
      Against Employees 235
      a. Criminal Charges 235
      b. Civil Proceedings 236
   3. Noncompete Agreements 236
      a. Interference With Contractual Relations 237
      b. Fraud 237
   4. Unemployment and Workers' Compensation
      Proceedings 238

12. Avoiding Exposure to Workplace Tort Liability: Practical Suggestions 244
A. Properly Screening for Unfit Applicants 245
B. Counseling, Supervising, and Terminating
   Unfit Employees 250
C. Using Disclaimers in Recruitment and Hiring 252
D. Avoiding Employee Detrimental Reliance 254
E. Properly Conducting Drug and Alcohol Testing 256
F. Properly Investigating Employee Misconduct 257
G. Minimizing Defamatory and Other Actionable
   Statements About Employees 259
H. Avoiding Unnecessary Inquiries About and Disclosure
   of Personal Employee Matters 261
I. Minimizing Abusive and Harassing Treatment
   of Employees by Supervisors and Co-Workers 263
J. Converting Terminations Into Resignations 265

K. Obtaining Releases From Employees 266
L. Qualifying Postemployment References 266
M. Avoiding Other Post-Termination Tortious Conduct ... 268
N. Other Practical Suggestions 269

13. Litigating Workplace Tort Actions 271
A. Overview 271
B. Multiple Tort and Other Employment Claims 271
C. Selection of Defendants 274
   1. Suing the Individual Wrongdoer 274
   2. Suing the Corporate Parent: Deeper Pockets 274
D. Jurisdiction 275
E. Employer Defenses 276
   1. Workers' Compensation 276
   2. Preemption 278
      a. NLRA Preemption 278
      b. LMRA Preemption 278
      c. ERISA Preemption 280
      d. Other Sources of Preemption 281
   3. No *Respondeat Superior* or Employer
      Ratification 282
   4. Arbitration 283
   5. Consent and Release 284
   6. Contributory and Comparative Negligence 285
   7. Other Defenses 286
F. Pretrial Discovery 286
G. Pretrial Motions to Dismiss and Motions
    for Summary Judgment 288
H. Jury Trials 289
I. Compensatory and Punitive Damage Awards 289
J. Attorneys' Fees 291
K. Out-of-Court Settlements 292
L. Settlement Agreements 293
   1. Legal Consideration 294
   2. Valid Waivers and Releases 294
   3. Confidentiality 295
   4. Employment References 295
   5. Additional Settlement Provisions 296

14. Other Significant Legal Issues 301
A. Personal Liability of Managers 301
B. Defendant Conflicts of Interest 302
C. Insurance Considerations 303

Appendices 305

    Appendix A. Criminal Record Inquiries 307
        Selected State Statutes 307
        Federal Law Under Title VII 314

    Appendix B. Polygraph Examinations 315
        Selected State Statutes 315
        Federal Law 320

    Appendix C. Consumer Credit Reports 322
        Selected State Statutes 322
        Federal Law 324

    Appendix D. Drug Testing 326
        Selected State Statutes 326
        Selected Federal Laws 330

    Appendix E. AIDS Testing 334
        Selected State Statutes 334
        Federal Law 339

    Appendix F. Smoking in the Workplace 341
        Selected State Statutes 341

    Appendix G. Employee Access to Personnel Records ... 348
        Selected State Statutes 348

    Appendix H. Blacklisting of Employees 355
        Selected State Statutes 355

Table of Cases 359

Index 369

About the Authors 383

Introduction

A. The Emergence of Workplace Torts

In the 1980s, employers witnessed the emergence of a different breed of employee lawsuit—one that is vastly different from the more traditional lawsuit brought under a host of federal and state statutes prohibiting discrimination and retaliation in employment and otherwise governing employer conduct in the workplace.[1]

In contrast to these federal and state statutes, which are the result of legislation enacted into law, the courts have recognized a number of civil actions based not on legislation but rather on the "common law" of the states. These common law theories of liability are, in turn, subsumed under the law of "torts."[2]

A tort is a civil wrong. It arises when one party breaches a legal duty it owes to another party, and the other suffers harm or damages as a result of the breach.[3] Torts include:

- negligence (including negligent hiring and retention),
- fraud and misrepresentation,
- defamation,
- infliction of emotional distress,
- assault and battery,
- false imprisonment,
- invasion of privacy,
- interference with contractual relations, and
- abuse of process and malicious prosecution.

Because the common law of torts involves "judge-made" principles of law, there are no statutes or regulations to read. Rather, practitioners must examine judicial decisions to comprehend the nature, scope, and contours of each tort, particularly as they apply in the employment context.[4]

B. Employer Liability for Workplace Torts

An employer may be liable for the torts of its employees under the doctrine of *respondeat superior*. Under this well-established doctrine, an employer will generally be liable for an employee's tortious conduct committed within the scope of his or her employment.[5] The courts have broadly construed the phrase "within the scope of employment." For example, an employee's acts may be within the scope of employment even though forbidden or consciously criminal or wrongful.[6] A failure to act may also be within the scope of employment.[7]

Even when an employee engages in tortious conduct *outside* the scope of his or her employment, the employer may still be liable if the employee *appeared* to act or speak on behalf of the employer.[8] Likewise, an act performed outside the scope of employment may subject an employer to liability if the management of an employer "ratifies" or condones the tortious conduct.[9] In that circumstance, the employer's ratification is regarded in the same light as if the tortious conduct had been initially authorized by the employer. Ratification of an unauthorized act can even be inferred from a failure to repudiate the tortious conduct.[10]

In addition, an employer may be liable for the tortious conduct of its employees, even if outside the scope of employment, if the employer was negligent or reckless.[11] Thus, an employer may be held liable for harm or injury caused by its employees if the employer was negligent or reckless in the employment of improper persons, in the supervision of its employees, or in permitting or failing to prevent negligent or tortious conduct by its employees.[12]

C. Workplace Torts Based on Intentional or Reckless Conduct

Most of the initial lawsuits for workplace torts were brought by employees against their employers to seek redress for the *intentional* or *reckless* conduct of their co-workers. Employers have historically been held liable for the conduct of their employees acting within the scope of their duties or in furtherance of the employers' interests.[13] While employers frequently argue that intentional or reckless acts of misconduct are neither within the scope of employment nor in furtherance of the employers' interests, the courts usually uphold jury verdicts imposing liability upon employers for most acts of employee misconduct committed at work.

A large number of employee lawsuits involving intentional or reckless misconduct of co-workers have resulted in six- and seven-figure jury verdicts against employers. Such cases have involved:

- employees with violent propensities who *intentionally* assaulted co-workers or customers;
- managers who *intentionally* or *recklessly* made false accusations that other employees were drug users, thieves or liars;
- executives who *intentionally* misled employees with promises of nonexistent bonuses, benefits, or continued employment;
- supervisors who *intentionally* harassed or sexually assaulted subordinates or subjected them to outrageous conditions of employment; and
- security agents who *intentionally* threatened employees with physical harm or held them against their will during company investigations.

Some torts, such as assault and battery, false imprisonment, interference with contractual relations, malicious prosecution, and abuse of process, require an employee to show that an employer, through one or more of its agents, was motivated by an improper intent or purpose. The more common torts, however, such as negligent hiring and retention, fraud and misrepresentation, defamation, infliction of emotional distress, and invasion of privacy, while often accompanied by an improper intent, do not require a showing of intentional wrongdoing for an employee to recover.[14]

D. Workplace Torts Based on Negligence or Carelessness

In the past few years, more and more employee lawsuits for workplace torts have sought to impose liability upon employers for injuries caused by the *negligent* and *careless* conduct of co-workers—conduct that is far more commonplace than intentional acts of misconduct. Further, even though acts of employee negligence and carelessness are not intended to cause harm or injury to co-workers or others, such conduct may nonetheless subject employers to substantial liability. Examples of such unintentional conduct include:

- negligent retention or supervision of unsafe or incompetent employees;

- inadequate supervision, training, and assignment of employees;
- indifference to warning employees of a known risk of harm;
- failure to provide a smoke-free workplace;
- careless administration of polygraph examinations;
- negligently furnishing alcohol to intoxicated employees and failure to provide alternative transportation home;
- innocent misrepresentations of company benefits or the economic condition of the employer;
- incomplete investigation of employee misconduct; and
- improper disclosure of employees' private lives to co-workers and others without a need to know.

To underscore the application of negligence to the employment context, the judiciary has also begun to permit recovery by employees for *negligent* misrepresentation and *negligent* infliction of emotional distress. These new torts require no showing of intentional wrongdoing—and mere carelessness or oversight may be sufficient to establish employer liability.[15]

In addition, a new twist in the law of defamation—*compelled self-publication*—has now become a viable back-door approach by employees to challenge many termination decisions that are otherwise insulated from judicial scrutiny.[16] Employers can no longer protect themselves against potential liability to terminated employees simply by declining to respond to postemployment reference checks or by providing only "name, rank, and serial number" information to prospective employers. Rather, employees are now challenging their terminations by filing defamation lawsuits against their former employers based solely on the employee's *own* repetition to a prospective employer of the reasons given by the former employer for the employee's discharge. This emerging theory of defamation, together with a deluge of lawsuits based on common forms of inadvertence by human resource professionals, has rendered the employee relations function a veritable mine field for those unfamiliar with these emerging areas of employer liability.

E. The Scope of Workplace Torts

Lawsuits for workplace torts span the full spectrum of the employment relationship, from recruitment to postemployment references, including hiring, applicant screening, job assignments, performance evaluations, drug and alcohol testing, smoking in the workplace, sexual harassment, exposure to workplace dangers, AIDS in the workplace, investigation of employee misconduct, honesty testing, employee assistance programs, termination of employees and supervisors, and enforcement of noncompetition provisions in employment contracts.

These types of employee lawsuits frequently contain a multitude of different tort claims. For example, female employees who have been sexually harassed by male supervisors have brought actions for negligent hiring and retention, assault and battery, intentional infliction of emotional distress, and invasion of privacy. Similarly, employer investigations of workplace misconduct have led to tort actions by employees for fraud, defamation, false imprisonment, invasion of privacy, infliction of emotional distress, assault, battery, and false imprisonment, where company investigators have:

- made false promises to those who cooperate in the investigation,
- falsely accused employees of workplace theft or drug use,
- needlessly inquired into an employee's private affairs,
- threatened or caused physical harm to the employee under investigation, or
- physically detained an employee against his or her will.

Further, tort actions are often coupled with a claim under a federal statute, such as Title VII, or a state wrongful discharge claim.[17]

F. The Challenge of Workplace Torts

Unlike lawsuits commenced under some federal and state employee relations statutes, this new type of employee lawsuit entitles the employee or injured party to a trial by jury.[18] Further, where a tort is committed with an improper motive, or simply a conscious disregard for the interests of others, *unlimited* punitive damages are available.[19] Hence, employers today are routinely facing the specter of jury awards totaling hundreds of thousands and sometimes millions of dollars in damages.

By suing an employer for a number of different torts, an employee can maximize the likelihood that at least one of the claims will survive a pretrial motion for summary judgment and ultimately be presented to a sympathetic jury. If more than one tort claim reaches the jury, an employee may recover compensatory and punitive damages for each.

In addition to the corporate liability of employers, supervisors are subject to *personal liability* for their tortious actions against employees, and many juries have awarded compensatory and punitive damages against offending supervisors and officials of the company. Punitive damages, moreover, can far exceed the compensatory damages awarded.

To avoid a jury trial and the risk of an adverse judgment, employers may seek to settle lawsuits in advance of trial. Many offended employees, however, appear to be more interested in vindication of "principle" than monetary satisfaction. For example, a former employee of a major oil company turned down an offer of $350,000 to settle his lawsuit for fraud. After a jury awarded him $10.1 million in damages, the employee remarked that he had declined to settle because he only "wanted [his] name cleared . . . to see them to be shown guilty."[20]

Whether an employee is genuinely interested in vindication or just wants a shot to hit the "lottery" with a jury, the fact remains that the amount of money it takes to settle a workplace tort case is often far greater than the amount needed to settle a typical employment discrimination case.

On the other hand, some employers who have rejected what appear to be unreasonable settlement demands by plaintiffs have been subjected to jury awards of compensatory and punitive damages as high as ten times the rejected settlement figure. In a negligent hiring action against a nonprofit corporation, for example, a jury returned a verdict for nearly $5 million in damages after the employer rejected a $500,000 offer to settle the case.[21]

G. Responding to the Challenge

Employers are not without defenses against these emerging theories of employer liability. For example, workers' compensation laws can, in certain instances, preclude an employee's lawsuit based on some of these torts. In addition, the defense of preemption may be used by employers to fend off an employee's state law tort action. Under this defense, a tort action may be "preempted" if it is also covered by a federal or state labor, employment, pension, or welfare benefit statute that precludes all other civil actions for the same wrong.

One sort of "defense" that seems to be disappearing is the de facto judicial deference historically provided to some employers, particularly health care facilities and universities, in their treatment of employees.[22] Indeed, it is becoming increasingly evident that employee lawsuits for workplace torts have become widely accepted by the judiciary. Thus, where employers in the past had been able to obtain pretrial dismissals of many employee tort actions, courts are now more inclined to allow these lawsuits to be presented to a jury. Further, even if an employer prevails in an action for negligent hiring, fraud, defamation, or another emerging workplace tort, it must still pay its attorneys' fees and other costs of defending an employee lawsuit, including money spent by supervisors and company officials on management issues related to the suit, that can far exceed actual monetary damages paid to the employee.

H. The Need for Preventive Measures

The most practical and sensible way for an employer to respond to the challenge of workplace torts is to take preventive measures to minimize the likelihood that its personnel will engage in certain types of negligent or intentional conduct that can form the basis for such a lawsuit. Many practical measures are available to employers who wish to limit their exposure to workplace torts. Indeed, if the employers involved in the lawsuits reported in this book had followed the precautions described in Chapter 12 below, many of those actions would never have been filed.

Still, the practical steps outlined in this book will not fully insulate employers from these types of lawsuits. Rather, managers, human resource professionals, and corporate counsel need to familiarize themselves with the pertinent legal principles discussed below, and review the illustrative cases summarized in this book. Only then will employers become aware of the scope of these emerging areas of employer liability and be capable of recognizing the variety of events that breed lawsuits for workplace torts.

I. Overview

Part One of this book, covering the first ten chapters, deals with emerging theories of employer tort liability.[23] Each chapter begins with a brief overview of the tort as it applies to the employment context, and then describes the general principles of law applicable to each tort. Where one or more trends in the law have arisen with respect to a particular tort, a brief discussion of the trend is included in the chapter. Finally, each chapter includes summaries of illustrative cases pertaining to each tort. This is the heart of Part One—the judicial decisions that define the nature, scope, and contours of each workplace tort. Over 175 illustrative case summaries are included.

Part Two provides the reader with a practical guide to workplace torts. Chapter 11 discusses which workplace torts arise in common employment contexts, starting with applicant screening and hiring and ending with termination and postemployment matters, such as job references. Chapter 12 focuses on avoiding exposure to workplace torts, and contains over 200 practical suggestions for practitioners. Chapter 13 deals with litigating workplace tort actions and addresses many of the considerations that face lawyers and nonlawyers alike when litigating—and settling—lawsuits alleging workplace torts. Finally, Chapter 14 reviews several other significant issues, including personal liability of managers for workplace torts and insurance considerations.

The book concludes with several appendices that summarize selected state and federal statutes governing criminal record inquiries, polygraph examinations, consumer credit reports, drug testing, and AIDS testing, as well as state laws regarding smoking in the workplace, employee access to personnel records, and blacklisting of employees.

Notes

1. The principal federal labor and employment statutes include the National Labor Relations Act of 1935 (NLRA), as amended; the Fair Labor Standards Act of 1938 (FLSA), as amended; the Labor Management Relations Act of 1947 (LMRA), as amended; Title VII of the Civil Rights Act of 1964 (Title VII), as amended; the Age Discrimination in Employment Act of 1967 (ADEA), as amended; the Occupational Safety and Health Act of 1970 (OSHA), as amended; the Rehabilitation Act of 1973, as amended; the Employee Retirement Income Security Act of 1974 (ERISA), as amended; and the Americans With Disabilities Act of 1990 (ADA).
2. Some state legislatures have also enacted laws to supplement or supplant the common law of torts. Counsel should therefore review state statutory law as well when advising management on the law of workplace torts.
3. *See* W. KEETON, PROSSER AND KEETON ON THE LAW OF TORTS at 2 (5th ed. 1984).
4. Some states have codified and modified a few common law torts, principally the tort of invasion of privacy, which is also the subject of the constitutions of certain states, such as California. Practitioners should check the statutory and constitutional law of all applicable states.
5. *See* Restatement (Second) of Agency § 219(1).
6. *See* Restatement (Second) of Agency §§ 230, 231.

Introduction xxvii

7. *See* Restatement (Second) of Agency § 232.
8. *See* Restatement (Second) of Agency § 219(2).
9. *See* Restatement (Second) of Agency §§ 82, 218.
10. *See* Restatement (Second) of Agency § 94.
11. *See* Restatement (Second) of Agency § 219(2)(b).
12. *See* Restatement (Second) of Agency § 213.
13. *See* Restatement (Second) of Agency §§ 219(1), 228.
14. This book does not address the tort of wrongful discharge, which is a form of intentional tort. In some states, an action for wrongful discharge may be a tort, a breach of contract, or a statutory violation. The broad subject of wrongful discharge, including public policy torts, is addressed in W.J. HOLLOWAY AND M.J. LEECH, EMPLOYMENT TERMINATION: RIGHTS AND REMEDIES (BNA Books 1985, new edition forthcoming).
15. See Chapter 2, section C., and Chapter 3, section C.
16. See Chapter 3, section D.9.
17. Although wrongful discharge is regarded by some courts as a new type of tort, it is not included in this book because that topic has been the subject of numerous other publications.
18. Prior to the enactment of the Civil Rights Act of 1991, there was no right to a jury trial under either Title VII or the ADA. Plaintiffs alleging intentional discrimination under Title VII and the ADA are entitled to a trial by jury.
19. Although the Civil Rights Act of 1991 allows plaintiffs to recover punitive damages for employment discrimination, the amount of punitive damages, as well as compensatory damages covering emotional distress, is limited to $300,000 for employers with more than 500 employees; $200,000 for employers with more than 200 but fewer than 501 employees; $100,000 for employers with more than 100 but fewer than 201 employees; and $50,000 for employers of 100 or fewer employees. Many of the cases reported in this book involve punitive damages awarded far in excess of the limits contained in the Civil Rights Act of 1991, which has no application to state law tort claims. Punitive damages remain unlimited for workplace torts.
20. 12 CONN. L. TRIBUNE No. 29, at 1 (July 28, 1986), reporting *Dowie v. Exxon Corp.* (D. Conn. 1986), summarized in Chapter 2, section D.1.b.
21. Sallaz v. G-H-I Housing Corp., No. 86-66859 (Tex. Dist. Ct. Harris County 1986), summarized in Chapter 1, section D.1.c.
22. *See* University of Pa. v. EEOC, 493 U.S. 182 (1990).
23. Chapter 10 deals with an emerging *non*-tort theory of liability, the Racketeer Influenced and Corrupt Organizations Act, 18 U.S.C. § 1962, commonly referred to as RICO. RICO is included in this book because of its recent emergence in employee lawsuits against employers. In addition to the torts discussed in Chapters 1–9, there are a few lesser known torts that are recognized in some states, such as prima facie tort and civil conspiracy. These torts can also be asserted against employers.

Part One

Emerging Theories of Employer Tort Liability

Chapter 1

Negligent Hiring and Other Forms of Employer Negligence

A. Overview

The negligence theory of liability is increasingly being used in litigation by plaintiffs who have been injured or damaged by unfit or unsuitable employees, and by employees who seek an alternative or additional legal ground on which to challenge adverse employment decisions.

The last several years have witnessed a proliferation of lawsuits against employers for negligent hiring, negligent retention, and negligent supervision of dangerous or untrustworthy employees who engage in criminal, violent, or other wrongful acts. Frequently, the injuries for which plaintiffs seek recovery are assaults, thefts, and frauds upon co-workers, clients, and customers of an employer. In addition, more and more negligent retention lawsuits are also being brought to recover damages for sexual harassment of female employees who claim that their employers had knowledge that the harassing supervisor or co-worker had a propensity toward or history of engaging in sexual harassment.

B. Trends in the Law

The torts of negligent hiring, negligent retention, and negligent supervision are not confined to cases involving injuries caused by violent, criminal, or harassing conduct. Rather, these theories of liability are now being used by plaintiffs to recover damages for the negligent hiring of *incompetent* employees who should never have been hired in the first place,[1] and for negligent retention or supervision of *unsafe workers* whose on-the-job negligence causes injury to co-workers or third parties.[2]

Other forms of employer negligence have also become the subject of lawsuits. A few employees have commenced actions for negligent performance evaluation, claiming that their superiors failed to properly evaluate their job performance or warn them of possible discharge unless their performance improved.[3] These lawsuits initially met with some judicial approval, but most courts have now retreated from acceptance of this new tort.

Nevertheless, the judiciary has endorsed a variety of other causes of action for employer negligence:

- negligent failure to warn employees of a co-worker's violent or dangerous tendencies,[4]
- negligent failure to provide a smoke-free workplace,[5]
- negligent polygraph administration,[6]
- negligent furnishing of alcohol to intoxicated employees,[7] and
- negligent failure to provide alternative transportation home to an overworked and exhausted employee.[8]

And the variety of employer negligence claims is likely to increase, as more and more employees and others are seeking to expand an employer's duty of care to compensate them for all types of workplace-related harm. These actions reflect our nation's increasing willingness to regard employers as "insurance carriers" that should provide for the welfare of their workers and should compensate employees, clients, and customers for all types of harm caused directly or indirectly by those who work for employers.

C. General Principles of Law

1. Negligent Hiring, Retention, and Supervision

An employer has a duty to protect its employees, customers, clients, and visitors from injury caused by employees the employer knows, or *should know,* pose a risk of harm to others. This duty arises from common law and is breached by an employer who fails to protect its workers and customers from unreasonable risk of harm inflicted by unfit employees.[9] When an employer breaches that duty, it may be liable for damages under the torts of negligent hiring, negligent retention, or negligent supervision. These torts will be collectively referred to below as *negligent hiring*.

The tort of negligent hiring is recognized in almost every state. This emerging theory of employer liability is distinguished from the established legal doctrine of *respondeat superior,* where an employer is held liable for the wrongs or negligence of an employee acting *within* the scope of the employee's duties.[10] In contrast, under the theory of negligent hiring, an employer may be liable for the acts of an employee acting *outside* the scope of his or her employment.[11] Thus, an employer cannot escape liability for negligent hiring simply because an employee's violent or criminal acts occurred well after the employee's shift ended, happened miles away from the place of employment, and were inconsistent with his or her duties as an employee.[12]

For an employer to be liable for negligent hiring, a plaintiff first must prove that the employee who caused the injury was unfit for hiring or retention,[13] or was fit only if properly supervised.[14] An employee's fitness will depend, of course, on the nature of the employment and the risk posed by the employee to those who foreseeably could come into contact with the employee. For example, an employee who provides services in customers' homes poses a greater risk of harm to others than a worker who has no contact with patrons.[15]

Next, the plaintiff must prove that the employer's hiring or retention of the unfit employee, or the failure to properly supervise the employee, was the proximate cause of the plaintiff's injuries.[16] In other words, the injured party must show a connection, or *nexus,* between the injury and the employment of the unfit employee. For example, if an office equipment technician goes to a ball game and assaults a spectator rooting for the visiting team, the technician's employer is unlikely to be liable for negligent hiring, because no connection exists between the injury and the technician's employment. But, if the same technician follows a customer home one night and assaults the customer due to a disagreement that arose during a service call earlier that day, a connection can be shown between the injury and the technician's employment. In that case, the technician's employer may be liable for negligent hiring.

Finally, an injured plaintiff must prove that the employer knew or should have known of the employee's lack of fitness.[17] This is the issue most often in dispute in negligent hiring cases. Typically, the employer is unaware of the employee's unfitness. Thus, an employer's liability for negligent hiring frequently depends on whether it can be proved that the employer *should have known* of the employee's unfitness.

In contrast to negligent hiring, liability for *negligent retention* typically arises when an employer retains an employee despite actual knowledge of the employee's lack of fitness.[18] For example, where an employer has received complaints about a supervisor's sexual harassment of a female subordinate, yet retains the supervisor in employment or fails to take other corrective measures to abate the harassment, an employer may become liable for negligent retention if the harassment continues.[19]

Usually the employee relations or human resources manager is ultimately responsible for screening out unfit applicants. Thus, many lawsuits for negligent hiring focus on the role of the human resources department. Did it act imprudently in failing to contact all prior employers,[20] neglecting to verify the trustworthiness of an applicant,[21] or ignoring an obvious or not-so-obvious gap in employment?[22] Did it permit the retention of an employee despite reason to believe that the employee was unfit or unsuitable for the job?[23] These kinds of issues are for a jury to decide. Where an innocent plaintiff has suffered a grievous injury or substantial loss at the hands of an unfit employee, juries are often inclined to "second-guess" an employer's hiring, retention, and supervision of the unfit worker.[24]

2. Other Forms of Employer Negligence

Employees have attempted to expand the law of negligence to cover an array of workplace injuries or loss of employment. As noted above, a few courts have endorsed such attempts by recognizing the torts of negligent performance evaluation, negligent failure to provide a smoke-free workplace, negligent failure to warn of workplace dangers, negligent administration of polygraph examinations, negligent furnishing of alcohol to intoxicated employees, and negligent failure to provide alternative transportation home.[25]

Negligence is defined as conduct that falls below a standard of care established by law to protect others against unreasonable and foreseeable risk of harm.[26] To recover damages on a negligence theory, a plaintiff must first establish the existence of a duty.[27] This is frequently a thorny legal issue in those cases where an employee seeks to expand the law of negligence into new areas of the workplace. For example, several courts have struggled to determine whether an employer owes a legal duty to an employee to properly evaluate his or her performance.[28] And different courts have also reached contrary decisions as to whether there is a duty to warn employees of a co-worker's violent or dangerous propensities.[29]

A plaintiff then must show that the employer breached the duty,[30] and that the breach was the proximate cause of his or her damages or injury.[31] A breach can occur by affirmative acts that create an unreasonable risk of harm to another, or a failure to act where there is a duty to do so.[32] In cases involving a negligent failure to act, the amount of evidence sufficient to establish proximate cause is frequently relaxed, as many courts are extremely generous in permitting such cases to be submitted to a jury—even where it is extremely speculative whether performance of the act would have prevented the injury.[33]

D. Illustrative Cases

The cases summarized in this chapter are grouped by the following categories of employer negligence:

- Negligent Hiring:
    - incompetent employees,
    - unsafe employees,
    - dangerous employees, and
    - untrustworthy employees;
- Negligent Retention:
    - unsafe employees,
    - supervisors who sexually harass subordinates,
    - dangerous employees, and
    - untrustworthy employees;
- Negligent Supervision:
    - unsafe employees,
    - dangerous employees, and
    - supervisors who sexually harass subordinates;
- Negligent Failure to Warn;
- Negligent Performance Evaluation;
- Negligent Failure to Provide a Smoke-Free Workplace;
- Negligent Polygraph Administration;
- Negligent Furnishing of Alcohol to Intoxicated Employees; and
- Negligent Failure to Provide Alternative Transportation Home.[34]

Several of the cases in this chapter involve more than one form of employer negligence. For example, some negligent retention cases also involve claims for negligent hiring, and some negligent supervision cases also involve claims for negligent retention. Indeed, in at least one reported case, an injured party sued an employer for *negligently hiring* an unfit employee by not properly performing a comprehensive reference check, *negligently retaining* the employee by continuing his or her employment after learning that the employee was unfit for the job, and *negligently supervising* the employee by not seeking to control or supervise the job performance of the unfit employee.[35]

Because negligent hiring and retention cases frequently deal with physical injury or death caused by unfit employees, a number of the cases summarized in this chapter involve multimillion-dollar jury awards and settlements, including a $16 million settlement agreed to by a company that permitted one of its drivers to operate a delivery vehicle despite knowledge of the driver's drug and alcohol abuse;[36] a $3.7 million settlement, following a $5 million jury award, agreed to by the parent corporation and its housing subsidiary, which failed to conduct a criminal record search of one of its maintenance employees;[37] a $3.5 million jury award against a railroad corporation that failed to warn a supervisor about a subordinate's known violent tendencies;[38] and a $2.5 million jury award against a municipality for failing to evaluate a utility worker's past criminal record.[39]

1. Negligent Hiring

a. Incompetent Employees

Hospital Settles $3.5 Million Suit for Negligently Hiring Kidney Transplant Coordinator

A medical center sought to fill a position for coordinator of its kidney transplant unit. It hired an ex-policeman, who had no medical training and had cataracts. One of the transplant recipients who received a donor kidney after the coordinator was hired was a 53-year-old senior vice president of a bank. Two months after the transplant, however, the kidney was removed when the banker became ill.

X-rays of the kidney revealed that it was cancerous. The patient was diagnosed as having cancer, which spread to his brain and caused his death several months later. The source of the cancer was the donor kidney, as a subsequent review of the donor's medical charts revealed that the donor's kidney was cancerous.

The banker's widow filed a lawsuit against the medical center for $3.5 million. She claimed that her husband's death was caused by the hospital's negligent hiring of the transport coordinator, who was not only unskilled in reading medical charts but was unable to do so by virtue of his cataracts. The hospital settled before trial in an agreement that was sealed by order of the court. *Kolator v. State*, No. 71232 (N.Y. Ct. Cl. Apr. 8, 1988).

Hospital Sued for Negligent Hiring of Nurse Who Allegedly Pushed Baby Back Into Womb

One morning at 6 a.m. an expectant mother started to deliver her baby in a hospital delivery room. The baby's head was visible and was partially out of the mother's body. A nurse was present but no doctor was in attendance, so the nurse allegedly "pushed the baby back into the womb." This unorthodox method of childbirth allegedly resulted in injury to the child, severely retarding the baby's growth.

The parents of the child commenced an action against the hospital for medical malpractice and negligent hiring of hospital personnel. They alleged that the hospital had failed to use due care by hiring a nurse who was incompetent. The hospital contended that all of the claims were barred by the statute of limitations, but the lower court rejected this defense.

On appeal, an appellate court concluded that the medical malpractice claim was barred by the applicable statute of limitations. However, the appellate court permitted the negligent hiring claim to proceed to trial because it was subject to a longer statute of limitations.

The hospital had argued that the negligent hiring allegation was part and parcel of the malpractice claim, which was subject to a shorter statute of limitations period than a cause of action for negligence. The court held, however, that the negligent hiring claim was independent of the malpractice claim, since "liability may be imposed upon a hospital for its failure to employ competent staff for the treatment of patients." *DeLeon v. Hospital of Albert Einstein College of Medicine*, 164 A.D.2d 743, 566 N.Y.S.2d 213 (1st Dep't 1991).

b. Unsafe Employees

Passenger Bitten by Boarding Agent Who Tested Positive for AIDS Antibody Sues Airline for $12 Million

A passenger arrived at O'Hare Airport in Chicago only a few minutes before her flight was scheduled to depart. The ticket agent advised her to proceed directly to the departure gate. At the gate, the boarding agent refused to allow her to board the flight because she had no boarding pass. The passenger protested and the boarding agent closed the door to the jetway.

When the passenger asked for the agent's name, he refused to tell her. She then grabbed his arm. According to the passenger, the agent then kicked her in the shins and bit her hand. When the passenger requested that the airline test the boarding agent for the AIDS antibody, a test was administered and the result was positive.

Claiming that she has been placed in fear for her life, the passenger sued the airline. She charged the airline with negligently hiring the boarding agent and sought $12 million in damages. The passenger contended that, as a common carrier, the airline had the highest duty to safeguard its passengers from health and safety risks and that the airline "knew or should have known that [the agent] had been exposed to a deadly virus and that he is a violent person and is unfit for his job." The case was removed to federal court, where it reportedly is still pending. *Doe v. American Airlines,* No. 86 C 7801 (Cook County, Ill. 1986), reported in 173 Daily Lab. Rep. A-5 (1986).

Jury Awards $500,000 Against Employer Who Failed to Check Driving Record of Unsafe Driver

A man was hired as a driver for a telephone pole company. Before he was hired, he was interviewed by a company recruiter, who failed to ask to see his driver's license and failed to ascertain if he had received any traffic tickets. The driver said he had driven for another company for four months, but, in fact, he had worked for the company for only two months. Further, he had received at least five speeding tickets in the previous 18 months.

About a week after he began driving a truck for the employer, he hit several cars when driving too fast to stop behind stalled traffic. The driver of one of the cars suffered personal injuries, including two cracked teeth and injuries to cervical muscles and nerves, which required hospitalization, traction, therapy, and medication.

The injured car driver sued the telephone pole company for negligent hiring. He also sued the truck driver for ordinary negligence. A jury rendered a verdict in favor of the injured driver—it awarded him almost $250,000 in compensatory damages, assessed $250,000 in punitive damages against the employer, and assessed $50,000 in punitive damages against the truck driver. On appeal, the jury verdicts were upheld. The appellate court noted that the punitive damage awards were appropriate because the employer's conduct endangered the lives of others. *North Houston Pole Line Corp. v. McAllister,* 667 S.W.2d 829 (Tex. Ct. App. 1983).

Camp May Be Liable for Negligent Hiring of Unsafe Ranger Who Kept Guns in Living Quarters

A Boy Scout camp hired a ranger to perform maintenance and repair work. While the ranger's nephew was visiting his uncle's living quarters at the camp, he was shot with one of his uncle's guns by a camp counselor with whom he was playing. The camp allegedly had been aware that the ranger possessed and used guns.

The boy and his mother sued The Boy Scouts of America, a boy scout council, the camp counselor who shot the boy, and the boy's uncle. They alleged that the camp was negligent in hiring the ranger because it knew he had possessed and used guns in the past. The lower court granted the defendants' motion for summary judgment, and an intermediate appellate court affirmed.

The New Jersey Supreme Court reversed, expressly recognizing the tort of negligent hiring. It held that an employer may be liable for the negligent hiring or retention of an incompetent, unfit, or dangerous employee for injuries to third persons proximately caused by such negligence. The court noted that the employee conduct that forms the basis for the cause of action need *not* be within the scope of employment. Thus, the camp could be liable simply by hiring an employee for whom it provided lodging on the grounds of the camp and by knowing the employee was in possession of dangerous weapons. *DiCosala v. Kay,* 91 N.J. 159, 450 A.2d 508 (1982).

c. Dangerous Employees

Failure of Fast-Food Chain to Contact All References Listed by Applicant Results in $210,000 Award for Negligent Hiring

A nationwide fast-food chain operates a "McJobs" program in conjunction with state agencies to provide jobs to the mentally handicapped and developmentally disabled. A retarded 37-year-old man who was referred to the restaurant chain by the Colorado Division of Vocational Rehabilitation previously had been convicted for child molestation and was on parole. The state agency failed to inform the fast-food chain of the employee's prior criminal conviction.

The manager of the restaurant hired the applicant but failed to contact all of the references listed by the applicant on the application form. While still a trainee for the fast-food provider, the employee assaulted a three-year-old boy in the restroom of the restaurant.

The parents of the boy sued the fast-food chain for negligent hiring, contending that if all of the references had been contacted, the restaurant would have learned of the employee's child molestation conviction. The boy's parents also sued the state of Colorado. The restaurant argued that its contract with the state agency required the state to provide "appropriate applicants." The jury found that the state of Colorado was 55 percent at fault, and the fast food chain was 45 percent at fault, and assessed damages at $210,000. *R.M. v. McDonald's Corp.*, No. 89-CV-17012 (Colo. Dist. Ct. Mar. 8, 1991), reported in 53 Daily Labor Report A-6 (1991).

Parent Corporation Settles for $3.7 Million After Jury Awards $5 Million in Damages for Fatal Assault by Paroled Employee

A 15-year-old girl went to visit her blind sister at an apartment complex for the handicapped operated by a not-for-profit housing corporation. The girl was raped and murdered by the housing corporation's maintenance man. He had previously been convicted for the abduction and murder of a young woman, but had been paroled for that offense almost 20 years before.

The parents of the girl brought an action against the housing corporation and its parent corporation, alleging that its subsidiary was negligent in hiring the maintenance employee. The defendants agreed to settle the case for the limit of their insurance coverage—$500,000—but the insurance company declined to settle. The case was then tried to a jury, which awarded the girl's parents $4 million in actual damages, $200,000 in punitive damages, and $750,000 in interest and funeral expenses. After the subsidiary and parent corporations appealed the verdict, the parties reportedly settled for $3.7 million. *Sallaz v. G-H-I Housing Corp.*, No. 85-66859 (Tex. Dist. Ct. Harris County 1986).

Twenty-Minute Interview of Delivery Person May Be Inadequate to Fulfill Supermarket's Duty of Care to Customers

A supermarket chain in New York City provided home delivery service to its customers. Applicants for home delivery positions were interviewed by the personnel director. One of the applicants completed an application form stating that he had never been convicted of a crime. In fact, the applicant had previously been convicted of robbery.

After conducting a 20-minute interview of the applicant, the personnel director hired him—before checking his references. On his fourth day of employment, the employee raped and robbed a customer in her home after he gained access to her apartment while making a delivery.

The woman sued the supermarket for negligent hiring. The employer made a motion for summary judgment, arguing that the supermarket had no affirmative duty to investigate the employee's criminal background before hiring him and had no reason to believe that the employee was violent.

The court denied the motion. It held that when an establishment provides delivery services, it has a duty to its customers to employ safe help to make deliveries. Here, the court noted, the personnel director conducted "a cursory 20-minute interview" and failed to check employment references before employing a delivery person who would be provided by customers with access to their homes. In these circumstances, the court ruled, a jury could reasonably infer that the supermarket failed to exercise due care and caution required by the nature of the job and the consequences of employing an unsuitable or unfit person for the position. The case was reportedly settled for a six-figure amount. *Rosen-House v. Sloan's Supermarket*, N.Y.L.J., Sept. 27, 1988, at 18, col. 4 (Sup. Ct. New York County), *aff'd mem.*, 148 A.D.2d 1020, 540 N.Y.S.2d 120 (1st Dep't 1989).

Employer of Ex-Offenders Cannot Escape Liability by Relying on State-Licensed Agency to Screen Applicants

Following a request at a Rotary Club luncheon by the director of "Stepping Stones," a state-licensed residential treatment center for juveniles, a laundromat owner agreed to hire a number of Stepping Stones residents to work at his place of business. The initial selection of juveniles regarded as suitable for employment was done by Stepping Stones counselors without the participation of the prospective employer. The owner of the laundromat told the director of the agency that he "didn't want any troublemakers," but he never interviewed any of the juveniles sent to work at his business.

One of the Stepping Stones juveniles employed by the laundromat had been "in trouble" since he was 13 years old, although he had never been charged with any criminal conduct involving violence. One evening while working at the laundromat the juvenile severely beat a customer on the head and face with his fists and a hammer.

The customer filed suit against the laundromat and the rehabilitation agency. A settlement was reached between the victim and Stepping Stones, but not with the laundromat. The employer filed a motion for summary judgment, claiming that public policy concerns for fostering innovative release and rehabilitation programs for criminal offenders override an employer's common law duty to hire competent, nonvicious employees. The trial court agreed and entered summary judgment in favor of the employer.

On appeal, the appellate court reversed. It held that while it may be reasonable in some instances for an employer to rely on the screening techniques and judgment of professionals at a residential treatment center for troubled youths, a jury may reasonably conclude that *some* inquiry on the part of the employer was necessary in this case, particularly where the laundromat was open at night and the juvenile was essentially unsupervised. In addition, the appellate court noted, the owner never asked the assailant about his background and failed to inquire whether any of the juveniles referred for employment were known as "troublemakers." The case was reportedly settled. *Nigg v. Patterson*, 226 Cal. App. 3d 551, 276 Cal. Rptr. 587, 6 IER Cases 65 (1990), *superseded,* 279 Cal. Rptr. 99, 806 P.2d 841 (1991).

Mail Room Clerk Who Assaulted Secretary at Home May Subject Employer to Liability

A secretary was employed by a large chemical manufacturer at its corporate headquarters. A mail room clerk who had been convicted of rape and robbery also worked for the firm. The mail clerk's duties required him to circulate among the employees at the headquarters facility, during which time he came in contact with the secretary. His assigned duties also allegedly provided him with the opportunity to learn the name and home address of the secretary. One evening, he followed her home and fatally assaulted her in her apartment. He was later convicted of murder.

The parents of the secretary brought an action against the employer for negligent hiring, and the employer made a motion to dismiss. The lower court granted the motion and dismissed the action. On appeal, however, an appellate court reversed. It held that where a plaintiff can show that the employer knew or should have known of an employee's dangerous proclivities, the employer may be liable for negligent hiring if its negligence in hiring the employee was the proximate cause of the injury and was foreseeable. The appellate court concluded that, based on the allegations that the employer should have known of the mail clerk's violent propensities, the parents were entitled to proceed with their claim for negligent hiring. *Gaines v. Monsanto Co.*, 655 S.W.2d 568 (Mo. Ct. App. 1983).

Tavern Owner Prevails in Suit by Customer Assaulted by Bartender Hired After Reference Check

A customer of a tavern, who had "had a few words" with the bartender the evening before, decided to return to the tavern the next day. The bartender, who evidently was angered to see the customer return so soon, shot the customer twice. The bartender had a prior criminal record of which the tavern owner was not aware. The tavern owner had, however, asked the former owner about previous employees when he purchased the tavern, and the bartender was recommended by the former owner as a good worker and a person the new owner should employ.

The customer brought an action for negligent hiring. The lower court entered judgment in favor of the tavern owner at the end of the trial, and an appellate court affirmed. It concluded that the employer's investigation was sufficient to avoid a breach of duty, notwithstanding the failure to inquire into the bartender's criminal record, because the employer's inquiry did not reveal any facts that placed or should have placed the tavern owner on notice that the employee was potentially dangerous. Accordingly, the tavern owner was not held liable under the doctrine of negligent hiring. *Evans v. Morsell*, 284 Md. 160, 395 A.2d 480 (1978).

Gaps in Employment History Required Apartment Owner to Check Manager's Criminal Record

An apartment manager assaulted and raped a female tenant after gaining access to her apartment with a passkey issued to him by his employer. The employer's agent had interviewed the employee but did not check the references he supplied on his employment application. The employee indicated on his application that he had been convicted of crimes he described as "traffic tickets." This was neither questioned nor investigated by the employer.

In fact, the employee was on parole at the time he was hired—a fact he did not disclose. The employer did contact the owner of an apartment building where the employee had been a manager for a short time, and a car wash where he had worked for three months, and he ran a credit check in the states where the employee had resided most recently. The employer did not learn, however, that the employee had been discharged from the Army after only 14 months and had only a three-month work history in the state where he lived for the five years following the Army discharge; nor did it look into any facts regarding his out-of-state references.

In the tenant's action for negligent hiring, the jury rendered a verdict against the employer, and an appellate court affirmed. It held that the employer's limited investigation did not furnish a sufficient basis for a reasonable employer to conclude that the employee was reliable. Thus, the court stated, reasonable care required the employer to investigate further the possibility that the employee had a criminal record. Had such an inquiry been made, the court noted, the employer would have discovered that the employment gaps occurred because the employee had been in jail.

Although it may have been difficult to obtain information on the employee's criminal history from various state law-enforcement authorities, the court noted that the services of nationwide private investigation agencies are available at relatively modest fees. The court further noted that although such a search might not have revealed a conviction in a state in which the applicant had not indicated he had lived, the fact that a bona fide attempt was made to ascertain this information would have been a significant factor in determining whether the employer exercised the degree of care necessary to avoid liability. *Ponticas v. K.M.S. Investments*, 331 N.W.2d 907 (Minn. 1983).

Authors' Note: The use of criminal record information is frequently governed by state law. In addition, federal and state nondiscrimination laws may also regulate the use of criminal record information. Appendix A sets forth a summary of the laws in selected states governing the request for and use of arrest and conviction information of employees and applicants for employment, as well as a brief review of federal law under Title VII governing employment decisions based on arrest and conviction information. *See also* Appendix C, which deals in part with investigative consumer reports.

Customer Assaulted at Home by Employee May Recover Against Company

A customer contracted with a termite and pest control company to provide regular pest control service in her home. As a result of representations from the contractor that its employee was honest, reliable, and trustworthy, the customer allowed the employee into her home, where he physically assaulted her.

The customer sued the pest control company, seeking over $100,000 in damages. The lower court dismissed the case, but an appellate court reversed and remanded it for trial. The appellate court stated that if the customer could prove her allegations, she could recover damages under the theories of negligent hiring and retention. *Abbott v. Payne,* 457 So. 2d 1156 (Fla. Dist. Ct. App. 1984).

Taxi Company May Be Liable for Driver's Theft of Passenger's Pants

A passenger in a taxi was driven to his home, paid the fare, and exited the cab. He apparently declined to give the taxi driver a tip. The driver assaulted the customer with an iron bar, took his pants and their contents, and drove away. The driver later was convicted of assault.

The customer filed a lawsuit for negligent hiring. The employer filed a motion to dismiss, which was denied by the lower court. An appellate court affirmed and held that the passenger was entitled to a trial before a jury. The court stated that the employer could be held liable for the negligent hiring of the taxi driver if the passenger could prove that the company had failed to investigate prospective drivers to determine whether they were dangerous. *Burch v. A&G Assocs.,* 122 Mich. App. 798, 333 N.W.2d 140 (1983).

Developer May Be Liable for Failure to Reexamine Employee's Fitness Before Transferring Him to New Job

A developer of condominiums hired an employee to perform yard work. The developer gave its managing agent no instructions on how to conduct job interviews, and the employment application form did not request a history of criminal convictions. The agent neglected to contact any former employers or references of the employee.

Three weeks later, the managing agent transferred the employee from an outdoor to an indoor job, which gave him access to tenants' apartments. The employee subsequently assaulted a tenant, allegedly after using a passkey to gain entrance. Unknown to the employer, the employee had been convicted previously of breaking and entering and assault with intent to murder in the second degree.

In the ensuing action for negligent hiring, the trial court entered summary judgment in favor of the employer, but an appellate court reversed. It found that the possibility of "intimate contact" with tenants was a factor to be considered in determining the degree of inquiry required of the employer. Had the employee continued to work at his outside yard-maintenance job, the court noted, an independent inquiry of his past may not have been required. Once the employer transferred him to an indoor job, however, the employer was duty-bound to make a reasonable inquiry about his background, including contacting previous employers and personal references.

The court also noted that unless something in the employee's background was suspect, no criminal record inquiry was required. Finally, the court noted that the cost of obtaining criminal record information would be relevant to the issue of the employer's liability. *Williams v. Feather Sound,* 386 So. 2d 1238 (Fla. Dist. Ct. App. 1980), *review denied,* 392 So. 2d 1374 (Fla. 1981).

d. Untrustworthy Employees

Temporary Hire Must Pass Trustworthiness Test if Allowed in Customer Homes or Businesses

To help him in making a furniture delivery to the home of a customer, a driver employed by the furniture store hired a temporary employee without conducting any investigation or inquiry into the employee's background. At the time of the delivery, the employee stole personal property of the purchaser.

In an action by the customer against the store for negligent hiring, the court awarded judgment against the employer. It held that an employer that gives its drivers authority to hire additional employees "off the street" will be liable for negligent hiring where the employer fails to ensure that proper standards are used in hiring such workers. *Weiss v. Furniture in the Raw,* 62 Misc. 2d 283, 306 N.Y.S.2d 253 (Civ. Ct. Queens County 1969).

Real Estate Firm Liable for $175,000 Where It Knew Its Agent Had Previously Engaged in Forgery

In the course of a real estate transaction, a seller was defrauded by a real estate agent when the agent forged certain signatures on a sales contract. The real estate company that employed the agent had helped the employee obtain a real estate license despite knowing that the agent had previously forged signatures on other documents and had been convicted of passing checks with insufficient funds.

The seller brought an action for negligent hiring and retention against the real estate company. After trial, the court awarded the seller $150,000 in compensatory damages and $25,000 in punitive damages against the employer.

An appellate court affirmed. It held that although the employee acted outside the scope of her employment, the real estate company was liable for negligent hiring and retention because it should have known that the employee might engage in forgeries or frauds in connection with the sale of real estate. *Pruitt v. Pavelin,* 141 Ariz. 195, 685 P.2d 1347 (1984).

2. Negligent Retention

a. Unsafe Employees

Delivery Company That Knew or Should Have Known of Driver's Substance Abuse Settles Suit for $16 Million

A company that delivers telephone books employed a number of drivers. One of the drivers showed a pattern of drug and alcohol abuse, yet his employer allowed him to continue to drive a company truck. After commencing work one day, the driver stopped at a suburban liquor store and purchased a pint of vodka. Having consumed the alcohol, he decided to drive into downtown Washington, D.C. to visit his wife at work. While en route, the driver lost control of his vehicle on a crowded city street, rammed into a dozen cars, and finally hit a 34-year-old woman, dragging her along the street and severely injuring her left leg.

The woman filed a negligent retention suit against the driver's employer, claiming that the employer knew or should have known about the driver's alcohol and drug problem. During the course of pretrial discovery, the woman's attorney also learned that the employer had failed to check the employee's driving record, which would have revealed that his driver's license had been suspended in another state. Only days before the case was scheduled to go to trial, the company reached a settlement with the injured pedestrian valued at $16 million. *Redd v. Product Dev. Corp.,* No. 89-1119 (D.C. Super. Ct. 1990).

b. Supervisors Who Sexually Harass Subordinates

Employer's Termination of Sex Harasser Too Late to Avoid Liability for Punitive Damages

A manager of a textile plant repeatedly made sexually suggestive remarks and gestures toward a female supervisor over a period of two years. His lewd comments included references to male and female genitalia and his willingness to save her job from layoff if she had sex with him.

The female supervisor complained about the plant manager's misconduct to her immediate superior, a department head, but he failed to take any further action because the plant manager was his superior as well. Finally, the plant's personnel manager was informed about the complaints of harassment. Senior management was then notified of the complaints and, after an investigation, the offender was involuntarily terminated.

Three months later, when the plant underwent a reduction in force, the female supervisor elected retirement with severance pay over returning to a nonsupervisory hourly position in the plant. She then filed an action against her former employer and the plant manager for negligent retention, infliction of mental and emotional distress, and invasion of privacy.

A jury returned a verdict in her favor, finding that the employer had negligently retained the plant manager in its employ. The jury found, however, that the female supervisor was *contributorily negligent* and only awarded her $10,000 in compensatory and $50,000 in punitive damages.

The employer appealed, arguing that it could not be held liable where it promptly discharged the offending plant manager as soon as senior management learned of the sexual harassment. The appellate court disagreed. It held that after the female supervisor complained to her immediate superior, it was his obligation to report the allegations of sexual misconduct to higher company authorities. By failing to do so, the employer breached its duty to the plaintiff. *Brown v. Burlington Indus.*, 93 N.C. App. 431, 378 S.E.2d 232 (1989), *review dismissed*, 326 N.C. 356, 388 S.E.2d 769 (1990).

Employer May Be Liable for Negligent Retention of Supervisor Who Harassed Employee

A counter operator in a fast-food restaurant was subjected to lewd and obscene comments by her supervisor, who repeatedly made sexual advances toward her, placed his hands on the private parts of her body, and on one occasion dropped his trousers in her presence. These advances were repelled by the counter operator, but the improprieties continued until she resigned. The employee alleged that incidents of similar misconduct by the supervisor previously had been reported to the employer.

The counter operator brought an action against the employer and her supervisor for negligent retention and assault. The defendants' motion for summary judgment was granted by the trial court, which held that the counter operator's claims were barred by the state workers' compensation law.

On appeal, however, an appellate court reversed. It first held that the counter operator's claims were not barred by the workers' compensation law because the alleged acts of the supervisor did not arise out of the counter operator's employment. Rather, the appellate court held that the harassment constituted willful acts of a third person engaged in for "personal reasons," which removes the case from the domain of the workers' compensation law.

The appellate court then held that although the counter operator could not maintain her claim of assault against the employer, she could proceed with her claim of negligent retention. The court concluded that an employer may be liable for negligent retention if it retained the supervisor in a supervisory position "with notice of his proclivity to engage in sexually offensive conduct directed against female employees." After the appellate court's decision was affirmed by the Georgia Supreme Court, the case was reportedly settled during retrial for $125,000. *Cox v. Brazo,* 165 Ga. App. 888, 303 S.E.2d 71, *aff'd,* 251 Ga. 491, 307 S.E.2d 474 (1983).

c. Dangerous Employees

Failure of Personnel Department to Evaluate Worker's Past Criminal Record Leads to $2.5 Million Award

Pursuant to a state-mandated work relief program requiring the employment of persons receiving public assistance, including ex-convicts, the City of New York hired a welfare recipient to serve as a utility worker in its Parks Department. The worker, who had previously been convicted and served a lengthy prison sentence for attempted rape, robbery, and grand larceny, falsely stated on his application form that he had never been arrested or convicted. Although his fingerprints were taken at the time he applied for a job, he commenced work before his fingerprints were processed by the police department.

Four months later, the police department processed his fingerprints and sent the utility worker's "rap sheet" to the city's personnel department. Despite a detailed set of personnel procedures for determining the types of jobs suitable for applicants with criminal records, the personnel department took no action after it learned that the employee was an ex-convict and had lied about his past criminal record. Three months later, the utility worker sexually assaulted a nine-year-old girl in the maintenance shed at the playground where he had been assigned.

The parents of the victim brought suit against the City of New York for negligent retention of the utility worker. A jury initially rendered a verdict of $2.5 million for the victim, but an appellate court reversed the judgment and remanded the case for a second trial. The city then offered to settle the case for $300,000, but that offer was rejected by the parents. A new trial was held, and a second jury awarded the victim $3.5 million, which was reduced by the trial court to $2.5 million.

On appeal to the highest court in the state of New York, the $2.5 million award was affirmed. While noting the importance of employing former inmates and reintegrating them into society, the New York Court of Appeals held that such a worthy objective cannot excuse a municipal employer from failing to comply with its own procedures requiring informed discretion in the placement of individuals with criminal records. According to the court, if the city's personnel department had at least *considered* whether the worker's criminal record warranted his removal from the job, it would have been insulated from liability under the doctrine of governmental immunity. By ignoring the problem, however, it not only forfeited its governmental immunity but also breached its duty of care to prevent harm to those who would foreseeably come into contact with the worker. *Haddock v. City of N.Y.*, 75 N.Y.2d 478, 553 N.E.2d 987, 554 N.Y.S.2d 439, 5 IER Cases 358 (1990).

$750,000 Awarded Against Employer for Retaining Employee Who Inflicted "Judo Chops" on Customer

A customer entered a car rental office to rent a vehicle for the weekend. Since the customer did not have two credit cards in his possession, company policy required him to pay a deposit of $75 instead of the $20 deposit he had paid in the past. The customer attempted to persuade the employee to accept the smaller deposit, but the employee refused.

An argument ensued and, as the customer turned to leave, the employee struck him with a blow to the back of his head, knocking him to the floor. As the customer lay on the floor, the employee repeatedly kicked him and hit him with "judo chops."

The customer brought a civil action for negligent retention. The trial produced evidence of the employee's irascible nature, inability to get along with subordinates, propensity to "blow up," and occasional use of profane and threatening language when speaking to customers. In addition, the evidence showed that the car rental company had taken no disciplinary action against the employee either before *or* after the incident. A jury awarded the customer $350,000 in compensatory damages against the employer and employee and $400,000 in punitive damages against the employer. The awards were upheld on appeal. *Greenfield v. Spectrum Inv. Corp.*, 174 Cal. App. 3d 111, 219 Cal. Rptr. 805 (1985).

Employer May Use Negligent Retention Theory As a Defense to a Wrongful Discharge Claim

A federal employee was discharged from his job following a violent physical assault on a supervisor and a rampage through the office during which he damaged and destroyed equipment. The employee claimed that his violent behavior was the result of a handicap, described as an "adjustment disorder with mixed disturbance of emotion and conduct and a compulsive personality disorder." The employee filed suit against his employer under the federal Rehabilitation Act of 1973, claiming that the government wrongfully terminated his employment. The employee contended that his employer was obligated by law to accommodate his handicap by transferring him or his supervisor to another position.

The government filed a motion for summary judgment, arguing that it was not required to retain or transfer an employee who demonstrated a propensity for physical violence—even if the employee's behavioral tendencies were caused by a handicapping mental illness. The court agreed, holding that "one who is unable to refrain from doing physical violence to the person of a supervisor, no matter how unfair he believes the supervision to be or how provocative its manner, is simply not otherwise qualified for employment." *Adams v. Alderson*, 723 F. Supp. 1531 (D.D.C. 1989), *aff'd*, No. 89-5265 (D.C. Cir. Apr. 10, 1990).

d. Untrustworthy Employees

Security Agency Must Pay $300,000 to Client Robbed by Guard With "Sticky Fingers"

A manufacturer of gold sunglass frames for the federal government retained a security firm to provide guard services for its facility. A guard employed by the security firm was involved in three thefts of gold used to make the frames. When it hired the guard, the security company requested the employee's police records but did not contact character references he listed and did not ask his previous employers about his honesty and trustworthiness. In addition, a supervisor had reason to suspect the security guard of having "sticky fingers" in connection with a theft of the proceeds of a vending machine.

The manufacturer brought suit against the security firm on theories of negligent hiring, negligent retention, and negligent supervision. After trial, the jury awarded the manufacturer over $300,000 in damages.

An appellate court upheld the verdict, stating that when an employee is being hired for a sensitive occupation, mere lack of negative evidence may not be sufficient to meet the employer's obligation of reasonable care. The court also said an employer's duty to guard against negligent hiring does not end when an applicant is selected for hire. Rather, the court said, an employer has a continuing duty to retain in its service only those employees who are fit and competent, and to supervise carefully any employee *suspected* of wrongdoing. *Welsh Mfg. v. Pinkerton's, Inc.*, 474 A.2d 436 (R.I. 1984).

3. Negligent Supervision

a. Unsafe Employees

Estate of Customer Gets $100,000 but Cannot Reach Deeper Pockets of Oil Company

A motorist pulled into a gas station to fill up his car with fuel. Instead of pumping gasoline, the gas station attendant shot and killed the motorist. The estate of the customer brought suit against the oil company and the gas station. During the course of the lawsuit, the estate learned that the attendant had previously discharged his gun at the station. The gas station agreed to pay the deceased's estate $100,000 in settlement of the claim against it. The oil company, however, filed a motion for summary judgment, which was granted by the lower court.

On appeal, the appellate court affirmed. It held that because the employee charged with the fatal shooting was an employee of the gas station and not of the oil company, the oil company could not be held liable for the action of the attendant. In rendering its opinion, the court stated that the oil company could have been liable under the theory of negligent supervision and retention—*if* it employed the gas station attendant—provided that the customer demonstrated that the employer knew or should have known that its employee had behaved in an unsafe, dangerous, or otherwise incompetent manner, and that the employer, armed with that actual or constructive knowledge, failed to supervise the employee adequately. *Giles v. Shell Oil Corp.*, 487 A.2d 610 (D.C. 1985).

Baseball Club Cleared of Negligent Supervision Claim by Fan Claiming He Was Hit With a Bat by Two Minor Leaguers

During the eighth inning of a Fourth-of-July minor-league baseball game, a patron moved to the third base line and began heckling players sitting in the bullpen. He accused the players of "stealing the local women" and remarked that he would show the players what "West Virginia manhood was like" by "blowing off" the players' heads.

The heckler was then asked to leave by the pitching coach. After the game, the patron encountered the players in the parking lot and a fight broke out. The patron was left with a broken jaw which, he claimed, resulted from one of the players striking him in the face with a baseball bat.

The patron brought suit against the parent baseball team for $2 million in compensatory and punitive damages. He claimed that the team was negligent in failing to supervise, train, and control its players, and in failing to instruct them in the manner, care, and conduct in which they were to treat patrons involved in sensitive situations.

The baseball club made a motion to dismiss the complaint. The court granted the motion, concluding that because attacks on spectators by baseball players are "virtually unheard of," the players' alleged conduct was not reasonably foreseeable. The court therefore declined to impose upon the club a duty to instruct its players on how to handle hecklers. *Simmons v. Baltimore Orioles*, 712 F. Supp. 79, 4 IER Cases 572 (W.D. Va. 1989).

b. Dangerous Employees

County Pays $440,000 in Damages for Failure to Properly Supervise Ex-Convict Employed in Vocational Rehabilitation Program

A county government entered into an agreement with a community college to conduct a program to teach construction skills to 60 individuals, half of whom were former or current prison inmates. Among the people hired by the manager of the program and his assistants was a man who had been previously convicted of second-degree murder.

Most of the job center's employees were aware that vandalism was rampant at the training site. At one point, the employee with the second-degree murder conviction told a co-worker he would kill the person responsible for the vandalism. This comment was known to management. Moreover, the county had assigned the employee to live at the training program job site with the assistant director, so that one of them always would be on the premises to protect it against vandalism and theft. The employee learned that a certain boy had been responsible for the vandalism. He caught the boy, sexually assaulted him, and then murdered him.

The parents of the murdered boy brought a negligent supervision and wrongful death action against the county. The trial court granted summary judgment in favor of the employer. On appeal, the judgment was reversed and the case was remanded for trial.

The appellate court determined that a genuine issue of fact existed as to whether the slaying of the boy was foreseeable. The court also noted that a suspected vandal arguably would be within the class of persons subjected to an increased risk of harm by the negligent assignment of security duties to an employee known to have dangerous propensities. The parties reportedly settled before trial for $440,000. *Henley v. Prince George's County*, 305 Md. 320, 503 A.2d 1333 (1986).

Public Employer May Be Liable Where It Ignored Patients' Complaints About Doctor's Behavior

An inmate patient at a correctional facility claimed to have been sexually assaulted by a physician employed by the New York State Department of Correctional Services. The department had received previous complaints about the physician from other inmate patients.

The inmate brought an action against the state for negligent retention of the physician and failure to supervise him properly. The trial court refused to dismiss the claim and the appellate court affirmed. It held that where an employer fails to respond to patient complaints previously lodged against an employee, a patient is entitled to recover damages for negligent retention and supervision of the unfit employee. *Mercer v. State*, 125 A.D.2d 376, 509 N.Y.S.2d 103 (2d Dep't 1986).

c. Supervisors Who Sexually Harass Subordinates

Employee Sexually Harassed by Superior May Maintain Claim for Negligent Failure to Adequately Train and Supervise Managers

A female security specialist for a utility company experienced unwelcome sexual harassment and physical contact by her manager for a period of six months. The manager allegedly called her at home, followed her during off-work hours, appeared uninvited at her home, delivered sexually suggestive notes to her, ordered her to drive with him to remote rural areas, touched her body in offensive ways without her consent, and detained her against her will in confined quarters late at night. Finally, just before her termination from employment, her manager allegedly called her into his office, detained her, and made her sit in a confined room for hours while he verbally and emotionally abused her and then allegedly coerced her into signing a "settlement and release."

The security specialist commenced a lawsuit against her employer for sexual harassment in violation of Title VII. In addition, she sued her employer for a variety of state law claims: negligent failure to adequately train and supervise the offending manager, breach of employment contract, breach of implied covenant of good faith and fair dealing, intentional and negligent infliction of emotional distress, invasion of privacy, battery, false imprisonment, and fraud.

The employer filed a motion to dismiss all of the state law claims on the ground that the state's antidiscrimination law preempted all tort and contract claims under state law. The court disagreed, holding that the antidiscrimination act did not preempt an independent state law tort or contract claim where the employee seeks to remedy a type of injury that is different than the injuries covered by the antidiscrimination law. With that in mind, the court dismissed the state law contract claims for termination of employment in breach of contract and breach of implied covenant of good faith and fair dealing because the antidiscrimination law provided a remedy for improper discharge. The court concluded, however, that the antidiscrimination law did not preempt any of the state law tort claims because each of the torts sought to remedy an injury other than sexual harassment or improper termination.

As to the employee's claim for negligent failure to train and supervise, the court concluded that employers have an obligation to provide a reasonable amount of training and supervision to supervisory employees to ensure they carry out their duties without endangering their subordinates. According to the court, this includes training and supervision as to the unlawful and prohibited practice of sexual harassment. The court therefore held that the employee could proceed with her failure to train and supervise claim.

Likewise, the court permitted the employee to proceed with her intentional and negligent infliction claims (based on the verbal and emotional abuse she suffered in her supervisor's office on the day of her termination); the invasion of privacy claim (based on the supervisor's intrusion into her private life by calling her at home and following her during off-work hours); the battery claim (based on the nonconsensual offensive touching by the supervisor); the false imprisonment claim (based on the wrongful detention of the employee in confined quarters late at night and in the supervisor's office on the day she was terminated); and the fraud claim (based on the fraudulent inducement of the female employee to sign a "settlement and release"). *Davis v. Utah Power & Light Co.*, 5 IER Cases 1713 (D. Utah 1988).

4. Negligent Failure to Warn

Employer Liable for $3.5 Million for Failure to Warn Supervisor of Employee's Known Violent Tendencies

After an Amtrak superintendent reprimanded a railroad employee for having been in a restaurant eating breakfast when he was supposed to have been at work, the employee returned to the superintendent's office a few hours later carrying a loaded shotgun. The employee fired two shotgun blasts at the superintendent, striking him in the leg and kneecap. The employee had previously engaged in violent conduct at Amtrak, but that fact was never reported to Amtrak supervisory personnel.

The superintendent commenced an action against Amtrak. He claimed that if he had been forewarned of the employee's violent tendencies, he would have taken precautions to avoid injury. A jury agreed, awarding the superintendent $3.5 million in damages.

Although the verdict was overturned by the trial judge, it was reinstated on appeal. The appellate court held that in cases involving a negligent failure to act, courts have been generous in permitting the evidence to be presented to a jury, even "though it is often a pretty speculative matter whether precaution would in fact have saved the victim." *Smith v. National R.R. Passenger Corp.*, 856 F.2d 467 (2d Cir. 1988).

Employer Sued by Sex Harassment Victim for Negligent Failure to Warn of Supervisor's Known Offensive Behavior

After receiving complaints about a supervisor's sexually suggestive remarks and unwelcome touching of female clerical workers, senior managers of a computer company cautioned the supervisor not to engage in conduct that could be regarded as sexual harassment. Subsequently, when the supervisor interviewed a female applicant for a word-processor position, he allegedly asked her what she would do if she were subjected to sexual harassment in the workplace. Shortly after the word processor was hired, the supervisor allegedly made sexually suggestive innuendos to her and began to touch her despite her strenuous objections—although the word processor acknowledged that she did not bring these matters to the attention of management.

One month later, during a snowstorm that caused the office to close early, the word processor accepted a ride to her home from the supervisor. Upon arriving at her home, she claimed that the supervisor insisted upon entering her apartment and grabbed her and then began kissing her despite her demands to stop. Eventually the word processor persuaded the supervisor to leave. She reported the incident the next day.

Senior management commenced a formal investigation, leading to disciplinary action against the supervisor and a warning that he would be terminated for any recurrences or retaliation against the word processor. Nevertheless, the word processor resigned her employment and filed suit against the computer company and the supervisor.

In addition to sexual harassment and constructive discharge claims under Title VII, the word processor sued for negligent failure to warn. She claimed that her employer had an affirmative duty to warn her about a supervisor's known offensive and harassing behavior. The lower court dismissed that claim.

On appeal, the appellate court remanded the state law claim for negligent failure to warn. The appellate court directed the lower court to afford the word processor an opportunity to clarify the precise nature of her claim and to demonstrate whether it was a valid cause of action in Virginia. In an unpublished decision by the lower court, the employee's failure-to-warn claim was dismissed. *Paroline v. Unisys Corp.*, 900 F.2d 27 (4th Cir. 1990)(*en banc*), *vacating in part* 879 F.2d 100 (4th Cir. 1989), *on remand*, No. 88-0063-A (E.D. Va. July 13, 1990).

5. Negligent Performance Evaluation

Terminated Employee Recovers Damages for Employer's Failure to Inform Him That Discharge Was Being Contemplated

A long-term employee of a manufacturing company served as the company's manager of manufacturing. He was given generally favorable job evaluations by his superior, the vice president of manufacturing, for the first eight years. In the ninth year, the vice president of manufacturing was replaced. The manager of manufacturing expressed great disappointment at not being named as the new vice president, and he allowed his disappointment to adversely affect his work performance and attitude.

When the new vice president completed an annual performance evaluation for the manager, the vice president commented on the manager's strengths and weaknesses, including his poor attitude and lack of cooperation. Although the vice president met with the manager to discuss the performance evaluation, the vice president did not show him the evaluation, nor did he disclose to the manager that the company was contemplating termination of the manager if his performance did not dramatically improve. Several months later, the manager was terminated for poor attitude, lack of leadership, and lack of cooperation.

The manager commenced an action in federal court against his employer for age discrimination, wrongful discharge, and negligent job evaluation. The district court dismissed the age discrimination claim. It also dismissed the wrongful discharge claim, finding that although the employer was contractually obligated by its employee handbook to terminate managers only for cause, the employer had good cause for discharge.

The district court held, however, that the employee stated a claim for negligent performance evaluation. It concluded that because the employee handbook provided that annual employee evaluations were intended to benefit employees, the employer had a duty to use ordinary and reasonable care in performing the annual evaluations.

In reviewing the evidence, the district court found that the vice president of manufacturing had breached that duty by failing to warn the manager, at the time of his annual performance review, that he might be terminated if his job performance did not rapidly and dramatically improve. The court calculated the manager's compensatory damages at $210,000 and assessed his mental distress damages at $150,000. But, since the district court determined that the manager was contributorily negligent, it reduced the total damages award against the employer by 83 percent. *Chamberlain v. Bissell Inc.*, 547 F. Supp. 1067 (W.D. Mich. 1982).

Negligent Performance Evaluation Claim Limited Where Employee Alleges Breach of Duty Distinct From Contractual Obligation

A machine operator failed to appear for at least two consecutive weekend overtime shifts. Missing overtime was a violation of the rules of conduct established in the employer's handbook for employees. The employee had previously violated a number of other employee rules, including low productivity, quitting early, and poor attitude. The employer's president decided to recommend discharge of the operator. He made his recommendation to an employee committee composed of the operator's co-workers. The committee approved the employee's termination.

The employee filed a lawsuit alleging wrongful discharge and negligent performance evaluation. His wrongful discharge claim was premised on the termination procedures of the employee handbook, which, he claimed, his employer was contractually bound to follow but had failed to adhere to. The employee's negligent evaluation claim was based on the performance evaluation provisions of the same employee handbook. The employee alleged that his evaluations, which led to his discharge, were misleading, inaccurate, and negligently compiled.

The lower court dismissed the employee's wrongful discharge claim but directed that his cause of action for negligent evaluation be tried to a jury. On appeal, an appellate court reversed on the negligent evaluation claim. It ruled that prior judicial opinions recognizing the tort of negligent evaluation had incorrectly permitted a tort action based on breach of contract.

The appellate court held that where an employee claims that his or her employer is *contractually* bound to follow certain procedures in an employment manual, the employee cannot also claim that the employer *negligently* failed to follow the procedures in the handbook. A negligent evaluation claim, the appeals court held, can only be maintained if the employee alleges that the employer breached a duty of care distinct from the breach of a contractual duty to the employee. *Loftis v. G.T. Prods.*, 167 Mich. App. 787, 423 N.W.2d 358, 3 IER Cases 641 (1988).

Authors' Note: The tort of negligent performance evaluation has not received a favorable reception in the courts after *Loftis*.

6. Negligent Failure to Provide a Smoke-Free Workplace

Court Recognizes Tort of Negligent Failure to Provide Reasonably Smoke-Free Workplace

A Washington state social services employee worked in an office environment that continuously exposed her to cigarette and tobacco smoke. She complained to her supervisors that constant exposure to cigarette smoke was having an adverse effect on her health. Her employer, though, failed to take any steps to correct the problem. As a result of her exposure to tobacco smoke in the workplace, she developed chronic obstructive pulmonary disease. The employee resigned after her physician advised her that she should not continue to perform her job unless the state provided her with a clean-air working environment.

The employee filed a claim for workers' compensation, but it was denied on the grounds that her lung disease was not the result of a work-related injury, nor did pulmonary lung disease constitute an industrial injury. Unable to obtain workers' compensation benefits, the employee sued the state for negligently failing to provide her with a smoke-free environment.

Although the lower court dismissed her claim, her cause of action for negligence was reinstated on appeal. In ruling in favor of the employee, the Washington Supreme Court stated that an employer has an affirmative and continuing duty to provide all employees with a reasonably safe place to work. This common law duty, it held, includes a duty to provide a working environment reasonably free from tobacco smoke pollution. The court noted that the employer's duty does not require it to provide a smoke-free environment for each employee no matter what the cost; if, however, an employer is aware of an individual employee's special or particular sensitivity to tobacco smoke, it has a common law duty to take reasonable steps to accommodate the employee's sensitivities. The parties reportedly settled the case. *McCarthy v. State,* 110 Wash. 2d 812, 759 P.2d 351, 3 IER Cases 710 (1988).

Authors' Note: See also *Carroll v. Tennessee Valley Authority,* summarized in Chapter 4, where an employee's claim against her employer for negligent failure to provide a smoke-free workplace was dismissed—although the court permitted the employee to proceed with a claim against her employer for intentional infliction of emotional distress.

7. Negligent Polygraph Administration

Lawsuit for Negligent Administration of Polygraph Exam May Proceed to Trial Where Consent and Release Form Executed by Employee May Be Invalid

Due to losses of merchandise, a lumber company scheduled polygraph examinations for several employees, including an employee with multiple sclerosis (MS). The employer was aware that the employee had MS. Immediately before administering the test, the employer obtained the employee's signature on a form consenting to the examination and releasing the lumber company and the company that employed the polygraph examiner from all claims. The employee claimed that he believed his job would be terminated if he did not sign the release and take the polygraph exam.

The employee advised the polygraph administrator that he had MS and was taking a drug called prednisone. The administrator said he would determine at a later time whether the medication could affect the polygraph results. The polygraph administrator reported to the employer that the employee had been deceptive during the examination, but noted that the results were questionable due to his uncertainty as to the effect of the employee's illness and medication on the test results.

Another exam was scheduled but was canceled when the employee's physician advised the lumber company that the employee was not physically fit for a second test. After a brief absence from work caused by his illness, the employee returned to work for a month, only to be told by the lumber company that he was being terminated because he was physically unfit for his duties.

The employee brought a suit for negligent administration of the polygraph examination, defamation, and intentional infliction of emotional distress. Holding that the consent and release form signed by the employee was valid, the trial court dismissed the negligent administration and defamation causes of action. A jury, however, returned a verdict in favor of the employee on the intentional infliction of emotional distress claim.

On appeal, the appellate court reversed the trial court's rulings. First, it dismissed the intentional infliction claim, holding that the mere scheduling of a second exam did not constitute outrageous conduct. Next, the appellate court reinstated both the negligent administration and defamation claims, holding that the validity of the consent and release form was a question for the jury. The appellate court stated that the consent form would only be regarded as valid if it was executed by the employee free of duress and with full knowledge of its terms. Since the employee presented evidence to the contrary, the matter was an issue to be decided by a jury. The case was reportedly settled after appeal. *Mechanics Lumber Co. v. Smith*, 296 Ark. 285, 752 S.W.2d 763, 3 IER Cases 891 (1988).

Authors' Note: The federal Employee Polygraph Protection Act, 29 U.S.C. sections 2001–9, limits and governs the request for and use of polygraph examinations. It does not, however, preempt state law tort claims regarding polygraph examinations. See 29 U.S.C. section 2009. Some states also have enacted laws limiting and governing the request for and/or use of polygraph examinations. Appendix B sets forth the laws regarding polygraph examinations in selected states and briefly outlines the restrictions set forth in the federal polygraph protection law.

8. Negligent Furnishing of Alcohol to Intoxicated Employees

Employer May Be Liable for Negligently Furnishing Alcohol to Employee at Employer-Hosted Banquet

An employee for an aluminum company attended a banquet provided by the company to honor its long-term employees. The banquet was held at an inn. At the banquet, the company provided its employees with dinner, champagne, wine, and mixed drinks. The employee arrived at 7 p.m. and by 8:30 p.m. had consumed at least ten drinks. He continued his drinking, although at a slower pace, until he left the banquet at 10:30 p.m. He then entered his car and drove away. He ended up driving the wrong way on a freeway off-ramp, striking a motorcycle and seriously injuring the motorcyclist.

The injured motorcyclist filed suit against the driver's employer and the inn for negligently furnishing alcohol to an intoxicated person. The lower court granted the defendants' motion for summary judgment, which was affirmed by an intermediate appellate court.

On further appeal, summary judgment in favor of the defendants was reversed. The Washington Supreme Court held that because the motorcyclist had presented witnesses who testified that the employee was intoxicated when he left the banquet, it was up to the jury to decide whether the employer and/or the inn knew or should have known that the employee was intoxicated. The appeals court also concluded that the fact that the employer did not sell or serve the alcohol to its employees was irrelevant, since the employer's managers were present at the banquet and could have ordered that service be denied. *Dickinson v. Edwards,* 105 Wash. 2d 457, 716 P.2d 814 (1986).

Authors' Note: The issue of an employer's liability for furnishing liquor to its intoxicated employees has received varied treatment by the courts, depending on the state involved and the existence of certain tavern-owner laws. For example, liability was imposed on an employer under North Carolina law in *Chastain v. Litton Systems*,[40] and under Texas law in *Otis Engineering Corp. v. Clark*,[41] but no duty of care was found to exist under Minnesota law in *Meany v. Newell*[42] and under Michigan law in *Millross v. Plum Hollow Golf Club*.[43]

9. Negligent Failure to Provide Alternative Transportation Home

Motorists Injured by Exhausted Employee May Recover Damages Against Employer

A laborer for a railroad reported to work at the railway depot at 7 a.m. The depot was 50 miles from his house. After working for three hours at the depot, the laborer and several other co-workers were transported to the site of a train derailment. Upon arriving, the laborers were directed to repair the track and remove debris caused by the derailment. Much of the work involved heavy manual labor. The work was continuous, except for intermittent periods when the workers were required to step out of the way of heavy equipment.

The work continued long past the laborer's normal 3:30 p.m. quitting time. At 10 p.m. that night, the laborer told his foreman that he was tired and wanted to go home. The foreman told him not to leave. After a meal break at about 1 a.m. of the next day, the laborer once again was directed to return to work.

He continued to work, repairing the derailment, until 9:30 a.m., when he finally told the road master that he was too tired to continue to work. The laborer asked for a ride to his car, which he had parked at the train depot. When he arrived, he got into his car and started to drive home—but never arrived. He fell asleep at the wheel of his car and caused an accident, seriously injuring the driver and passenger in another vehicle.

The motorists filed an action for negligence against the railroad company and the laborer, claiming that the railway willfully, negligently, and "with a conscious disregard for the rights and safety of others," ordered the laborer to work for almost 27 straight hours without rest and then failed to provide either rest or alternative transportation home when it knew or should have known that the laborer constituted a menace to the safety of the public. After the close of evidence at trial, the railroad asked the trial court to enter judgment in its favor on the ground that it owed no duty of care toward the motorists. The trial court agreed with the railroad and entered judgment in its favor.

The judgment was reversed on appeal. The appellate court observed that the legal concept of "duty" was an evolving one and the current emphasis "has ... shifted toward the goal of compensating victims of tortious conduct." It then noted that the railroad's conduct not only involved a failure to take appropriate precautionary measures (such as providing the employee with alternative transportation home or an area to rest before driving home), but also included the affirmative conduct of requiring the employee to work unreasonably long hours and then "setting him loose on the highway." In these circumstances, particularly where it was reasonably foreseeable that the laborer would be unable to drive home safely, the appeals court held that the railroad had a duty of care to the injured motorists. *Robertson v. LeMaster,* 171 W. Va. 607, 301 S.E.2d 563 (1983).

Notes

1. *See* cases summarized in section D.1.a. of this chapter.
2. *See* cases summarized in sections D.2.a. and D.3.a. of this chapter.
3. *See* cases summarized in section D.5. of this chapter.
4. *See* cases summarized in section D.4. of this chapter.
5. *See* case summarized in section D.6. of this chapter.
6. *See* case summarized in section D.7. of this chapter.
7. *See* case summarized in section D.8. of this chapter.
8. *See* case summarized in section D.9. of this chapter.
9. *See* Restatement (Second) of Torts § 282.
10. *See* Restatement (Second) of Agency §§ 219(1), 228. *See also* Introduction, Section B.
11. *See* Restatement (Second) of Agency § 219(2): "A master is not subject to liability for the torts of his servants acting outside the scope of their employment, *unless:* ... (b) the master was negligent or reckless." (emphasis added.) *See also* Restatement (Second) of Agency § 213, comment d; Restatement (Second) of Torts § 317.
12. *See* Gaines v. Monsanto Co., 655 S.W.2d 568 (Mo. Ct. App. 1983), summarized in section D.1.c. of this chapter.
13. *See* DiCosala v. Kay, 91 N.J. 159, 450 A.2d 508 (1982), summarized in section D.1.b. of this chapter.
14. *See* Henley v. Prince Georges County, 305 Md. 320, 503 A.2d 1333 (1986), summarized in section D.3.b. of this chapter.
15. *See* Rosen-House v. Sloan's Supermarket, N.Y.L.J., Sept. 27, 1988, at 18, col. 4 (Sup. Ct. New York County), *aff'd mem.,* 148 A.D.2d 1020, 540 N.Y.S.2d 120 (1st Dep't 1989), summarized in section D.1.c. of this chapter.
16. *See* Gaines v. Monsanto Co., 655 S.W.2d 568 (Mo. Ct. App. 1983), summarized in section D.1.c. of this chapter.
17. *See* Ponticas v. K.M.S. Inv., 331 N.W.2d 907 (Minn. 1983), summarized in section D.1.c. of this chapter.

18. *See* Restatement (Second) of Torts § 317, comment c.
19. *See* cases summarized in section D.2.b. of this chapter.
20. *See* Williams v. Feather Sound, 386 So. 2d 1238 (Fla. Dist. Ct. App. 1980), *review denied*, 392 So. 2d 1374 (Fla. 1981), summarized in section D.2.c. of this chapter.
21. *See* Weiss v. Furniture in the Raw, 62 Misc. 2d 283, 306 N.Y.S.2d 253 (Civ. Ct. Queens County 1969), summarized in section D.1.d. of this chapter.
22. *See* Ponticas v. K.M.S. Inv., 331 N.W.2d 907 (Minn. 1983), summarized in section D.1.c. of this chapter.
23. *See* Welsh Mfg. v. Pinkerton's, Inc., 474 A.2d 436 (R.I. 1984), summarized in section D.2.d. of this chapter.
24. *See* Greenfield v. Spectrum Inv. Corp., 174 Cal. App. 3d 111, 219 Cal. Rptr. 805 (1985), summarized in section D.2.b. of this chapter.
25. *See* cases summarized in sections D.4.–9. of this chapter.
26. Restatement (Second) of Torts § 282.
27. Restatement (Second) of Torts §§ 328A(a), 328B(b).
28. *Compare* Chamberlain v. Bissell, Inc., 547 F. Supp. 1067 (W.D. Mich. 1982) *with* Loftis v. G.T. Prods., 167 Mich. App. 787, 423 N.W.2d 358, 3 IER Cases 641 (1988). Both cases are summarized in section D.5. of this chapter.
29. *Compare* Smith v. National R.R. Passenger Corp., 856 F.2d 467 (2d Cir. 1988) *with* Paroline v. Unisys Corp., 900 F.2d 27 (4th Cir. 1990)(*en banc*), *vacating in part* 879 F.2d 100 (4th Cir. 1989), *on remand*, No. 88-63-A (E.D. Va. July 13, 1990). Both cases are summarized in section D.4. of this chapter.
30. Restatement (Second) of Torts §§ 328A(b), 328C(b).
31. Restatement (Second) of Torts §§ 281(c), 328A(c).
32. Restatement (Second) of Torts § 284(a), (b).
33. *See* Smith v. National R.R. Passenger Corp., 856 F.2d 467 (2d Cir. 1988), summarized in section D.4. of this chapter.
34. Two other forms of employer negligence—negligent misrepresentation and negligent infliction of emotional distress—are discussed in Chapter 2, section C., and Chapter 4, section C., respectively.
35. *See* Welsh Mfg. v. Pinkerton's, Inc., 474 A.2d 436 (R.I. 1984), summarized in section D.2.d. of this chapter.
36. *See* Redd v. Product Dev. Corp., No. 89-1119 (D.C. Super. Ct. 1990), summarized in section D.2.a. of this chapter.
37. *See* Sallaz v. G-H-I Housing Corp., No. 85-66859 (Tex. Dist. Ct. Harris County 1986), summarized in section D.1.c. of this chapter.
38. *See* Smith v. National R.R. Passenger Corp., 856 F.2d 467 (2d Cir. 1988), summarized in section D.4. of this chapter.
39. *See* Haddock v. City of N.Y., 75 N.Y.2d 478, 553 N.E.2d 987, 554 N.Y.S.2d 439, 5 IER Cases 358 (1990), summarized in section D.2.c. of this chapter.
40. 694 F.2d 957 (4th Cir. 1982), *cert. denied*, 462 U.S. 1106 (1983).
41. 668 S.W.2d 307 (Tex. 1983).
42. 367 N.W.2d 472 (Minn. 1985).
43. 429 Mich. 178, 413 N.W.2d 17 (1987).

Chapter 2

Fraud and Misrepresentation

A. Overview

Employer liability for fraud and misrepresentation has been the focus of considerable litigation in the past few years. Most frequently, claims arise when an employer makes false promises or misstatements of fact to an applicant during the recruitment and hiring process in order to persuade the applicant to accept a job with the employer.

Most employee claims for fraud and misrepresentation involve false promises regarding the terms or conditions of employment, such as bonuses, profit sharing, salary, commissions, reimbursement of relocation expenses, promotions, work schedules, length of employment, and job responsibilities. Employee lawsuits have also been brought by strike replacements who have been told that their jobs are "permanent," only to be replaced by the striking workers at the conclusion of the strike.

Another form of hiring fraud involves misleading or erroneous statements about the employer's profitability or economic stability. This type of fraud is likely to be the subject of a lawsuit where an employee resigns from a job with one employer to accept a seemingly better position with a new employer, only to be laid off by the new employer because of undisclosed financial difficulties that existed or were anticipated at the time of hiring.

Lawsuits for employer fraud have also involved false promises or misrepresentations intended to persuade employees not to seek employment elsewhere or to forgo job opportunities with other employers. Cases have also arisen where an employer falsely represents that it will provide a specific level of pension benefits or misrepresents that medical benefits will continue. In addition, employer fraud can arise where an employer terminates an employee after falsely promising that the employee would not be discharged if he or she cooperated in an investigation of workplace misconduct, fraudulently induces employee resignations, and fraudulently conceals information from employees about illnesses caused by hazardous workplace substances.

B. General Principles of Law

Generally, the essential elements in an action for fraud or misrepresentation are:

(1) a false representation of fact, opinion, intention, or law;
(2) knowledge or belief that the information is false;
(3) intent to induce another to act, or to refrain from acting, in reliance upon the false representation;
(4) causing the other to act, or refrain from acting, in reasonable reliance upon the false representation; and
(5) damage to the other person resulting from reliance upon the false representation.[1]

Thus, where an employer or its agent states to an employee that he or she will be given job security to induce the employee not to accept a position with a competitor, the employer will be liable in an action for fraud if it knew the employee would eventually be replaced and the employee, in reliance on that statement, declined the other offer.[2] Likewise, an employee who took a lie detector test based on the representation that he would retain his job if the results were negative could pursue a fraud claim where his employer terminated him the day after the test results failed to show he had answered the questions deceptively.[3]

An employer may be liable for fraud not only where its agent knew or believed the representation was false, but also where the agent did not have confidence in the accuracy of the representation or did not have a basis for making the statement.[4] Even ambiguous statements can subject an employer to liability if one interpretation of the representation would be false, and if the representation is made without regard to how it will be understood by an employee.[5] Further, representations that are misleading because the employer fails to state additional or qualifying information (*i.e.*, "half-truths") are also actionable under the tort of fraud.[6]

For a misrepresentation to subject the employer to liability, however, it must be *material*. "Material" is defined as a matter of importance in determining one's choice of action.[7] An employer's liability under the law of fraud is not confined, though, to misrepresentations of material information. *Concealment* of material information may also subject an employer to liability for fraud.[8] Liability for fraudulent concealment may arise, for example, where the failure to disclose material information will cause a prior statement to be misleading, or where after-acquired information renders a prior statement untrue or misleading.[9]

Employee fraud claims are frequently accompanied by an action for breach of contract. In those cases, even if the employee fails to prove the employer knowingly intended never to fulfill its promise, the employee can still recover damages in a breach of contract action based on the promise itself.[10] In that event, although the employee will not be entitled to punitive damages for the intentional tort of fraud, the employee will still be able to recover his or her compensatory damages for a breach of contract. Thus, given the current state of the law in this area, employers should take special care not to make any promises they will be unable to fulfill.

C. Trend in the Law: Negligent Misrepresentation

A new and significant development in this area of the law is the emergence of the tort of negligent misrepresentation in the employment context. No intent is necessary to establish liability under this tort; thus, *innocent* misrepresentations to employees are actionable, as long as the employee can show that the employer knew or *should have known*, in the exercise of reasonable care and competence, that the representation made to the employee was false.[11] For example, a high-school principal who neglected to state that his assurance of continued employment was based on the continuation of past levels of enrollment may be liable for damages if the teacher is not hired the next year due to a decline in enrollment.[12]

Courts have also recognized claims for negligent misrepresentation where an employer's representative, in attempting to recruit an employee, states that the potential employer's relationship with its sole supplier is stable when in fact it is tenuous,[13] or states that a financially troubled employer is profitable when it has only made money during the past two months.[14]

Similarly, courts have also recognized claims for negligent misrepresentation where an employer induces an employee to accept a severance package based on the employer's inflated estimate of the level of pension benefits the employee would receive for early retirement,[15] or when an employer fails to fulfill a promise to "bridge" an employee's past years of service for pension benefit purposes—where the employer's representative who made the statement should have known that the pension plan could not horor the employee's prior years of service.[16]

D. Illustrative Cases

The cases summarized below are grouped into the following categories of employer fraud and misrepresentation:
- Fraudulent Recruitment and Hiring:
  - misrepresentations of employer's business or profitability, and
  - misrepresentations of terms or conditions of employment;
- Fraudulent Retention of Employees;
- Misrepresentations Regarding Employee Benefits;
- Fraudulent Employee Assignments;
- Fraudulent Employee Investigations;
- Fraudulent Inducement of Employee Resignations; and
- Fraudulent Concealment of Workplace Illnesses.

In some of the cases reported in this chapter, the employees alleged not only fraud but negligent misrepresentation as well.[17] In this fashion, even if an employee is unable to prove that the employer *knew* its representations were false, the employee can still recover for negligent misrepresentation if he or she can prove that the employer *should have known* its statements were false. In one such case, a jury returned a verdict against the employer in the amount of $2.7 million for negligently misrepresenting that the relationship between the employer and its sole supplier of goods was stable when in fact it was shaky.[18]

In another case summarized below, a jury returned a $10.1 million award of damages against an employer for luring a senior executive away from a competitor with false promises of, among other things, hefty bonuses and participation in profit plans.[19] Other large jury awards against employers include a $1.3 million verdict for fraudulent concealment of a workplace-related disease;[20] a $750,000 punitive damage award for inducing an executive to remain employed by falsely promising him a bonus worth $30,000;[21] a $600,000 award against an employer that directed an employee to engage in fraudulent pricing practices;[22] and a $450,000 award for failing to disclose to an employee, who was eventually laid off, that the employer was experiencing severe financial difficulties at the time she was hired.[23]

1. Fraudulent Recruitment and Hiring

a. Misrepresentations of Employer's Business or Profitability

Failure of Employer to Disclose Financial Difficulties During Job Interview Results in $450,000 Jury Award

The president of a computer services company that was experiencing serious financial difficulties interviewed an applicant for the position of sales manager. A few months before the interview, the president had concluded that if efforts to rehabilitate the business did not succeed, the company might have to shut down in six months.

During the interview, the applicant asked the president about the company's financial status. The president stated that the company had no detailed financial reports. He also stated that the company was owned by a multimillion-dollar parent corporation and referred the applicant to a magazine article that commented favorably on the company's likelihood of success. The applicant was offered the position; she accepted it and relocated from New Orleans to Denver at a salary of $45,000 per year.

The company continued to experience serious financial difficulties and, only three months after the applicant was hired as sales manager, three dozen employees were laid off. Four months later, the sales manager was permanently laid off as well.

The sales manager filed an action against the computer company for fraudulent concealment, claiming that if, during the hiring process, the employer had disclosed to her that the company was in serious financial difficulty, she would not have accepted the offer and relocated to Denver. A jury awarded her $450,000 in damages: $90,000 in compensatory damages and $360,000 in punitive damages.

On appeal, the employer asserted that it had no duty to disclose any financial information or plans to an applicant during the interview process, especially where such disclosure involves confidential information that may be useful to competitors. The appellate court disagreed and upheld the $450,000 jury award. It held that an employer has a duty to disclose to an applicant "facts—even facts which are confidential—basic to the transaction" where it has stated other facts that it knows will create a false impression. *Berger v. Security Pac. Information Sys.*, 795 P.2d 1380, 5 IER Cases 951 (Colo. Ct. App. 1990).

$2.7 Million Jury Verdict for Negligent Misrepresentation Remanded for New Trial

A vice president of a domestic automaker was recruited by a major distributorship of a foreign car manufacturer to serve as the executive vice president for the distributorship. During the course of negotiations, the owner of the distributorship represented that the executive vice president would (1) report directly to the owner, (2) not be required to perform the duties of general manager, (3) receive equity participation in all future business ventures of the distributorship, and (4) be provided with a $200,000 life insurance policy. The owner also made two other representations to the executive vice president that the distributorship's franchise with Toyota was stable, and the owner's relationship with the general manager for the distributorship was amicable.

During his first days on the job, the new executive vice president discovered that the owner's relationship with both the foreign car manufacturer and the general manager had been troubled for some time. Eventually, the owner dismissed his general manager and required the executive vice president to assume the duties of general manager. Subsequently, the owner hired another high-ranking employee to whom the executive vice president was directed to report. Construing that new reporting relationship as a constructive discharge, the executive vice president resigned from his job. At the time he quit he had not been provided with the $200,000 life insurance policy he was promised and was not, as promised, included as an equity participant in an automobile venture organized by the owner during the employee's tenure as executive vice president.

The executive vice president brought an action for breach of contract, fraud, and negligent misrepresentation against his employer and the owner of the distributorship. Although the jury returned a verdict in favor of the employer on the fraud count, it awarded the executive vice president $221,000 on his breach of contract claim and $2.7 million on his negligent misrepresentation claim. The employer appealed, claiming that none of the six representations to which the executive vice president pointed could form the basis for a claim of negligent misrepresentation.

On appeal, the appellate court held that while none of the first *four* representations could form the basis for a claim of negligent misrepresentation, the final *two* representations, those pertaining to the stability of the distributorship's franchise with the foreign-car manufacturer and the owner's relationship with the general manager, if made, were legally sufficient to sustain the verdict. Accordingly, the court remanded the negligent misrepresentation claim for a new trial based solely on those two representations. *Weisman v. Connors,* 312 Md. 428, 540 A.2d 783, *rev'd and remanded on remand,* 76 Md. App. 488, 547 A.2d 636 (Ct. Spec. App. 1988), *cert. denied,* 314 Md. 497, 551 A.2d 868 (1989).

Partial Truth About Company's Profitability Not Sufficient to Defeat Claims for Fraud and Negligent Misrepresentation

During the course of interviewing an applicant for the position of Director of Industrial Sales, the personnel director allegedly described the employer as a "profitable company." After the interview, the employer offered the job to the applicant, who accepted the offer and relocated from Seattle to Cleveland to join the company. Eight months later, the employee was laid off.

The employee filed an action for fraud, negligent misrepresentation, and breach of contract. He claimed that the personnel director had misrepresented the financial position of the employer by failing to disclose during the interview that the company had lost money in each of the two prior years. In response, the employer filed a motion for summary judgment, arguing that the personnel director's statements were accurate inasmuch as the company earned profits during the two months immediately preceding the interview.

The court denied the motion and directed that the case proceed to trial. It noted that an employer is under a duty to make full disclosure of facts "where necessary to dispel misleading impressions which might have been created by . . . partial revelation of facts." The court therefore concluded that trial was warranted on the fraud and negligent misrepresentation claims since the personnel director had made factual statements about the company's financial condition without explaining that his description of the firm as "profitable" pertained only to a very limited period of time. *Harlan v. Intergy, Inc.,* 721 F. Supp. 148, 4 IER Cases 497 (N.D. Ohio 1989).

b. Misrepresentations of Terms or Conditions of Employment

Jury Awards $10.1 Million for Luring Executive Away From Competitor With False Promises

A large corporation wooed a national sales manager away from one of its major competitors, holding out the prospect of a division presidency, an eventual salary of $100,000 a year, hefty bonuses, and a profit participation program that could ultimately be worth up to $1 million. The executive was hired as a vice president, but claimed that another recruit was also lured to the company with the same promise of becoming the division president. Further, the employee claimed that the profit participation program was abandoned and the promised bonuses were not forthcoming. He also claimed that the division for which he was hired was dissolved by the corporate parent and that it knew that the division's dissolution was likely because of financial difficulties that were never disclosed to the executive during the course of his interviews. Eventually, after the executive complained to senior management and to the company's board chairman, the employee was dismissed.

The executive filed suit for fraud and breach of contract. At trial, the employee introduced a letter from one of the employer's personnel executives, stating that "[s]everal individuals were falsely led to make major career decisions" based on promises by corporate personnel. The letter also warned that lawsuits might be brought by executives who were promised millions of dollars in bonus and profit-sharing programs that never materialized. The jury deliberated for only nine hours, and returned a verdict for over $10.1 million, including $9 million in punitive damages. After the company appealed the verdict, the parties settled for an undisclosed seven-figure sum. *Dowie v. Exxon Corp.*, 12 Conn. L. Trib. No. 29 (July 28, 1986), at 1.

Company Liable for Fraud Where Vice President Made Promise to Rehire Employee but Had No Authority to Make Such Promise

A plant manager for a manufacturer of shoe soles had been employed by the company for four years when he was terminated from employment. After working at another company for five years, he was contacted by his former employer and asked to return. He initially refused to do so, but did agree to serve as a consultant for six weeks. At the end of the six-week period, a vice president of the sole manufacturer told the employee, who was 57 years old at the time, that if he agreed to work in a full-time regular position with the company, he could remain with the firm until he was 65 and could stay beyond age 65 if he wanted to. The employee accepted the offer and began to serve as manager of the injection mold department.

After several months, the employee learned that the injection mold work was going to be transferred to another facility in a different state. Although he offered to move to the other state, the company advised him that it had already hired another person to serve as manager of the injection mold department at the other location. The employee's job was thereafter continued on a week-to-week basis, and he was eventually terminated less than a year after he had been rehired by the company.

The employee filed a lawsuit against the employer for fraud, breach of contract, and negligent infliction of emotional distress. After all evidence was presented at trial, the trial court granted judgment for the employer on the claim for negligent infliction, but submitted the fraud and breach of contract claims to the jury. The jury then returned a verdict in favor of the employee, awarding him $110,000 in compensatory damages and $35,000 in punitive damages.

An appellate court affirmed the verdict in favor of the employee on the fraud claim. It held that, based on the evidence introduced at trial, the jury could have reasonably concluded that the employer's vice president made the promise of continued employment until age 65 either (1) knowing that he had no authority to make such a promise and failing to disclose to the employee that he lacked the authority to fulfill the promise, or (2) knowing that the company only intended to retain the employee for a short period of time. In either case, the appellate court concluded, the employee had established a cause of action for fraud and was therefore entitled to an award of compensatory damages. The court did, however, reverse the jury's award of punitive damages, holding that the vice president's conduct was not malicious or motivated by ill will. *Boivin v. Jones & Vining, Inc.*, 578 A.2d 187, 6 IER Cases 48 (Me. 1990).

Employer May Be Liable for Fraud If Manager Knowingly Misrepresents Duties, Responsibilities, or Salary Potential of Job

A female employee worked for over 20 years at the aircraft engine division of a major industrial corporation, serving in a supervisory position in the word-processing unit. When the division decided to reorganize its word-processing activities, her job was eliminated. After discussions with her manager, the employee accepted a transfer to a newly created position called "Word Processor Analyst." According to the employee, her manager offered her a "first crack" at this new job, which, he said, would involve innovative use of word-processing equipment, significant supervisory responsibilities, further opportunities for salary enhancement, and a chance to work directly under the manager.

Instead, the employee claimed, she was asked to perform menial clerical chores for a lower-level manager. And when she applied for a transfer to a higher-level job, a male applicant received the promotion.

The employee filed an action against her employer and manager for sex discrimination and fraud. She claimed that she was discriminatorily denied the promotion and placed in a "dead-end" job because of her sex. She claimed that her manager promised her a job with innovative duties, supervisory responsibilities, and enhanced salary potential while knowing that the job would not provide such opportunities.

The employer filed a motion for summary judgment, seeking dismissal of the claim for fraud. The court denied the motion. It stated that while false statements of conditions to exist in the future are usually not actionable, reliance on false representations concerning future events may be justifiable where the party making the representations exercises control over the occurrence of the future event. The court held that the employee may recover for fraud upon proof that her manager, who was in a position to exercise control over the future conditions of the employee's job, knowingly misrepresented either the potential benefits of the job or his own intent to provide them, and that the employee relied on those representations to her detriment. *Della Croce v. General Elec. Co.*, 2 IER Cases 1548 (D. Mass. 1988).

Unfulfilled Promise by Vice President to "Go to Bat" for Employee Can Result in Recovery for Fraud

For over two months, an Illinois resident interviewed and negotiated with a nationwide nursing home enterprise for the position of acquisition director for its western division in Fresno, California. The applicant met with officials of the employer in Illinois, California and finally in Jackson, Mississippi. During the meeting in Mississippi with one of the employer's vice presidents, the applicant was orally offered the position of acquisition director. The offer was then confirmed in a letter, which also provided that the company agreed to pay the employee's relocation expenses. The employee accepted the offer and relocated his family from Illinois to California. Four months later the employee was fired, only a few days after he requested that the company purchase his unsold house in Illinois.

The employee sued the employer in federal district court in Illinois for $300,000 in damages for fraud, alleging that the employer had misrepresented that it would purchase the employee's Illinois home after he commenced working for the employer in California. In his deposition, the employee testified that during the meeting in Mississippi, he told the employer's vice president that he was only willing to undertake the risk of selling his house for 90 days. He also testified that the vice president replied, "[I'll] go to bat for you in 90 days" and "buy your home."

The employer filed a motion for summary judgment. The district court granted the motion and the employee appealed. On appeal, the employer contended that any representations made to the employee about the sale of his house were "promises of events to occur *in futuro*," which should not form the basis for a cause of action for fraud. The appellate court disagreed, holding that a promise made with no intention of performing it is actionable fraud where the other party relies on it as an inducement to enter into an agreement. The appeals court further held that the employee's deposition testimony was sufficient to send the case to a jury to decide whether the vice president made the alleged promise and, if so, whether he knew the promise to be false at or soon after he made it and failed to disclose that fact to the employee. *Palmer v. Beverly Enters.*, 823 F.2d 1105, 3 IER Cases 218 (7th Cir. 1987).

Sales Employee Who Accepted Job Offer for Daytime Work May Maintain Action for Fraud Where She Was Required to Work Evenings Instead

A sales employee who interviewed for a job in a furniture store was told by the sales manager that her hours would be from 8:30 a.m. to 5:30 p.m. Tuesday through Saturday, and that she would receive an eight-percent commission on all in-store sales. The employee accepted the offer, quit her old job, and relocated closer to her new employer. When she began work, however, she was informed by the sales manager that she would have to work evenings and would receive a commission of less than eight percent. She quit her new job less than two weeks later.

The sales employee brought an action for fraud against the store and its sales manager, together with an action for breach of contract.

The lower court granted the defendants' motion for summary judgment, and the employee appealed. The employer argued on appeal that the action for fraud was properly dismissed because the employment was at-will and, hence, the terms of employment could be modified by the employer at any time.

The appeals court disagreed, holding that even at-will employees have a right to rely on representations by an employer about the terms and conditions of employment. The court concluded that the action for fraud could be maintained by the employee because the record contained sufficient evidence to support an inference that the sales manager intended to change the employee's terms of employment once she began her new job. *Albrant v. Sterling Furniture Co.*, 85 Or. App. 272, 736 P.2d 201, *review denied*, 304 Or. 55, 742 P.2d 1186 (1987).

Although Broken Promises Did Not Constitute Fraud, Podiatrist May Still Recover Damages for Breach of Contract

A podiatrist entered into an employment contract with the president of a podiatry services corporation. The contract provided for a base salary "plus such bonuses as shall be approved by the Board of Directors from time to time provided that if any such bonuses are approved, employee's bonus shall be equal to twenty-five percent (25%) of the total bonus so declared for all employees." The employment relationship deteriorated and the podiatrist was terminated. No bonus was paid.

The podiatrist brought suit for fraud and breach of contract, claiming that the president induced him to accept employment based on fraudulent promises regarding the bonus. The court held that in the absence of any proof that, at the time the agreement was entered into, the employer did not intend to fulfill its contractual obligation to pay a bonus, the podiatrist could not prevail in his action for fraud. Rather, the court stated, the podiatrist was limited to his damages under the contract. *Higgins v. Lawrence,* 107 Mich. App. 178, 309 N.W.2d 194 (1981).

Strike Replacements Promised "Permanent" Employment but Terminated at the End of a Strike May Maintain $500,000 Misrepresentation Claim Against Employer

Twelve employees were hired by an employer as permanent replacements for employees who were on strike against the employer for a new contract. The 12 employees had responded to an advertisement in a local newspaper, which stated, in part, "Openings Available for Qualified Persons Looking for Employment to Permanently Replace Striking Warehouse and Maintenance Employees." Shortly after they were hired, the union filed an unfair labor practice charge against the employer.

In order to convince the strike replacements that their jobs were not in jeopardy, the employer distributed a letter addressed "to all permanent employees," assuring them that their positions were secure. The union and the employer subsequently agreed on the terms of a new contract and a resolution of the unfair labor practice charge. As part of the settlement agreement, the employer agreed to reinstate at least 35 of the striking employees. To make room for them, the employer laid off the 12 replacements.

The strike replacements filed suit against the employer for breach of contract and fraud, seeking $250,000 in compensatory damages and $250,000 in punitive damages for the tort claim. They claimed that the employer knew that its promise of permanent employment was false, and that the strike replacements would detrimentally rely on the promise in accepting the offer to work behind the picket line. The trial court held that the replacements' claims were preempted by the National Labor Relations Act (NLRA), but an appellate court reversed.

The case proceeded to the United States Supreme Court, which held that the strike replacements' claims were not preempted by the NLRA. The Supreme Court stated that although the labor laws permit an employer to hire permanent replacements, those same laws may not be invoked to nullify an employer's valid promise of permanent employment. The Supreme Court suggested that employers protect themselves from such lawsuits by making all offers of employment to strike replacements subject to both a strike settlement agreement and an NLRB order that the strikers (if they are adjudged by the Board to be unfair labor practice strikers) be reinstated. *Belknap, Inc. v. Hale,* 463 U.S. 491, 113 LRRM 3057 (1983).

Fired Strike Replacements Receive Compensatory and Punitive Damages in Action for Fraudulent Misrepresentation

At the expiration of a collective bargaining agreement, union employees of a meat-packing company went on strike and set up pickets outside the plant entrance. Management determined that to remain in operation during the strike, it would have to hire new employees and use supervisory personnel on the kill floor. Several strike replacements were hired during the first week of the strike;

each was promised that he would not be fired in the event the strike was settled. The strike was settled 12 days after it started. The strike replacements were laid off at the end of their shift on the following day.

The strike replacements filed an action for fraud and breach of contact against the employer. The case was tried to a jury, which returned a verdict awarding both compensatory and punitive damages to each of the strike replacements.

On appeal, the jury verdict was upheld. The appellate court stated that the jury could have reasonably concluded that the employer fraudulently misrepresented to the strike replacements that they would have permanent positions, intending all along to use them only as strike replacements and to terminate their positions when the strike was settled. *Verway v. Blincoe Packing Co.*, 108 Idaho 315, 698 P.2d 377 (1985).

2. Fraudulent Retention of Employees

False Promise to Pay $30,000 Bonus Results in Punitive Damage Award of $750,000

A Texas travel company executive and the company president conducted lengthy negotiations regarding the executive's continuation of employment after the expiration of his two-year employment contract. The parties reached an oral agreement on salary and discussed a proposed bonus plan. Under the plan, the executive would be paid a five-percent bonus on any improvement over the company's net operating loss in the prior year. The bonus would be paid when a profit was realized.

The company president instructed the executive to formalize their bonus arrangement in writing. The executive did so and then gave it to the company president. The plan was modified by the company attorney but never returned to the executive. When the executive made further inquiry, the company president stated that he had no intention of honoring the bonus plan.

The executive brought an action for fraudulent misrepresentation and breach of an oral contract. The jury found that the company president had made a false promise he never intended to keep and that the executive relied on it to his detriment. The jury awarded the executive $30,000 in compensatory damages (the amount of the promised bonus) and $750,000 in punitive damages for fraudulent misrepresentation, but the trial court reduced the amount of the punitive damages award. Although an intermediate appellate court reversed the jury's verdict, the Supreme Court of Texas affirmed the judgment in favor of the employee. Further, it remanded the case to the intermediate appellate court to determine whether the trial court had erroneously reduced the $750,000 punitive damages award. *Spoljaric v. Percival Tours,* 708 S.W.2d 432 (Tex. 1986).

Teacher May Recover for Principal's Negligent Misrepresentation Regarding Continued Employment

A high school language teacher was employed under two successive one-year contracts. Toward the end of the second contract period, the teacher's principal told her that there would be "no problem" with her teaching certain courses the following year, that everything "looked fine" for rehire the next year, and that she should continue her planning for the exchange program for the following year. Shortly thereafter, a notice was posted that stated "all present faculty members will be offered contracts for next year." Less than one month later, though, the teacher was informed that her contract would not be renewed due to staff cutbacks as a result of declining enrollment.

The teacher brought an action for negligent misrepresentation and breach of contract. The lower court dismissed both causes of action. An intermediate appellate court reinstated the claims, but on further appeal only the negligent misrepresentation claim was permitted to proceed. The appellate court held that because the principal should have known that his hiring plans were contingent on student enrollment levels for the following year, his statements, while not intentionally false, constituted negligent misrepresentations for which damages may be recovered. *D'Ulisse-Cupo v. Board of Directors,* 202 Conn. 206, 520 A.2d 217, 2 IER Cases 948 (1987).

Japanese Employer May Be Liable for Fraud After Breaking Employment "Marriage"

The national sales manager of a Japanese electronics firm retained an executive search firm to assist him in seeking new employment opportunities. After interviewing with a major competitor of his employer, he was offered a comparable position but was assured that he would become a vice president within a reasonable period of time. He accepted the offer and submitted a letter of resignation to the president of his company. The president then called him into his office, told him he was personally insulted by his resignation, ripped up the resignation letter, and told the sales manager that he had a job for the rest of his life because the company, according to the president, would not fire any of its managers.

Based on these statements by the company president, the sales manager revoked his acceptance of the competitor's offer. He then informed the company vice president that he had done so. The vice president assured him that "he was married to the company and that no divorce was allowed." A few days later, the sales manager advised the executive search firm that he had revoked his acceptance of the competitor's offer. The recruiter advised him, however, that his employer was actively seeking to replace him.

The sales manager immediately confronted the company's vice president with the information from the recruiter. The vice president told him that the company was not seeking to replace him and the recruiter just wanted to earn a fee by placing the sales manager with another firm. Only four months later, though, the employee was terminated without cause.

The sales manager commenced a lawsuit against the employer for fraud, breach of contract, defamation, outrage, and tortious interference. He alleged that the company had been seeking to replace him while simultaneously inducing him to stay with the firm and forgo other valuable employment opportunities. He claimed that he reasonably relied to his detriment on the deceitful misrepresentations of the company president and vice president.

The lower court dismissed all of the sales manager's claims on summary judgment. An intermediate appellate court reinstated the sales manager's claims for fraud, breach of contract, and tortious interference, and that ruling was affirmed on further appeal. As to the fraud claim, the appellate court held that the employee was entitled to present his claim to a jury because there were material issues of fact regarding every element of a cause of action for fraud: the employer's false representation, its knowledge of the falsity, the employee's reasonable reliance on the false representations, and damages resulting therefrom. *Shebar v. Sanyo Business Sys.*, 111 N.J. 276, 544 A.2d 377, 3 IER Cases 1385 (1988).

3. Misrepresentations Regarding Employee Benefits

Employee May Maintain Action for Fraud and Negligent Misrepresentation Where Employer Failed to "Bridge" Employee's Past Years of Service for Pension Purposes

A welding supervisor worked for a steel company at its Brooklyn shipyard for 12 years until the shipyard was shut down and the supervisor was laid off. Thirteen years later, the company offered the employee a job as a welding and burning supervisor at its Hoboken,

New Jersey yard. The employee claimed that a company representative told him at the time he was offered reemployment that the employer would "bridge" his 13-year break in service by treating his 12 years of prior employment as part of his continuous service with the employer. He also claimed that an employer representative told him that he would be provided with sufficient employment time to qualify for a fully vested pension.

The employee accepted the offer and worked there for four and a half years, until the employer closed that shipyard and again laid him off. The employee received no pension benefits from the employer after his termination from employment.

The employee brought an action for fraud, negligent misrepresentation, and breach of contract, claiming that he accepted reemployment and resigned his employment elsewhere in reliance on the alleged representations, which the employer knew or should have known were false.

The employer filed a motion for summary judgment, urging dismissal of the claims on the basis of ERISA preemption. The court disagreed. It held that where an employee neither seeks benefits *under a plan* nor seeks damages for refusal to provide benefits *under a plan,* state law claims for fraud, negligent misrepresentation, and breach of contract are not preempted by ERISA. As the court noted, ERISA does not preempt an employee's lawsuit for damages *from the employer* arising from the company's failure to bridge his years of service and to retain him as an employee long enough for his pension to vest. *McNamee v. Bethlehem Steel Corp.,* 692 F. Supp. 1477 (E.D.N.Y. 1988).

Employee May Obtain Damages for Misrepresentations Regarding Promised Increase in Pension Benefits

A senior executive of a truck trailer manufacturer was a long-term participant in a company-sponsored pension plan. After the manufacturer was acquired by a multinational corporation, the executive learned that the pension benefits available under the parent corporation's pension plan were far superior to the benefits under the manufacturing subsidiary's plan. He claimed that he was told by the parent corporation's chairman of the board and the subsidiary's manager of employee relations that the benefits available under the parent subsidiary's pension plan would be made equal to the benefits under the parent corporation's pension plan. The executive agreed to continue his employment based on this promise of an enhanced pension benefit. When the executive resigned, however, he was advised that he would be receiving the regular pension benefits available under the subsidiary's pension plan.

The executive sued the parent corporation under ERISA for interference with his attainment of superior pension benefits under the corporate pension plan, and for benefits under the corporate pension plan. In addition, he sued the parent corporation and the subsidiary's personnel manager for fraud, claiming that he continued his employment based on the defendants' misrepresentations that the pension benefits he would be receiving under the subsidiary's plan would be equal to the superior benefits available to comparable salaried executives under the parent corporation's pension plan.

The employer filed a motion for summary judgment, contending that the fraud claim was preempted by ERISA. The court denied the motion. It noted that if the executive succeeded in proving his allegations of fraud, compensatory damages would be paid directly to him by the corporate parent, *not* out of any pension plan. It therefore held that the fraud claim was not preempted by ERISA simply because the subject of the deception was pension benefits. As the court stated, "Like promises for a raise in salary, a promotion, or the use of tickets to a baseball game, [the] employer's promise to provide the plaintiff with certain benefits at some unknown time in the future, upon which plaintiff could reasonably rely, is the essence of the fraud involved." *Greenblatt v. Budd Co.*, 666 F. Supp. 735 (E.D. Pa. 1987).

Widow of Employee Recovers $121,000 in Damages for False Assurances That Employee's Medical Coverage Would Continue

A salaried salesman for a farm equipment company was hospitalized on and off for several years. About the time that the company's farm equipment business began to decline, company officials determined that the salesman was "not paying his way." The employer thus decided to convert the salesman from his salaried status to that of an unsalaried, commissioned independent contractor. When the employee's wife inquired about continuation of health benefits, she claimed she was told "not to worry" because her husband's group employee medical coverage would continue. Shortly thereafter, the salesman became ill again and subsequently died. His wife submitted claims for medical coverage, but she was denied benefits under the plan. She claimed that she never received a notice of termination of insurance.

The salesman's widow commenced an action against the employer for equitable estoppel, which is similar to an action for negligent misrepresentation. A jury awarded the salesman's widow $121,000 in damages, and the verdict was upheld on appeal. The appellate court held that where an employer misrepresents to an employee that his or her medical coverage will continue, the employer is liable for damages where the misrepresentation would reasonably lead the employee to conclude that there was no need to seek medical coverage elsewhere. *Cory v. Binkley Co.*, 235 Kan. 906, 684 P.2d 1019 (1984).

Authors' Note: Termination of medical benefits provided under an ERISA plan requires compliance with the federal COBRA law, including notification of termination of coverage and an opportunity for the employee to pay the full cost of his or her medical insurance. See 29 U.S.C. sections 1161–68 and 26 U.S.C. section 162(k). State laws may also require such notification.

4. Fraudulent Employee Assignments

Employee Recovers $600,000 Where He Was Told by Superiors That the Fraudulent Pricing Practices He Was Asked to Perform Were Necessary to Ensure a "Fair Profit"

An employee of a major industrial manufacturer worked in the accounting department. A few years after he was hired, he was asked to provide a cost breakdown for military contracts and federal government procurements. He was occasionally directed to revise his figures upward to increase the number of man-hours allocated to particular projects. When the employee questioned this practice, he was advised by his superiors that this was an established practice for government contractors to ensure a "fair profit." He was also told, "You have been asked to do a job, do it."

Eventually, the company commenced an internal investigation of its pricing practices. The employee fully cooperated in the investigation and willingly divulged information about how he performed his cost breakdowns. Shortly thereafter, the employee was told that he was being terminated and that his name was being supplied to the federal government for possible criminal investigation and indictment. The employee was eventually granted immunity from prosecution in exchange for his testimony regarding the division's pricing irregularities.

The employee filed an action against his former employer for fraud, intentional infliction of emotional distress, defamation, promissory estoppel (detrimental reliance), and breach of contract. A jury returned a general verdict for $600,000 in favor of the employee, finding for him on his fraud, intentional infliction, and promissory estoppel claims.

On appeal, the appellate court upheld the jury's verdict on the fraud and intentional infliction claims. As to the action for fraud, the appeals court held that such an action may be maintained where the false representations of an employer expose an employee to potential criminal liability. In this case, the court held, the employee had presented sufficient evidence to the jury that his employer had represented to him that the illegal pricing practices he was asked to perform were perfectly legitimate. Because the appellate court reversed on the promissory estoppel claim, though, it remanded the case for a new trial on damages because it could not determine to what extent the jury's award of damages was influenced by the promissory estoppel claim. *Russ v. TRW*, 59 Ohio St. 3d 42, 570 N.E.2d 1076, 6 IER Cases 769 (1991).

5. Fraudulent Employee Investigations

Special Agents "Railroaded" Into Reporting Financial Irregularities May Recover Damages for Fraud

Four special agents of a railroad, after being assured by the railroad's comptroller that "no one would lose their jobs," informed the railroad's internal auditing department that they had information concerning fraudulent misappropriation of railroad funds and services by their supervisors. Relying on this assurance of no retaliation, the special agents revealed the alleged misappropriation of funds.

Subsequently, the special agents began to experience subtle forms of retaliation, such as a change in their hours of employment. They reported this to one of the railroad's vice presidents, to whom the special agents also revealed other financial improprieties. He, too, assured them that they would not be retaliated against or suffer loss of employment. Eventually, however, one of the special agents was fired and the others were told that their jobs would be abolished or they would be transferred to another state.

In the agents' actions for fraud and wrongful discharge, the trial court granted summary judgment to the railroad. On appeal, the judgment was reversed. The appellate court held that where employees are assured that they will not suffer reprisals for disclosing improprieties, the employees may recover damages for fraud if they face retaliation for having done so. *Mueller v. Union Pac. R.R.*, 220 Neb. 742, 371 N.W.2d 732 (1985).

Union Employee's Fraud Claim Based on Inconclusive Results of Polygraph Exam Preempted by Federal Labor Law

An employee of a trucking company was seen by a security guard attempting to take gas from one of the company's service vehicles. The employee admitted to taking the gas but claimed that he did so to refuel a work-related vehicle. Several days after the incident, the employee's supervisors approached him, and when they were not satisfied with the explanation he gave, he was terminated.

The employee then filed a grievance with his union. In response to his grievance, his supervisor offered him the following options: resign, be fired and proceed with a grievance, or submit to a polygraph exam which, if negative, would result in his reinstatement. The employee agreed to take the test even though the collective bargaining agreement governing his employment prohibited the use of polygraph exams as a condition of employment. The test proved inconclusive, but the employee was not reinstated.

The employee filed an action against his employer in state court for fraud, misrepresentation, defamation, breach of contract, negligent and intentional infliction of emotional distress, and breach of an implied covenant of good faith and fair dealing. In his claim for fraud, the employee alleged that his employer had no intention of reinstating him when it offered him the opportunity to take the polygraph exam.

The employer removed the case from state to federal court, and then made a motion for summary judgment. The court held that the employee's state law fraud claim was preempted by federal labor law because the use of polygraphs was a matter dealt with in the collective bargaining agreement. As such, the employee's claim was subject to resolution through the grievance and arbitration provisions contained in the labor contract. *Jeffers v. Convoy Co.*, 636 F. Supp. 1337, 1 IER Cases 919 (D. Minn. 1986).

Authors' Note: See Appendix B and the Authors' Note in Chapter 1, section D.7., regarding the federal Employee Polygraph Protection Act, 29 U.S.C. sections 2001–09, and selected state laws limiting and governing the use of polygraph examinations.

6. Fraudulent Inducement of Employee Resignations

Employee May Recover Damages Where He Resigned Based on Employer's Inflated Estimate of His Future Pension Benefit

A long-term foreman for a newspaper was offered a "buyout" package whereby he would resign his employment in exchange for a $50,000 lump-sum payment, enhanced severance pay, and continuation of medical and life insurance benefits. He was given one week to decide whether to accept or decline the offer.

In an effort to determine whether he could afford to resign his $50,000-per-year job, the foreman asked the employer's pension manager to tell him what his monthly pension benefit would be if he accepted the buyout offer. The pension manager advised the foreman that his monthly benefit would be $1049 per month "in rough figures." Following receipt of this information from the employer's pension manager, and after consultation with his financial adviser, the foreman accepted the buyout offer and then applied for early retirement. When he began receiving his monthly pension checks, however, they were for $774 per month, $275 per month less than the $1049 figure he had previously been given.

The foreman brought an action against the employer for negligent misrepresentation, claiming that he relied to his detriment upon the pension manager's negligent misstatement as to the value of his pension benefit in deciding to accept the buyout offer. The employer's pension manager conceded that the $1049 figure he communicated to the foreman was incorrect, and that his error resulted from undue haste. The foreman, in turn, conceded that all he was entitled to under the terms of the pension plan was the $774 monthly benefit he had been receiving. In his claim for negligent misrepresentation, therefore, the foreman did not seek to recover any additional benefits from the pension plan. Instead, he sought compensatory damages from his employer resulting from the relinquishment of his job, which had paid him a salary of $50,000 per year.

In response to the complaint, the employer filed a motion for summary judgment, arguing that the foreman's claim was preempted by ERISA and should thus be dismissed. The court denied the motion. It held that the employee could proceed with his negligent misrepresentation claim inasmuch as he was suing not as a participant of a pension plan but, rather, as an employee seeking economic damages from his employer based on false financial information negligently communicated to him by a representative of his employer. *Sandler v. New York News,* 721 F. Supp. 506 (S.D.N.Y. 1989).

60 *Employer's Guide to Workplace Torts*

Automaker May Be Liable for Fraudulently Inducing Employees to Resign

A subsidiary of an automobile manufacturer decided to lay off a large number of its unionized employees in response to an economic downturn in the industry. A committee made up of union and management representatives created the "Voluntary Termination of Employment Plan," which offered severance pay in lump-sum or two-year installments to employees who agreed to resign. Thirty-two of the employees who opted for severance pay under the plan subsequently sought reemployment with the company. Their requests were denied.

The 32 employees sued the company for fraud, claiming that the automaker had fraudulently induced them to opt for the severance plan with false promises regarding their future reemployment eligibility. The employer filed a motion for summary judgment, contending that the fraud action was preempted by the federal labor and pension laws, but the motion was denied. An appellate court agreed, holding that the fraud claim could be maintained because it was not preempted by the NLRA or ERISA. *Wells v. General Motors Corp.*, 881 F.2d 166, 4 IER Cases 1392 (5th Cir. 1989).

7. Fraudulent Concealment of Workplace Illnesses

$1.3 Million Jury Verdict Upheld for Fraudulent Concealment of Workplace-Related Disease

Six pipefitting employees at two New Jersey manufacturing plants worked in plants containing extensive piping insulated with an asbestos-containing material. Each employee received annual or semiannual physical examinations and chest X-rays from the company's doctors, who advised the workers that they were fit for continued asbestos-related duty and suffered from no relevant medical problems. The pipefitters continued to work in asbestos-exposed areas for several years, and each was eventually diagnosed by his own physician as suffering from asbestosis.

The six employees brought an action for fraudulent concealment against the company and its physicians. They claimed that earlier X-rays showed the presence of asbestosis-related symptoms, but that the physicians did not disclose this information to them. The employees also introduced evidence that the company, including its corporate physicians, knew of the dangers of prolonged asbestos exposure, yet they provided employees with minimal information concerning these risks. The case was tried to a jury, which returned a verdict of $1,382,500 in favor of the plaintiffs, including $200,000 in punitive damages for each of the six employees. The employer appealed.

On appeal, the appellate court affirmed the jury verdict. It noted initially that the employees' claim for fraudulent concealment required them to prove more than mere negligent misdiagnosis on the part of the company's doctors, because negligence would only entitle the employees to relief under the workers' compensation laws. In contrast, the appeals court noted, a claim for fraudulent concealment in these circumstances requires proof of aggravation of occupational disease or illness resulting from the employer's fraudulent concealment of already-discovered disabilities.

In this case, the appeals court concluded, even though the employees had presented no *direct* evidence of intentional concealment, the *circumstantial* evidence presented by the employees and their witnesses was sufficient for a jury to infer that the employer or its physicians knowingly concealed relevant medical information from the workers. The appellate court therefore upheld the jury awards, which were also affirmed on further appeal to the New Jersey Supreme Court. *Millison v. E.I. du Pont de Nemours & Co.*, 226 N.J. Super. 572, 545 A.2d 213 (App. Div. 1988), *aff'd*, 115 N.J. 252, 558 A.2d 461 (1989).

Notes

1. Restatement (Second) of Torts § 525.
2. *See* Shebar v. Sanyo Business Sys., 111 N.J. 276, 544 A.2d 377, 3 IER Cases 1385 (1988), summarized in section D.1.b. of this chapter.
3. *See* Jeffers v. Convoy Co., 636 F. Supp. 1337, 1 IER Cases 919 (D. Minn. 1986), summarized in section D.5. of this chapter.
4. *See* Restatement (Second) of Torts §§ 526(b), (c).
5. *See* Restatement (Second) of Torts § 527.
6. *See* Restatement (Second) of Torts § 529.
7. *See* Restatement (Second) of Torts § 538.
8. *See* Restatement (Second) of Torts § 550.
9. *See* Restatement (Second) of Torts § 551. A cause of action for equitable estoppel may also be brought on the basis of misrepresentations, whether intentional or innocent. *See* Cory v. Binkley Co., summarized in section D.3. of this chapter.
10. *See* Weisman v. Connors, 312 Md. 428, 540 A.2d 783, *rev'd and remanded on remand*, 76 Md. App. 488, 547 A.2d 636 (Ct. Spec. App. 1988), *cert. denied*, 314 Md. 497, 551 A.2d 868 (1989), summarized in section D.1.a. of this chapter; *and* Higgins v. Lawrence, 107 Mich. App. 178, 309 N.W.2d 194 (1981), summarized in section D.1.b. of this chapter.
11. *See* Restatement (Second) of Torts § 552, comments (e) and (f).

12. *See* D'Ulisse-Cupo v. Board of Directors, 202 Conn. 206, 520 A.2d 217, 2 IER Cases 948 (1987), summarized in section D.2. of this chapter.
13. *See* Weisman v. Connors, 312 Md. 428, 540 A.2d 783, *rev'd and remanded on remand,* 76 Md. App. 488, 547 A.2d 636 (Ct. Spec. App. 1988), *cert. denied,* 314 Md. 497, 551 A.2d 868 (1989), summarized in section D.1.a. of this chapter.
14. *See* Harlan v. Intergy, Inc., 721 F. Supp. 148, 4 IER Cases 497 (N.D. Ohio 1989), summarized in section D.1.a. of this chapter.
15. *See* Sandler v. New York News, 721 F. Supp. 506 (S.D.N.Y. 1989), summarized in section D.6. of this chapter.
16. *See* McNamee v. Bethlehem Steel Corp., 692 F. Supp. 1477 (E.D.N.Y. 1988), summarized in section D.3. of this chapter.
17. *See* Harlan v. Intergy, Inc., 721 F. Supp. 148, 4 IER Cases 497 (N.D. Ohio 1989), summarized in section D.1.a. of this chapter; *and* McNamee v. Bethlehem Steel Corp., 692 F. Supp. 1477 (E.D.N.Y. 1988), summarized in section D.3. of this chapter.
18. *See* Weisman v. Connors, 312 Md. 428, 540 A.2d 783, *rev'd and remanded on remand,* 76 Md. App. 488, 547 A.2d 636 (Ct. Spec. App. 1988), *cert. denied,* 314 Md. 497, 551 A.2d 868 (1989), summarized in section D.1.a. of this chapter.
19. *See* Dowie v. Exxon Corp., 12 Conn. L. Trib. No. 29 (July 28, 1986), at 1, summarized in section D.1.b. of this chapter.
20. *See* Millison v. E.I. du Pont de Nemours & Co., 226 N.J. Super. 572, 545 A.2d 213 (App. Div. 1988), *aff'd,* 115 N.J. 252, 558 A.2d 461 (1989), summarized in section D.7. of this chapter.
21. *See* Spoljaric v. Percival Tours, 708 S.W.2d 432 (Tex. 1986), summarized in section D.2. of this chapter.
22. *See* Russ v. TRW, 59 Ohio St. 3d 42, 570 N.E.2d 1076, 6 IER Cases 769 (1991), summarized in section D.4. of this chapter.
23. *See* Berger v. Security Pac. Information Sys., 795 P.2d 1380, 5 IER Cases 951 (Colo. Ct. App. 1990), summarized in section D.1.a. of this chapter.

Chapter 3

Defamation

A. Overview

The number of defamation actions filed by employees against employers has surged during the past few years. These actions have arisen in a broad range of employment-related matters, including evaluations, workplace investigations, disciplinary warnings, terminations, postemployment references, and administrative proceedings before unemployment and workers' compensation boards.

These lawsuits have involved employer statements regarding illegal drug use, alcohol abuse, theft, fraudulent conduct, incompetence, and sexual harassment. Even the AIDS epidemic has become the subject of employee lawsuits for defamation.

B. General Principles of Law

There are two types of defamation actions: libel (written or printed defamation) and slander (spoken defamation).

A communication is defamatory if it tends to harm the reputation of another in a way that lowers him or her in the estimation of the community, or deters others from associating or dealing with him or her.[1] Statements that adversely reflect upon an employee's job fitness or abilities are defamatory; so too are statements that an employee has engaged in criminal conduct (such as using illicit drugs), is dishonest or lacks integrity, or has a loathsome disease (such as AIDS or venereal disease).[2]

Injury to reputation is a necessary element of an action for defamation. Often, though, injury to reputation will be presumed from the nature of the statements themselves, such as statements that an employee is incompetent or "a zero."[3]

A defamatory statement about an employee is not actionable unless it is "published" to another party.[4] For example, a communication between a supervisor and a personnel director or between a human resource assistant and a prospective employer constitutes a publication. Even a communication from a manager to his or her secretary may constitute a publication in some jurisdictions.[5]

Of course, a defamatory statement published to another person is not actionable unless it is false.[6] Truth is an absolute defense to a claim of defamation.[7] Publication of a truthful statement, however, can be the basis of an action for intentional infliction of severe emotional distress, invasion of privacy, or interference with contractual relations, all of which are discussed at length in other chapters of this book.

There are a number of defenses to an action for defamation. As noted above, truth is an absolute defense. So too is consent.[8] But the defense most often asserted in employer defamation cases is privilege.

A privilege may be *absolute* or *qualified*. An *absolute privilege* is generally accorded to statements made by legislators during legislative proceedings as well as communications made by lawyers, judges, parties, and witnesses in the course of, or leading up to, judicial or administrative proceedings.[9]

Significantly, employers have been afforded a qualified privilege to "defame" an employee.[10] This qualified privilege permits an employer to publish false and defamatory statements about an employee, *but only if* the employer can show that the statement: (1) was made with a good-faith belief in its truth; (2) served a business interest or had a business purpose; (3) was limited to the business interest or purpose to be served; (4) was made on a proper occasion; and (5) was published to proper parties only.[11]

An employer can abuse this qualified privilege, however, by failing to properly verify the facts underlying the defamatory statement[12] or by overpublicizing the defamatory statement to employees or third parties who do not have a legitimate business interest in the subject matter of the defamatory statement.[13] Where an employer abuses its qualified privilege to defame an employee, it loses the privilege (and often the lawsuit). This is the most frequently litigated issue in employee defamation cases.

Finally, although "malice" must be proven in defamation actions against the media,[14] malice or ill will is generally *not* a necessary element in employee defamation suits. Nonetheless, if malice or ill will is proven by an employee, the employer forfeits its qualified privilege and will be held liable if the employee proves that the defamatory statement is false.[15]

C. Trend in the Law: Compelled Self-Publication

Perhaps the most important development in this area of employer liability is the emergence of the theory of *compelled self-publication*.[16] This theory, sometimes called *self-defamation* or *compelled defamation*, arises when an employer advises an employee that he or she has been terminated for a reason that is both false and defamatory. In seeking new employment, the employee is then "compelled" to communicate that defamatory reason to prospective employers. Thus, an employer can now be held liable for defamation even if, as a matter of policy, it merely confirms dates of employment or provides *no* information to prospective employers.

The significance of this development in the law of defamation is that employees can now challenge their terminations in court—even if the state in which the termination occurred generally provides no remedy for "wrongful discharge." For even if an employer is conscientious in limiting postemployment references and refrains from publishing the grounds for an employee's termination, the employee can literally "create" his or her own defamation claim by publishing the grounds for his or her termination to a prospective employer. This requires employers to be more vigilant than ever in ensuring that the grounds for an employee's termination are not only valid but also capable of being sustained in a court of law.

D. Illustrative Cases

The cases summarized in this chapter are grouped by the following categories of employer defamation:
- Defamation in Workplace Investigations of Employee Misconduct:
  - illegal drug use and sales,
  - theft and fraudulent conduct, and
  - sexual harassment;
- Defamatory Evaluations and Warnings;

- Defamatory Statements Regarding Employees With AIDS;
- Defamation in Group Employee Meetings;
- Defamation in Internal Memos;
- Defamation in Company Newsletters;
- Unprivileged Defamatory Statements;
- Defamatory Postemployment References;
- Defamation by Compelled Self-Publication; and
- Defamatory Statements in Post-Termination Proceedings.

Although some employer defamation cases involve communications that are wholly unrelated to an employee's termination, such as a supervisor's false statement to an employee's co-workers that the employee has AIDS, most defamation cases by employees involve communications pertaining to the grounds for an employee's termination.

For example, a court upheld a jury verdict of $1.9 million against an employer that advised a prospective employer that an employee was a "zero" and implied that he had been discharged for serious misconduct.[17] Another court upheld a jury verdict of $350,000 in favor of an employee whose supervisor announced at a meeting of his co-workers that the employee had been fired for drunkenness on a business trip, where the employee was able to prove to a jury that he had not been drinking.[18] In another case, a jury awarded an employee $250,000 for recklessly providing a defamatory employment reference based solely on "office gossip."[19] And in a case of compelled self-publication, several employees were awarded $900,000 in damages by a jury when *they* advised prospective employers that they had been fired for "gross insubordination" because they refused to change their expense reports to delete charges that the employer had disallowed.[20]

While some of the employer defamation lawsuits summarized below include a claim for wrongful discharge or breach of contract, it is by no means necessary for an employee to demonstrate that he or she was improperly terminated in order to succeed in a claim for defamation. Instead, the employee need only allege that the grounds for discharge were false and that agents of the employer published the false grounds in communications either inside or outside the company—or that the employee was compelled to publish the false grounds to prospective employers.[21] Hence, as the cases summarized in this chapter show, the tort of defamation can provide employees with an *indirect* means to challenge their terminations.

1. Defamation in Workplace Investigations of Employee Misconduct

a. Illegal Drug Use and Sales

Employer Liable for $200,000 in Damages for Communicating "False Positive" Drug Test Result

A railroad employee was tested for drugs after an on-the-job accident. The report stated that a "trace" of methadone was found in the employee's urine. The personnel manager was advised by the testing physician that a "trace" meant only that it was *possible* that the employee was a heroin or methadone user. Nonetheless, the personnel manager prepared a written accident report that stated, "The drug screening test was positive for Methadone. Methadone is a drug which is often used to give to heroin addicts." The report was sent to officials of the employer who routinely received accident reports.

The employee learned of the report and caused a second test to be taken. This test showed that the first was a "false positive." The employee was, nevertheless, terminated for violation of safety rules. The employee sought assistance from the United States Department of Labor (DOL), which requested information about the employee's termination. The employer's director of labor relations wrote to the DOL that "traces of methadone were present in [the employee's] system."

The employee filed an action for defamation against the personnel manager, the director of labor relations, and the employer itself. After a jury trial, the employee was awarded $150,000 in compensatory damages and $50,000 in punitive damages. On appeal, the appellate court affirmed the award, finding that the jury could reasonably conclude that the defendants "made false statements in writing that [the employee] was a narcotics user when they knew better." *Houston Belt & Terminal Ry. v. Wherry*, 548 S.W.2d 743 (Tex. 1976), *appeal dismissed*, 434 U.S. 962 (1977).

Employer Assessed Damages for False Accusations of Drug Use and Theft

A bank collection manager was summoned to a meeting with a vice president and bank investigator to discuss "improprieties" discovered in the course of an investigation conducted by bank officials. The employee's immediate supervisor also was present at the meeting. During the meeting, the investigator stated, "I have enough against you for an indictment," and threw an envelope containing foil packets on the table. He then said, "Come on, ... you know what these are. Have you ever used cocaine?" The vice president also accused the manager of stealing a truck. The following day, he was terminated for cause. The employee claimed that these statements falsely suggested criminality on his part.

The manager filed an action for slander against the employer, the vice president, and the bank investigator. A jury found that the statements in question were uttered solely out of malice and were injurious to the collection manager. The jury then awarded the manager $55,000 in compensatory damages and $133,000 in punitive damages, but those awards were reduced by the trial court.

An intermediate appellate court affirmed the finding of liability, as did the New York Court of Appeals, the highest state court. It held that while statements made in an investigatory meeting are subject to a qualified privilege, the privilege will be lost where the purpose of the defamatory statements was, as here, to injure the employee's career. The Court of Appeals then sustained the award of compensatory damages, but reversed the punitive damages award. *Loughry v. Lincoln First Bank, N.A.*, 67 N.Y.2d 369, 494 N.E.2d 70, 502 N.Y.S.2d 965 (1986).

Employees Sue Based on Anonymous Letter Implicating Them in Drug Dealing, but Suit Is Dismissed

The personnel manager of an electronics company received an anonymous letter slipped under her office door. The letter claimed that two employees of the company were selling drugs on the employer's premises. After discussing the contents of the letter with her superiors, the personnel manager discussed the matter privately with each of the two employees identified in the letter. She advised them about the contents of the letter and warned them that being caught selling drugs would be grounds for dismissal. She then told the employees that she had no reason to believe that the allegations in the letter were true, that the matter would remain private, and that no adverse action would be taken against them. Indeed, the employees remained employed by the company.

The employees filed an action for defamation against the personnel manager and employer. In response to the employer's motion for summary judgment, the two employees claimed that the employer and personnel manager lost their qualified privilege because they acted with malice. Specifically, the employees alleged that the day before they were told about the letter, another employee approached one of them and requested a "joint." They inferred from this incident that the employee who asked them for marijuana was being used improperly as part of the employer's investigation.

The court granted the employer's motion and dismissed the case. On appeal, an appellate court affirmed the dismissal, concluding that the employees' claim of malice was based on nothing more than mere suspicion and surmise. The court also noted that malice could hardly be found when the personnel manager kept the contents of the letter private and assured the employees that they would not lose their jobs. *LaScala v. D'Angelo*, 104 A.D.2d 930, 480 N.Y.S.2d 546 (2d Dep't 1984).

b. Theft and Fraudulent Conduct

Supervisor's Failure to Verify Damaging Facts Can Result in Liability for Defamation

An employee for a telephone company was issued a corporate credit card for company purchases only. The employee provided the card number to an artwork dealer solely to verify his identity. He allegedly told the dealer that under no circumstances were any charges to be put on the card. The artwork company nonetheless placed a $2,670 charge on the corporate credit account. The assistant manager immediately arranged for a credit, and a credit letter was promptly sent to the employee.

The employee then brought the credit letter to his supervisor's attention. The supervisor called the artwork dealer and spoke with one of its representatives. Thereafter, a senior manager for the company terminated the employee for using his credit card in an effort to defraud his employer.

The employee brought an action against the company, asserting 13 causes of action arising out of his termination from employment, including defamation, breach of contract, sex discrimination, retaliation, interference with prospective economic relations, and intentional infliction of emotional distress. The employee alleged that his employer was liable for defamation because his supervisor falsely stated to the senior manager of the company who terminated the employee that he had improperly charged artwork to the credit card.

The employer filed a motion for summary judgment, urging dismissal of all 13 claims for relief. As to the defamation claim, the employer argued that there can be no "publication" of communications between two agents of the same corporation. The court disagreed, holding that a defamatory statement may be "published" by one agent of a corporation to another. The employer also argued that the alleged defamatory communication was privileged, because the supervisor had a duty to report the matter to a senior manager.

The court observed, however, that such a privilege is a conditional one that can be destroyed by recklessness in failing to conduct a thorough investigation into the subject matter of the communication. Accordingly, although the court granted summary judgment in favor of the employer on 12 of the 13 counts, it denied summary judgment on the defamation claim. It held that there were factual issues to be resolved by a jury as to whether the supervisor failed to investigate the credit card incident thoroughly and failed to verify the facts before communicating to the senior-level manager that the employee had intended to defraud his employer. *Howcroft v. Mountain States Tel. & Tel. Co.*, 712 F. Supp. 1514, 4 IER Cases 1225 (D. Utah 1989).

c. Sexual Harassment

Employee Who Claims Employer Falsely Accused Him of Sexual Harassment May Recover Damages for Defamation

A supervisor for an insurance company was accused by his employer of sexually harassing a female employee in his division by allegedly asking her out socially, touching her offensively, making sexual advances and comments, and sending sexually oriented notes to employees in his division. He claimed that the accusations were false, that the employer wrongfully discharged him based on the false accusations, and that the defamatory reason for his termination was disseminated throughout the company.

The supervisor brought an action for breach of employment contract, wrongful discharge, and defamation. The employer filed a motion to dismiss the complaint as to the defamation claim, arguing that the allegedly defamatory comments enjoyed an absolute privilege. The court disagreed. It held that the employer enjoyed only a qualified privilege, which could be abused by publication of the supervisor's alleged sexual harassment to fellow employees. *Gonzalez v. CNA Ins. Co.*, 717 F. Supp. 1087 (E.D. Pa. 1989).

2. Defamatory Evaluations and Warnings

Employer That Used "Bell Curve" in Performance Reviews Sued by Employees Who Received Subpar Evaluations

An employer instituted a policy that required the use of a "bell curve" in evaluating the job performance of management employees. The effect of the policy was that some managers would receive subpar evaluations. Certain managers who received the poor evaluations allegedly were denied promotions and pay increases and were demoted.

The affected employees commenced an action for defamation because the evaluations were shown to others at the company. The lower court granted the employer's motion to dismiss, and an appellate court affirmed. It held that an employer has a qualified privilege to show allegedly defamatory performance evaluations to others in the company when such conduct serves the employer's legitimate interest in determining the fitness of its employees to perform their jobs. *McCone v. New England Tel. & Tel. Co.*, 393 Mass. 231, 471 N.E.2d 47 (1984).

Employee May Recover Damages Where Employer Disseminated Warning Letter Accusing Him of "Opening Company Mail"

Several years after a truck driver began his employment with an express delivery company, he was elected shop steward. Just before his vacation, the driver was told to see his foreman, who handed him a warning letter. The letter stated that he violated company policy by "opening company mail."

After unsuccessfully challenging the warning with several of his superiors, the warning letter was placed in his personnel file. Within a few days, many of the driver's fellow employees had heard about the warning letter and discussed it over the citizens' band radio. The driver claimed that he told no one about the allegations other than his girlfriend.

The driver then instituted a lawsuit for defamation against his employer. The lower court dismissed the action, but the appellate court reversed. It first noted that although a warning letter to an employee is a privileged communication, the privilege may be lost if it is abused by dissemination of the letter to fellow employees. The court held that the words "opening company mail" may be defamatory. It therefore remanded the case to the lower court for a trial. *Agriss v. Roadway Express*, 334 Pa. Super. 295, 483 A.2d 456 (1984).

3. Defamatory Statements Regarding Employees With AIDS

False Accusation of AIDS May Result in Employee's Recovery Against Employer for Slander

A meat cutter for a supermarket alleged that a co-worker called him at home to inquire about his absence from work. He claimed that he told the co-worker he had been hospitalized for a ruptured hernia and one of his roommates was being tested for AIDS. The employee further alleged that the co-worker then informed the employee's supervisor that the employee might have AIDS and might have been exposed to AIDS by his roommate. The employee was called into his supervisor's office and asked if he had AIDS. He denied that he did. The employee allegedly was told that he could either voluntarily resign or be terminated for reasons of health. He chose to be terminated.

The employee filed an action for slander against his employer and supervisor. He also filed an action for discrimination on the basis of a perceived handicap. The trial court entered summary judgment in favor of the defendants, but the employee appealed. On appeal, summary judgment was reversed on the defamation claim because the employer and supervisor had failed to raise the defense of a qualified privilege in their answer to the complaint.

A concurring judge, though, noted that there was sufficient evidence in the record to defeat the assertion of a qualified privilege. Specifically, the employee presented evidence of ill will toward him by the co-worker, who told him that he lost his job because of his life-style, not because of anything the co-worker had stated to the employee's supervisor. Moreover, although the employee had told the co-worker that one doctor *thought* that the employee's roommate *might* have AIDS, the co-worker told the employee's supervisor that the employee lived with an individual who *did* have AIDS. According to the concurring judge, this statement by the co-worker raised a question of fact as to whether the co-worker acted with knowledge of the falsity of his statement, with reckless disregard of whether it was false, or with a high degree of awareness of its probable falsity. The statements by the co-worker were, in fact, false, as neither the employee nor his roommate had AIDS. *Little v. Bryce,* 733 S.W.2d 937 (Tex. Ct. App. 1987).

4. Defamation in Group Employee Meetings

Employer Held Liable for $350,000 in Damages for Statement That Manager Was Fired for Drunkenness

A general manager of a paper products company was discharged by his superior for alleged drunkenness at a public bar and for using profane language and engaging in misbehavior in the presence of other employees who were together on a business trip. The manager had received a previous warning from his superior, a division director, for using profanity and arguing with company employees after the manager admittedly consumed too much alcohol on another business trip. His superior based the decision to discharge the manager on an anonymous letter describing the manager as drunk, loud, and profane. The other workers who were present at the bar, however, denied that the manager was drunk or had acted improperly.

The division director never spoke to the manager about the incident at the bar or sought to determine the identity of the anonymous letter's author. Nonetheless, after terminating the manager, the director assembled over 100 of the division's workers and advised them that the manager had been fired because he had been "drunk," misbehaved in a bar and had a "drinking problem." The director then stated that the company "looks unkindly on this kind of conduct."

In his action against the employer for defamation, a jury awarded the manager $350,000 in damages. On appeal, the appellate court noted that an employer has a qualified privilege to disseminate to its employees a certain amount of information regarding the discharge of another employee to further its legitimate interests in upholding work rules. The appellate court concluded, however, that an employer may abuse the privilege if the employer did not have a reasonable and good faith belief in the truth of the defamatory statement. Here, the court noted, the director did not even seek to determine who had written the anonymous letter, despite statements from those who were present at the bar that the manager was not drunk. The court held that a jury could reasonably conclude that the conduct by the division director abused the employer's privilege.

The appellate court also held that the director's statements to over 100 division workers, many of whom were rank-and-file employees who had no contact with the manager, likewise abused the employer's privilege. According to the court, a "simple statement" to employees—that the manager had been terminated because of a dispute with higher management over the conduct of his job—would have served the business needs of the employer. *Benassi v. Georgia-Pacific,* 62 Or. App. 698, 662 P.2d 760, *modified on other grounds,* 63 Or. App. 672, 667 P.2d 532, *review denied,* 295 Or. 730, 670 P.2d 1035 (1983).

Employee Who Made Unauthorized Duplicate of Key May Still Recover Damages for Slanderous Remarks Made at Meeting of Employees

A claims analyst for a physicians' service was periodically required to work on Saturdays. Pursuant to company practice, a supervisor would lend her a key to open the office. Company policy forbade employees to make copies of keys. On one Saturday that the employee worked, it was discovered that she had an unauthorized key. She admitted that she had made a copy of a key but refused to divulge who had given her an original.

The claims analyst was discharged the following Monday. Later in the day a meeting was called of all claims department personnel. At the meeting a vice president stated that an unidentified employee was discharged that day because she had an unauthorized key and that several items of company property had been missing prior to that date. The claims analyst was the only employee who was dismissed that day.

The claims analyst brought a slander suit against her employer and its vice president, claiming that the statements at the meeting implied her criminality. A jury awarded her damages. On appeal, the appellate court held that because the vice president admitted that he only had a suspicion—and not a reasonable basis—to believe that the employee had stolen any property from the employer, the employer had abused its qualified privilege to defame the employee. The court held that the vice president's claim that he did not intend to accuse the plaintiff was not relevant, as "his statements to the claims department employees served to accuse her of theft" even though her name was not actually used. *Worley v. Oregon Physicians Servs.,*

69 Or. App. 241, 686 P.2d 404, *review denied,* 298 Or. 334, 691 P.2d 483 (1984).

5. Defamation in Internal Memos

Secretary Who Pieced Together Scraps of Paper Found in Office Trash Can Recovers Over $100,000 for Defamatory Statements

A secretary who worked in the finance department of a television station cooperated in an investigation conducted by the Minnesota Human Rights Department regarding two sex discrimination complaints filed against her employer by employees of the station. Thereafter, the secretary encountered "communication problems" with her co-workers. She requested a transfer, but her request was denied. The secretary's supervisor encouraged her to leave her job, but she refused. Shortly thereafter, the secretary noticed scraps of paper with her name on them in a wastepaper basket near a photocopy machine. Pieced together, the scraps formed a memo that read:

> [N]ot a good asset to the department. Single mother of two, she will be a little tough to eliminate. [H]as been in the middle of two legal disputes within the company regarding the termination, etc., of other employees. I am building the appropriate file and [would] like to replace her with a top notch secretary, possibly one from [within the] building.

When the supervisor learned the secretary had obtained pieces of the memo from the trash can, the supervisor fired her summarily and sent a memorandum to the head of the station's finance department, stating that the secretary "retrieved a piece of personal correspondence from my waste bin." The supervisor also advised senior management at the station in a memorandum that the secretary had been fired for "gross misconduct."

The secretary sued the station for defamation based on the memorandum sent by her supervisor to the finance department head. She also sued for breach of an implied covenant of good faith and fair dealing as well as sex, marital status, and reprisal discrimination. A jury returned a verdict in her favor on the defamation claim for $12,000 in compensatory damages and $500,000 in punitive damages. The employer appealed.

The appellate court upheld the jury's finding of liability on the defamation claim. It concluded that the written accusations that the secretary retrieved personal correspondence from a supervisor's wastebasket and was fired for gross misconduct were sufficiently harmful to the secretary's reputation to support a claim for defamation.

While the appellate court noted that the written statements were privileged, it held that there was sufficient evidence to sustain the jury's finding that the supervisor made the defamatory statements in the memo with actual malice. In that regard, the appeals court stated that actual malice could be demonstrated by the supervisor's expressed intent to replace the secretary after "building the appropriate file," which resulted from the secretary's cooperation with the state human rights department. The appellate court, however, reduced the jury's $500,000 award of punitive damages to $100,000. *Bradley v. Hubbard Broadcasting*, 471 N.W.2d 670 (Minn. Ct. App. 1991).

Memo Referring to Professor as "Incompetent" May Constitute Actionable Defamation if Statement Was Knowingly False

A professor was terminated from his post as vice president for student affairs by the college president. In seeking ratification of his decision by the college's board of trustees, the president of the college submitted a memorandum to the trustees that allegedly contained blatant falsehoods about the professor, including statements that the professor was "incompetent."

The professor commenced an action for defamation against the college and its president, and also asserted claims for breach of contract and interference with contract. After the defamation claim was dismissed, the professor appealed. The appellate court noted that charges of incompetence by an employer are per se defamatory, as the statements reflect adversely on one's chosen occupation. The court stated, though, that when such charges are made by an employer, their communication to others may be privileged—unless made with knowledge of their falsity or with malice. In this case, the appeals court held, the professor's allegations that the college president made *knowing* falsehoods that he was incompetent would, if proven, be sufficient to establish a claim for defamation. *Holland v. Kennedy*, 548 So. 2d 982 (Miss. 1989).

Dictation of Termination Letter With False Reasons for Discharge Can Furnish Grounds for Defamation

A sales representative had been employed by a design firm for six years. The company policy provided that a limit of $5,000 in commissions could be earned from a single customer during the fiscal year. Because the sales representative handled only a few large accounts, he objected to this policy and sought an increase due to his special circumstances. The employer decided to terminate him when he refused to accept the company's offer of $10,000 per year in commissions.

The employee's supervisor dictated a termination letter, which was typed by the supervisor's secretary. It was then placed in the employee's personnel file and distributed only to two senior officers of the company. The letter, which was also sent to the employee, stated that he had been discharged for "failure to increase business as a Major Projects Sales Representative."

The employee sued for defamation. A jury found that the employer abused its qualified privilege because it acted with actual malice. The jury then awarded the employee $70,000 in compensatory damages and $125,000 in punitive damages. The employer appealed, but an intermediate appellate court upheld the jury award. It remarked that even the dictation of a letter to a secretary, whether transcribed or not, constitutes a publication that can form the basis for an action for defamation.

The appellate court also stated that the jury could have reasonably concluded that the employer acted with malice, since the jury found that the reason given for termination was knowingly false. On further appeal, however, the Minnesota Supreme Court reversed, holding that there was insufficient evidence in the record to establish that the employer had acted with malice. *Frankson v. Design Space Int'l*, 380 N.W.2d 560 (Minn. Ct. App.), *rev'd in relevant part*, 394 N.W.2d 140 (Minn. 1986).

6. Defamation in Company Newsletters

Defamatory Statement in Company Newsletter May Result in Damages for Libel

Two years before commencing his employment with a wood and lumber company, an employee was injured when he fell through a "waferboard" on the roof of a garage he was building for his home. He sustained numerous injuries, including broken ribs, a broken bone in his back, and a broken heel. After recovering from the injuries, the employee applied for employment with the company that manufactured the waferboard. On his employment application, the employee completed a medical form, where he stated "no" to questions regarding back trouble, bone fractures, and X-rays of his back. In the question regarding hospitalization, however, the employee answered "yes" and wrote "fall off roof." He also advised the company that he had previously fallen off a roof and broken some bones including his ribs and a heel.

A year later, the employee filed a products liability action against the company, alleging that it had negligently manufactured the waferboard involved in the fall from his roof. He alleged in his complaint that he suffered permanent disabilities as a result of the fall, and he sought compensatory and punitive damages. The complaint was served on the personnel manager of the plant where the employee worked. The personnel manager compared the allegations in the products liability complaint against the answers provided by the employee on the medical record portion of the application form. Based on the discrepancy the personnel manager suspended the employee pending an investigation into possible fraud regarding his employment forms. Three weeks later the employee was terminated.

Shortly thereafter the company published a plant newsletter containing a section entitled "Comings and Goings." Next to the employee's name the newsletter stated, "Terminate . . . Falsification of Emp. Forms." Approximately 160 copies of the newsletter were made available in the company lunchroom to the 160 or so workers at the plant. The workers, however, were not restricted from taking the newsletter home and frequently took their copies out of the workplace. A copy reached the local hospital where the employee's wife worked, and two of her co-workers read the reference to the reasons for her husband's termination.

The employee filed an action for defamation, invasion of privacy, and wrongful discharge. The employer raised the defense of conditional privilege, asserting that it was privileged to make good faith communications to its employees concerning the reason for the discharge of one of their co-workers. In response, the employee argued that even if the communication in the newsletter regarding the reasons for his termination was privileged, the company abused the privilege by excessive publication of the newsletter to persons who did not have a need to know of the reasons for the termination.

The jury returned a verdict of $50,000 for defamation and $50,000 for invasion of privacy. On appeal, the appellate court upheld the application of a conditional privilege for both the defamation and invasion of privacy claims, but concluded that the issue of excessive publication must be tried to the jury. Although the court noted that an employer is entitled to use a method of publication that results in an *incidental* communication to persons outside the scope of the privilege, the issue as to whether the employer overpublicized the reasons for the employee's discharge was for the jury to decide. *Zinda v. Louisiana Pac. Corp.*, 149 Wis. 2d 913, 440 N.W.2d 548, 4 IER Cases 703 (1989).

7. Unprivileged Defamatory Statements

Supervisor's Remark to Customer That Employee Was "Caught Stealing" Was Not a Privileged Communication

An employee worked as a weigher for a grain purchasing company. His duties included weighing trucks both before and after the grain was unloaded into the grain elevator. After the grain company discovered that the quantity of grain in its grain elevator was substantially less than the quantity of grain indicated on its weight records, the company conducted a covert investigation.

On several consecutive evenings when the employee was on duty, two company supervisors "staked out" the grain elevator and allegedly observed the employee allowing drivers to drive their loaded trucks over the company's scales without dumping their grain. The employee then filled out purchase tickets for the trucks as though the grain had been dumped.

A few days later, the employee's supervisor told one of the company's customers that the employee "will not be with us long because [he] was caught stealing." The customer replied, "[H]ow could [he] steal grain?" The supervisor replied, "I don't know." Shortly thereafter, the president and a vice president of the company met with the employee in the company's offices to discuss the issue of the stolen grain. A polygraph operator was present. During the meeting, the president accused the employee of stealing the grain, but the employee denied the accusation. Later that day, the company president discharged the employee.

The employee brought a defamation action against his employer, the president, and his supervisor. He alleged that the president's statements in the presence of the polygraph operator and his supervisor's statements to the customer regarding his alleged theft of grain were false and defamatory. The defendants filed a motion for summary judgment, claiming that all of the statements in question were privileged. The lower court agreed, and granted summary judgment for the employer.

On appeal, the appellate court upheld the grant of summary judgment as to the statements by the company president. It held that absent any showing of actual malice, the statements made in the presence of the polygraph operator were privileged. However, the appellate court reversed as to the statements made by the employee's supervisor to one of the company's customers that the employee "was caught stealing." It held that no privilege exists as to communications between a supervisor and a customer where such statements were not part of any investigation, where the supervisor had no business interest in making such a communication, or where there was no duty to do so. The appeals court remanded the case for trial as to the issues of the employer's and supervisor's liability for the defamatory statements made to the company's customer. *Nelson v. Lapeyrouse Grain Corp.*, 534 So. 2d 1085, 5 IER Cases 1812 (Ala. 1988).

Co-Worker's Statement During Coffee Break That Salesman Was Fired for "Not Working" Not Privileged

After 18 years of employment for a pharmaceutical company, a sales representative was terminated for allegedly falsifying doctor call reports. Subsequently, his superior made statements to several doctors that the employee had been terminated for "falsifying records and spending work time in his personal pursuits." Further, a co-worker told a medical center employee during a coffee break that the sales representative had been fired for "not working." The former employee stated that while he never discussed his termination with anyone other than his family, he was told by several industry salesmen that his termination was the "talk of the town" and that he had been terminated for falsifying reports and not doing a good job.

The former employee filed suit against the pharmaceutical company for defamation and breach of contract. He claimed that his former supervisor and a former co-worker made statements, while acting within the course of their employment, which were not only false but were made without any valid business purpose. Those statements, the former employee claimed, deprived him of the benefits of public confidence and injured him in his occupation and professional reputation. At trial, the jury awarded the former sales representative $250,000 for defamation and $300,000 for breach of contract.

An intermediate appellate court upheld the jury verdict on appeal. As to the defamation claim, the court held that while defamatory statements made to third-party physicians *during* an investigation of doctor call reports would generally be privileged, such statements to physicians made *after* the investigation had concluded were *not* within the scope of any privilege. Further, the statement made during a coffee break by one of the salesman's former co-workers was likewise not privileged.

On further appeal, the employer finally succeeded in reversing the jury's verdict. The appeals court held that the evidence introduced at trial established that the statements made by the salesman's supervisor and co-worker, although unprivileged, were nonetheless *truthful* statements of fact. Hence, the employer established an absolute defense to the employee's claim for defamation. *Brannan v. Wyeth Laboratories,* 516 So. 2d 157, 3 IER Cases 61 (La. Ct. App. 1987), *reversed in relevant part,* 526 So. 2d 1101, 3 IER Cases 609 (La. 1988).

8. Defamatory Postemployment References

Salesman Called "a Zero" in Postemployment Reference Awarded $1.9 Million

Several months after an insurance salesman began his employment, the president of the insurance company reduced the salesman's salary and cut his commission because he purportedly failed to produce sufficient income. A few months later, the salesman was fired.

When the salesman was unable to obtain other employment, he hired an investigator to learn what the insurance company was saying about him. The investigator called several of the company's employees and represented to them that the salesman was being considered for a position of trust and confidence. One of the salesman's former co-workers told the investigator that the salesman was "untrustworthy . . . not always entirely truthful . . . disruptive . . . paranoid . . . hostile and was guilty of padding his expense account." Another former co-worker described the salesman as "horrible in a business sense, irrational, ruthless, and disliked by office personnel." He also described the salesman as "a zero."

In addition, when a prospective employer asked an official of the company why the salesman had been terminated, the company official said the salesman had not reached his production goals. When pressed for more information, the official commented, "I can't go into it." Based on these comments, the prospective employer decided not to hire the salesman.

In his action for defamation, a jury awarded the salesman $1.9 million, including $1.3 million in punitive damages. An appellate court upheld the verdict on appeal. The court stated that it was reasonable for the jury to have found that the personal verbal attacks on the salesman were false and defamatory to the extent they injured his reputation. The appellate court also held that the company official's statements to the prospective employer that "I can't go into it" falsely implied that the salesman had been terminated for serious misconduct. *Frank B. Hall & Co. v. Buck*, 678 S.W.2d 612 (Tex. Ct. App. 1984), *cert. denied*, 472 U.S. 1009 (1985).

Employment Reference Based on "Office Gossip" Results in $250,000 Award for Defamation

After a year on the job, a project manager for a construction company was terminated for "lack of work." The project manager called a business acquaintance at another construction company to find out if any work was available with that firm. The other firm offered the project manager a job on a construction project, subject to approval of the owners of the project.

One of the owners of the project called the project executive of the construction company that had laid off the project manager, and the project executive stated as follows:

(1) [The project manager] seemed detail oriented to the point of losing sight of the big picture.
(2) He had a lot of knowledge and experience on big jobs.
(3) With a large staff might be a very competent P.M. [project manager].
(4) Obviously he no longer work[s] for us, and that might say enough.

The project executive, however, had never supervised, evaluated, read an evaluation of, or worked with the project manager. His remarks were based entirely on the "general impression" he had developed from "hearing people talk about" the project manager at work. Nonetheless, the project executive did not advise the owner of the project that he had no firsthand knowledge of the project manager's work performance; nor did he acknowledge that his information was based solely on unsubstantiated office rumor. Instead, he led the owner of the project to believe that he had actually worked with the project manager on a construction project.

When the owner of the project did not hire him, the project manager filed a lawsuit for defamation against his former employer after he learned that the project executive had made negative comments about him to one of the owners of the project. A jury returned a verdict in favor of the project manager, awarding him over $370,000 in damages against his former employer. The trial court reduced the award to $250,000. The employer appealed.

The appellate court first addressed the employer's argument that the statements contained in the postemployment reference were protected by a qualified privilege. The appellate court concluded, however, that the employer had abused its qualified privilege by acting with gross indifference or recklessness as to the truth of the statements conveyed to the prospective employer. As the court stated, "[I]n short, this is a case of pure 'rumor' or 'gossip' or 'scuttlebutt' conveyed as fact, without any disclaimer or explanation." The court therefore affirmed the jury's verdict as well as the court's award of damages. *Sigal Constr. Corp. v. Stanbury*, 586 A.2d 1204, 6 IER Cases 201 (D.C. App. 1991).

Bus Driver Who Refused to Alter Time Cards Recovers $90,000 in Damages for Defamatory Postemployment Reference

A bus driver employed by a school district was paid in accordance with a designated "route time" for the route she drove. The driver's route time was designated by the school district as 90 minutes. She was paid for 90 minutes of working time regardless of the actual time it took her to drive. Drivers were required to fill in their time cards for the designated route time.

After a study was undertaken of the driver's route, her route time was cut to 75 minutes. The driver was informed of the change and instructed to mark her time cards accordingly. Upset over the change, the driver declined to do so and instead marked her time card with the actual time it took her to drive the route. When she refused to alter her time card to reflect only 75 minutes of work, her supervisor issued a written warning for "falsifying information on time cards."

After the driver continued to refuse to alter the time cards, she was first suspended and then terminated. When she attempted to obtain employment with another school district, her former employer stated that she was terminated "for recording the incorrect time on time cards."

The bus driver commenced a defamation action against the school district. A jury awarded her $90,000, including $31,000 in punitive damages. On appeal, the appellate court upheld the verdict and award of damages. It concluded that because the postemployment reference was susceptible to more than one meaning, it was not unreasonable for the jury to infer that the statement imputed dishonest acts to the employee. The court observed that "[t]his case demonstrates how mountains can be built from molehills." *Vinson v. Linn-Mar Community School Dist.*, 360 N.W.2d 108 (Iowa 1984).

Employee Who Was Told His Performance Was Favorable May Recover Damages for Negative Reference

A sales representative was employed by a company for 16 years. When a new district manager was hired as the employee's boss, the two did not get along and the employee was asked to resign in lieu of termination. When the employee resigned, the district manager stated that he had a favorable impression of the employee's capabilities and would give him a good recommendation to prospective employers. Thereafter, the employee sought new employment through an employment agency. When the agency asked the district manager about the employee, he stated that the employee "was a poor salesperson and was not industrious."

In the employee's action for defamation, a jury awarded him $37,500. An appellate court upheld the award, finding that the district manager's disregard for his promise to the employee constituted an abuse of the qualified privilege. *Stuempges v. Parke, Davis & Co.*, 297 N.W.2d 252 (Minn. 1980).

Editor's Comparison of Former Sports Columnist With His Replacements, as Well as Opinion That Columnist Was "On the Downswing," May Each Constitute Actionable Defamation

A 57-year-old columnist for a national sports newspaper was replaced by several younger writers after 22 years of service. In a letter to the editor, the paper was asked by a reader why it replaced the longtime columnist. The sports editor wrote, "I know Joe brightened a lot of hearts through his column through the years, but we felt it was time to make a change, with more energetic columnists who attend more events and are closer to today's sports scene." The president of the newspaper was also quoted in *USA Today* as saying, "Those who seemed to have reached maturity and are on the downswing are giving way to some of the up-and-coming young writers who we think deserve a chance."

The columnist commenced an action against the paper, its editor, and its president for defamation and age discrimination. After summary judgment was granted in favor of the defendants, the columnist appealed. As to the defamation claim, the defendants asserted on appeal that the comments by the editor and president were privileged as *opinions*. The appellate court concluded that the editor's response to the reader's letter, although expressed as an opinion, created a reasonable inference, by negative implication, that the columnist did not work hard, did not attend sports events very frequently, or was out of touch with current sports personalities, all of which are derogatory and actionable defamation if untrue.

Likewise, the appellate court concluded that the president's alleged comment to *USA Today*, where he expressed his opinion that the columnist was "on the downswing," was capable of implying that the columnist's writing and reasoning abilities had deteriorated or that the quality of his work had declined. Accordingly, the appeals court reversed the lower court's dismissal of the defamation claims and remanded the case for further proceedings.

After the case was remanded, the paper filed another motion for summary judgment. Because the columnist, who was a public figure, failed to proffer any evidence that the statements by the editor and president were made with actual malice, the court granted the defendants' motion for summary judgment. This second summary judgment was upheld on appeal. *Falls v. Sporting News Publishing Co.*, 834 F.2d 611, 2 IER Cases 1239 (6th Cir. 1987), *on remand*, 714 F. Supp. 843 (E.D. Mich. 1989), *aff'd mem.*, 899 F.2d 1221 (6th Cir. 1990).

Authors' Note: For many years, the courts held that statements of fact could be actionable defamation but *opinions* could not. In 1990, however, the United States Supreme Court held in *Milkovich v. Lorain Journal Co.*[22] that the perceived distinction between "opinion" and "fact" was an "artificial dichotomy." Rather, any statement, even one expressed as an "opinion," can amount to actionable defamation if it reasonably implies a false assertion of fact.

Employee May Recover for Defamatory Reference Despite Signed Release on Application Form

An employee formerly employed by a freight company attempted to obtain new employment with another company. He completed and signed an employment application authorizing the prospective employer to obtain information from previous employers and releasing all parties from all liability for any damage that might result from the dissemination of the information. The prospective employer called the prior employer and was given statements which, if not true, were clearly defamatory.

The former employee brought an action for defamation. The former employer claimed that the release signed by the employee protected it from such a lawsuit. The court disagreed. It held that the release contained in the application form was unenforceable because it was against public policy for a party to try to absolve itself from tortious conduct. *Kellums v. Freight Sales Centers,* 467 So. 2d 816 (Fla. Dist. Ct. App. 1985).

9. Defamation by Compelled Self-Publication

Employer Liable for Defamation Resulting From Employees' "Compelled Self-Publication"

Several employees of a life insurance company were sent on a business trip. Prior to the trip, they were given oral instructions concerning meal allowances and tips and were also given a $1,400 travel advance with no further instructions. When the employees returned, they were asked to file expense reports. They attempted to reconstruct their expenses, but their expense reports were rejected as erroneous. The employer then sought to recover approximately $200 from each of the employees. After they each refused to change their expense reports, they were fired for "gross insubordination."

When the employees sought to obtain new employment, they were asked about the reason for their termination. They truthfully advised the prospective employers of the reasons given by their prior employer for their terminations.

The employees filed a defamation action against their former employer. A jury returned a verdict for the employees and awarded all of them $900,000 in compensatory and punitive damages. On appeal, an intermediate appellate court affirmed the jury verdict.

The employer then appealed to the Minnesota Supreme Court, claiming that the verdicts in favor of the employees should be overturned because there was no publication of the defamatory statements by the employer. The Minnesota Supreme Court disagreed with the employer and upheld the jury's verdicts. It held that when defamatory statements are made to a terminated employee, publication is assumed since the employee will be compelled to state the reason for his discharge in subsequent employment interviews. The court noted that the "compelled self-publication" doctrine "provides a significant new basis for maintaining a cause of action for defamation."

The court did, however, vacate the jury's award of punitive damages. It concluded that punitive damages will not be allowed in defamation actions based on the doctrine of "compelled self-publication."

According to the court, to allow punitive damages in defamation actions where the *employee* publishes the defamatory statements may actually tend to encourage the self-publication of defamatory employment references. *Lewis v. Equitable Life Assurance Soc'y*, 389 N.W.2d 876, 1 IER Cases 1269 (Minn. 1986).

Employer May Be Liable for Defamation Where Employee Is Falsely Accused of Accepting Cash Gifts

A territory manager for an oil company was the subject of an internal investigation into alleged violations of the company's policies against accepting cash gifts. At a meeting called to discuss the manager's conduct, the employee was advised that the company had received information that he had accepted large cash gifts from oil company dealers. During the course of the meeting, the district manager and the corporate supervisor of investigations told the territory manager, "We know you have taken money from dealers." The district manager then stated, "We got you, son."

The district manager and supervisor of investigations told the employee that the matter would be investigated further. The next day, however, the territory manager was fired. The following month, the district manager met with several of the oil company's dealers to discuss problems in the district. The district manager allegedly told the dealers that "[w]e have gotten rid of a cancer."

In his search for new employment, the territory manager claimed that because of his sudden departure from the company after years of service, he felt compelled to repeat to prospective new employers the statements made to him by the company's district manager regarding his termination.

The territory manager brought an action for defamation against his employer, the district manager, and the supervisor of investigations. The defendants filed a motion for summary judgment. The court first held that the territory manager had introduced sufficient evidence to establish an action for defamation by compelled self-publication. According to the court, the law will not require an employee to fabricate a story to prospective new employers about the circumstances surrounding his discharge.

Second, the court held that the alleged statement by the district manager to the dealers about "[getting] rid of a cancer" would not be privileged if the employer could not show that it had been prompted by an essential business duty. The court therefore denied the defendants' motion for summary judgment and set the case for trial. *Elmore*

v. *Shell Oil Co.*, 733 F. Supp. 544, 5 IER Cases 185 (E.D.N.Y. 1988).[23]

10. Defamatory Statements in Post-Termination Proceedings

Filing of Required Securities Form Stating That Terminated Dealer Was Under "Internal Review for Fraud" Results in $100,000 Arbitration Award Against Employer

A securities firm terminated a securities dealer hired to manage its insurance products division after it learned that the dealer had also established his own general insurance agency. As required by the National Association of Securities Dealers (NASD), the firm filed with the NASD a Uniform Termination Statement (Form U-5) to record the dealer's termination.

When the firm was unable to locate certain files for which the dealer had been responsible, it asked the dealer to return the files. Although the dealer claimed that the files were used in connection with his own insurance agency, he nonetheless agreed to make the information contained in the files available to the firm—provided that it signed a release and agreed to indemnify the dealer against any and all claims.

Instead of complying with the dealer's demand, the securities firm filed a statement of claim with the Arbitration Department of the New York Stock Exchange, since the firm and the dealer had agreed to arbitrate all disputes that arose between them. In addition, the securities firm filed an amended Form U-5, noting the commencement of the arbitration and stating that the dealer was under "internal review for fraud or wrongful taking of property, or violating investment related statutes, regulations, rules or industry standards of conduct."

The securities dealer denied the allegations in the statement of claim and served a counterclaim upon the securities firm, not only claiming that he had been wrongfully discharged but also alleging that he had been defamed by the filing of the amended Form U-5 and the statement of claim. The arbitration panel found in favor of the dealer, awarding him $56,000 for wrongful discharge, $100,000 for defamation, $14,000 for attorneys' fees, and $100,000 in punitive damages.

The securities firm filed a petition in federal district court to vacate the arbitration award, contending that its filing of the amended

Form U-5 and its statement of claim were both protected by an *absolute* privilege. The court disagreed. It held that regardless of whether the filing of the amended Form U-5 was required by a public or private duty, such a filing was protected only by a *qualified* privilege, which could be overcome by a showing of actual malice.

The court likewise held that the filing of a statement of claim with the Arbitration Department of the New York Stock Exchange did *not* enjoy an absolute privilege; rather, the securities firm only enjoyed a qualified privilege, which could be lost by a showing of actual malice or a lack of probable cause. Since malice and probable cause are issues of fact, and because a reviewing court may not overrule an arbitrator's finding of fact, the district court upheld the defamation award. The court did, however, vacate the award of punitive damages, holding that state law prohibited the award of punitive damages by an arbitrator. *Fahnestock & Co. v. Waltman*, No. 90 Civ. 1792 (S.D.N.Y. Aug. 23, 1990), *aff'd*, 935 F.2d 512 (2d Cir.), *cert. denied*, 112 S. Ct. 380 (1991).

Employees Sue Employer for Statements Made to Unemployment Board, but Claims Are Dismissed

Two employees, husband and wife, were terminated by their employer. When each applied for unemployment benefits, the state unemployment compensation commission sent their former employer a request for wage and separation information. On one form, the employer wrote that the wife had been discharged due to "a drastic reduction in sales" and "a lack of capability." On the other form, the employer wrote that the husband had been "discharged for cause," and attached a letter stating that he had been fired "for a cause so serious as to affect the company's integrity."

The husband and wife commenced an action for defamation against the employer and their superior who filled out the forms. The court held that when an unemployment compensation commission requests separation information, the statements made in response are entitled to a qualified privilege. Here, no recovery was permitted because the court found that the husband and wife had failed to show that their former employer acted with any improper purpose or made an excessive publication to uninterested parties. *Rogozinski v. Airstream by Angell*, 152 N.J. Super. 133, 377 A.2d 807 (Law Div. 1977), *modified on other grounds*, 164 N.J. Super. 465, 397 A.2d 334 (App. Div. 1979).

Damages May Be Awarded When Employer Repeats Defamatory Remarks Made to Workers' Compensation Board

An employee for a shipping company received injuries while driving a truck in the course of his employment. In a report filed with the state Department of Labor and Employment, the employee's manager stated that the driver had been intoxicated at the time of the accident. The employer also remarked to other people that the driver was intoxicated while driving his truck.

The driver sued the employer and the manager for defamation, alleging that the statements made to the Department of Labor and Employment and to third persons defamed him. The court held that while the statements made in the worker's compensation board report were subject to an absolute privilege, repetition of these statements to third parties was not entitled even to a qualified privilege. Thus, the court held, the employee may recover if he can prove the falsity of the statements. *Dorr v. C.B. Johnson, Inc.*, 660 P.2d 517 (Colo. Ct. App. 1983).

Employee May Sue Employer for Libel Based on Bill That Implied He Engaged in Theft of Services

Concerned about the tampering and theft of electricity by employees, a utility company implemented an inspection program that involved checking the residential meters of the company's own employees for tampering. One of the meters checked belonged to a meter reader who had been employed by the company for 25 years.

When the employee's meter was first checked, no irregularities were found. But when the utility subsequently discovered that the employee's meter had been replaced only three days before the inspection, the old meter was retrieved and tampering was discovered. The employer terminated the employee and sent a letter detailing the company's charges to the meter reader's home. The letter, which stated that the employee was being charged for unmetered service due to tampering with the employee's meter, was also circulated to three employees in the utility's security and billing departments.

The employee filed an action for libel. A jury returned a verdict in favor of the employee, but the trial court reduced the amount of the damage award to $1, concluding that because the letter did not state that the employee actually engaged in a theft of services, the employee was only entitled to nominal damages. On appeal, an appellate court reversed. It held that even though the letter did not specifically charge the crime of larceny, it sufficiently detailed the specifics of the crime and, thus, was defamatory per se. Therefore, the court concluded, the employee was not limited to an award of nominal damages. *Battista v. United Illuminating Co.*, 10 Conn. App. 486, 523 A.2d 1356, *cert. denied*, 204 Conn. 802, 525 A.2d 1352 (1987).

Notes

1. *See* Restatement (Second) of Torts § 559.
2. *See* Restatement (Second) of Torts §§ 569, comment g; 571–73.
3. *See* Restatement (Second) of Torts § 569, comment e; *see also* Frank B. Hall & Co. v. Buck, 678 S.W.2d 612 (Tex. Ct. App. 1984), *cert. denied*, 472 U.S. 1009 (1985), summarized in section D.8. of this chapter.
4. *See* Restatement (Second) of Torts § 558(b).
5. *See* Frankson v. Design Space Int'l, 380 N.W.2d 560 (Minn. Ct. App.), *reversed in relevant part*, 394 N.W.2d 140 (Minn. 1986), summarized in section D.5. of this chapter.
6. *See* Restatement (Second) of Torts § 558(a).
7. *See* Restatement (Second) of Torts § 581A.
8. *See* Restatement (Second) of Torts § 583.
9. *See* Restatement (Second) of Torts §§ 585–88.
10. *See* Restatement (Second) of Torts § 595, comment i.
11. *See* Restatement (Second) of Torts §§ 599, 600, 603–05.
12. *See* Restatement (Second) of Torts § 600(b); Howcroft v. Mountain States Tel. & Tel. Co., 712 F. Supp. 1514, 4 IER Cases 1225 (D. Utah 1989), summarized in section D.3. of this chapter.
13. *See* Restatement (Second) of Torts § 604; Benassi v. Georgia-Pacific, 62 Or. App. 698, 662 P.2d 760, *modified on other grounds*, 63 Or. App. 672, 667 P.2d 532, *review denied*, 295 Or. 730, 670 P.2d 1035 (1983), summarized in section D.4. of this chapter.
14. *See* New York Times v. Sullivan, 376 U.S. 254 (1964).
15. *See, e.g.*, Bradley v. Hubbard Broadcasting, 471 N.W.2d 670 (Minn. Ct. App. 1991), summarized in section D.5. of this chapter.
16. *See* cases summarized in section D.9. of this chapter.
17. *See* Frank B. Hall & Co. v. Buck, 678 S.W.2d 612 (Tex. Ct. App. 1984), *cert. denied*, 472 U.S. 1009 (1985), summarized in section D.8. of this chapter.
18. *See* Benassi v. Georgia-Pacific, 62 Or. App. 698, 662 P.2d 760, *modified on other grounds*, 63 Or. App. 672, 667 P.2d 532, review denied, 295 Or. 730, 670 P.2d 1035 (1983), summarized in section D.4. of this chapter.
19. *See* Sigal Constr. Corp. v. Stanbury, 586 A.2d 1204, 6 IER Cases 201 (D.C. App. 1991), summarized in section D.8. of this chapter.
20. *See* Lewis v. Equitable Life Assurance Soc'y, 389 N.W.2d 876, 1 IER Cases 1269 (Minn. 1986), summarized in section D.9. of this chapter.
21. Because an employer will almost always raise the defense of privilege, however, the employee can only prevail if the employer fails to establish that the communications in issue were privileged or if the employee can demonstrate that the employer abused its privilege.
22. 497 U.S. 1 (1990).
23. *But see* Weintraub v. Phillips, Nizer, Benjamin, et al., 172 A.D.2d 254, 568 N.Y.S.2d 84 (1st Dep't 1991).

Chapter 4

Infliction of Emotional Distress

A. Overview

Employees who experience what they perceive to be abusive conduct by their supervisors or co-workers are increasingly commencing lawsuits against their employers for intentional infliction of emotional distress. Because of its broad definition, this tort is applicable to many aspects of the employment relationship, including job assignments, workplace environment, evaluations, demotions, and termination.

Claims of intentional infliction of emotional distress most frequently involve verbal or physical harassment by superiors or co-workers, threatening or offensive investigations of employee misconduct, knowingly false accusations of dishonesty, and abusive and reckless methods of termination. Recently, employees have also been using this tort to challenge employers that make improper use of employee assistance programs, use unreasonable drug testing procedures, and fail to prevent employee exposure to secondhand smoke.

B. General Principles of Law

The tort of intentional infliction of emotional distress, also known in some states as the tort of *outrage*, allows recovery for intentional actions deemed to be so shocking and outrageous, and so extreme in degree, as to exceed all bounds of decency and to be regarded as atrocious and utterly intolerable in a civilized society.[1]

The term "outrageous" is a subjective notion that fails to describe a particular act or series of acts that may render a defendant liable for compensatory and punitive damages. The issue of liability is therefore open to a societal definition of what constitutes "outrageous" behavior.[2]

In the employment context, the types of conduct most frequently found to be outrageous involve abusive actions by supervisors.[3] Further, conduct may be judged outrageous where a supervisor or coworker acts with knowledge that an employee is particularly susceptible to emotional distress.[4]

Although these guidelines are somewhat vague, liability for this tort will not be found for "mere insults, indignities, threats, annoyances, petty oppressions, or other trivialities."[5] To give further meaning to the scope of this tort, it is said that "[t]he rough edges of our society still need filing down and in the meantime, plaintiffs must necessarily be expected and required to be hardened to a certain amount of rough language, and to occasional acts that are definitely inconsiderate and unkind."[6]

A claim for intentional infliction of emotional distress need not, however, be based on *intentional* misconduct. Rather, an employee can prevail on such a claim merely by showing that the employer's agent *recklessly* inflicted emotional distress upon the employee.[7] "Recklessness" is defined as a conscious disregard of a high probability that physical harm or emotional distress will follow.[8]

Finally, to succeed in a claim for intentional infliction, the plaintiff must prove that he or she suffered *severe* emotional distress.[9] In many cases, however, the extreme and outrageous character of the defendant's conduct can raise an inference that severe distress has occurred.[10]

C. Trend in the Law: Negligent Infliction of Emotional Distress

Employees have recently begun to assert claims against employers for *negligent* infliction of emotional distress. This tort differs substantially from the tort of *intentional* infliction of emotional distress. Most significantly, the tort of negligent infliction does not require a showing of outrageous conduct by the employer. Instead, an employee can recover for negligent infliction if the employer's agent failed to use ordinary and reasonable care not to cause the employee to suffer foreseeable emotional distress.[11]

For example, an employee forced to produce a urine sample for a drug test in front of four company representatives who were directly observing employees as they provided urine samples was awarded $125,000 in damages for negligent infliction of emotional distress—even though his claim for intentional infliction was dismissed.[12] Similarly, a female employee who filed both intentional and negligent infliction claims based on her inability to breast-feed her baby after learning of her termination from employment could maintain a claim for negligent infliction of emotional distress, but not a claim for intentional infliction.[13] And an African-American employee who claimed he suffered psychological trauma as a result of workplace harassment and discriminatory treatment may recover damages for negligent infliction even though his Title VII claims were dismissed.[14]

It is anticipated that employees will commence an increasing number of negligent infliction claims in the 1990s, or add a negligent infliction claim to an intentional infliction action as a "backup" cause of action. While the opportunity for recovering punitive damages is very slight in a negligent infliction action—in contrast with the routine recovery of punitive damages in successful intentional infliction claims—compensatory damages can nevertheless be very substantial in any case where the employee has suffered *severe* emotional distress.

D. Illustrative Cases

The infliction of emotional distress cases summarized in this chapter fall into the following categories:

- Demotions, Negative Job Evaluations, and Undesirable Work Assignments;
- Sexual Harassment;
- Other Forms of Workplace Harassment;
- Abusive Investigations of Employee Misconduct:
  - unwarranted threats of criminal prosecution, and
  - improper use of polygraph examinations;
- Unreasonable Drug Testing Techniques;
- Improper Use of Employee Assistance Programs;
- Workplace Injuries and Illnesses;
- Smoking in the Workplace; and
- Abusive, Reckless, Discriminatory, and Negligent Methods of Termination.

The cases summarized in this chapter include a number of million-dollar jury verdicts for intentional infliction of emotional distress. In one case, a $3.1 million jury award was upheld on appeal where an employer totally humiliated a senior vice president by demoting him to a janitor's position.[15] In another case, $5.3 million was awarded to an executive where his employer terminated him on the basis of a false performance evaluation created solely as a pretext to fire the executive for his homosexual activities.[16] A $1.3 million jury award was also upheld on appeal where an employee's supervisor, in violation of a state law prohibiting employers from requiring employees to take polygraph exams, tried to force the employee to resign her job after she refused to take a lie detector test.[17] And in a loss of consortium action filed by the wife of an employee who was continually harassed and humiliated at work, an appellate court upheld a $1.5 million jury award in her favor.[18]

In each of these cases, as well as in many others summarized in this chapter, the enormous jury awards were based in large measure on the severity of the emotional distress suffered by the oppressed employee. Indeed, as a practical matter, the more severe the emotional distress suffered by the employee, the more likely a court or jury will find that the conduct by the employer was outrageous.

1. Demotions, Negative Job Evaluations, and Undesirable Work Assignments

Vice President Recovers $3.1 Million for "Total Humiliation" Resulting From Demotion to Janitor's Job

A 60-year-old vice president and assistant to the president of a paper company had received favorable performance evaluations for several years. When a new 42-year-old president assumed control of the company, though, the vice president was deliberately given the "silent treatment" by the new president, who made known his desire to bring in "new blood" and to develop a "young team" at the company. The president also began dismantling the vice president's job by removing his responsibilities and assigning them to younger employees. Shortly thereafter, the vice president went on three months of disability leave for a medical problem unrelated to his work.

After returning from his disability leave, the vice president was confronted by the president and given three options: relocating and taking a sales job at half his pay; termination with three months' pay; or accepting a demotion to a warehouse supervisor's position at the same salary but with none of the benefits he had enjoyed for many years, including a management bonus, company car, country club membership, and company expense account. The vice president chose the warehouse position, an entry-level job requiring no more than one year's experience in the paper industry.

The former vice president's new supervisor promptly embarked on a course of harassment against him, calling him an "old man" and a "goldbrick." He also placed him in charge of housekeeping but did not assign any employees to assist him. He was, therefore, required to sweep the floors and clean up the employees' cafeteria himself.

Within four months' time, the former vice president began to suffer severe depression. He consulted a psychiatrist who diagnosed him as suffering from reactive depression due to on-the-job stress. The psychiatrist also advised him to resign his job. Two months later, after having quit his job, the former vice president suffered a psychotic manic episode and was involuntarily hospitalized. Over the next two years, he was hospitalized again and given electroconvulsive shock therapy. His mental illness did not go into remission until four years after it began.

The former vice president filed a claim for age discrimination and intentional infliction of emotional distress. The jury returned a verdict in his favor on his intentional infliction claim for $3.1 million: compensatory damages of $850,000 and punitive damages of $2.25 million. The jury also awarded him over $300,000 on his age claim.

On appeal, the employer argued that the verdict in favor of the former vice president on his intentional infliction claim should be reversed because his evidence of outrageous conduct was the same as that used in his age discrimination claim. The appellate court disagreed. It found that the nature of the evidence presented at trial took the case out of the realm of an ordinary employment discrimination dispute and placed it in the category of outrageous behavior. Affirming the jury verdict, the court stated, "[I]t is difficult to conceive of a workplace scenario more painful and embarrassing than an executive, indeed a vice president and assistant to the president, being subjected before his fellow employees to the most menial janitorial services and duties of cleaning up after entry level employees: the steep downhill push to total humiliation." *Wilson v. Monarch Paper Co.*, 939 F.2d 1138, 6 IER Cases 1344 (5th Cir. 1991).

Acrophobic Photographer Assigned High-Rise Work May Recover Damages

A photographer worked for a major military contractor for over 23 years. He suffered from a fear of heights, a condition known to other employees in his employer's photography department. He claimed his previous supervisor did not assign him to work at heights, but that his new supervisor, knowing of his fear, nevertheless directed him to perform high-rise work.

The photographer further claimed that when he declined the assignment, his supervisor demanded that he perform the work or be forcibly removed from the work site. Although the photographer did not perform the work, he claimed the supervisor's conduct caused him severe emotional distress and anxiety that required him to be hospitalized.

The photographer sued his supervisor for intentional infliction of emotional distress. The supervisor filed a motion for summary judgment, but the court denied the motion and set the case for trial. The court held that because reasonable persons could differ as to whether the supervisor's alleged conduct was "heartless, flagrant, and outrageous," it was for the jury to decide whether the supervisor's conduct was so extreme as to result in liability. *Brown v. Ellis*, 40 Conn. Supp. 165, 484 A.2d 944 (1984).

Unjustified Job Evaluation May Entitle Worker to Recovery of Damages

A city employee was allegedly subjected to numerous instances of workplace harassment, including being placed in job assignments for which he was not trained, falsely lowering his job performance evaluations, and ridiculing and harassing him.

The employee sued the city for intentional infliction of severe emotional distress, seeking compensatory and punitive damages for his injuries. The trial court dismissed the complaint, but an appellate court reversed, noting that the false job evaluation and alleged acts of ridicule and harassment may be sufficiently extreme and outrageous for the employee to recover. *Dixon v. Stuart*, 85 N.C. App. 338, 354 S.E.2d 757 (1987).

Threat to Schedule Worker on "Graveyard" Shift to "Get Rid of" Him May Be Sufficient to Recover for Intentional Infliction

A grocery store worker alleged that his supervisor engaged in a course of conduct designed to embarrass and humiliate him and told him that she intended to "get rid of" him. He alleged that the supervisor insulted, ridiculed, and criticized him and his wife, alone and in front of other employees and customers. She also allegedly threatened to reduce his work hours and scheduled him for "graveyard" shifts as well as other shifts that she knew conflicted with his religious obligations.

The employee brought a religious discrimination claim against his employer, as well as a common law claim for intentional infliction of emotional distress. The employer filed a motion to dismiss, contending that the intentional infliction claim could not be maintained because the factual basis for that claim was the same as for the discrimination claim. The court disagreed, holding that the employee could proceed with his claim for intentional infliction of emotional distress, since his tort action required proof of facts beyond those necessary to make out the religious discrimination claim. *Malone v. Safeway Stores,* 698 F. Supp. 207, 2 IER Cases 1470 (D. Or. 1987).

Union Official May Sue Union for Referring Him to Jobs for Which He Was Not Qualified

A local union officer was subjected to a campaign of personal abuse by other union officials because he disagreed with them on internal union policies. He claimed that the officials removed his name from the top of the out-of-work list and placed it at the bottom, referred him to jobs of short duration when more desirable work was available, and referred him to jobs for which he was not qualified.

The local union officer sued his union and the other union officials who, he claimed, caused him to suffer severe emotional distress. At trial, a jury awarded the plaintiff $7,500 in actual damages and $175,000 in punitive damages. The verdict, however, was overturned by a state appellate court on the basis that the state law claim was preempted by federal labor law. The United States Supreme Court reversed, holding that the state law claim was not preempted because the outrageous conduct was of such a substantial and enduring quality that "no reasonable man in a civilized society should be expected to endure it." The Supreme Court remanded the case on the issue of damages. *Farmer v. United Bhd. of Carpenters, Local 25,* 430 U.S. 290, 94 LRRM 2759 (1977).

Employee's Wife Awarded $1.5 Million for Loss of Consortium Resulting From Emotional Distress of Husband Humiliated at Work

An employee for an envelope manufacturer had worked for the company for 29 years. He had overcome a background of adversity, including birth defects and childhood deafness, to become a head adjuster responsible for several envelope-making machines. Trouble began, however, when the company implemented a new policy mandating overtime when too few employees volunteered. The head adjuster worried about having to work overtime immediately after his regular eight-hour shift, because he not only suffered from backaches but also had lost four fingers in an industrial accident many years earlier.

After the employee refused to work overtime on several occasions, his supervisor gave him a verbal warning—a step that could lead to his eventual dismissal under the collective bargaining agreement between the employer and his union. His supervisor and other company supervisors thereafter began to taunt, harass, and humiliate him. Among other things, a supervisor told the employee to demonstrate, in front of his assembled co-workers, how his lack of fingers put added strain on his back—an order that the employee took as a deliberate effort to humiliate him. His supervisor also assigned particularly slow workers to operate the machines of which the head adjuster was in charge, and eventually demoted him to work in the tool crib—a low-level job with no responsibilities other than to hand out tools to other employees.

These and other similar forms of harassment eventually caused the employee to suffer a serious emotional breakdown, preventing him from working or maintaining ordinary human relationships. The employee's wife was forced to become, in effect, his caretaker.

Although the employee sought compensation under the state workers' compensation law, his wife filed a loss of consortium lawsuit against her husband's employer. She alleged that her husband's employer had negligently or intentionally inflicted severe emotional distress upon her husband, thereby causing her to suffer mental anguish as a result of observing the effects of the job-related emotional stress upon her husband. The wife also presented evidence by an expert witness that her marriage was reduced to a relationship similar to a wife whose husband had Alzheimer's disease. A jury awarded the wife $1.5 million in damages.

On appeal, the employer claimed that the spouse's claim was preempted by the federal Labor Management Relations Act because the warning and demotion were purportedly implemented pursuant to the governing collective bargaining agreement. The appeals court, however, refused to address the preemption issue, concluding that the employer's failure to raise that defense until after the jury verdict was rendered constituted a waiver of that defense.

The employer also argued that the jury's award of damages was excessive. The appeals court disagreed, concluding that the $1.5 million award was justified in light of the fact that the marriage had changed from a source of joy to a nursing relationship. *Sweeney v. Westvaco Co.*, 926 F.2d 29, 6 IER Cases 289 (1st Cir.), *cert. denied*, 112 S. Ct. 274 (1991).

Fire Department Captain Sues After Suffering Stroke Caused by Demotion and Harassment

A captain in a fire department was heavily involved in union activities. As reprisal for these activities, his supervisor, an assistant chief, devised a new personnel procedure that resulted in the captain receiving poor performance evaluations even though he had previously received excellent ones. The assistant chief also sent the captain a letter telling him to appear at a disciplinary hearing on the false basis that he had lied on his workers' compensation papers.

Following a hearing, the captain was demoted to engineer, publicly stripped of his captain's badge, and assigned to menial tasks. He also was ordered to return to duty from sick leave and was assigned to an entry-level position. Finally, after his blood pressure rose due to the ongoing harassment, the employee suffered a stroke that left him completely paralyzed.

The captain sued his employer in state court for intentional infliction of emotional distress, seeking damages for total and permanent mental and physical disability. In addition, the captain's wife sued the employer for loss of consortium and intentional infliction of emotional distress.

The employer filed a motion for summary judgment, contending that the captain's claim for intentional infliction of emotional distress must be dismissed because his exclusive remedy was under the state's workers' compensation law. The trial court agreed and granted summary judgment in favor of the employer. An intermediate appellate court affirmed. The captain then appealed to the California Supreme Court, which likewise affirmed the grant of summary judgment in favor of the employer. It held that when misconduct by a supervisor consists of actions that are a normal part of the employment relationship, such as demotions, promotions, criticism of work, and friction in negotiations over grievances, an employee who suffers emotional distress may not avoid the exclusive remedy provision of the workers' compensation law by characterizing the employer's decisions as unfair, outrageous harassment, or intended to cause emotional disturbance. *Cole v. Fair Oaks Fire Protection Dist.*, 43 Cal. 3d 148, 729 P.2d 743, 233 Cal. Rptr. 308, 1 IER Cases 1644 (1987).

2. Sexual Harassment

Employee Harassed by Supervisor After Terminating Their Voluntary, Consensual Sexual Affair Awarded $125,000 for Intentional Infliction

A female data processing employee and her supervisor engaged in a voluntary consensual relationship during her employment at a corporate data processing facility. After three years she terminated the relationship but continued to work at the company for the same supervisor.

When she refused to continue the relationship, the supervisor began to harass her. He withheld performance evaluations and salary reviews; made frequent sexual remarks to the female employee; touched her intimately; left sexual materials on her desk, including a book entitled *Sex Over Forty;* and "looked down [her] blouse and up [her] skirt." He continued to harass her for four years, causing the employee to suffer severe emotional harm.

The data processing employee filed a lawsuit for sexual harassment. She also filed a claim against her employer and supervisor for intentional infliction of emotional distress. In a nonjury trial, the court concluded that the supervisor's harassment constituted extreme and outrageous conduct and caused emotional distress that "no reasonable woman" could endure. The court awarded the employee $75,000 for emotional harm and $50.000 in punitive damages, finding that the supervisor's campaign of harassment was malicious. Finally, the court awarded the employee $17,000 for lost salary increases on her Title VII claim, for a total damage award of $142,000. *Shrout v. Black Clawson Co.*, 689 F. Supp. 774, 3 IER Cases 492 (S.D. Ohio 1988).

Sexually Harassed Employee Awarded $100,000 in Punitive Damages Where Employer Failed to Halt Harassment

An employee of a major cosmetics firm claimed that her manager had propositioned her and then threatened her if she did not spend the night with him. Later, at an awards picnic, after she had rejected the manager's proposition, he grabbed her and ran his hands over the intimate areas of her body. The employee reported these incidents to management but no action was taken for several months. In the interim the harassment continued, and the employee began to suffer high blood pressure, chest pains, and other symptoms of emotional distress.

The employee sued the company and the manager for intentional infliction of emotional distress and assault and battery. A jury awarded her $10,000 in compensatory damages and $100,000 in punitive damages against the employer on the intentional infliction claim, and $100 in compensatory and $1,000 in punitive damages against the manager on the assault and battery claim. An appellate court affirmed, holding that the company's failure to take appropriate action in response to the employee's complaints of sexual harassment by the manager constituted intentional infliction of emotional distress. The court further found that the manager's and employer's conduct was not accidental in nature so as to limit the employee's recovery to a workers' compensation claim under state law. *Ford v. Revlon, Inc.,* 153 Ariz. 38, 734 P.2d 580, 1 IER Cases 1571 (1987).

3. Other Forms of Workplace Harassment

Employer Liable for $275,000 Where Supervisor Planted Checks in Employee's Purse to Make It Appear She Was a Thief

A clerk in the administrative department of a credit company sought a promotion into the collection department. Her supervisor, the assistant manager, denied her request and advised her that "women usually don't go into that department." As a result, the clerk wrote a letter to the regional manager complaining about the lack of promotional opportunities for women in the company.

The following year, the clerk again requested a promotion into the collection department. Just as before, her request was denied, although she was given a promotion to a higher clerk position. Shortly thereafter, the assistant manager began to transfer the clerk from desk to desk within the administrative department and subjected her to "special" annual reviews periodically throughout the year. Her performance rating, which had been "satisfactory plus," was downgraded to "satisfactory."

Thereafter, while processing checks received in the mail, the clerk was informed that a check was missing. Ten days later, she discovered the missing check lying on top of the coin compartment in her own cash box. The day after the first check reappeared, the clerk discovered in her purse two more checks made out to the company. These two "check incidents" convinced the clerk that the assistant manager was attempting to "set her up" to prevent her transfer to the collection department. As a result, she began to experience insomnia, headaches, and nervousness, and felt paranoid about what would happen to her next at work.

After the clerk advised the regional manager of the two incidents, she received another "special" annual review, whereby her performance rating was further downgraded to "satisfactory minus." She was also told that she would be fired if her performance did not improve in 60 days. Her supervisors, however, refused to conduct a 60-day evaluation and gave her no reason for the delay. A month later, after she was given a final evaluation of "unsatisfactory," the clerk was fired. The clerk claimed that she continued to experience sleep problems, headaches, and nervousness, which allegedly contributed to her subsequent divorce.

The clerk filed an action for sex discrimination under Title VII as well as a claim for intentional infliction of emotional distress. A jury returned a verdict in her favor of $275,000 on her intentional infliction claim. The judge also found for the clerk on her Title VII claim.

On appeal, the employer argued that the conduct by the assistant manager was not outrageous. The appeals court disagreed. It held that there was sufficient evidence from which a jury could reasonably conclude that the assistant manager planted the checks to make it appear that she was a thief or to place her in fear of such an accusation. According to the court, these two "check incidents," even standing alone, were sufficient to constitute outrageous conduct. *Dean v. Ford Motor Credit Co.*, 885 F.2d 300, 4 IER Cases 1623 (5th Cir. 1989).

Harassment Resulting in "Psychological Trauma" May Not Violate Title VII, but May Result in Damages for Negligent Infliction of Emotional Distress

An African-American product engineer for an automobile maker experienced a series of allegedly harassing and discriminatory actions by his supervisor at work. He claimed that his supervisor used obscene language and spoke more harshly to him than to his white co-workers; failed to grant his request for a transfer; delayed his wage increase and gave him smaller raises than his white colleagues; and failed to complete his performance appraisals in a timely fashion. The engineer began to suffer constant fatigue, severe anxiety, exhaustion, nervousness, and suicidal thoughts, all of which resulted from a clinically diagnosed case of major depression. Eventually, the engineer was granted permanent disability benefits under the automaker's retirement plan for salaried employees.

The engineer filed an action in federal court under Title VII for discriminatory treatment and a hostile work environment on the basis of race. He also filed a state law tort claim for negligent infliction of emotional distress. He claimed that the employer was aware, through its own records, of the damaging effect to his "psyche" that was caused by the actions and inactions of his supervisor.

The employer made a motion for summary judgment as to all of the engineer's claims. Although summary judgment was granted on the engineer's claim under Title VII for workplace harassment, it was denied as to the engineer's claim for negligent infliction of emotional distress. The employer had argued that the engineer's claim for negligent infliction should be dismissed under state law because the emotional distress he allegedly suffered did not result in and was not accompanied by physical injury. The court disagreed. It held that the engineer's claim that he suffered "psychological trauma" as a result of the allegedly discriminatory treatment he received at work from his supervisor was sufficient to maintain a claim for negligent infliction. At trial, however, a jury rejected the engineer's claim of negligent infliction of emotional distress. *Payne v. General Motors Corp.*, 5 IER Cases 1081, 53 FEP Cases 471 (D. Kan. 1990), *aff'd mem.*, 943 F.2d 57 (10th Cir. 1991).

Racial Insults and Slurs by Supervisor May Constitute Outrageous Conduct

An African-American employee of a large manufacturing company claimed that his supervisor said "that he did not like Blacks," and had insulted him and his race by making statements such as "Black people in general don't like to work."

The employee sued the employer, claiming that these remarks constituted intentional infliction of emotional distress. The trial court granted the employer's motion for summary judgment, but an appellate court reversed. It noted that a supervisor's intentional use of racial slurs and insults against an employee may constitute outrageous conduct. Accordingly, the court remanded the case for trial. *Robinson v. Hewlett-Packard Corp.*, 183 Cal. App. 3d 1108, 228 Cal. Rptr. 591 (1986).

Disability Plan Beneficiary May Not Maintain Suit Against Trustees and Plan Administrator for Intentional Infliction

An employee beneficiary under a self-funded employee benefit plan received disability benefits for about five-and-a-half years. She alleged that she was constantly harassed by her employer and the insurance company during this period and that the harassment caused her and her son emotional distress and allegedly precipitated her divorce. She also claimed that her employer and the insurance carrier continuously requested unnecessary medical reports, refused to provide her attorney with copies of her claim file, and unjustifiably withheld benefit payments on two occasions.

The employee sued her employer, its former parent company, and the insurance company for intentional infliction of emotional distress under state law and for breach of various fiduciary duties under the federal Employee Retirement Income Security Act (ERISA). The lower court dismissed the employee's state law tort claims, holding that the employee could not maintain her state law claim for intentional infliction because her allegations fell within the scope of ERISA's preemption clause, which provides that "any and all State laws insofar as they may now or hereafter relate to any employee benefit plan" are preempted. The dismissal of the state law tort claims was affirmed on appeal. *Powell v. Chesapeake & Potomac Tel. Co.*, 780 F.2d 419 (4th Cir. 1985), *cert. denied*, 476 U.S. 1170 (1986).

4. Abusive Investigations of Employee Misconduct

a. Unwarranted Threats of Criminal Prosecution

Damage Award Upheld for Employee Threatened With Prosecution for Alleged Theft

Following the discovery of cash register shortages, the security director of a department store accused a sales employee of stealing money. He also threatened her with criminal prosecution and imprisonment.

The employee claimed that the security director tried to frighten her and make her an example for other employees. The employee was told, among other things, "We are talking about embezzlement, which is punishable by years in jail," and "We know you have been stealing money." The employee asserted that the security director made the allegations without any evidence as to her guilt or innocence, and that she was then placed under surveillance until she was forced to quit her job.

The employee filed an action for intentional infliction of emotional distress against the store and the security officer. The jury returned a verdict in favor of the employee and awarded her compensatory damages. An appellate court affirmed the jury's verdict, noting that the jury reasonably could have concluded that the security officer made his threats without ample evidence of the employee's guilt. The court stated that, in those circumstances, "defendants' method of interrogation was an extraordinary transgression of contemporary standards of civilized conduct toward an employee." *Hall v. May Dep't Stores Co.*, 292 Or. 131, 637 P.2d 126 (1981).

b. Improper Use of Polygraph Examinations

Jury Awards $1.3 Million Against Employer for Harassing and Firing Employee Who Refused to Take Lie Detector Test

An employee of a Maryland pharmacy was regarded as a serious and dedicated worker. After an inventory shortage was discovered at the pharmacy, she was asked by her supervisor to submit to a polygraph exam, even though Maryland law prohibited employers from requiring that employees take such tests as a condition of continued employment.

When the employee refused to take the exam, she was told that her hours would be reduced, her store keys would be taken, and she would be transferred. Finally, the supervisor tried to force her to resign before he fired her outright. As a result of the supervisor's conduct, the employee, who suffered from a preexisting nervous condition, was deeply disturbed, took large amounts of medication, slept most of the day, became a recluse, and could no longer perform routine household chores.

The employee brought an action for intentional infliction of emotional distress against her employer and supervisor. A jury awarded her $300,000 in actual damages and $1 million in punitive damages. On appeal, the appellate court held that the jury had properly found that the supervisor's conduct was outrageous and that the evidence showed that the employee suffered severe emotional distress.

The appeals court also found that the award of $1 million in punitive damages against the pharmacy was appropriate where the employer, through its supervisor, tried to force the employee to resign, even though he knew of her devotion to her job, and where the employer, through its officers, was aware of the statute prohibiting employers from requiring employees to take polygraph exams. *Moniodis v. Cook*, 64 Md. App. 1, 494 A.2d 212, 1 IER Cases 441, *cert. denied*, 304 Md. 631, 500 A.2d 649 (1985).

Authors' Note: A number of states have enacted laws that, like the federal Employee Polygraph Protection Act, 29 U.S.C. sections 2001–09, limit and regulate the request for and use of polygraph examinations (see Appendix B). Many of these state laws, like the federal law governing polygraph examinations, not only provide a statutory remedy for violation of the law, but also permit employees to bring tort claims against their employers for abusive polygraph examinations.

Jury Awards $100,000 to Employee Who Suffered Nightmares After Polygraph Exam

A bank teller was asked by her employer to submit to a polygraph exam because several deposits from an account were missing. The employer's request violated a state law prohibiting employers from soliciting or requiring a polygraph or any test designed to determine an employee's honesty.

For sixteen months after taking the exam, the employee suffered nightmares in which the polygraph test chair turned into an electric chair. She also became withdrawn, tired, and gained weight. The employee had had a rigid moral and religious upbringing and interpreted the request to take the polygraph exam as an accusation of dishonesty.

The employee sued the bank in state court for intentional infliction of emotional distress. The jury awarded her close to $100,000 in damages, costs, and attorneys' fees. The award was upheld on appeal. *Kamrath v. Suburban Nat'l Bank*, 363 N.W.2d 108 (Minn. Ct. App. 1985).

Polygraph Exam May Lead to Liability Even Though Employee Signed Release Before Taking Test

An assistant restaurant manager was asked by his employer to take a polygraph exam after $250 was found missing from the restaurant's safe. A state law prohibited an employer from requiring an employee to take a polygraph exam as a condition of continued employment. When the employee appeared for the exam, he was told by the test administrator that he had to sign a form that purported to release the employer from liability for the administration of the test. The employee signed the form, failed the test, and was terminated.

The employee brought an action against his employer and the investigative agency for intentional infliction of emotional distress, defamation, invasion of privacy, negligence, and wrongful discharge.

The trial court found that the employee did not produce sufficient evidence to show that his employer crossed the line from *requesting* that the employee take a polygraph exam to *requiring* the employee to submit to it.

An appellate court reversed on appeal, holding that the determination as to whether the employer *required* the employee to submit to a polygraph exam was an issue for the jury to decide. The court also stated that it would be appropriate for the jury to take into account the disparate positions of power between the employee and employer when determining whether the employee signed the release in the belief that his continued employment depended on it. *Leibowitz v. H.A. Winston Co.*, 342 Pa. Super. 456, 493 A.2d 111 (1985).

5. Unreasonable Drug Testing Techniques

Employer That Required Employee to Provide Urine Sample Under Direct Observation of Company Representative Liable for $125,000 in Damages

In order to control suspected drug use among its offshore employees, a drilling company implemented a comprehensive drug testing program for its Gulf of Mexico operations. The cornerstone of the policy was the administration of unannounced urinalyses to all personnel who worked on the company's drilling rigs. To ensure against adulteration or substitution of the urine specimens, at least one company representative observed all employees as they provided samples. The company regarded direct observation as a critical component of its drug testing program.

One of the employees, a barge engineer, tested positive for drugs. A second test was then administered, which showed an unacceptably high level of marijuana in the engineer's urine. As a result, the engineer was discharged.

The engineer filed an action against the company, challenging the implementation and administration of the drug testing program. He asserted claims for intentional infliction of emotional distress, negligent infliction of emotional distress, invasion of privacy, defamation, and wrongful discharge. At trial, the engineer testified that he was "disgusted by the whole idea of someone being paid to look at [his] penis while [he] urinated." The employer prevailed on the engineer's claims for wrongful discharge, intentional infliction of emotional distress, and defamation. The jury found in favor of the engineer on his invasion of privacy claim, although it awarded him only $1 in damages.

On the engineer's claim for negligent infliction of emotional distress, however, the jury returned a verdict against the employer in the amount of $125,000. In answering the special verdict questions, the jury found that the employer had breached its duty to use reasonable care not to cause serious emotional distress to its employees by implementing and administering a drug testing program based on the direct observation of employees providing urine samples. The jury then found that a reasonable person in the plaintiff's position would be seriously distressed by the direct observation of his act of urination.

On appeal, the employer argued that the jury's award on the negligent infliction claim should be reversed, because the emotional distress purportedly suffered by the barge engineer was neither foreseeable nor reasonably anticipated. According to the company, it was hardly foreseeable that a barge engineer (and ex-Marine) employed on an offshore oil rig would suffer serious psychological distress by a co-worker's observation of him providing a urine sample as part of a drug testing program. The appeals court disagreed and upheld the jury's verdict on the claim for negligent infliction of emotional distress. *Kelley v. Schlumberger Technology Corp.*, 849 F.2d 41, 3 IER Cases 696 (1st Cir. 1988).

6. Improper Use of Employee Assistance Programs

Supervisor's Misguided Attempt to Enroll Nonalcoholic Employee in Alcohol-Dependency Program Results in $130,000 Award for Reckless Conduct

A top salesman for a regional telephone company began to experience bouts of severe depression. Although he had quit drinking alcoholic beverages seven years earlier, he once again began to drink beer when alone in his hotel room at nights. Because he was concerned over his depression and sudden change in alcohol consumption, the salesman consulted his personal physician. After conferring with a psychologist, his doctor briefly admitted the salesman to a hospital for depression. A psychiatrist on staff at the hospital prescribed medication for depression. At no time did any of the doctors diagnose the salesman as an alcoholic.

Following his discharge from the hospital, the salesman met with his supervisor to discuss his hospitalization. Prior to this meeting, the salesman's wife had expressed concern to the supervisor about her husband's drinking. During their meeting, the supervisor suggested that the salesman meet with a counselor of the employee assistance program (EAP), which was operated by a different company that provided services pursuant to contract with the employer.

The salesman met with the EAP counselor, who inquired about the salesman's prior history of drinking and his recent change in drinking habits. The salesman then met with both the EAP counselor and the supervisor. The EAP counselor announced to the salesman that he was an alcoholic, and, with the concurrence of the salesman's supervisor, told him that he had to enroll in an inpatient alcohol treatment program for 30 days or face termination of employment. The salesman was told to make a decision before leaving the office. When he asked if he could postpone his decision, the supervisor told the salesman that postponement would be regarded as rejection of the treatment program offer. He then turned in his equipment and his supervisor told him he was fired. This resulted in a worsening of the employee's depression, requiring further medical treatment.

The salesman brought an action in court for intentional infliction of emotional distress against his employer, his supervisor, the EAP counselor, and the company that employed the counselor. The jury returned a verdict against all of the defendants, awarding the salesman $30,000 in compensatory damages and $100,000 in punitive damages.

On appeal, the defendants argued that there was no evidence that any of the actions undertaken by the EAP counselor or supervisor was done willfully or intentionally for the purpose of producing mental anguish on the part of the salesman. The appeals court disagreed and sustained the jury's verdict. It stated that recovery may be based on intentional *or reckless* conduct that causes severe emotional distress. The court defined "reckless conduct" as actions that show a deliberate disregard of a high probability that emotional distress will follow. The appeals court then held that the jury could reasonably have found the conduct of the supervisor and EAP counselor extreme and outrageous, since they knew that the salesman was suffering from severe depression and was particularly susceptible to emotional distress at the time of the confrontation. *Wangen v. Knudson*, 428 N.W.2d 242 (S.D. 1988).

7. Workplace Injuries and Illnesses

Football Player Awarded $70,000 After Erroneous Public Disclosure of Fatal Blood Disease

A professional football player signed three one-year player contracts with the team and the league. Each contract contained a standard NFL injury-benefit provision, allowing a person injured in performance of his contract to receive his salary for its duration. The player suffered a severe shoulder injury during his first season with the football team.

While he was hospitalized, the player was found to have a blood clot in his lung. After informing the team of his intention to resign, he was asked to submit to an examination by a second physician. The second physician diagnosed the player as suffering from an abnormal blood disease that predisposed him to blood clots, and recommended that the player not be allowed to continue playing contact sports.

After learning that the player had been advised to quit, a sports columnist telephoned the team physician to confirm his medical problems. The physician was quoted in the *Philadelphia Bulletin* as stating that the player was suffering from polycythemia vera. When the player contacted his personal physician to find out what this meant, he was told that polycythemia vera was a fatal blood disease. He testified that for some time thereafter he was depressed and frightened at the prospect of his imminent death. At first he refused to submit to further tests, but when he finally did, it was discovered that he did not have the disease. Nonetheless, he claimed that he remained frightened.

The football player brought suit against the team and the league, alleging intentional infliction of emotional distress. A jury awarded him $10,000 in compensatory damages and almost $60,000 in punitive damages. On appeal, the appellate court upheld the jury's award, holding that reckless conduct that causes severe emotional distress renders an actor as liable as if he had acted intentionally. Moreover, the court found that the award of punitive damages was not excessive. *Chuy v. Philadelphia Eagles Football Club*, 595 F.2d 1265 (3d Cir. 1979).

8. Smoking in the Workplace

Employer May Be Liable for Intentional Infliction Where Supervisor Harassed Employee Following Requests for a Smoke-Free Workplace

An employee of the Tennessee Valley Authority (TVA) worked for many years in a small and poorly ventilated office that she shared with co-workers who smoked at work. The employee began experiencing problems with her breathing. After consulting several doctors who warned her against further exposure to tobacco smoke, the employee submitted several written requests to her supervisor for a smoke-free work environment. The employee claimed that her supervisor ignored her requests, told fellow workers about her smoke complaints, and retaliated against her by giving her poor performance ratings and verbally harassing her in front of her co-workers.

The employee sued the TVA in federal court for negligence in failing to maintain a smoke-free work environment and for intentional infliction of emotional distress, seeking compensatory and punitive damages. Her husband also sued her employer for loss of consortium. The TVA filed a motion to dismiss the complaint in its entirety.

The court ruled that the employee's negligence claim could not be pursued against the TVA, a federal governmental entity, because claims of workplace negligence are barred by the Federal Employees' Compensation Act (FECA). The court concluded, however, that FECA did not preclude her cause of action for *intentional* infliction of emotional distress, since injury from intentional acts is not covered by FECA. The court also held that the doctrine of official immunity, which is generally applicable to lawsuits premised on the conduct of federal officials, did not bar the intentional infliction claim, because the kind of harassment and intimidation alleged by the employee had no connection to the supervisor's duties and responsibilities. *Carroll v. Tennessee Valley Auth.*, 697 F. Supp. 508, 3 IER Cases 149 (D.D.C. 1988).

Authors' Note: See also *McCarthy v. State,* summarized in Chapter 1, where an employee was permitted to maintain an action against her employer for negligent failure to provide a smoke-free workplace. Many states, as well as some municipalities, currently have statutes limiting and restricting smoking in the workplace. Some of these laws provide a comprehensive enforcement scheme and preempt state law tort claims by workers harmed by secondhand smoke.

9. Abusive, Reckless, Discriminatory, and Negligent Methods of Termination

Executive Awarded $5.3 Million in Tort Damages for Employer's False Evaluation Used as a Pretext to Terminate Him for Homosexual Activities

A senior executive for an oil company subsidiary had a distinguished 19-year career marked by consistently high evaluations of his work. The executive inadvertently misplaced at work an extra copy of a private memo that he had typed on his employer's word processor concerning the "house rules" for homosexuals in attendance at a private party the executive planned to attend. The "house rules" were designed to encourage "safe sex" by the attendees of the party. The executive's secretary found the memo and handed it to the president of the subsidiary, who had not previously known that his subordinate was a homosexual.

The president, together with other officials of the company, originally planned to use the contents of the memo and its presence in the office as justification for terminating the executive. They ultimately decided, however, to terminate the executive by creating a false, unsatisfactory evaluation of the executive's work performance. The president placed the fabricated performance evaluation in the executive's personnel file and then terminated him on the basis of unsatisfactory job performance. The president also refused to afford the executive any notice period before actual termination, told the unemployment compensation board that the executive had resigned, and advised at least one executive headhunter of the memo and its contents. The termination also created a lasting estrangement between the executive and his father, who was a retiree of the company.

The executive commenced an action against the oil company and its subsidiary, alleging a variety of tort claims including intentional infliction of emotional distress. After a nonjury trial, the court awarded the executive $3.3 million in compensatory damages on his tort claims. In addition, after concluding that the employer's termination of the executive was malicious, oppressive, deceitful, and cruel, the court also awarded him $2 million in punitive damages on his intentional infliction claim. Finally, the court awarded the executive $2.5 million in damages for breach of an implied covenant of good faith, resulting in a total award of $7.8 million in damages. *Collins v. Shell Oil Co.*, 56 FEP Cases 440 (Cal. Super. Ct. Alameda County 1991).

TV Anchorwoman's Inability to Breast-Feed Her Baby After She Was Told of Termination May Give Rise to Negligent Infliction Claim

On the day she arrived home from the hospital with her second child, a television news anchorwoman in Topeka, Kansas, was informed by the station manager that she had been terminated from her job. The station manager thought it best not to advise the anchorwoman that she was being replaced by a male newscaster until after she gave birth and had returned from the hospital. He also went to her home so that he could personally deliver the news of her termination. He notified her of the decision in a polite manner without any derogatory or demeaning comments. Six weeks later, the anchorwoman became unable to lactate, which prevented her from continuing to breast-feed her new baby.

The anchorwoman filed a lawsuit against the television station for intentional and negligent infliction of emotional distress. She claimed that, as a direct result of her employer's conduct, she suffered severe mental distress and physical injury, including the inability to lactate. The anchorwoman also filed a state law claim against the station and its general manager for fraud. She alleged that only four months before her termination, the general manager had fraudulently induced her to sign an employment contract that prohibited her from working for another station, knowing all along that she would be replaced within a few months. Finally, the anchorwoman filed a claim against the station under Title VII, alleging that her employer had discriminated against her on the basis of her sex by replacing her with a man.

The station and its general manager filed a motion for summary judgment on the anchorwoman's tort claims. The court held that the employer's conduct was not so extreme or outrageous as to permit recovery for *intentional* infliction of emotional distress, concluding that the conduct was, at most, unthoughtful and tactless. The court held, however, that the anchorwoman stated a claim for *negligent* infliction, based on the emotional distress caused by her inability to lactate.

The court also held that the anchorwoman could recover for fraud against her employer and the station manager if she could prove her allegation that the station manager had decided not to retain her before the time she executed the restrictive covenant. The case was reportedly settled for a six-figure sum. *Freeman v. Kansas State Network,* 719 F. Supp. 995, 5 IER Cases 155 (D. Kan. 1989).

Employer May Be Liable Where Supervisor Sent Employee to Seminar He Knew Had Been Cancelled

An occupational therapist was employed by a convalescent home. After the administrator of the home instituted certain treatment program changes, which the therapist regarded as improper, she notified the administrator by letter that she had decided to resign. In her letter, the therapist detailed the reasons for her belief that the changes to the treatment program violated state laws and the standards of practice of the American Occupational Therapy Association.

A week earlier, the therapist had registered for an out-of-town seminar for occupational therapists. The conference was to be held two days after she gave notice of her resignation. Nonetheless, when she submitted her resignation, the administrator told her that she could attend the conference. At the time, the administrator allegedly knew that the conference had been cancelled, but never told the therapist.

The therapist traveled to the site of the seminar two days later, only to learn that it had been cancelled. When she returned to work the following day, the administrator notified the therapist that she had been fired for "engag[ing] in the commission of felony or theft, in connection with . . . a fraudulent scheme to obtain salary from the [employer] by enrolling in classes which had been cancelled." Thereafter, the therapist claimed, the administrator falsely told others that the therapist was dishonest, untrustworthy, a thief, and incompetent. As a result, the therapist alleged, she suffered extreme emotional pain in the form of fear, anxiety, anger, humiliation, and depression.

The therapist filed a lawsuit for wrongful discharge. She also added a claim against her employer and the administrator for intentional infliction of emotional distress. The lower court dismissed both counts of the complaint. On appeal, the appellate court upheld the dismissal of the wrongful discharge claim because the employee had actually resigned. As to the intentional infliction claim, however, the appeals court reversed. It held that a supervisor's conduct of sending an employee to a conference, knowing that it had been cancelled, for the purpose of setting her up to be fired for theft or dishonesty, is an extraordinary transgression of the bounds of socially tolerable conduct. Accordingly, the appeals court remanded the case for trial. *McCool v. Hillhaven Corp.*, 97 Or. App. 536, 777 P.2d 1013, 4 IER Cases 1026, *review denied*, 308 Or. 593, 784 P.2d 1100 (1989).

Long-Term Employee May Maintain Claim for Negligent Infliction Based Solely on Allegation That He Became Depressed Following Termination

A jeans manufacturer terminated one of its Texas sales representatives after eleven years of employment with the company. As a result of his termination, the salesman alleged that he suffered severe emotional distress. He subsequently filed an action in federal court for intentional and negligent infliction of emotional distress and age discrimination.

The company filed a motion for summary judgment on all claims. The employer argued that the court should dismiss the claim for intentional infliction of emotional distress because the mere fact of termination after eleven years of employment could not be regarded as outrageous. The employer also maintained that the salesman had failed to demonstrate that he had suffered the type of severe emotional distress necessary to recover under the tort of negligent infliction.

The court agreed with the manufacturer that the termination alone would not satisfy the requirement of outrageousness to sustain a claim for *intentional* infliction of emotional distress. The court refused, however, to dismiss the salesman's *negligent* infliction claim. It concluded that whether the plaintiff had suffered emotional distress that was severe enough to permit recovery for negligent infliction is a question of fact for a jury to determine. According to the court's ruling, the salesman may be entitled to recover damages on his claim for negligent infliction of emotional distress if he is able to prove to a jury that his termination caused him to feel anger, depression, embarrassment, and shock. *Abston v. Levi Strauss & Co.*, 684 F. Supp. 152, 3 IER Cases 1329 (E.D. Tex. 1987).

Black Employee May Maintain Intentional Infliction Claim Based on Discriminatory Termination for Falsifying Employment Application a Decade Ago

An African-American employee of a regional telephone company was discharged after ten years of employment when her employer discovered that she had lied on her employment application concerning her prior criminal record. The employee brought an action against her employer in federal court for racial discrimination under 42 U.S.C. section 1981 and for intentional infliction of emotional distress, claiming that she was discriminatorily discharged because equally deceptive white employees who lied about their criminal records were not fired.

The lower court dismissed the employee's claim for racial discrimination under section 1981 (because, at the time, section 1981 did not apply to termination of employment) and the claim for intentional infliction. A federal appellate court, however, reversed the lower court's decision on the tort claim. It held that an intentionally discriminatory termination *may* give rise to a claim for intentional infliction of emotional distress. *Walker v. South Cent. Bell Tel. Co.*, 904 F.2d 275, 5 IER Cases 1373 (5th Cir. 1990).

Firing Workers in Alphabetical Order May Subject Employer to Damages

The manager of a restaurant called all of the waitresses to a meeting one day. The waitresses were told that someone was suspected of stealing, but the identity of that person was not known. As a result, the manager threatened that all of the waitresses present would be fired in alphabetical order until the person responsible for the theft was discovered. The manager then fired the waitress whose name was first in alphabetical order.

The terminated waitress sued both the restaurant and its manager, alleging that the manager's conduct was reckless, extreme, outrageous, and intended to cause emotional distress. A lower court dismissed the waitress's complaint, holding that damages for emotional distress are not compensable absent a manifestation of physical injury. On appeal, the lower court's dismissal was reversed. The appeals court held that one who, by extreme and outrageous conduct, causes severe emotional distress to another, is subject to liability for the emotional distress even though no bodily harm may result. *Agis v. Howard Johnson Co.*, 371 Mass. 140, 355 N.E.2d 315 (1976).

Notes

1. The Restatement (Second) of Torts § 46(1) defines the tort as follows: "One who by extreme and outrageous conduct intentionally or recklessly causes severe emotional distress to another is subject to liability for such emotional distress, and if bodily harm to the other results from it, for such bodily harm."
2. *See* Restatement (Second) of Torts § 46(1), comment d.
3. *See* Restatement (Second) of Torts § 46, comment e.
4. *See* Restatement (Second) of Torts § 46, comment f.
5. *See* Restatement (Second) of Torts § 46, comment d.
6. *See* Restatement (Second) of Torts § 46, comment d.
7. *See* Restatement (Second) of Torts § 46, comment i; Wangen v. Knudson, 428 N.W.2d 242 (S.D. 1988), summarized in section D.6. of this chapter.
8. *See* Restatement (Second) of Torts §§ 46, comment i, and 500, comment a.
9. *See* Restatement (Second) of Torts § 46(1).
10. *See* Restatement (Second) of Torts § 46, comment j.
11. *See* Kelley v. Schlumberger Technology Corp., 849 F.2d 41, 3 IER Cases 696 (1st Cir. 1988), summarized in section D.5. of this chapter.
12. *See* Kelley v. Schlumberger Technology Corp., 849 F.2d 41, 3 IER Cases 696 (1st Cir. 1988), summarized in section D.5. of this chapter.
13. *See* Freeman v. Kansas State Network, 719 F. Supp. 995, 5 IER Cases 155 (D. Kan. 1989), summarized in section D.9. of this chapter.
14. *See* Payne v. General Motors Corp., 5 IER Cases 1081, 53 FEP Cases 471 (D. Kan. 1990), *aff'd mem.*, 943 F.2d 57 (10th Cir. 1991), summarized in section D.3. of this chapter.
15. *See* Wilson v. Monarch Paper Co., 939 F.2d 1138, 6 IER Cases 1344 (5th Cir. 1991), summarized in section D.1. of this chapter.
16. *See* Collins v. Shell Oil Co., 56 FEP Cases 440 (Cal. Super. Ct. Alameda County 1991), summarized in section D.9. of this chapter.
17. *See* Moniodis v. Cook, 64 Md. App. 1, 494 A.2d 212, 1 IER Cases 441, *cert. denied*, 304 Md. 631, 500 A.2d 649 (1985), summarized in section D.4. of this chapter.
18. *See* Sweeney v. Westvaco Co., 926 F.2d 29, 6 IER Cases 289 (1st Cir.), *cert. denied*, 112 S. Ct. 274 (1991), summarized in section D.1. of this chapter.

Chapter 5

Invasion of Privacy

A. Overview

Employees have become increasingly sensitive about their rights of privacy in the workplace. This increased sensitivity occurs at the same time employers are expanding preemployment inquiries, instituting drug testing programs, and automating the retrieval of employee-specific information.

Invasion of privacy lawsuits have focused primarily on public disclosures by employers of private facts regarding their employees, such as an employee's psychiatric or medical condition. In addition, invasion of privacy actions have dealt with intrusions into an employee's privacy, such as unauthorized entry into a worker's locker or home or an inquiry into an employee's sexual affairs.

Protection of workplace privacy also has become the subject of increased federal and state legislation covering such areas as the use of drug and alcohol testing, polygraph examinations and other honesty tests, telephone surveillance, monitoring of video display terminal operators, and criminal record inquiries. AIDS testing and exposure to the AIDS virus also have become the subjects of new legislation. All of these subjects of recent legislation are also fertile grounds for lawsuits for invasion of privacy.

B. General Principles of Law

An individual's privacy interest is premised on his or her "right to be let alone." This interest is protected in some jurisdictions not only by the common law, but also by statute, public policy, and/or state constitution. In addition, various federal statutes protect an individual's privacy interest, as does the Fourth Amendment of the United States Constitution, which is applicable to public employees.[1]

There are four types of state law torts that are frequently referred to as actions for "invasion of privacy."[2] The first tort is the appropriation of another person's name or likeness. This right is similar to a property right in that it consists of the individual's exclusive use of his or her identity. The case law in this area generally involves whether a defendant used a plaintiff's name, picture, or other likeness for commercial use without the plaintiff's consent.[3] This tort generally is not applicable to the employment context.

A second tort generally recognized under the invasion of privacy concept is "false light publicity," where a person *publicly* attributes to the plaintiff certain characteristics, conduct, or beliefs that are false, so that the plaintiff is placed before the public in a "false light."[4] To be actionable, the false light in which the plaintiff is placed must be highly offensive to a reasonable person, and the defendant must or should have known that he or she was placing the plaintiff in the false light.[5] Although similar to defamation, this tort involves a person's interest in being left alone, whereas defamation pertains to an individual's interest in a good reputation.[6]

The tort of false light publicity arises in the employment context where, for example, an employer terminates an employee in such a manner as to imply that he engaged in misconduct or a breach of ethics,[7] or where a supervisor falsely states to a subordinate in front of other employees that the subordinate's wife is sexually promiscuous.[8] The tort can even arise where an employer falsely states in a public manner that a female employee filed a baseless claim of sexual harassment.[9]

A third type of privacy action is the tort of public disclosure of private facts. This tort, which is the most frequently asserted cause of action by employees for invasion of privacy, arises where someone publicizes a facet of another person's private life that is not of legitimate concern to the public.[10] It usually arises where an employer unreasonably or unnecessarily publicizes an employee's sexual, financial, familial, or medical affairs, such as an employee's infection with the AIDS virus or his or her psychiatric diagnosis.[11] The publicity need not be widespread; disclosure to an employee's co-workers may be sufficient to satisfy the requirement that the private matters be publicized.[12]

The fourth type of invasion of privacy action is intrusion upon another's seclusion. This tort arises where someone intentionally intrudes, physically or otherwise, upon the solitude or seclusion of another person or upon his or her private affairs or concerns.[13] The intrusion becomes actionable if it would be regarded as highly offensive to a reasonable person.[14] An actionable intrusion may arise, for example, when an employer searches an employee's locker, desk, files, or mail, or enters an employee's home.[15] It may also arise when an employer unreasonably inquires into an employee's private affairs, such as an employee's sexual interests or other matters unrelated to the employee's job.[16]

In workplace privacy actions, the most significant factual issue in determining liability is whether the person who allegedly committed the invasion of privacy had a legitimate reason to inquire into or disclose a matter that the employee regards as private. Where no legitimate purpose is served, such as when a supervisor unnecessarily inquires into an employee's sexual affairs[17] or when a manager discloses an employee's psychiatric history to the employee's co-workers,[18] an employer may become liable in damages for invasion of privacy.

C. Illustrative Cases

The invasion of privacy cases summarized in this chapter fall into the following categories:

- Disclosure of Employees' Medical or Mental Condition;
- Disclosure of Personal Matters About Employees;
- Inquiries Into Employees' Private Affairs;
- Searches of Employee Lockers and Mail; and
- False Light Publicity.

Because invasion of privacy claims embrace different types of torts, the cases summarized in this chapter include not only statements about employees that are alleged to be *false*, but also statements about employees acknowledged to be *true*.

Some invasion of privacy cases have resulted in substantial awards of damages, such as a $358,000 jury award for an inappropriate inquiry during a polygraph examination into an employee's past drug use and into other private matters that were unrelated to the employee's job.[19] Most invasion of privacy claims, though, have so far resulted in more modest awards of damages, such as the $100,000 award against an employer that searched an employee's locker and purse at work without her consent.[20] Nonetheless, invasion of privacy claims are no less costly to defend than any other employee tort actions, and employers may spend more to defend these types of cases than to satisfy a potential judgment in favor of an employee.

1. Disclosure of Employees' Medical or Mental Condition

Employee Afflicted by AIDS-Related Complex May Maintain Claim Where Employer Disclosed Medical Condition to Employee's Co-Workers

A repair technician for a telephone company requested permission to be absent from work for two medical appointments. His supervisor granted the requests. But when the repair technician asked permission to be absent for another medical appointment, the supervisor asked the repair technician to tell him why. The technician protested, but the supervisor promised to keep the information confidential. The employee told his supervisor that he had been diagnosed as having AIDS-related complex.

The supervisor disclosed this information to his superiors. Thereafter, company managers informed employees in large group meetings that the repair technician had AIDS. The technician subsequently received calls from his co-workers threatening to lynch him if he returned to work. The technician decided not to return to work.

The technician brought a lawsuit for invasion of privacy under state law. He alleged that his employer violated his right to privacy by forcing him to disclose information about his medical condition and then disclosing the information to other employees. The technician claimed that the disclosures were not reasonably necessary to safeguard substantial or legitimate business interests of the employer.

The employer filed a motion to dismiss the complaint, which included a state law claim for employment discrimination on the basis of handicap and disability. The court denied the employer's motion, ruling that the issue of the legitimacy of the employer's business interest in disclosing the information to the employee's co-workers was a question of fact to be determined at trial. *Cronan v. New England Tel. Co.*, 41 FEP Cases 1273 (Mass. Super. Ct. Suffolk County 1986).

Employer That Disclosed Employee's Mastectomy to Co-Workers May Be Liable for Invasion of Privacy

An employee of an electronics firm advised a company nurse about three medical leaves of absence she would need over a two-year period to undergo a mastectomy and reconstructive surgery. The company nurse advised the employee that her medical condition would be kept confidential. Subsequently, though, a co-worker informed the employee that she had been told at work of the employee's mastectomy. The employee claimed that, as a result of the disclosure at work and her belief that many of her co-workers were aware of her medical condition, she suffered severe physical, mental, and emotional distress that forced her to take an early retirement.

The employee filed an action against her employer for two forms of invasion of privacy: public disclosure of private facts and unreasonable intrusion into the seclusion of another. The court granted the employer's motion to dismiss. On appeal, the employer argued that the employee's claim for public disclosure of private facts was properly dismissed for two reasons: first, there was no widespread disclosure of the employee's medical condition; and second, the matter disclosed would not be objectionable or highly offensive to a reasonable person.

The appeals court disagreed. It held that the "public disclosure" requirement of the tort can be satisfied by proof of disclosure to even a few fellow employees at work. It also held that whether the disclosure of an operation of such a personal nature would be highly offensive to a reasonable person presents a question of fact for the jury to determine. The appellate court therefore reversed the lower court's dismissal of the public disclosure of private facts claim, and remanded it for trial.

The appeals court did, however, affirm the dismissal of the claim for unreasonable intrusion. It held that the dissemination of information *voluntarily* disclosed to the employer by the employee was not an intrusion or prying into the seclusion of another. *Miller v. Motorola*, 202 Ill. App. 3d 976, 560 N.E.2d 900, 5 IER Cases 885 (1990).

Disclosure of Employee's Mental State May Result in Damages for Invasion of Privacy

An employee of a major computer manufacturer had used the company's "open-door" policy several times over a seven-year period to lodge complaints about his performance evaluations and to inform management that his suggestions for improving internal policy were missing from his files. During the same period, the employee had complained to his supervisor that he was suffering from nervousness, headaches, and loss of sleep.

The supervisor referred the employee to a local physician who was under contract to the employer. After examining the employee, the physician telephoned the employee's supervisor and advised her that she thought the employee was "paranoid" and should see a psychiatrist. The supervisor made a note for her files and then relayed the information to the director of personnel, who subsequently sent a memorandum to several managers regarding the employee's mental condition.

Over the next several days, two of the managers made telephone calls to members of the corporate in-house medical staff, advising them that the local physician thought the employee was "paranoid." The in-house physicians then called the local physician, who confirmed her medical opinion and the need for treatment by a psychiatrist. An in-house doctor recommended to the employee that he take a three-month medical leave of absence, and the employee followed the physician's suggestion.

The company's medical records policy provided that all medical information contained in an employee's medical file, including information from a local physician under contract to the company, would remain confidential and would not be released without the employee's consent—except in the case of an emergency or where required by law. Company policy also prohibited managers from communicating directly with local physicians under contract to the employer, unless the employee consented. It was undisputed that the employee never consented to the release of any medical information or to any communications between the local physician and company management.

The employee filed a lawsuit in federal court for invasion of privacy against his employer, his supervisor, and the local physician. The court granted the defendants' motion for summary judgment. On appeal, the federal appellate court first addressed the claim against the employer and the supervisor. It held that an employer's intracorporate communication of private facts about an employee may constitute an invasion of privacy if the employee's individual right to privacy outweighs the employer's legitimate business need to disseminate private information that could affect the employee's work. The appellate court noted, however, that an employer may not be able to demonstrate a need to disclose an employee's medical condition where the company's managers obtained and disseminated the medical information in violation of its own policies.

The appellate court next addressed the employee's claim against the local physician. It held that a physician may be liable for invasion of privacy for disclosure of medical information to a patient's employer if the physician owes a duty of confidentiality to the employee. The court noted that a duty of confidentiality arises whenever an employee has reason to believe that a physician-patient relationship has been established. The appellate court therefore remanded the case for trial on the employee's claim against his employer and supervisor as well as his claim against the local physician. *Bratt v. IBM*, 785 F.2d 352 (1st Cir. 1986).

Authors' Note: The Americans With Disabilities Act of 1990 (ADA) regulates not only employer inquiries regarding employee disabilities, but also the retention, use, and disclosure of employee medical information obtained by employers.[21] State laws may also regulate an employer's conduct in the area of employee medical information.

2. Disclosure of Personal Matters About Employees

Employee Sues for $20 Million After Husband Commits Suicide Upon Hearing From Employer That She Was Absent From Work at Night, but Case Is Dismissed

A female employee of a bakery who worked the 11:30 p.m. to 7:30 a.m. shift apparently was with her lover on several nights instead of being at work. Her husband called the bakery one evening and was told that his wife was absent. The next day, he went to the bakery and spoke with the assistant personnel manager who, after reviewing her personnel file, allegedly informed the employee's husband of several other times she had been absent from work. The husband committed suicide two days later, leaving a note that he wanted his wife to be happy without him.

The female employee sued the bakery and the assistant personnel manager in state court for invasion of privacy and the wrongful death of her husband, seeking $20 million in damages. She alleged that the assistant personnel manager impermissibly intruded upon her seclusion by revealing her absences to her husband. She further claimed that, as a result of her husband's suicide, she had experienced mental pain and suffering. The court granted summary judgment for the employer, and the employee appealed.

In affirming the grant of summary judgment for the defendants, the appellate court noted that information in an employee's personnel file is generally considered confidential and, therefore, cannot be disclosed. The court held, however, that the statements made by the assistant personnel manager, even though they disclosed confidential personal information, were *privileged* under state law, since they were made in response to an inquiry regarding the employee's welfare. The appellate court also noted that the husband just as easily could have tried to call his wife at work on those nights and found out that she was not there. *Kobeck v. Nabisco, Inc.*, 166 Ga. App. 652, 305 S.E.2d 183, 1 IER Cases 200 (1983).

Jury Awards Teachers $225,000 in Suit Against School District for Publicizing Their Drunk Driving Accident, but Verdict Is Reversed on Appeal

Three high school teachers were involved in an alcohol-related accident following a retirement party where they had been drinking. Students from the school were in the crowd that gathered at the scene of the accident. Accounts of the incident, including interviews with school board officials, were published by the local media. The school district subsequently disciplined the teachers. In addition, the teacher who was driving the car was prosecuted for driving under the influence of alcohol, although she was acquitted at trial.

The teachers sued the school district, claiming that the publication of the incident by school officials was an invasion of their privacy. A jury awarded the teachers a total of $225,000. An appellate court, however, overturned the verdict. It held that the teachers had failed to prove invasion of privacy by publication of private facts because the accident, as well as the school district's campaign to stop drinking and driving, were public knowledge. The court also noted that the disciplinary record of the teachers constituted public information under applicable state law. *Trout v. Umatilla County School Dist.*, 77 Or. App. 95, 712 P.2d 814 (1985), *review denied,* 300 Or. 704, 716 P.2d 758 (1986).

Employer Sued for Disclosing Financial Information About Former Employee to IRS, but Disclosure Did Not Constitute Invasion of Privacy

In response to a summons, an employer disclosed financial information to the Internal Revenue Service (IRS) about a former employee. The information consisted of forms and ledgers showing all compensation paid to the former employee, the reimbursements he claimed, and the expenses he charged.

The employee sued his former employer for invasion of privacy. The court granted the employer's motion for summary judgment. On appeal, an appellate court affirmed. It concluded that the employer was not liable for invasion of privacy because the employer had been served with a summons to produce the records and notified the employee that it would provide the records to the IRS unless instructed by a court not to comply with the summons. The court held that the employee's right to privacy in the records was outweighed by the interest of the IRS in pursuing a legitimate investigation of the employee's tax liability. *Wells v. Premier Indus. Corp.*, 691 P.2d 765 (Colo. Ct. App. 1984).

Hospital Prevails in Suit for Disclosure of Personnel Director's Separation Agreement

A university hospital disclosed the terms of a former personnel director's separation agreement with the hospital to one employee at a staff meeting and to another employee who had made an inquiry about the personnel director's departure. The employee sued the university, claiming that the disclosure was an invasion of her privacy by giving publicity to private matters.

The court granted the employer's motion for summary judgment, holding that the employee had failed to state a valid claim for invasion of privacy under state law. The court concluded that it was not unreasonable for an employer to disclose information regarding the reasons for which the personnel director left her position and the terms of her separation agreement to an employee who asked and to another employee at a regular staff meeting conducted by the hospital. The court further concluded that such limited disclosure would not constitute the type of widespread "publicity" necessary to prove a claim for invasion of privacy. Finally, the court held that the matter disclosed would not be highly offensive to an ordinary person. *Wells v. Thomas*, 569 F. Supp. 426 (E.D. Pa. 1983).

Authors' Note: It may be advisable for an employer *not* to disclose to other employees this type of information about an employee's separation, unless there is a valid business purpose for such disclosure.

3. Inquiries Into Employees' Private Affairs

Manager Asked About Drug Use and Other Private Matters During Polygraph Exam Awarded $398,000 for Invasion of Privacy

A long-term manager of a fast-food restaurant was discharged for poor performance and for violating company policy against the use of drugs. The manager claimed that he was actually discharged for failing to promote one of his subordinates, who was the godson of one of the business' owners. The manager's superior had confronted him about rumors that he was using drugs. The manager submitted to a polygraph exam, allegedly under threat of losing his job, and purportedly failed the test. The manager alleged that during the polygraph exam he was asked questions regarding past drug use as well as other matters unrelated to his employment that he was entitled to keep private.

The manager sued his employer in state court for invasion of privacy and defamation. The employer removed the case to federal court. After a week-long trial the jury found that the manager had been terminated for reasons unrelated to his alleged use of drugs; that the employer had invaded his privacy; and that the employer had defamed the manager by falsely stating that he had used drugs. The jury awarded the manager $398,000 in damages on the invasion of privacy claim and $50,000 in damages on the defamation claim.

On appeal, the employer argued that because the company's personnel manual prohibited drug use by employees, the manager impliedly gave the employer permission to conduct whatever investigations it deemed necessary, including a polygraph exam inquiring about the manager's use of drugs and other private matters. The appellate court rejected this novel argument and upheld the jury's findings that the investigation was "highly offensive" and invaded the manager's privacy by inquiring into matters unrelated to his job. *O'Brien v. Papa Gino's of America,* 780 F.2d 1067, 1 IER Cases 458 (1st Cir. 1986).

Employer May Be Liable for Invasion of Privacy by Allegedly Inducing Physician to Reveal Results of Drug Screening Test

While working at a glass plant, an employee who became ill was taken by ambulance to the emergency room of a local hospital. There, he was examined and treated by a hospital physician, who ordered that a blood and urine sample be taken from the employee for a drug/alcohol screen. The results of the screen revealed the presence of marijuana.

Approximately one week later, the employee was fired from his job for violation of the plant rule dealing with working while under the influence of drugs. The employer based its decision on the results of the drug/alcohol screen, which was provided to it by the hospital physician. This information had been specifically requested from the physician by officials in the employer's employee relations department.

The employee commenced an action against his employer for invasion of privacy, claiming that his employer had intruded upon his seclusion by requesting and obtaining confidential drug screen results without his consent. The employer filed a motion for summary judgment, which was denied. The court first pointed out that a state law provision prohibits physicians from disclosing medical information without a patient's consent, except to protect individual or public welfare. The court then held that the interest of the employer in ensuring that an employee is fit for work cannot justify an employer's inducement of a physician to breach his statutory duty of confidentiality. Although the employer had a perfectly valid and permissible objective of determining whether the employee was fit for work, the court stated that it may not achieve that lawful objective by means involving an unwarranted and unreasonable intrusion into an employee's private affairs. *Neal v. Corning Glass Works Corp.*, 745 F. Supp. 1294, 5 IER Cases 1636 (S.D. Ohio 1989).

Company President Violates Employee's Right to Privacy by Asking Her About Her Sex Life

A female employee of a maintenance firm claimed that the company president invaded her psychological seclusion by asking her constantly about "what positions" she used with her husband and demanding that she have oral sex with him at least three times a week to maintain her job. The company president harassed her in this fashion several times a week, she alleged, and papered the windows in his office in the belief that she ultimately would submit to his demands.

The employee sued her employer and the company president in federal court, bringing a state law claim for invasion of privacy together with a Title VII action for sexual harassment. A jury awarded her $25,000 in damages. An appellate court upheld the jury award, concluding that the employee's interest in her psychological seclusion had been violated. *Phillips v. Smalley Maintenance Servs.*, 711 F.2d 1524, 1 IER Cases 221 (11th Cir. 1983).

Employer and Supervisor Sued for Disclosing Employee's Psychiatric History to Co-Workers, but Court Dismisses Case

Information about an employee's psychiatric treatment was included in his medical records at work. The employee's supervisor allegedly looked into his medical records and learned about his visits to a psychiatrist. The employee also claimed that his supervisor told some of the employee's co-workers about his psychiatric problems and treatment.

The employee sued his employer and supervisor for unreasonable intrusion upon his seclusion and unreasonable publicity of private facts. The court granted the employer's motion for summary judgment on both claims. An intermediate appellate court reversed, but on further appeal the lawsuit was dismissed. The appellate court held that although the employee's psychiatric treatment may be a private matter, it may also be a legitimate concern to a supervisor, thereby justifying an inquiry into the employee's medical records at work. The court also held that the employer could not be liable for unreasonable disclosure of private facts where only a small group of co-workers was made privy to the employee's private affairs. *Eddy v. Brown,* 715 P.2d 74 (Okla. 1986).

4. Searches of Employees' Lockers and Mail

Employer Liable for $100,000 in Punitive Damages for Searching Employee's Locker and Purse

A department store provided an employee with a personal locker on which she had installed her own lock. After security personnel alerted management that an unidentified employee had stolen some merchandise and price-marking equipment, the store manager searched the employee's locker as well as her purse without her consent. When confronted by the employee, the store manager denied that a search had occurred.

The employee sued her employer for invasion of privacy on the ground that her employer wrongfully intruded upon her seclusion by searching her personal locker and purse, which was inside the locker. A jury awarded the employee $8,000 in actual damages and $100,000 in punitive damages for invading an area where she had a reasonable expectation of privacy.

On appeal, an appellate court held that the mere suspicion that an unidentified employee had stolen goods from the store was insufficient to justify the search of the employee's locker and purse without her consent. It also held that where an employee, with the employer's knowledge, purchases and uses his or her own lock on a locker at work, the employee manifests, and the employer recognizes, an expectation that the locker and its contents will be free from intrusion and interference.

The appeals court, however, remanded the case to the trial court because the judge had failed to properly instruct the jury that there could be no recovery for invasion of privacy based on an intrusion upon seclusion unless the intrusion was highly offensive to a person of reasonable sensitivities. *K-Mart Corp. v. Trotti,* 677 S.W.2d 632 (Tex. Ct. App. 1984), *writ denied,* 686 S.W.2d 593 (Tex. 1985).

Authors' Note: Public employees are also protected by the Fourth Amendment of the United States Constitution from unreasonable work-related searches of their desks, file cabinets, and other work areas where governmental employees have a reasonable expectation of privacy.[22]

Employee May Recover for Invasion of Privacy Arising From Unauthorized Reading of Personal Mail Sent to His Place of Work

An officer of a corporation sued a fellow officer for invasion of privacy on the ground that the defendant intruded upon his seclusion by reading his personal mail delivered to the corporation's place of business.

A lower court dismissed the claim, but an appellate court reversed. It held that the plaintiff sufficiently stated a cause of action for invasion of privacy because his mail was addressed to him and marked "personal." The court found that under state law the plaintiff retained a reasonable expectation of privacy in his mail, even though the conduct occurred in a business environment. *Vernars v. Young,* 539 F.2d 966 (3d Cir. 1976).

Co-Workers' Entry Into Employee's Home Leads to Jury Award Against Employer for Invasion of Privacy

After a telephone company employee failed to report to work on time, his co-workers went to his trailer home and observed empty liquor bottles strewn about. The co-workers returned later that day with another witness. When the employee did not respond to their knocking, they entered the trailer, where they allegedly noticed an empty whiskey bottle. The co-workers reported this information to their employer, who terminated the employee.

The employee brought an action against his employer and his co-workers for invasion of privacy. A jury awarded him $15,000 in damages. On appeal, the appellate court rejected the defendants' argument that they should not be held liable, because they entered the employee's home out of concern for his well-being. Instead, the court found that the co-workers physically intruded upon the employee's home without justification. *Love v. Southern Bell Tel. & Tel. Co.*, 263 So. 2d 460 (La. Ct. App.), *writ denied*, 262 La. 1117, 266 So. 2d 429 (1972).

5. False Light Publicity

Attorney General Who Stated in Press Conference That Former Clerk's Sexual Harassment Claim Was "Unfounded" May Be Liable for Invasion of Privacy

A clerk employed in the Office of the Attorney General for the state of Kansas sued the Attorney General and others in his office for sexual harassment on the job. The case was settled, but the terms of the settlement were not revealed to the press or public. One of the terms of the settlement was that the parties agreed to keep the terms confidential.

Questions were raised in the press and state legislature as to how much money was paid to the clerk, whether public funds were used, and why the terms were not disclosed. The Attorney General, who was considering a bid for the Kansas gubernatorial race, expressed concern that publicity might damage his campaign. In an effort at "damage control," the Attorney General held a news conference. His chief aide began the conference by stating that only private funds were used for the settlement, and that the clerk was paid $24,000 to withdraw her claim. The chief aide also stated that "[t]he case was totally without merit, and preposterous allegations [were made]." The Attorney General then added, "the allegations in the suit were totally unfounded."

The clerk then commenced a second lawsuit against the Attorney General and his chief aide, claiming that both defendants invaded her privacy and committed the tort of false light publicity by stating that her initial lawsuit was "without merit" and "totally unfounded." The Attorney General and his aide filed motions for summary judgment. They contended that the false light claim should be dismissed because their comments were merely opinions, not statements of fact, and because the clerk had failed to show that the defendants acted with malice.

The court first noted that the tort of false light publicity, like an action for defamation, requires the matter published to be untrue. But whereas an action for defamation seeks redress for injury to reputation, the court stated that a claim for false light publicity seeks damages for mental distress resulting from being exposed to public view in a false light.

The court then addressed the arguments of the defendants. It held that the statements by the Attorney General and his aide were not opinions. They did not preface their statements with the phrase "in my opinion," nor did they state that they "believed" the clerk's sexual harassment suit to be without merit or totally unfounded. Rather, they stated that the allegations "were" baseless, and, as such, their comments were statements of fact.

The court next held that the clerk need not prove malice in order to prevail on her false light claim, since malice need only be proven with respect to statements *about* public figures, not statements *by* public figures. The court therefore denied the defendants' motion for summary judgment, concluding that the clerk was entitled to present to a jury her claim for false light publicity and would be entitled to damages if she could prove that the statements by the Attorney General and his aide were not only highly offensive, but untrue as well. *Tomson v. Stephan,* 696 F. Supp. 1407, 4 IER Cases 1648 (D. Kan. 1988).

Authors' Note: In 1990, the United States Supreme Court in *Milkovich v. Lorain Journal Co.* concluded that any statement, even one expressed as an opinion, is actionable if it reasonably implies a false assertion of fact.[23] In some states, though, a "pure opinion" may *not* be the subject of an action for defamation.

Employer May Be Liable for False Light Publicity by Escorting Employee out of Building in Plain View of Other Employees

A trader for a major securities firm voiced objection to his superiors about several trading practices that he believed were in violation of the rules of the Chicago Board of Trade as well as federal laws governing the commodities exchange. Rather than discontinuing those practices, the securities firm decided to terminate the trader. In plain view of his co-workers, the trader's superiors made a surprise visit to his office, refused to allow him to speak to his staff, remained with him while he packed up his personal belongings, interrogated his fellow employees about entries in his travel and entertainment expense reports, and then escorted him out of the building.

The trader brought an action against his employer for false light publicity, claiming that the cumulative impact of this series of acts was to create a false impression among his co-workers that the trader had engaged in serious misconduct or a substantial breach of ethics precipitating his discharge. The employer filed a motion to dismiss the complaint, but the court denied the motion. It held that the series of acts leading up to and surrounding the trader's termination, including escorting the employee from the building in front of the other employees, could convey the false and offensive message to many of the trader's co-workers that his discharge was due to unscrupulous conduct on his part. *Zechman v. Merrill Lynch, Pierce, Fenner & Smith*, 742 F. Supp. 1359, 5 IER Cases 1665 (N.D. Ill. 1990).

Supervisor's Remark Implying Whorish Conduct by Employee's Wife Results in Awards for Actual and Punitive Damages

A dock worker for a freight company was involved in a verbal altercation with his supervisor. The heated discussion escalated into a verbal assault upon the dock worker in which the supervisor made vulgar and provocative remarks to the employee about his wife. The supervisor said, in an extremely crude manner, that he had "heard that the other night [your] wife was [engaging in oral sex]" with three other workers. The remark was uttered at the dock worker's place of employment and was heard by other employees.

The dock worker filed a lawsuit against his employer for invasion of privacy and intentional infliction of emotional distress. His wife also sued the employer for defamation and invasion of privacy. The dock worker alleged that the verbal assault by the supervisor was part of an intended plan by management to harass workers who had challenged work rules and working conditions on the job. His wife alleged that she was defamed and publicly placed in a false light.

Although the jury returned a verdict against the wife on her claim for defamation, it returned a verdict in her favor on her claim for invasion of privacy, awarding her $20,000 in actual damages. The jury also returned a verdict in favor of the dock worker on his claims for intentional infliction and invasion of privacy. It awarded him nominal damages of only $1 on each of his two claims, but added $50,000 in punitive damages.

On appeal, the employer argued that the dock worker's claims were preempted by federal labor law, because the comments about his wife grew out of a dispute between the dock worker and his supervisor over work rules and working conditions governed by a collective bargaining agreement. The appeals court disagreed, concluding that even if the vulgar remarks were part of a plot by management to get rid of troublemakers who protested working conditions, preemption would not apply given the "particularly abusive manner" in which the alleged plan was carried out. The court then affirmed the jury verdicts and awards, holding that the supervisor's statement was an outrageous invasion of the privacy of the dock worker and his wife. *Keehr v. Consolidated Freightways*, 825 F.2d 133, 2 IER Cases 565 (7th Cir. 1987).

Notes

1. *See* O'Connor v. Ortega, 480 U.S. 709, 1 IER Cases 1617 (1987); National Treasury Employees Union v. Von Raab, 489 U.S. 656, 4 IER Cases 246 (1989); Skinner v. Railway Labor Executives' Ass'n, 489 U.S. 602, 4 IER Cases 224 (1989).
2. *See* Restatement (Second) of Torts § 652A.
3. *See* Restatement (Second) of Torts § 652C.
4. *See* Restatement (Second) of Torts § 652E.
5. *See* Restatement (Second) of Torts § 652E(a).
6. W. KEETON, PROSSER AND KEETON ON THE LAW OF TORTS § 117, at 864 (5th ed. 1984).
7. *See* Zechman v. Merrill Lynch, Pierce, Fenner & Smith, 742 F. Supp. 1359, 5 IER Cases 1665 (N.D. Ill. 1990), summarized in section C.5. of this chapter.
8. *See* Keehr v. Consolidated Freightways, 825 F.2d 133, 2 IER Cases 565 (7th Cir. 1987), summarized in section C.5. of this chapter.
9. *See* Tomson v. Stephan, 696 F. Supp. 1407, 4 IER Cases 1648 (D. Kan. 1988), summarized in section C.5. of this chapter.
10. *See* Restatement (Second) of Torts § 652D.
11. *See* cases summarized in sections C.1. and C.2. of this chapter.
12. *See* Miller v. Motorola, 202 Ill. App. 3d 976, 560 N.E.2d 900, 5 IER Cases 885 (1990), summarized in section C.1. of this chapter.
13. *See* Restatement (Second) of Torts § 652B.
14. *See* Restatement (Second) of Torts § 652B.
15. *See* cases summarized in section C.2. of this chapter.
16. *See* cases summarized in section C.3. of this chapter.
17. *See, e.g.,* Phillips v. Smalley Maintenance Servs., 711 F.2d 1524, 1 IER Cases 221 (11th Cir. 1983), summarized in section C.3. of this chapter.
18. *See* Eddy v. Brown, 715 P.2d 74 (Okla. 1986), summarized in section C.3. of this chapter.
19. *See* O'Brien v. Papa Gino's of America, 780 F.2d 1067, 1 IER Cases 458 (1st Cir. 1986), summarized in section C.3. of this chapter.
20. *See* K-Mart Corp. v. Trotti, 677 S.W.2d 632 (Tex. Ct. App. 1984), *writ denied*, 686 S.W.2d 593 (Tex. 1985), summarized in section C.4. of this chapter.
21. *See* ADA § 102(c).
22. *See* O'Connor v. Ortega, 480 U.S. 709, 1 IER Cases 1617 (1987).
23. 497 U.S. 1 (1990).

Chapter 6

Assault and Battery

A. Overview

While civil actions for assault and battery are not typically associated with the workplace, employees are increasingly asserting such claims against their employers. The most common use of these torts by employees is to seek damages against employers for sexual harassment involving offensive contact by supervisors and co-workers.

Employees have also begun to sue their employers for assault and battery in connection with drug testing, polygraph exams, and investigations of employee misconduct. Employees have even used these torts to seek recovery for exposure to toxic substances.

B. General Principles of Law

The torts of assault and battery encompass an individual's right to be free from an unwanted, nonconsensual contact with his or her body, or from a fear of that contact.[1] Assault protects the person's right to be free from a reasonable *fear* or *apprehension* of the contact, while battery protects the person's right to be free from the *actual* contact.[2]

The tort of assault has two elements: the apprehension of contact, and the intentional conduct of another person in instilling that apprehension.[3] The first element is satisfied by any act that reasonably instills the apprehension that immediate physical contact will result, such as shaking a fist at someone or pointing a gun in another person's face.[4] Thus, no actual contact is necessary to state a claim for assault. The second element, intent, is satisfied if the act is carried out to arouse the apprehension that contact will result.[5] Threatening words alone cannot make a person liable for assault, but words can lend meaning to overt acts or circumstances that place another person in reasonable apprehension of harm and make the actor liable for assault.[6]

The tort of battery is defined as an intentional and unpermitted contact with the person of another.[7] A battery may occur by the mere touching of any part of another person's body or anything attached to the body, such as clothing or an object held in one's hand.[8] Actual physical harm, however, need not result; it is sufficient that the person was forced to endure a physical contact against his or her will.[9] Thus, employees exposed to toxic substances or subjected to polygraph exams or drug testing have brought actions for battery by claiming that they were forced to endure physical contact with the toxic substance or the equipment used in the examination or testing.[10]

C. Illustrative Cases

The cases summarized in this chapter fall into the following categories of workplace assaults and batteries:

- Sexual Harassment Battery;
- Drug Testing Battery;
- Polygraph Battery;
- Assault and Battery During Investigations of Workplace Misconduct;
- Battery by Exposure to Toxic Substances; and
- Other Workplace Assaults and Batteries.

In many cases, where an employee claims that he or she was subjected to offensive contact at work, the employee seeks recovery not only for assault and battery, but also intentional infliction of emotional distress. The cases summarized in this chapter include cases where the claim for intentional infliction of emotional distress was dismissed, but the assault or battery claim was upheld. Hence, most of the cases summarized below involve conduct that, although tortious, does *not* generally satisfy the standard of outrageous conduct, as required for recovery under the tort of intentional infliction of emotional distress (see Chapter 4, section B.). Thus, the torts of assault and battery frequently serve as "backups" to a failed claim for intentional infliction of emotional distress.

1. Sexual Harassment Battery

Bisexual Judge Who Kissed Male Court Reporter on the Lips Liable for $125,000 in Damages for Battery

A bisexual judge hired a male employee as his court reporter. During the first several months of the reporter's employment with the judge, the two men developed a friendship and often went out together outside of work. Their racquetball games and frequent lunches were followed by unannounced visits by the judge to the employee's home.

The judge eventually made propositions and advances toward the reporter. Although the employee claimed that he tried to make it clear to his employer that he wanted to continue the friendship on a business basis only, the judge persisted in making advances toward him. The sexual overtures culminated when the judge walked past the employee in his chambers and abruptly kissed him on the lips. The court reporter claimed that he suffered embarrassment and emotional distress as a result of the kiss.

The court reporter filed a lawsuit against the state and the judge, seeking damages for battery and intentional infliction of emotional distress. The trial court granted the judge's motion for summary judgment on the claim for intentional infliction of emotional distress, but not the battery claim, which was tried to a jury. The jury awarded the court reporter $50,000 in compensatory damages, $25,000 for future injury, and $300,000 in punitive damages. The trial court reduced the punitive damage award to $50,000 based on the judge's inability to pay, leaving a total award of $125,000.

On appeal, the court upheld the jury's finding that the judge had committed a battery by kissing the court reporter on the lips. It also upheld the award of $125,000 in damages. *Johnson v. Ramsey County,* 424 N.W.2d 800, 3 IER Cases 629 (Minn. Ct. App. 1988).

"Practical Jokes" Resulting in Offensive Contact May Subject Employer to Liability for Battery and Invasion of Privacy

A female employee of a paper company was subjected to various acts of sexual harassment and physical abuse by her male co-workers over a period of several years. The female employee, however, did not report to management any of the harassment or misconduct engaged in by her co-workers. The only acts reported to management involved the final two acts of physical harassment, where a male co-worker twice lifted the female employee in and out of a hopper and touched her breasts, and later placed an air hose, which the two had been using to blow dust off themselves, between the female worker's legs.

The female employee brought an action against her employer for sexual harassment under Title VII, as well as state law claims for battery, invasion of privacy, and intentional infliction of emotional distress. The employer filed a motion for summary judgment on all claims. The court dismissed the Title VII claim because the employee failed to introduce any evidence that the company knew or should have known of the harassing conduct, and took prompt remedial action after notification by the employee.

As to the state law tort claims, the court held that the one-year state statute of limitations for battery and invasion of privacy precluded the employee from maintaining a battery or invasion of privacy claim for any offensive contacts that occurred more than one year before the date that the employee filed her complaint in court. The only offensive contacts that occurred within a year of the filing of her complaint were the hopper and air hose incidents.

The employer asserted that it could not be held vicariously liable for the acts of the offending co-worker because such conduct was outside the scope of his employment. The court disagreed, concluding that the issue as to whether the co-worker's offensive touchings were "connected in time, place and causation" with employment duties or in furtherance of the employer's objectives was an issue to be decided at trial by a jury.

The court then examined the individual tort claims. After noting that the tort of battery requires an *intent* to cause the plaintiff to suffer a harmful or offensive contact, it stated that the intention need not be malicious, nor must the perpetrator intend to inflict actual damage. Rather, "[t]he defendant may be liable although intending nothing more than a ... practical joke." The court therefore denied the employer's motion for summary judgment and set the case down for trial on the claim of battery.

Similarly, after noting that the right to privacy has been defined as "the right to be let alone," the court also set down for the trial the employee's invasion of privacy claim. Lastly, although the court expressed doubt that the employee's claim for intentional infliction of emotional distress could be proven at trial, it set down that claim for trial as well. *Waltman v. International Paper Co.*, 3 IER Cases 1336 (W.D. La. 1988), *rev'd in part on other grounds*, 875 F.2d 468 (5th Cir. 1989).

Employee May Recover Against Employer Where Supervisor Had Practice of "Rubbing Up Against Her" in Office

A long-term employee with a good work record served as a secretary to the employer's controller until she was terminated for "negative attitude towards company—chronic complainer." She alleged that her boss repeatedly made sexually offensive comments and suggestions to her and "made a practice of touching her and rubbing up against her in the office." One month after the employee complained to the personnel manager, she was fired.

In the employee's action for assault and battery against the employer and its controller, the trial court granted the company's motion for summary judgment. On appeal, an appellate court reversed. It held that even though the alleged physical touching was not to any "private area" of her body, it is for the jury to decide whether the touching and "rubbing" over a lengthy period of time "would be offensive to an ordinary person not unduly sensitive to his [or her] dignity." Further, the employee presented evidence that the company had failed to take prompt action when she complained, and had experienced similar problems with the controller in the past. The appellate court stated that this evidence could lead a jury to conclude that the employer ratified the controller's conduct, especially where it discharged the harassed female employee and retained the alleged harasser. Such ratification, the court held, could render the employer liable for assault and battery based on the controller's offensive contact. *Newsome v. Cooper-Wiss, Inc.*, 179 Ga. App. 670, 347 S.E.2d 619 (1986).

Supervisor Who Overlooks "Innocent Friendly Gesture" May Impose Liability on Employer

A receptionist for a major steel company was allegedly subjected to numerous indignities at the hands of her immediate supervisor. The employee claimed that, over a 15-month period, her supervisor subjected her to sexually explicit language, off-color jokes and sexual innuendos, and frequent intrusions into her marital affairs. Additionally, the receptionist claimed that her supervisor touched her buttocks without her consent. This was admittedly witnessed by the supervisor's boss, an official of the company, who described it as "an innocent friendly gesture."

The receptionist sued her employer in federal court under Title VII of the Civil Rights Act of 1964 for sexual harassment and for assault and battery. The lower court granted summary judgment in favor of the employer on the assault and battery claims, holding that the supervisor was not acting within the scope of his employment or in furtherance of the employer's interests. On appeal, however, an appellate court reversed. It held that the company official's failure to take any action after witnessing the incident could create an inference that the employer did not object to, and therefore ratified and condoned, the supervisor's actions. Accordingly, the receptionist was entitled to present her case for assault and battery to a jury. *Davis v. United States Steel Corp.*, 779 F.2d 209, 39 FEP Cases 955 (4th Cir. 1985).

Male Employee Grabbed and Pinched by Co-Worker May Recover Damages Against His Employer for Assault and Battery

A male employee of a mortgage company was grabbed between the legs by a male co-worker, who also pinched his buttocks, tried to mount him, and made sexually suggestive remarks. The employee had complained to two of his supervisors about the co-worker's conduct and the distress he was suffering, but neither supervisor took any action to stop the conduct.

The employee brought an action for assault and battery and intentional infliction of emotional distress against his employer and the offending co-worker. The employer filed a motion for summary judgment, claiming that the co-worker's conduct was outside the scope of his employment and was not ratified by the employer. The lower court granted the motion.

On appeal, the appellate court reversed. It held that the employee had introduced sufficient evidence to submit to a jury the issues of whether the employer had knowledge of the misconduct and ratified the co-worker's actions by condonation. The appellate court also held that the employee's claims for assault and battery and intentional infliction were *not* barred by the exclusive remedy provisions of the state workers' compensation law, because the co-worker's conduct toward the employee was not a normal part of an employment relationship. *Hart v. National Mortgage & Land Co.*, 189 Cal. App. 3d 1420, 235 Cal. Rptr. 68 (1987).

Workers' Compensation Law Bars Claim for Battery Where Employer Was Never Informed of Sexual Harassment

Two female employees who worked in a convenience store claimed that while their supervisor was performing his supervisory duties, he intentionally pinched, grabbed, and patted their shoulders and buttocks against their will. One of the employees also claimed that while she was stocking a cooler with beer and milk, her supervisor unbuttoned her blouse, grabbed her breasts, and tore the zipper off her pants.

Both employees sued their employer and supervisor for assault and battery. Before trial, the court entered summary judgment in favor of the employer, holding that the employees' claims were barred because the state workers' compensation law provided the exclusive remedy for injury from such conduct. On appeal, an appellate court affirmed. It found that because no complaints of misconduct had been reported to a responsible official of the employer (with the exception of the "cooler" incident, after which a manager attempted to investigate the allegations), the employer "could be guilty of only simple negligence," for which the workers' compensation law provides an exclusive remedy. *Schwartz v. Zippy Mart,* 470 So. 2d 720 (Fla. Dist. Ct. App. 1985).

Insurance Company Must Defend and Indemnify Employer in Lawsuit Alleging Sexual Harassment Battery at Work

A female executive secretary who claimed that she was sexually harassed filed a lawsuit against her employer for battery. She alleged that a male co-worker committed repeated acts of sexual harassment by "offensively touch[ing] [her] rear end and breasts." She further alleged that her employer's senior management was aware of this offensive conduct but took no remedial measures. As a result, she claimed that she suffered serious emotional distress and disruption of her personal life.

Upon receipt of the court complaint, her employer notified its general liability insurance carrier of the lawsuit. The carrier had issued a policy to the employer requiring it to pay "all sums the insured shall become legally obligated to pay as damages because of bodily harm by accident or disease." The insurance company refused to defend the action or indemnify the company for any loss arising from the lawsuit, claiming that emotional distress and mental anguish did not constitute "bodily injury." Thereafter, the employer entered into a settlement agreement with the executive secretary without the participation, consent, or approval of the insurance company.

The employer then filed a lawsuit against the insurance carrier, claiming that the insurer breached its duty to defend and indemnify under the policy. The employer sought to recover the money paid to the executive secretary to settle the case, as well as its legal costs.

Summary judgment was entered in favor of the insurance company, and the employer appealed. On appeal, the judgment was reversed. The appellate court noted that the judiciary has come to recognize that emotional distress can and often does have a direct effect on other bodily functions. The court therefore held that the term "bodily injury" in the insurance policy did include the emotional and psychological distress that allegedly resulted from the sexually harassing and tortious contact suffered by the executive secretary. *NPS Corp. v. Insurance Co. of N. Am.*, 213 N.J. Super. 547, 517 A.2d 1211, 2 IER Cases 471 (App. Div. 1986).

2. Drug Testing Battery

Union Employees' Suit for Assault and Battery in Connection With Drug Test Preempted by LMRA

Two union employees suspected of drug use were subjected to medical examinations during which they were required to provide blood and urine samples for use in drug tests. They later sued their employer for assault and battery and other state law torts in connection with the examinations.

The employer filed a motion for summary judgment, asserting that the state law tort claims were preempted by federal labor law because the employees had a right to file a grievance under the collective bargaining agreement covering the union-represented employees of the employer. The lower court granted the employer's motion for summary judgment. An appellate court affirmed. It noted that the governing collective bargaining agreement permitted the employer to require an employee to submit to a medical examination and a blood and urine test when the employee's physical condition and ability to work were called into question. The court therefore held that the employees' battery claims (that the employer improperly forced them to allow their bodies to be searched) were preempted by the Labor Management Relations Act (LMRA) and, as such, were required to be resolved not by a court, but by an arbitrator appointed under the grievance procedures of the collective bargaining agreement. *Strachan v. Union Oil Co.*, 768 F.2d 703, 1 IER Cases 1844 (5th Cir. 1985).

3. Polygraph Battery

Employer May Be Liable for Assault and Battery by Forcing Employee to Submit to Polygraph Test

A bus company discharged an employee because of his alleged failure to report $32.60 received from a shipping order. The employee agreed to take a polygraph test on the condition that if he passed he would be reinstated, but if he failed he would drop his union grievance. Before he took the test, the employee signed a release. The employee failed the test but later claimed that he was never informed of, and had not agreed to, the latter part of the bargain.

The discharged employee brought suit against his former employer, alleging assault and battery by the administration of a polygraph exam. The employer moved for summary judgment on the ground that the employee executed a waiver and release when he voluntarily submitted to the polygraph test.

The court held that there was a genuine issue of fact as to whether the employee signed a release and took the polygraph exam as a condition of continued employment. Pennsylvania law specifically prohibits an employer from *requiring* an employee to submit to a polygraph examination "as a condition for employment or continuation of employment." The court held that if the employee could prove to a jury that he was forced to undergo an examination in order to keep his job, the release would be invalid and he could maintain an action for assault and battery. *Smith v. Greyhound Lines*, 614 F. Supp. 558 (W.D. Pa. 1984), *aff'd mem.*, 800 F.2d 1139 (3d Cir. 1986).

Polygraph Exam Prompts Suit for Assault and Battery, but No Recovery Where Touching of Plaintiff Was Not Inappropriate

After discovering that certain receipts were missing, a restaurant executive told the associate manager of the restaurant that she had to submit to a polygraph examination or face termination from employment. After being subjected to a pretest procedure by the polygraph examiner where parts of the polygraph apparatus were physically placed in contact with the employee's body, she indicated she did not wish to proceed further with the test. The associate manager was discharged shortly thereafter.

The employee brought an action against her employer and the polygraph test administrator to recover for assault and battery and false imprisonment. The trial court granted the defendants' motions for summary judgment. On appeal, the appellate court affirmed, holding that there was no evidence of any inappropriate touching of the employee's person and no evidence that she was in fear of such offensive conduct. *Walden v. General Mills Restaurant Group*, 31 Ohio App. 3d 11, 508 N.E.2d 168 (1986).

4. Assault and Battery During Investigations of Workplace Misconduct

Employees Sue for Alleged Apprehension of Harm During Security Investigation Following Theft

Two couriers for an air express company were subjected to a security investigation following the theft of an expensive wristwatch entrusted to the company for overnight delivery. One employee claimed that during the investigation a company investigator pulled back his jacket to reveal a firearm he was carrying, placing the employee in apprehension of immediate harm. The other employee claimed that he was placed in apprehension of immediate harm when a company investigator braced himself against a wall and pushed the employee backward when he tried to leave the room.

Both employees commenced an action for assault and battery, as well as intentional and negligent infliction of emotional distress. At trial, the jury found that the employees had been assaulted and awarded them $50,000 in damages for their claims. The trial court, however, overturned the verdict, finding that the employees had failed to prove the genuineness of their alleged fear and intimidation. *Leahy v. Federal Express Corp.*, 613 F. Supp. 906 (E.D.N.Y. 1985).

Employee Recovers Damages for Assault and Battery During Theft Investigation

During an investigation by an employer into a disappearance of company funds, an employee of a grocery store was subjected to an interrogation. The employee claimed that during his questioning he was assaulted by two investigators of the employer. After the investigation, the employer brought suit against the employee for embezzlement. The employee counterclaimed for assault and battery.

A jury rendered a verdict in favor of the employee on the assault and battery claim and awarded him $15,000 in damages. The employer appealed, contending that the workers' compensation law provided the employee with his exclusive remedy, because the assault and battery was committed by a fellow employee. The appellate court rejected that argument and upheld the jury award. It stated that an employer cannot avail itself of the workers' compensation defense where its own investigators committed an assault and battery during an investigation. *Singer Shop-Rite v. Rangel*, 174 N.J. Super. 442, 416 A.2d 965 (App. Div.), *cert. denied*, 85 N.J. 148, 425 A.2d 299 (1980).

5. Battery by Exposure to Toxic Substances

By Assigning Workers to Clean Up PCB Spill Without Protective Clothing, Employer May Be Liable for Battery and Fraudulent Concealment

A transformer failure released a toxic level of polychlorinated biphenyls (PCBs) onto the floor of a mill in Oregon. After three attempts by hazardous waste specialists failed to reduce the PCB amounts to a nontoxic level, the company ordered two temporary employees to finish the cleanup, which required scrubbing the floor on their hands and knees over a period of five days. The company knew that the concentration of PCBs greatly exceeded exposure levels permitted by EPA standards, yet did not provide the employees with any protective clothing during the cleanup. The company also knew that the employees' work clothes had become soaked with PCBs.

The temporary employees filed a claim in federal district court against the employer for battery and fraudulent concealment. The district court dismissed the battery claim, which was based on the employees' contention that their employer intentionally caused them to come into contact with toxic levels of PCBs by assigning them to clean up the spill without providing them with protective clothing. The court concluded that the employees introduced no evidence that the company's actions were *intended* to injure the workers. Rather, according to the court, exposure to the PCBs was due to the employer's negligence. Therefore, the court held, the employees' exclusive remedy was under the state workers' compensation law, which covers workplace injuries caused by negligence.

The district court also dismissed the fraud claim, concluding that the claim was preempted by the federal Labor Management Relations Act (LMRA), because the assignment of duties was a subject covered by the governing collective bargaining agreement.

On appeal, the appellate court reinstated both the battery and fraud claims. It held that because the company assigned the task of toxic cleanup to two temporary workers who were unfamiliar with such work rather than contracting with a specialist as it had done in the past, a jury could infer that the employer *intended* to cause the two employees to come into contact with toxic levels of PCBs. Thus, the appeals court held, the state workers' compensation law would not preclude the employees' state law claim for battery.

The appellate court also held that the employees' fraud claim, based on the employer's knowing concealment of health and safety risks, was not preempted by the LMRA. The court stated that the employees could succeed on their fraudulent concealment claim if they could prove that the employer's failure to warn them of the risks involved in cleaning up PCBs constituted a fraudulent omission, upon which the employees relied to their detriment. *Gulden v. Crown Zellerbach Corp.*, 890 F.2d 195, 4 IER Cases 1761 (9th Cir. 1989).

Authors' Note: Some state "right to know" laws may also govern the disclosure of hazardous work assignments.

Employees Need Not Show Actual Intent to Injure in Toxic Tort Action Against Employer for Assault

A research chemist was employed by a major chemical company that manufactured "agent orange." The chemist commenced an action against his employer for assault and intentional infliction of emotional distress, alleging that his employer intentionally assaulted him and caused him to suffer severe emotional distress by causing him to be exposed to "agent orange." The trial court granted summary judgment in favor of the employer on both counts. It held that the chemist's action was barred by the exclusive remedy provision of the workers' compensation law, inasmuch as the employee could not demonstrate that the employer acted *intentionally* to harm him.

On appeal, an intermediate appellate court affirmed the dismissal of the assault claim but reinstated the claim for intentional infliction of emotional distress. On further appeal, the Supreme Court of Michigan reinstated the assault claim as well. It held that the workers' compensation defense would *not* bar the chemist's tort claims of toxic assault or intentional infliction of emotional distress if he could show that the employer knew that workplace injury or damage was substantially certain to result as a consequence of the company's actions. The appellate court concluded that where an employee can show such substantial certainty, the employer is deemed to have intended to cause the injuries. *Beauchamp v. Dow Chem. Co.*, 427 Mich. 1, 398 N.W.2d 882 (1986).

6. Other Workplace Assaults and Batteries

Grievance Committee Chairman Recovers Damages for Battery Instigated by Employer

A grievance committee chairman was asked by his employer to review a set of work rules. The chairman made certain changes to the rules because he felt they were not in compliance with the union labor contract. The employer's labor relations director disagreed with some of the changes, and this provoked a number of intimidating incidents allegedly performed at the employer's behest. In one such incident, the employee was purposely struck on his back and head by another employee operating a "clarifier" machine. The grievance committee chairman testified that he was not hurt by the machine, but introduced evidence that certain managers of the employer had offered $15,000 "to take care of ... troublemakers" and had instructed another worker on the day before the clarifier machine incident to "get the redhead son of a bitch off the job."

The grievance committee chairman sued the employer and the employee who operated the clarifier machine for battery. The jury returned a verdict in favor of the grievance committee chairman, awarding him actual and punitive damages of $120,000. After the award of damages was reduced by the trial court to $80,000, the employer appealed.

On appeal, the employer argued that the battery claim was preempted by the National Labor Relations Act (NLRA) and/or the Labor Management Relations Act (LMRA). The appellate court rejected that argument, holding that the employee's claim for battery was not preempted because it did not involve any questions involving the interpretation of the terms of the collective bargaining agreement.

The employer also argued that the grievance committee chairman had failed to prove a battery because he was admittedly not hurt by the clarifier machine. The appellate court disagreed. It held that actual injury to the body is not a necessary element of an action for battery. It is sufficient, the court held, if one merely lays his or her hands on another in a hostile manner, even if no damage results. According to the court, the wrong consists of the manner and spirit of the touching, and the question of bodily pain is important only as to the amount of damages. *Surrency v. Harbison*, 489 So. 2d 1097 (Ala. 1986).

Employer Not Liable for Supervisor's Unorthodox Approach of Reprimanding Employees by Physical Assault

A supervisor of a fried chicken chain attempted to reprimand one of the employees under his supervision for what he apparently regarded as an instance of unsatisfactory job performance. After making several disparaging remarks about the employee's personal life, the supervisor grabbed the employee by her shirt collar, threw her to the ground, and kicked her in the back.

The employer filed a motion for summary judgment, seeking dismissal of the tort claim on the ground that the alleged conduct was outside the scope of the supervisor's employment. The lower court granted the employer's motion.

On appeal, the appellate court noted that an employer is liable for the tortious conduct of one of its employees under the doctrine of *respondeat superior* if the employee's actions are within the scope of his or her employment or were subsequently ratified by the employer. The appellate court concluded that although the supervisor had the authority to engage in limited forms of disciplinary action in accordance with the established policies of the employer, the employee had failed to introduce any evidence that such authority included the unprovoked use of physical violence against a subordinate. Further, the court stated that no evidence was presented by the employee that the employer ratified or condoned the supervisor's conduct. The appellate court therefore held that no liability could be imposed upon the employer in this case under the doctrine of *respondeat superior*. *Hester v. Church's Fried Chicken,* 27 Ohio App. 3d 74, 499 N.E.2d 923 (1986).

Notes

1. *See* W. KEETON, PROSSER AND KEETON ON THE LAW OF TORTS §§ 9, 10 (5th ed. 1984).
2. *See* Restatement (Second) of Torts §§ 18, 21.
3. *See* Restatement (Second) of Torts § 21(1).
4. *See* W. KEETON, PROSSER AND KEETON ON THE LAW OF TORTS § 10, at 43 (5th ed. 1984).
5. *See* Restatement (Second) of Torts §§ 24, 32.
6. *See* Restatement (Second) of Torts § 31.
7. *See* Restatement (Second) of Torts § 13.
8. *See* W. KEETON, PROSSER AND KEETON ON THE LAW OF TORTS § 9, at 39 (5th ed. 1984).
9. *See* W. KEETON, PROSSER AND KEETON ON THE LAW OF TORTS § 9, at 41 (5th ed. 1984).
10. See sections C.2., C.3., and C.5. of this chapter.

Chapter 7

Interference With Contractual Relations

A. Overview

While the tort of interference with contractual relations arises most often in the business context, employees today are bringing this type of lawsuit against their employers more frequently than ever before. The tort of interference generally arises in three different employment contexts: where a supervisor or manager causes the termination or resignation of an employee; where a former employer provides an unfavorable postemployment job reference that results in the rejection of an employee for a position with a new employer; and where an employer seeks to enforce a noncompete provision in an employee's contract of employment.

Lawsuits for tortious interference with contractual relations also have been brought against supervisors and managers for interference with an employee's job performance and failing to assign an employee a proper work assignment. In addition, claims for tortious interference have been successfully brought against former and prospective employers for causing a current employer to terminate an employee. A tortious interference claim has even been brought by workers who lost their jobs as a result of a failed hostile takeover attempt.

B. General Principles of Law

To establish a cause of action for tortious interference with contractual relations, a person must *improperly* induce or cause a third party to breach or not to perform its contract with another person.[1] Similarly, a person may tortiously interfere with *prospective* contractual relations of another by improperly inducing or causing a third person not to enter into a prospective contractual relationship.[2] This tort is also referred to as interference with prospective economic advantage.

The key to liability under these torts of interference is whether the defendant acted improperly—in other words, did the defendant have *legal justification* to interfere with another's contractual or prospective contractual relationship?[3] There is no set formula for determining whether a person's interference with contractual or prospective contractual relations is lawful. A variety of factors are considered, such as the actor's motive, the interests sought to be advanced by the actor, and the interests of the parties to the contract.[4]

For example, as a general rule, an employer may provide truthful information or honest advice about a former employee to a prospective employer, even if by providing the information or advice the employer causes the prospective employer not to offer the employee a job.[5] Likewise, as a general proposition, an employer may enforce a lawful and valid noncompete provision in an employment agreement, even if the employer knows that by so doing it will interfere with an employee's opportunity to seek employment with a competitor.[6]

Tortious interference requires the defendant to have knowledge of the contractual or prospective contractual relationship and to *intend*, without legal justification, to interfere with the relationship. Hence, a party cannot recover damages for *negligent* interference with contractual or prospective contractual relations.[7]

Finally, tortious interference with contractual or prospective contractual relations applies only to third-party interference—that is, a party to a contract cannot tortiously interfere with his or her own contract. Hence, when an employee alleges that a superior interfered with his or her employment contract, the question that most often arises is whether the superior, as an agent of the employer, is considered to be a party to the contract, as opposed to a third party. As the cases in this chapter demonstrate, the answer to that question frequently depends on the status of the employee's superior, that is, whether the superior's conduct was within the scope of his or her employment, and, if so, whether the superior acted with malice.[8]

C. Illustrative Cases

The cases summarized in this chapter fall into the following categories of tortious interference:

- Interference by Causing the Termination of an Employee:
  - at the behest of an employee's supervisor,
  - at the behest of a former employer,
  - at the behest of a prospective employer, and
  - as a result of an unsuccessful takeover attempt;
- Interference With Job Performance;
- Interference by Improper Work Assignments;
- Negative Job References; and
- Unreasonable Enforcement of Noncompete Agreements.

Tortious interference cases have the potential to generate substantial jury awards in favor of employees, particularly where the interference results in a loss of employment. In one case summarized below, a jury awarded a senior executive $1 million in actual and punitive damages when the executive's former employer caused his new employer to fire him and effectively blacklisted him from employment in his chosen field.[9] In another case summarized below, a jury awarded $2.8 million to two midlevel managers who lost their jobs when another employer induced their current employer to terminate their employment.[10]

Several of the tortious interference cases summarized below involve jury verdicts assessing personal liability against supervisors or managers. For example, in one case a jury awarded an employee $230,000 in compensatory and punitive damages against the employee's supervisor, who maliciously recommended that the employee be terminated.[11] In another case, a hospital manager was held personally liable for interfering with a physician's emergency medical practice by refusing to assign him any medical responsibilities relating to emergency medicine.[12] And in one case where a superior provided a negative job reference for a former employee, a jury awarded the employee $100,000 in compensatory damages against both the former employer and supervisor, and $50,000 in punitive damages against the supervisor personally.[13]

1. Interference by Causing Termination of Employees

a. At the Behest of an Employee's Supervisor

Jury Awards Sales Consultant $230,000 in Damages Against Supervisor Who Maliciously Recommended That She Be Terminated

A beauty sales consultant for a line of cosmetics sold at a department store was subjected to a prolonged pattern of harassment by her supervisor at the store. Among other things, the supervisor undermined the sales consultant's efforts to generate sales by prohibiting her from using the telephone on the sales floor to solicit customers to come into the store. The supervisor also removed the beauty consultant's stool from behind her counter, even though the consultant needed to rest her ailing foot from time to time. In addition, the supervisor falsely accused the employee of improperly bringing merchandise home, never gave her a salary increase despite satisfactory sales, made critical remarks about her appearance, and laughed at her in front of a customer.

The sales consultant complained about her supervisor to the vice president for human resources, who advised the supervisor to stop "nitpicking" her subordinate and to "get off her back." Immediately thereafter, however, the supervisor changed the employee's work schedule by refusing to allow her to have Saturdays off. A few months later, the supervisor returned to the vice president for human resources and recommended that the beauty consultant be fired for unsatisfactory job performance and violation of a lunch hour rule. The vice president then called the employee into his office and terminated her. On the day the sales consultant was fired, the supervisor remarked to another worker that "I finally accomplished what I set out to do."

The sales consultant filed a lawsuit against the department store for wrongful discharge. In addition, she sued her supervisor and the vice president for human resources for tortious interference with her at-will employment contract with the store. Finally, she sued her supervisor for intentional infliction of emotional distress. Prior to trial, the claims against the department store and the vice president were dismissed, as was the employee's claim against her supervisor for intentional infliction of emotional distress. The tortious interference claim against her supervisor, however, proceeded to trial, and a jury entered a verdict in her favor for $165,000 in compensatory damages and $65,000 in punitive damages.

The supervisor asked the trial court to overturn the jury's verdict. She argued that (1) her conduct was privileged; (2) even if unprivileged, her conduct was not malicious; (3) a claim for tortious interference with contractual relations could not be maintained by an at-will employee; and (4) in any event, she was not a third party to the at-will employment contract but rather an agent of the employer and party to the contract.

The court first held that the supervisor was only entitled to a *qualified* privilege, which could be lost if the supervisor acted either outside the scope of her employment or within the scope of employment but with malice. The court then upheld the jury's verdict, concluding that although the evidence of malice was "marginal," there was sufficient evidence for the jury to have found that the supervisor's conduct was malicious. The court also concluded that an at-will employment relationship was not a bar to recovery for interference with contractual relations.

Finally, the court addressed the key issue in the case: whether a supervisor could be deemed a third party to a contract of employment. The court ruled that only a corporate officer, general manager or other person of such rank and position could be considered the "alter ego" of the employer and, hence, a party to the employment contract. In contrast, a person who was "merely a foreman, supervisor or manager" would not be regarded as a party to the contract; rather, such persons were third parties to a contract of employment. The court therefore held that although the supervisor had acted within the scope of her duties, she would be considered a third party to the contract because she was only a supervisor. The trial court did, however, substantially reduce the total amount of the consultant's compensatory and punitive damage awards against the supervisor from $230,000 to $80,000. *Sorrells v. Garfinkel's*, 2 IER Cases 618 (D.C. Super. Ct. 1987).

Employees Fired by General Manager May Recover Damages for Tortious Interference

Three employees of an electric company claimed that the general manager of the public utility directed them to engage in illegal and irregular business practices, including waiving extension fees for favored developers and awarding contracts for work without competitive bidding. These practices were the subject of an investigation by the state public utilities commission.

The three employees were terminated from employment for supposedly being "disloyal" to the general manager of the utility. The first employee was terminated after he expressed his opposition to the general manager's alleged practice of hiring employees who were loyal to the general manager but were not necessarily qualified for their jobs. The second employee was discharged the day after he testified truthfully before the public utility commission during the course of its investigation. And the third employee, an engineer, was terminated after a favored contractor complained to the general manager about the engineer, who had experienced difficulty persuading the contractor to comply with the contract requirements.

The three employees filed suit in state court against the public utility and the general manager for breach of an implied employment contract, wrongful discharge, tortious interference with contract, tortious interference with prospective financial advantages, and intentional infliction of emotional distress. After the court granted the summary judgment in favor of the defendants on all claims, the employees appealed.

As to the tortious interference claims, the appellate court held that an officer or director of a corporation generally will not be held personally liable for inducing the corporation's breach of an employment contract of an employee if the officer or director is acting within the scope of his or her official duties. The appellate court stated, however, that if the officer or director is motivated *solely* by a desire to induce the corporation to breach an employment contract of an employee, or to interfere in the contractual relationship between the corporation and the employee, the interference is improper. The appellate court therefore reversed the grant of summary judgment on the tortious interference claims. It concluded that because the issues of motivation and whether the officer was acting within the scope of his duties were disputed by the parties, such issues must be decided by a jury. *Cronk v. Intermountain Rural Elec. Ass'n*, 765 P.2d 619, 3 IER Cases 1049 (Colo. Ct. App. 1988).

b. At the Behest of a Former Employer

Executive Recovers $1 Million for Tortious Interference Where Former Employer Caused New Employer to Fire and Blacklist Him From Any Future Employment

The executive vice president of a major beef-producing company was abruptly fired from his job and ordered to leave the workplace immediately. He did so, but took his personal work files with him. The documents he removed contained confidential memoranda regarding the company's marketing, pricing, and sales strategies. Two years later, he turned those documents over to several attorneys who were representing several small meat-packing companies that were suing his former employer for antitrust violations.

At about the same time, a subcommittee of the United States House of Representatives initiated an investigation into the competitive posture of small meat packers and whether the current laws were sufficient to ensure healthy competition in the meat industry. The subcommittee subpoenaed a large number of documents under protective order in the antitrust case brought by the small meat-packing companies against the executive vice president's former employer, including the documents that he had provided to the attorneys for the plaintiffs. After examining the subpoenaed documents, the subcommittee subpoenaed the executive to testify before Congress. The subcommittee also invited the major beef producer to testify as to the significance of the subpoenaed documents, including those the former executive had taken when he was fired.

The beef-producing company chose not to send a representative to testify before the subcommittee. Instead, it responded through a letter sent by the company's president. In the letter, the company characterized its former executive vice president as a "disgruntled ex-employee" who "stole 7 boxes of [company] documents, many of a confidential business and legal nature." The letter also asserted that the former executive's testimony was "absolutely false, and ... constitutes perjury." The beef-producing company sent a copy of the letter to members of agriculture associations, professors at academic institutions, and about fifty members of the media.

Six days after his testimony before Congress, the former executive vice president, who was at this time employed by another large meat-packing company, was terminated from his employment without notice or warning. Thereafter, he was unable to obtain employment with any employer in the meat-packing industry.

He then commenced an action against the beef producer for libel and tortious interference with present and future contractual relations. A jury returned a verdict in favor of the executive for $7 million: $6 million in compensatory and punitive damages for libel; $650,000 in compensatory and punitive damages for tortious interference resulting from the termination of his employment relationship with the other meat-packing company; and $350,000 in compensatory and punitive damages for tortious interference with future contractual relations resulting from his being blacklisted from future jobs by the beef producer.

On appeal, the libel judgment was vacated and the defamation claim was remanded for a new trial because the lower court had improperly placed the burden on the beef processor to prove the truth of its statements about its former executive vice president, instead of placing the burden on the employee to prove the falsity of the statements. The judgments in favor of the employee for tortious interference, however, were upheld. The appellate court concluded that there was sufficient evidence presented at trial by the employee from which the jury could have reasonably concluded that the beef processor had placed undue pressure on the other meat packer to fire the former executive vice president. Likewise, the appellate court held that the jury could have reasonably found, based on the evidence presented at trial, that the major beef producer had effectively blacklisted the executive from the meat industry as a whole, making it clear to the executive that he would never again work in that industry. The court therefore affirmed the $1 million in injury awards for the tortious interference claims. *In re IBP Confidential Business Documents Litig.*, 797 F.2d 632, 1 IER Cases 871 (8th Cir. 1986), *cert. denied*, 479 U.S. 1088 (1987).

Employer Liable for Over $100,000 in Damages for Directing Contractor to Terminate Former Employee

A boilermaker employed by an oil company sued his employer for personal injuries sustained while working at a company refinery. He recovered $25,000 in damages. A year later, the boilermaker was hired by a contractor that had been retained by the oil company to build a hot oil treating plant at the refinery. The agreement between the oil company and the contractor provided that the contractor had the sole right to supervise, manage, and control performance of the work.

On his second day of work for the contractor, a safety representative for the oil company asked the boilermaker what he was doing at the refinery, and he responded that he was working there for the contractor. The safety representative then stated, "[N]ot if [I] have anything to say about it." The next day, the boilermaker was terminated by the contractor. His notice of termination stated that the discharge was pursuant to the directive of the oil company.

The boilermaker sued the oil company again, this time for tortious interference with his employment contract. At trial, the oil company denied that it instructed the contractor to terminate the boilermaker. It maintained that it did not want the boilermaker working at its refinery because it regarded him as a safety risk since he was allegedly unable to physically perform the work required. At the conclusion of the trial, the jury awarded the boilermaker $102,000 in compensatory and punitive damages.

On appeal to the Supreme Court of Texas, the oil company claimed that the tortious interference claim should have been dismissed because the boilermaker's contract of employment was terminable at will. The court disagreed and held that until terminated, an at-will employment contract is valid and subsisting and third parties are not free to tortiously interfere with such contracts. The court remanded the case, however, on the issue of legal justification.

On remand, the lower court ruled that the oil company's interest in assuring the safety of all persons working at the refinery was not equal or superior to the boilermaker's right to continued employment by the contractor. It therefore held that the oil company had failed to prove legal justification for its interference with the at-will employment contract of the boilermaker and reinstated the award of damages. *Sterner v. Marathon Oil Co.*, 767 S.W.2d 686, 4 IER Cases 592 (Tex. 1989).

c. At the Behest of a Prospective Employer

Managers Awarded $2.8 Million for Wrongful Interference by Corporation That Caused Employer to Terminate Them

Two transportation corporations that provided both rail and nonrail transportation services decided to merge. They sought approval from the Interstate Commerce Commission (ICC) to merge their rail operations but immediately merged their nonrail operations into a new company. During the pendency of the ICC approval proceeding, the vice president for employee benefits of the new company sent a confidential memorandum to the chief executive officer of the smaller company recommending that it institute a severance program to provide an incentive for as many employees as possible to terminate their employment with the smaller company. According to the memo, this would "avoid the higher expense" of the anticipated severance provisions required by law to be provided to employees terminated because of railroad mergers. The larger company estimated the cost of the ICC-mandated severance benefits to be upwards of $40 million.

Shortly thereafter, the chief executive officer of the smaller company wrote a confidential letter to the chief executive officer of the larger company setting forth a detailed proposal to close the regional public relations offices of the smaller company before the completion of the merger. The letter listed the names and detailed the exact severance packages to be offered to each of the regional public relations employees. Subsequently, the smaller company implemented a "voluntary" work force reduction program, advising employees that they could take part in the program or be terminated at a later date without benefit of the program.

The public relations manager for the Portland, Oregon regional office elected to participate in the program under protest, while the public relations manager for the Houston regional office rejected the offer. The Houston regional office was then closed down—before the ICC issued its merger decision. Ultimately, when the ICC issued its decision, it denied the merger request. The smaller company eventually merged, however, with another rail corporation.

The two public relations managers filed suit against the larger company and the new company. They claimed that the defendant corporations interfered with their economic relationship with the smaller company by causing the smaller company to terminate them *before* the ICC ruled on the merger request in order to evade the severance benefits to which they would have been entitled by law if the new company had terminated the two managers *after* the anticipated approval of the merger by the ICC.

The jury returned verdicts in favor of the two managers on their causes of action against both the larger and the new corporations. The jury awarded the managers over $2.8 million in damages: $450,000 in economic damages; $400,000 in damages for emotional distress; $1.2 million in punitive damages against the new corporation; and $800,000 in punitive damages against the larger company.

On appeal, an appellate court held that there was sufficient evidence to find interference and improper motive on the part of the defendant corporations. It therefore affirmed the verdict and the $2.8 million award in favor of the employees on their tortious interference claim. *Kraus v. Santa Fe S. Pac. Corp.*, 878 F.2d 1193 (9th Cir. 1989), *cert. dismissed*, 493 U.S. 1051 (1990).

d. As a Result of an Unsuccessful Takeover Attempt

Conglomerate That Attempted Hostile Takeover May Be Liable to Employees Laid Off by Targeted Company As Part of Takeover Defense

A diversified conglomerate commenced a hostile takeover attempt of a major fiberglass corporation. The conglomerate decided to put the fiberglass company "in play" by purchasing its voting stock. After acquiring sufficient stock through its own purchase and purchases of others on its behalf, the conglomerate announced its intention to purchase the fiberglass corporation. One month after announcing its intention to purchase, however, it sold all of its interest in the fiberglass company, allegedly earning a profit of approximately $30 million.

In the meantime, the fiberglass corporation attempted to defend against the takeover attempt. It instituted a recapitalization plan that left the company with a $2 billion debt. To raise cash to service this debt, the fiberglass corporation was forced to close several plants. This resulted in the layoff of employees at those plants.

The laid-off employees and their union brought an action in state court against the conglomerate. The employees and their union asserted claims for tortious interference with prospective economic advantage and for negligence, seeking both compensatory and punitive damages.

The plaintiffs claimed that the conglomerate's takeover attempt interfered with prospective economic advantages anticipated by the laid-off workers in their employment relationship with the fiberglass company. The plaintiffs further alleged that the conglomerate's actions were neither generally acceptable nor sanctioned by common morality or applicable legal rules, including the federal securities and antitrust laws.

The conglomerate removed the case to federal court, claiming that the lawsuit was preempted by either the federal securities laws or the Labor Management Relations Act (LMRA). A federal district court disagreed, and remanded the case back to the state court.

After the case was remanded, the conglomerate filed a motion to dismiss. As to the interference claim, the court first held that the complaint alleged sufficient facts to show that the former employees had a reasonable expectation of prospective economic advantage as employees of the fiberglass company. The court next held that the complaint sufficiently alleged that the defendant's interference with that economic advantage was done intentionally and without legal justification or excuse—and in violation of the federal securities and antitrust laws—with knowledge that the takeover attempt would cause harm to the former employees' prospective employment relationship with the targeted corporation. Finally, the court held that the complaint adequately alleged facts suggesting that the interference caused the loss of the workers' jobs, thereby depriving them of a prospective economic advantage.

Addressing the negligence claim, the conglomerate contended that it owed no duty to the employees of the targeted company. The court disagreed. It concluded that a duty might exist in the circumstances of this case, since a defendant owes a duty of care to take reasonable measures to avoid the risk of causing economic damages to particular plaintiffs whom the defendant knows are likely to suffer such economic damages from its conduct. *Glass Molders Int'l Union v. Wickes Cos.*, 707 F. Supp. 174, 4 IER Cases 1718 (D.N.J. 1989), *on remand*, 243 N.J. Super. 44, 578 A.2d 402, 5 IER Cases 1060 (Law Div. 1990).

2. Interference With Job Performance

Supervisors Not Liable for Tortious Interference When Acting Within Scope of Their Employment

A supply clerk was allegedly subjected to a course of unequal treatment and harassment by her supervisors, including being scheduled to work both Christmas Day and New Year's Eve for three straight years after she specifically requested that she be given one of those days off from work. As a result of the harassment, she claimed that she was forced to resign her position after she became nervous, developed high blood pressure, and had to be hospitalized.

The employee brought an action against her employer and its supervisors for tortious interference with her employment contract. The trial court entered a directed verdict in favor of the employer. On appeal, the directed verdict was upheld. The appellate court stated that an employer cannot be held liable for tortious interference with its own contracts. In contrast, though, the court held that corporate officers and employees may be *individually* liable for tortious interference with the contractual relations of their employer, but only when they act *outside* the scope of their employment. In this case, however, the court concluded that the evidence did not establish that the supply clerk's supervisors were acting outside the scope of their authority. Thus, they could not be held liable for tortious interference. *Hickman v. Winston County Hosp. Bd.*, 508 So. 2d 237 (Ala. 1987).

3. Interference by Improper Work Assignments

Hospital Manager Held Personally Liable for Damages by Interfering With Physician's Employment

A physician who served as director of emergency medical services at a municipal hospital had several work-related disputes with the manager of the department of health and hospitals. As a result of these disputes, which received attention in the press, the manager removed the physician from his post, assigned him to perform proctology, and gave him an office in a building known as the "boiler room." Thereafter, the physician filed a civil service grievance to challenge the validity of the manager's actions.

In lieu of pursuing the grievance to its conclusion, the physician entered into a settlement agreement with the hospital. According to the agreement, the physician was to serve as a consultant in emergency medicine for 15 hours a week for a period of one year. The manager, however, assigned the physician work that did not relate to emergency medical treatment. This prompted the physician to treat the settlement agreement as a nullity and to resign from the hospital staff.

The physician brought an action for interference with contractual relations against the manager. The physician alleged that the manager intentionally interfered with the physician's contractual relations with the hospital by failing to assign him to emergency medical work, thereby preventing him from performing his obligations under the settlement agreement. At trial, the jury found that the manager had acted for other than bona fide purposes, and awarded the physician damages against the manager.

On appeal, the manager claimed that he was not a third party to the settlement agreement because he was an employee and agent of the hospital. The court disagreed, holding that where the manager was acting outside the scope of his employment, he could be held personally liable for tortious interference. *Trimble v. City of Denver*, 697 P.2d 716 (Colo. 1985).

4. Negative Job References

Employee Recovers $150,000 for Interference and Defamation Resulting From Negative Postemployment Reference

An applicant for a security position with a major retailer was offered a job, subject to a routine investigation of his employment reference. When the applicant's former supervisor was asked to give a reference, he told the retailer that the former employee had been fired. He also stated that the applicant was the subject of an investigation into check forgeries that, he said, was being turned over to the district attorney's office. The job offer was then rescinded.

The former employee filed an action against his former supervisor and his former employer for interference with prospective contractual relations and defamation. His wife also sued for loss of consortium. At trial, the former employee proved that he and his supervisor had a continuing personality conflict; that he had not been fired, but rather had resigned; and that the supervisor never referred the forgery matter to the district attorney's office. The jury returned a verdict in favor of the employee on both his tortious interference and defamation claims. It awarded him $100,000 in damages against the employer and his supervisor, as well as $50,000 in punitive damages solely against the supervisor. Finally, the jury awarded his wife $35,000 for loss of consortium. The jury awards were upheld on appeal. *Geyer v. Steinbronn*, 351 Pa. Super. 536, 506 A.2d 901 (1986).

$86,000 Jury Award Based on Postemployment Reference Overturned on Appeal

An employee and his friend set out to find some automobile parts to repair the employee's car. After locating the parts, the employee and his friend decided to stop at "Daisy Mae's Cafe." A coworker of the employee was also at the cafe and had parked a company truck in the parking lot. Certain patrons in the bar observed the employee and his friend remove some company tools from the truck. This information was passed on to the police and to the company. When the employee reported for work the next day, he was met by two of his supervisors. He denied their allegations of theft; nonetheless, he was discharged for stealing company property.

When the employee sought new employment with a packing company, he stated on his employment application that he had been "laid off" from his last job. The employee signed the application form, which authorized his prospective employer to contact the employee's prior employers. When the employee's former employer was contacted, it stated that the employee had been terminated for "stealing company property." After this information was verified in writing, the prospective employer gave no further consideration to the employee's application for employment.

The employee filed an action against his former employer for tortious interference with prospective contractual relations and defamation. The jury returned a verdict in favor of the employee and awarded him $86,700 for both causes of action. On appeal, however, the award was reversed. The appellate court held that the former employer's interference was lawful. It stated that in the "world of trade and commerce, it is imperative that a prospective employer have access to information about an employee's prior work record ...." Even if the information about the employee were false, he could not recover damages for tortious interference where there was no evidence that the former employer's motive was improper. *Turner v. Halliburton Co.*, 240 Kan. 1, 722 P.2d 1106 (1986).

Employee May Recover Damages Where Division Managers Caused Another Division to Rescind Job Offer

A technical service engineer was employed in the pump division of a company. He was asked by his supervisors to determine why certain industrial pumps were not functioning correctly. After inspecting the pumps, he filed a report detailing the problem and criticizing the manufacture of the pump rods. His criticism antagonized the manager of the manufacturing department, who met with the engineer and "cursed [him] to high heaven for writing his report." Two months later, the manufacturing manager advised the technical service engineer that he was being transferred to the manufacturing department. The engineer objected, but was advised by the manager of industrial relations that he had no choice. Later, another argument ensued between the engineer and the manufacturing manager. During the argument, the engineer called his superior a liar, after which he was fired.

Before the engineer left work, a co-worker called the service personnel manager in the turbo division of the company and recommended the engineer for employment in that division. After an interview, the service personnel manager told the engineer that he wanted to hire him. Before the job offer was finalized, however, the group general manager of the pump division called a general manager of the turbo division and told him that it was "wrong for somebody who had been terminated because of insubordination to find in the same company an opportunity with more money." Thereafter, the service personnel manager called the engineer and told him that he had just received a call from the group general manager of the pump division, who said, "I'm not allowed to hire you, and if I do, he's going to take it up with the group vice president."

The engineer commenced an action for tortious interference with prospective contractual relations and wrongful discharge. On a motion for summary judgment, the employer prevailed. But on appeal, the appellate court reversed. It held that the group general manager of the pump division did not simply give honest advice to the turbo division regarding the engineer's job application; rather, he used his position to eliminate the engineer's job opportunity at the turbo division by threatening the service personnel manager if he hired the engineer. Such conduct, the court said, was improper and could form the basis for an award of damages for tortious interference.

Finally, the appellate court held that although the two divisions were part of a single corporation, they were, as a practical matter, two separate companies. Hence, the pump division could be considered a third party that interfered with the engineer's job opportunities elsewhere. *Yaindl v. Ingersoll-Rand Co.*, 281 Pa. Super. 560, 422 A.2d 611, 115 LRRM 4738 (1980).

5. Unreasonable Enforcement of Noncompete Agreements

Enforcement of Unreasonable Noncompete Provisions May Subject Bank to Liability

A trust officer of a bank was offered a job with another bank. She informed her employer that unless she received an immediate raise and an assistant, she would accept the other bank's offer. Her employer agreed to her terms and granted her a 23-percent increase. In return, it asked the employee to sign an employment contract. The contract contained a provision barring her from accepting employment within a 25-mile radius of the bank for a period of two years if she voluntarily terminated her employment with the bank. She protested the clause but signed it. Subsequently, the trust officer voluntarily quit her job. Because the bank had previously taken steps to enforce the noncompete provision against another employee who had signed a similar contract, the trust officer did not seek other employment for a two-year period.

The trust officer sued the bank for lost wages during the two-year period following her resignation from employment. The jury returned a verdict for the employee and awarded her $35,000 in lost income. On appeal, the appellate court affirmed. It stated that although an employer may have a justifiable reason to enter into and enforce noncompete agreements, an employer "must decide whether [its] covenant is sufficiently narrow to protect only legitimate business interests *in a reasonable fashion,* or risk ... damages if its existence interferes with an employment opportunity." The court acknowledged that its opinion may severely curb the use of restrictive covenants in future employment contracts, but nonetheless concluded that "frivolous noncompetition clauses in employment contracts" can subject an employer to liability. *Torbett v. Wheeling Dollar Sav. & Trust Co.,* 173 W. Va. 210, 314 S.E.2d 166 (1983).

Employees Who Were Told Noncompete Agreements "Not Worth a Damn" Get $120,000 in Damages

Each of the employees of a company in the business of selling liquefied petroleum gas (LPG) products was required to sign a new employment contract each year. The contracts contained a noncompetition provision that prohibited employees from seeking employment for a period of three years with any other LPG company within a 50-mile radius of the company. When two of the employees signed their last contract with the employer, a representative of the employer assured them that the covenant not to compete was "not worth a damn," that the contract was "just a piece of paper," and that "it won't hold up in court."

The two employees terminated their employment with the employer and sought employment with another LPG company located within the 50-mile radius the covenant specified. Upon learning this, the employer threatened to sue the prospective employer if it hired the two employees. Based on this threat, the prospective employer decided not to hire the two LPG employees.

The two employees brought an action against their former employer for intentional interference with prospective contractual relations and fraudulent inducement to enter into the employment contracts. At trial, a jury awarded the two employees $120,000 on their claims for tortious interference and fraud. The jury verdict was upheld on appeal. The appellate court held that the former employer's claim of legal justification was undermined by its representation that the noncompete agreements were "not worth a damn."

Empiregas, Inc. v. Hardy, 487 So. 2d 244 (Ala. 1985), *cert. denied*, 476 U.S. 1116 (1986).

Notes

1. Restatement (Second) of Torts § 766.
2. Restatement (Second) of Torts § 766B.
3. Restatement (Second) of Torts § 767.
4. Restatement (Second) of Torts § 767(b)–(d).
5. Restatement (Second) of Torts § 772.
6. Restatement (Second) of Torts § 767(d).
7. Restatement (Second) of Torts § 766C.
8. *See* cases summarized in section C.1.a. of this chapter.
9. *See* In re IBP Confidential Business Documents Litig., 797 F.2d 632, 1 IER Cases 871 (8th Cir. 1986), *cert. denied*, 479 U.S. 1088 (1987), summarized in section C.1.b. of this chapter.
10. *See* Kraus v. Santa Fe S. Pac. Corp., 878 F.2d 1193 (9th Cir. 1989), *cert. dismissed*, 493 U.S. 1051 (1990), summarized in section C.1.c. of this chapter.
11. *See* Sorrells v. Garfinkel's, 2 IER Cases 618 (D.C. Super. Ct. 1987), summarized in section C.1.a. of this chapter. The trial court, however, reduced the award to $80,000.
12. *See* Trimble v. City of Denver, 697 P.2d 716 (Colo. 1985), summarized in section C.3. of this chapter.
13. *See* Geyer v. Steinbronn, 351 Pa. Super. 536, 506 A.2d 901 (1986), summarized in section C.4. of this chapter.

Chapter 8

False Imprisonment

A. Overview

Employers sometimes are forced to detain and question employees suspected of wrongdoing. Typically, such questioning takes place when employee theft or assault is suspected or when employee safety is compromised by possible drug or alcohol abuse. Where an employer detains an employee to question him or her about suspected wrongdoing, the employee may bring a lawsuit for false imprisonment.

The tort of false imprisonment has also been applied in the employment context to challenge an employer's action of subjecting an employee to a polygraph examination. In addition, it has also been asserted against an employer who required a drug-addicted employee to attend a 24-hour-a-day drug rehabilitation program as a condition of continued employment.

B. General Principles of Law

False imprisonment is the intentional restraint by one person of the movement or physical liberty of another.[1] To establish the tort of false imprisonment, the party restrained must show that he or she was conscious of or harmed by the confinement.[2] Any period of confinement, no matter how brief, is sufficient to constitute a basis for liability for false imprisonment.[3]

"Imprisonment" does not necessarily mean incarceration—a person may be falsely imprisoned if his or her movements are restrained on an open street, in a traveling car, or if that person is compelled to go with someone against his or her will.[4] An employee even can be "restrained" if he or she is blocked from leaving a room because another individual, such as a supervisor, is standing between the employee and the only exit from the room.[5]

While the confinement must be intentional, it is not necessary that the defendant be motivated by malice. A personal hostility or desire to offend is not a necessary element of false imprisonment.[6] Rather, the defendant need only intend to confine another.[7]

The required confinement may result from actual or apparent physical barriers, physical force, threats of physical force, or through duress.[8] For example, an employer may be liable for false imprisonment if its security officers make menacing gestures to an employee during an investigation of a workplace theft and then threaten the employee with prosecution and jail.[9]

Voluntary consent is a complete defense to a claim of false imprisonment. For example, if an employee, of his or her own free will, agrees to surrender his freedom of movement by remaining in a room to prove his or her innocence, there is no imprisonment.[10]

C. Illustrative Cases

The cases summarized in this chapter fall into the following categories of false imprisonment:

- Unreasonable Detention of Employees During Workplace Investigations:
  - actual and apparent detentions, and
  - blocking an employee's egress from an office or work site;
- Polygraph Examinations; and
- Other Forms of False Imprisonment.

More often than not, claims for false imprisonment by employees are accompanied by claims for one or more other torts, such as defamation, infliction of emotional distress, assault and battery, or malicious prosecution.

When juries have returned verdicts in favor of employees for false imprisonment, the jury awards have involved, for the most part, relatively modest jury awards—at least in comparison to the jury awards for some of the other torts discussed in Part One of this book. With the exception of one jury award for $500,000, which was reversed and remanded by an appellate court,[11] none of the other false imprisonment cases reported below has resulted in jury awards in excess of $110,000.[12] Nonetheless, false imprisonment is one of the more troubling torts, especially when asserted by an employee who has been detained in connection with an investigation of workplace misconduct, because it may be maintained not only by employees who are innocent of wrongdoing, but by guilty workers as well.[13]

1. Unreasonable Detention of Employees During Workplace Investigations

a. Actual and Apparent Detentions

Abusive Detention and Escort to Police Station Results in $100,000 Jury Award for False Imprisonment

Two employees were employed as cashiers at a large department store. Each was physically detained in the store's personnel office by a loss prevention manager and an off-duty police officer who believed that one employee aided the other in stealing two cartons of cigarettes by not ringing up an employee purchase correctly. The purchasing employee maintained from the outset that she thought she bought five cartons of cigarettes and a package of diapers. After looking at the receipt a second time during the questioning, however, she realized that two cartons of cigarettes apparently had not been rung up.

Both employees immediately offered to pay for the cigarettes, but the loss prevention manager refused to accept payment. Instead, the loss prevention manager continued to physically detain both employees and kept accusing them in a loud and abusive manner of being thieves and liars. Eventually, both employees were escorted by the off-duty police officer out of the store and to the police station.

The two cashiers sued the department store for false imprisonment and malicious prosecution. A jury awarded both employees a total of $100,000 in damages on their false imprisonment claims. On appeal, the employer argued that the employees could not establish that their imprisonment was involuntary. The appellate court concluded, however, that their detention was indeed involuntary, noting that the employees were not compensated for the time spent during their questioning and were delivered into police custody.

The court also concluded that the department store had failed to establish any grounds for a reasonable belief that the employees had acted wrongfully. Thus, the court held, the store's actions against the two employees could not be viewed as lawful under a state statute that affords merchants the right to detain a person for a reasonable time upon a reasonable belief that a theft has occurred. *Redican v. K-Mart Corp.*, 734 S.W.2d 864 (Mo. Ct. App. 1987).

Employee Interrogated for Hours About Sexual Assault Awarded $500,000 for False Imprisonment, but Case Is Remanded

A computer operator employed by a major photographic products manufacturer reported to her supervisor that a head operator had sexually assaulted her. Two days later, the head operator was told by his division director that he wanted to speak with him regarding his promotion bid. When the two men reached the director's office, the head operator was introduced to the store security director and was asked if he would answer some questions. He said that he would. He was then asked numerous questions about the computer operator and was told that he would be prosecuted if he did not admit to sexually assaulting her.

During the questioning, the security director threatened the head operator with discharge, clenched his fists, and on several occasions yelled at the head operator to sit back down. After the head operator made several requests to leave the office to use the rest room, he was finally allowed to do so. When he returned, the questioning continued for another hour, making the total time for the interrogation approximately four hours.

Based on the computer operator's complaint, the employer filed a criminal complaint against the head operator for assault and battery and rape by an unnatural act. After a two-week criminal trial, the jury returned a verdict of not guilty.

The head operator and his wife then filed a civil action against the employer alleging false imprisonment, intentional infliction of emotional distress, defamation, malicious prosecution, violation of civil rights, and loss of consortium. At trial, the jury awarded him $500,000 on his false imprisonment claim, $1.5 million on his malicious prosecution claim, and $1 million on his defamation claim. His wife was awarded a total of $2 million for loss of consortium arising out of the various claims.

On appeal, however, all of the judgments were reversed, except for the false imprisonment claim, which was remanded for a new trial. The appellate court stated that the trial court had erroneously instructed the jury that a threat of discharge during an interrogation, standing alone, could constitute false imprisonment. Accordingly, the appellate court remanded the case for a new trial on the false imprisonment claim to determine whether the evidence, considered as a whole, demonstrated that the employer's conduct and actions created an atmosphere "conducive to a threat of physical confrontation." *Foley v. Polaroid Corp.,* 400 Mass. 82, 508 N.E.2d 72, 2 IER Cases 328 (1987).

Employer Liable for $110,000 in Damages for "Frightening" Four-Hour Interrogation of Employee

A 17-year-old cashier worked at a department store. The store's loss prevention manager arrived at the store to investigate employee thefts. He interviewed one of the cashier's co-workers, who admitted to a theft and implicated several other employees, including the cashier. The accusations, as reflected in a written statement given that day, charged the cashier with participation in the theft of money from the service desk cash register.

The cashier was told that she was wanted in an office at the rear of the store. In the office, the loss prevention manager, sitting behind a desk, subjected the cashier to an intensive, four-hour interrogation. During the interrogation, the cashier was lectured at length about theft. She claimed that she became "frightened" when the interrogator raised his voice, slammed his fist on the desk, and put his face close to hers. He also told the cashier that she was staying there until she confessed. The cashier began to shake and cry and became nervous and horrified.

The cashier sued the department store and its loss prevention manager for false imprisonment. Following a six-day jury trial, the cashier was awarded compensatory damages of $10,000 and punitive damages of $100,000. On appeal, the store argued that it was entitled to detain and interrogate the cashier in the manner it did by virtue of a statutory privilege given store owners by a state statute or, alternatively, by "a common law privilege granted to merchants to detain individuals suspected of theft based upon probable cause." The appellate court held that the statute and the common law privilege were applicable only to the theft of merchandise by customers, not the theft of money by employees, and upheld the jury verdict. *DeAngelis v. Jamesway Dep't Store,* 205 N.J. Super. 519, 501 A.2d 561 (App. Div. 1985).

Accused Employee May Not Recover for False Imprisonment Where She Voluntarily Stayed in Manager's Office to Prove Her Innocence

A jewelry store clerk was reportedly seen stealing a watch by a co-worker. After listening to the co-worker's allegation, a supervisor approached the clerk and stated that he wanted to give her a tour of the store. He escorted her into the store manager's office where, after the door was closed, he accused her of stealing the watch. The clerk denied the allegation and agreed to take a lie-detector test to prove that she did not steal the watch. The test results supported her claim of innocence.

The clerk brought suit against her employer and her supervisor for false imprisonment. At trial, the jury returned a verdict for the employer, finding that the clerk had not been restrained against her will. On appeal, the appellate court noted that the employee had not asked to leave the office and no threat was made to compel her to stay. Indeed, although she was tricked into the manager's office under the pretense of a tour, she also testified that she wanted to stay to prove her innocence. Accordingly, the jury's verdict in favor of the employer was affirmed. *Hardy v. LaBelle's Distrib. Co.*, 203 Mont. 263, 661 P.2d 35 (1983).

Security Officer's Threats of Prosecution and Jail Can Imply Restraint on Employee's Freedom

A cashier for a grocery store allegedly stole $5 from her cash register. Before she left the premises she was confronted by men who identified themselves as security and police officers. They asked her where the money was. After expressing puzzlement at the accusation, the cashier was escorted to the back of the store. She later alleged that the security officers made menacing gestures that gave her the impression that she was in custody. In addition, she said she was threatened with prosecution and jail. The grocery store fired the cashier ten minutes after the interrogation ended.

The cashier sued her former employer for false imprisonment and slander. The court granted the employer's motion for summary judgment on both claims. An appellate court reversed. The employer claimed on appeal that state law permitted it to detain the employee because it had probable cause to believe she had stolen the money. The appellate court held that even if the employer had probable cause, the employee could still recover for false imprisonment, because the conduct of the employer's security officers impliedly restricted the cashier's freedom. *Tumbarella v. Kroger Co.*, 85 Mich. App. 482, 271 N.W.2d 284 (1978).

Employee Who Signed Consent Form Before Questioning Has No Claim for False Imprisonment

An employee of a department store's tailor shop was suspected of stealing store merchandise by concealing goods beneath her clothing. She was summoned to the store security office, where she was interrogated intermittently for three hours by the store's security manager. Before the interrogation the employee had signed a form consenting to be questioned regarding matters of company business.

The employee brought suit against the store for false imprisonment. In affirming the lower court's grant of summary judgment in favor of the company, the appellate court stressed that the employer's interrogation was lawful, as the employee had signed a written form consenting to be questioned. In addition, the evidence did not establish that the employee had requested that the questioning be discontinued. On the contrary, the employee's testimony indicated that she wanted to stay to clear the matter up. *Crowe v. J.C. Penney, Inc.*, 177 Ga. App. 586, 340 S.E.2d 192 (1986).

b. Blocking an Employee's Egress From an Office or Work Site

Employer May Be Liable for False Imprisonment by Blocking Employee's Egress From Work Cubicle

A sales representative was at work in his cubicle one afternoon when his supervisor arrived with two co-workers carrying empty boxes. The supervisor, who had previously issued a written warning of dismissal to the sales representative, advised the employee that he was being terminated and directed him to gather his personal belongings, place them in the boxes, and leave the building under escort. The sales representative declined to gather his personal effects and asked to speak to a representative from the personnel department.

According to the employee, his supervisor became incensed. When the sales representative tried to telephone the personnel department, the supervisor prevented him from using the phone by grabbing his wrist and arm. And when the employee tried to call the personnel department from another telephone, one of the two co-workers allegedly blocked him with his body, thereby preventing the sales representative from leaving his cubicle.

The employee commenced a lawsuit against his employer and supervisor, asserting claims for false imprisonment, assault and battery, defamation, intentional infliction of emotional distress, breach of contract, and wrongful discharge. The lower court granted the defendants' motion for summary judgment as to all of the claims raised in the lawsuit, and the sales representative appealed.

The appellate court reversed on the false imprisonment claim. It held that there were genuine issues of fact for a jury to determine on the false imprisonment claim, including whether the sales representative was confined against his will for an unreasonable duration or in an unreasonable manner, and whether the supervisor had a legitimate business justification to do so. The appeals court also vacated the lower court's grant of summary judgment on the intentional infliction claim. *Uebelacker v. Cincom Sys.*, 48 Ohio App. 3d 268, 549 N.E.2d 1210, 3 IER Cases 1853 (1988).

Supervisor Falsely Imprisons Employee by Standing Between Her and Door

A service representative who had been employed by a telephone company for 15 years was asked one evening to join her supervisor in his office. Upon arrival, her supervisor and another manager informed her that she would no longer be working for the phone company and that she could choose to resign or be fired. The supervisor's decision apparently was based on poor performance rather than misconduct by the employee, who refused to resign.

During the next hour and a half, her superiors positioned themselves between the employee and the office door, attempting to coerce her into resigning. When she asked to leave, she was told in a loud, harsh voice to "sit down." She was allowed to leave the office to visit the bathroom and to call her husband. On both occasions, though, she was told by her supervisor that if she did not return, he would call the police.

The employee brought an action against her employer and her superiors for false imprisonment. The jury returned a verdict in favor of the employee for $7,500. On appeal, the appellate court noted that ample evidence had been presented from which to conclude that the employee had been confined intentionally against her will by her superiors' action of blocking her egress from the office. Accordingly, the jury's verdict was upheld, although the award of damages was remanded for modification. *Dupler v. Seubert*, 69 Wis. 2d 373, 230 N.W.2d 626 (1975).

2. Polygraph Examinations

Release Forms Bar Lawsuit by Employees Who Submitted to Polygraph Tests for Fear of Losing Their Jobs

Because a hotel robbery appeared to be an inside job, the hotel's owner requested that all employees take a polygraph test. Upset over being asked to participate, the hotel manager asked what would happen if she refused to take the test. The owner indicated she would lose her job. Although the hotel manager protested at the time the test was administered, she signed a written statement acknowledging that she did not take the test under coercion or duress. Based on the test result, the hotel manager was fired.

Shortly after her discharge the hotel manager filed suit against her employer alleging false imprisonment. She claimed that she signed the release forms and submitted to the polygraph exam under duress because her job depended on her submitting to the test. The jury agreed, and returned a verdict in favor of the employee for $12,000, including $7,000 in punitive damages.

On appeal, the appellate court reversed. It rejected the employee's argument and held that the release form signed by her was valid. *Columbia Sussex Corp. v. Hay*, 627 S.W.2d 270 (Ky. Ct. App. 1981).

3. Other Forms of False Imprisonment

Bizarre Horseshoe Acts of Co-Worker May Subject Employer to Liability for False Imprisonment

An employee of a manufacturing company claimed that a co-worker had set up a steel horseshoe target directly over his work space, forced him to remain confined there against his will, and repeatedly pounded a large sledgehammer against the target, causing the employee to suffer a loss of hearing, severe mental anguish, and physical pain and suffering.

The employee filed an action against his employer for false imprisonment, alleging that his employer condoned the co-worker's misconduct by taking no action against the offending employee. In defense, the employer argued that the false imprisonment claim should be dismissed because state law limits the employee's remedy to workers' compensation.

The lower court dismissed the employee's action, but an appellate court reversed. It noted that the applicable state workers' compensation statute does not cover tort actions when injury is caused by a "willful and unprovoked physical act of aggression." It also held that, although the co-worker did not actually touch the employee, the co-worker's actions could nonetheless be characterized as a willful act of physical aggression within the meaning of the law. Thus, the workers' compensation statute did not bar the employee's common law action against his employer for false imprisonment. *Iverson v. Atlas Pac. Eng'g*, 143 Cal. App. 3d 219, 191 Cal. Rptr. 696 (1983).

Employee Required to Attend 24-Hour Drug Rehab Program Sues for False Imprisonment

As a condition of his continued employment with a transportation company, an employee claimed he was required to attend a 24-hour-a-day drug rehabilitation program. He also alleged that, upon release from the program, he was forced to attend biweekly meetings of Alcoholics Anonymous or Narcotics Anonymous and weekly "after care" meetings.

The employee sued his employer for false imprisonment, claiming that his required attendance at the rehabilitation program constituted an intentional act of confinement against his will. He also asserted claims for intentional and negligent infliction of emotional distress and invasion of privacy. The case was reportedly settled for a substantial amount of money. *Pettigrew v. Southern Pac. Transp. Co.*, No. 849343 (Super. Ct. San Francisco County Nov. 25, 1985).

Employee Sues for False Imprisonment for Ride in Supervisor's Car to Retrieve Stolen Goods

An employee of a telephone company was detained by her superiors for questioning concerning the illegitimate use of company equipment. After the employee had voluntarily signed a confession, she was driven in her supervisor's car to her home to retrieve the equipment.

The employee brought suit against the phone company for false imprisonment. She claimed that she had been falsely imprisoned during the car ride from the office to her home. The jury returned a verdict for the employee, but the trial court granted the employer's motion to set aside the judgment. On appeal, the appellate court affirmed the trial court's decision in favor of the employer, finding that the employee's fear of being fired and her subjective belief that she had no choice but to go on the trip were not sufficient to make her confinement involuntary. *Faniel v. Chesapeake & Potomac Tel. Co.*, 404 A.2d 147 (D.C. 1979).

Notes

1. W. KEETON, PROSSER AND KEETON ON THE LAW OF TORTS § 11 (5th ed. 1984).
2. *See* Restatement (Second) of Torts §§ 35, 42.
3. *See* Restatement (Second) of Torts § 35 and caveat.

4. W. KEETON, PROSSER AND KEETON ON THE LAW OF TORTS § 11, at 47 (5th ed. 1984).
5. *See* Dupler v. Seubert, 69 Wis. 2d 373, 230 N.W.2d 626 (1975); *and* Uebelacker v. Cincom Sys., 3 IER Cases 1853 (Ohio Ct. App. 1988), both of which are summarized in section C.2. of this chapter.
6. *See* Restatement (Second) of Torts § 44.
7. *See* Restatement (Second) of Torts § 43.
8. *See* Restatement (Second) of Torts §§ 38–40A.
9. *See* Tumbarella v. Kroger Co., 85 Mich. App. 284, 271 N.W.2d 482 (1978), summarized in section C.1.a. of this chapter.
10. *See* Hardy v. LaBelle's Distrib. Co., 203 Mont. 263, 661 P.2d 35 (1983), summarized in section C.1.a. of this chapter.
11. *See* Foley v. Polaroid Corp., 400 Mass. 82, 508 N.E.2d 72, 2 IER Cases 328 (1987), summarized in section C.1.a. of this chapter.
12. *See* DeAngelis v. Jamesway Dep't Stores, 205 N.J. Super. 519, 501 A.2d 561 (App. Div. 1985) ($110,000 award), summarized in section C.1.a. of this chapter; *and* Redican v. K-Mart Corp., 734 S.W.2d 864 (Mo. Ct. App. 1987) ($100,000 award), summarized in section C.1.a. of this chapter.
13. *See* Tumbarella v. Kroger Co., 85 Mich. App. 482, 271 N.W.2d 284 (1978), summarized in section C.1.a. of this chapter. Even if the employer had probable cause to detain the employee, the employer's threats of prosecution and menacing gestures during the interrogation may result in damages in favor of the employee.

Chapter 9

Malicious Prosecution and Abuse of Process

A. Overview

After discovering that an employee has engaged in a criminal or wrongful act, an employer may consider filing criminal charges or commencing a civil action against the offending employee. Most criminal charges or civil actions filed by employers against employees involve allegations of employee theft of goods or funds from the employer. Employers have also instituted proceedings against employees for destruction of property belonging to the company or a co-worker, sexual abuse of co-workers, misappropriation of an employer's trade secrets or confidential information, and illegal use or sale of drugs.

When forced to defend against an unwarranted criminal charge or civil suit, or after prevailing in such a proceeding, an employee may consider filing his or her own lawsuit against the employer. In these circumstances, two tort theories are available to the employee: malicious prosecution and abuse of process.

B. General Principles of Law

An action for malicious prosecution can properly be commenced only *after* a legal proceeding has terminated in favor of the person against whom the proceeding was brought.[1] In contrast, an action for abuse of process may be properly started *before* the legal proceeding has concluded.[2]

In order to establish liability for *malicious prosecution*, a plaintiff must first show that the defendant initiated or procured the commencement of criminal proceedings or took an active part in the initiation or continuation of civil proceedings against the plaintiff. Next, the plaintiff must show that the proceedings terminated in his or her favor. Finally, the plaintiff must prove that the criminal or civil proceedings were initiated or procured "without probable cause and primarily for a purpose other than that of bringing an offender to justice... [or] securing the proper adjudication of the claim."[3]

For example, consider an employer who presses criminal charges or files a civil action against an employee in connection with misappropriation of funds. The mere fact that the employee is adjudged not guilty or is found not to be liable in the civil proceeding does not, in and of itself, establish liability for malicious prosecution.[4]

If, however, the employer did not have "probable cause" to believe that the employee misappropriated funds, the employer may be liable to the employee for malicious prosecution—assuming that the employee can demonstrate that the employer initiated the proceeding primarily for an improper purpose.[5] As a practical matter, a jury may infer an improper purpose merely from the fact that the employer did not have probable cause.[6] Hence, the key issue in an action for malicious prosecution is whether the employer had probable cause to believe that the employee committed a criminal or wrongful act.[7]

In order to establish a claim for *abuse of process*, a plaintiff must establish that the defendant used the legal process, either criminal or civil, "primarily to accomplish a purpose for which it was not designed."[8] Thus, the use of the legal process must be designed primarily to accomplish an immediate and illegitimate end that cannot be served by the lawsuit, such as obtaining a business advantage, compelling the payment of a different debt, extorting money, or obtaining sexual favors.[9]

An action for malicious prosecution or abuse of process is not only available to employees but to employers as well. As with defamation, an *employer* may bring a claim for malicious prosecution or abuse of process against an *employee* who has improperly instituted a lawsuit against the employer.[10]

C. Illustrative Cases

The tort of malicious prosecution has the potential to create catastrophic liability for an employer, particularly where the legal proceeding commenced against the employee is criminal in nature. Two of the cases summarized below vividly demonstrate the enormous risk involved in commencing criminal proceedings against employees.

In one case, a jury returned a $34 million verdict against an employer for instituting criminal proceedings against an employee for theft. The jury found that the employer had filed a criminal complaint against the employee in retaliation for the employee's refusal to sign false corporate income tax returns and his filing of a wrongful discharge and breach of contract action against the employer.[11]

In the other case, a jury returned a $1.5 million verdict against an employer for assisting a female employee in filing criminal charges of rape against a male employee who was indicted but finally acquitted after a two-week trial.[12] Although the verdict in the second case was reversed on appeal, the two cases illustrate that juries are not reluctant to award millions of dollars to employees whom they believe were wrongfully subjected to unwarranted criminal prosecution by their employers.

Employer's Criminal Complaint Against Vice President Who Refused to Sign Fraudulent Corporate Tax Returns Results in $34 Million Jury Verdict

A certified public accountant was employed by an independent oil and gas company as vice president for corporate taxes. He was responsible for signing and attesting to the truthfulness of his employer's federal income tax returns as well as other corporate documents and certifications required to be filed with various agencies of the United States government. After significant changes were made to the federal tax laws regarding the use of corporate property for noncorporate purposes, as well as the reporting requirements relating to such use, the vice president advised his superiors of the changes. He also objected to the expenditure of corporate funds for the personal use of company executives without proper reporting.

Despite his protestations, his superiors directed him to certify as accurate certain corporate tax returns and other documents to be filed with the IRS and other agencies of the federal government—even though the documents contained false statements classifying personal expenditures as corporate expenses. For example, the tax returns falsely claimed that purely personal trips taken by the vice president's superiors were instead related to the corporation's business. When he refused to make these and other false certifications and to sign a false tax return, the vice president was terminated.

A year later, the vice president filed a civil complaint in state court for wrongful discharge against his former employer as well as the chief financial and chief executive officers of the company. Shortly thereafter, the company instituted a proceeding against the vice president with the State Board of Public Accountants, seeking revocation of his license as a certified public accountant. The company also filed a criminal complaint against the vice president, alleging that he had changed and destroyed data on a computer disk belonging to the company. He was subsequently indicted and jailed, but the criminal case was eventually dismissed.

The vice president then amended his state court civil complaint by adding claims for malicious prosecution and abuse of process. After a lengthy trial, a jury returned a verdict in favor of the employee for over $48 million on his claims. Of the $48 million awarded, $34 million was awarded on the malicious prosecution and abuse of process counts consisting of $12 million in compensatory damages against the employer, including past and future mental anguish and injury to reputation; $20 million in punitive damages assessed against the company; and $2 million in punitive damages assessed against the two individual defendants. The case was settled before appeal in a confidential settlement agreement. *Sims v. Kaneb Servs.*, No. 86-2474 (Tex. Dist. Ct. Harris County Dec. 1, 1989), reported in 4 IER No. 23, at 2 (1989).

Employee Recovers $100,000 After Being Acquitted on Criminal Charges Filed by Employer

An assistant manager of a restaurant chain was accused by the employer's loss prevention manager of stealing money over a period of several days from the daily receipts placed in the restaurant's safe. The employee advised the manager that she was not at work on one of those days and that six other employees knew the combination to the safe. The loss prevention manager did not, however, investigate the employee's employment history or personal background or interview any other employees.

Instead, the loss prevention manager terminated the assistant manager and filed a criminal complaint charging her with the theft of funds. Thereafter, the employee was tried on criminal charges. The first jury could not reach a verdict, and a mistrial was declared. She was retried by a second jury, which acquitted her.

The assistant manager then sued her employer for malicious prosecution, slander, intentional infliction of emotional distress, and wrongful discharge. Each of the claims was dismissed by the trial court except her claim for malicious proscecution. The jury returned a verdict in her favor on that claim and awarded her $100,000 in damages.

On appeal, the verdict was upheld. The appellate court held that the jury properly found that the criminal proceedings were initiated with undue haste and without adequate investigation, on insufficient grounds, and without probable cause. The court also held that an improper purpose could be inferred from the absence of probable cause. *Wainauskis v. Howard Johnson Co.*, 339 Pa. Super. 266, 488 A.2d 1117 (1985).

Employee May Maintain Malicious Prosecution and False Arrest Claims Following Dismissal of Criminal Charges Filed by Employer

A machinist employed by a brewery was accused by three employees of slashing the tires of a co-worker's car, which was parked in the company parking lot. After the employees reported the incident to plant management an investigation followed, and police officers arrested the machinist at the plant. He was charged with destruction of property and appeared in court, but the charges were eventually dismissed.

As a result of the incident, the brewery terminated the machinist for violating company policy prohibiting malicious mischief. He filed a grievance in accordance with the procedures set forth in the governing collective bargaining agreement. The arbitrator sustained his grievance and ordered his reinstatement with back pay and retroactive seniority.

The machinist then filed a lawsuit in state court against his employer and the three employees who accused him of slashing the tires. He sued for malicious prosecution, false arrest, intentional infliction of emotional distress, tortious interference with contractual relations, slander, and wrongful discharge. The defendants removed the case from state to federal court and then filed a motion to dismiss, contending that all of the claims were preempted by the Labor Management Relations Act (LMRA).

The court granted the motion to dismiss, concluding that each of the machinist's claims was preempted by the LMRA because they related to events surrounding an alleged violation of the collective bargaining agreement. On appeal, an appellate court affirmed the lower court's preemption holding as it applied to all of the machinist's claims *except for* the malicious prosecution and false arrest counts. The appeals court held that, unlike the other claims, these two causes of action did not require reference to or interpretation of the collective bargaining agreement. Therefore, the employee could proceed in court with his malicious prosecution and false arrest claims. *Johnson v. Anheuser Busch, Inc.*, 876 F.2d 620, 4 IER Cases 709 (8th Cir. 1989).

Department Store Must Pay Cashiers $160,000 in Damages for Malicious Prosecution Where Its Manager Insisted That Cashiers Be Arrested But Never Showed Up in Court

As noted in Chapter 8, two cashiers for a department store were detained by a loss prevention manager in connection with their alleged theft of two cartons of cigarettes. The cashiers insisted that the two cartons of cigarettes were mistakenly placed in a shopping bag without being rung up for sale. At the conclusion of the investigation, the loss prevention manager called the police and told an officer that he wanted the two cashiers to be taken to jail and wanted the other employees to see them taken away. The police advised the loss prevention manager that there was no need to arrest the cashiers, but the loss prevention manager insisted that the police officer fill out a summons against the two cashiers.

The two cashiers were arrested in the loss prevention manager's office, led through the store by the police, and then placed in the back of a paddy wagon. They were taken to the police station, fingerprinted, and charged with theft. Both employees appeared when their case was called at municipal court, but no one from the employer appeared to testify against them. The charges were therefore dismissed.

The two cashiers brought an action against the department store for malicious prosecution and false imprisonment. The jury returned a verdict in their favor on both counts, but awarded only $1,000 to each employee on the malicious prosecution claims.

On appeal, the appellate court first rejected the employer's argument that the malicious prosecution and false imprisonment claims were barred by the state workers' compensation law. The appellate court then held that even though the cashiers admitted that two cartons of cigarettes had not been paid for, the jury could have reasonably concluded that the employer did *not* have reasonable cause for filing the criminal charges against the cashiers. Finally, the court remanded the malicious prosecution claims for a new trial, inasmuch as the jury awards of $1,000 were so low as to "shock the conscience of the court."

On remand, a jury again found in favor of the two cashiers on their malicious prosecution claims. This time, however, the jury awarded both employees a total of $160,000 in damages, $50,000 each in actual damages and $30,000 each in punitive damages. Those verdicts were affirmed on appeal. *Redican v. K-Mart Corp.*, 734 S.W.2d 864 (Mo. Ct. App. 1987).

Employee Counterclaims for Malicious Prosecution After Employer Sues for Misappropriation of Funds

A gas station manager was accused by her employer of misappropriating gas station products and cash receipts. A number of other employees, though, had access to the storeroom where the money and goods were kept. Nevertheless, the employer filed criminal charges against the manager. After she was arraigned and pled not guilty, the charges were dropped by the district attorney.

The employer also filed a civil action against the employee, alleging that she had misappropriated $10,000 in goods and funds. The employee filed a counterclaim against her employer for defamation and malicious prosecution (relating to the criminal proceeding).

The jury returned a verdict in favor of the employee on the employer's action for misappropriation of property, but also returned a verdict in favor of the employer on the employee's claim for malicious prosecution. On appeal, the appellate court upheld the verdicts. It found that despite the district attorney's decision not to prosecute the employee, the employer had probable cause to believe that the manager had committed a theft. *Young Oil Co. v. Durbin*, 412 So. 2d 620 (La. Ct. App. 1982).

Jury Returns $1.5 Million Verdict Against Employer for Malicious Prosecution, but Verdict Is Overturned on Appeal

As discussed in Chapter 8, a computer operator employed by a photographic products company reported to her supervisor that a head operator had sexually assaulted her. A few days later the head operator was questioned about the accusation but denied the charges.

After advising the computer operator that the accused had denied any wrongdoing, the employer's corporate security officer brought the computer operator to the police department and introduced her to police personnel. The computer operator provided a sworn statement to the police, which the corporate security officer read and witnessed. Criminal complaints were issued the next day from the local district court charging the head operator with assault, battery, and rape by virtue of an unnatural act. A grand jury thereafter returned an indictment on all three counts. After a two-week trial, the jury returned a verdict of not guilty.

The head operator thereafter began an action for malicious prosecution, false imprisonment, defamation, intentional infliction of emotional distress, and loss of civil rights, and his wife brought an action for loss of consortium. The jury in the civil case awarded the head operator $1.5 million on his malicious prosecution claim and $1.5 million on his other claims. It also awarded his wife $2 million for loss of consortium. The trial judge, however, overturned the award as to each of the claims, including the cause of action for malicious prosecution.

On appeal, the appellate court upheld the trial court's decision dismissing the jury award on the malicious prosecution claim. The appeals court held that the employee could not prevail on his claim for malicious prosecution where the employer relied in good faith on the accuser's allegation of sexual assault. *Foley v. Polaroid Corp.*, 400 Mass. 82, 508 N.E.2d 72, 2 IER Cases 328 (1987).

Notes

1. *See* Restatement (Second) of Torts §§ 658, 672(b), and 674(b). In the noncriminal context, the tort is also called "wrongful use of civil proceedings." *See* Restatement (Second) of Torts § 674.
2. *See* Restatement (Second) of Torts § 682, comment a.
3. *See* Restatement (Second) of Torts §§ 653, 674.
4. *See* Restatement (Second) of Torts §§ 657, comment a; and 659.
5. *See* Restatement (Second) of Torts §§ 653(a), 674(a).
6. *See* Wainauskis v. Howard Johnson Co., 339 Pa. Super. 266, 488 A.2d 1117 (1985), summarized in section C. of this chapter.
7. "Probable cause" as applied to the institution or initiation of *criminal* proceedings is defined as correctly or reasonably believing that the person accused has acted in a particular manner, that such acts constitute the offense charged, and that the person charging the offense is sufficiently informed as to the law and the facts to justify the prosecution. *See* Restatement (Second) of Torts § 662. "Probable cause" as applied to the institution or initiation of *civil* proceedings means a reasonable belief in the existence of facts on which the claim is based; and either correctly or reasonably believing that under those facts the claim may be valid under applicable law, or believing so on the advice of counsel, sought in good faith and given after disclosure of all known relevant facts. *See* Restatement (Second) of Torts § 675.
8. *See* Restatement (Second) of Torts § 682.
9. *See* Restatement (Second) of Torts § 682 illustrations.

186   *Employer's Guide to Workplace Torts*

10. *See, e.g.,* Grell v. Poulsen, 389 N.W.2d 661 (Iowa 1986).
11. *See* Sims v. Kaneb Servs., No. 86-2474 (Tex. Dist. Ct. Harris County Dec. 1, 1989), reported in 4 IER No. 23, at 2 (1989), and summarized in this chapter.
12. *See* Foley v. Polaroid Corp., 400 Mass. 82, 508 N.E.2d 72, 2 IER Cases 328 (1987), summarized in this chapter.

Chapter 10

RICO

A. Overview

In 1985, the United States Supreme Court held that the Racketeer Influenced and Corrupt Organizations Act (RICO)[1] was applicable to civil lawsuits, that it should be "read broadly," and that a defendant in a civil RICO action need not be associated with organized crime.[2] Because RICO allows treble damages as well as attorneys' fees for prevailing plaintiffs, a number of employees are now appending a RICO claim to their state law tort actions or are suing for a RICO violation alone. These types of lawsuits, even if unsuccessful, can be severely damaging to a corporation's goodwill, inasmuch as RICO is also a preferred statute for prosecuting notorious organized crime figures.

RICO actions by employees are most likely to arise as a result of employer fraud, corruption, or criminal misdeeds. Typically, employees bring RICO claims where they have been terminated from their jobs after discovering or disclosing a RICO violation perpetrated by agents of the employer. RICO claims may also be maintained by employees who have been terminated for refusing to participate in illegal or fraudulent conduct or physically coerced by union or employer representatives in an effort to "persuade" the employee to withdraw a criminal charge or pay money to a union or employer representative.

While a RICO action is not technically a tort, but rather a statutory wrong, it has been included in this book because of its recent emergence in the employment context.

B. General Principles of Law

In a civil action under RICO, a plaintiff essentially must prove that the defendants engaged in a pattern of racketeering activity related to the affairs of an enterprise affecting interstate or foreign commerce. A plaintiff also must prove that the racketeering activity proximately caused him or her to suffer injury to his business or property.[3]

A "pattern" of racketeering activity is defined in RICO as requiring at least two acts of racketeering activity occurring within ten years of each other.[4] "Racketeering activity" may be mail fraud, wire fraud, theft, obstruction of justice, or a number of other state and federal criminal acts.[5]

C. Illustrative Cases

The RICO cases summarized below fall into the following categories:

- Opposition to or Disclosure of Illegal Activities;
- Refusal to Participate in an Illegal Scheme; and
- Physical Coercion of Employees.

Because of the very technical pleading requirements set forth in RICO, most RICO claims have been dismissed by the courts. Where a RICO action survives a motion to dismiss or a motion for summary judgment, however, the potential for a large damage award is enhanced by the treble damages provision of RICO. That potential was realized in the first case summarized below, where a jury issued a $69 million verdict against an employer who terminated two employees for opposing illegal activities perpetrated by the employer.

1. Opposition to or Disclosure of Illegal Activities

Two Vice Presidents Who Objected to Illegal Foreign Payments Awarded $69 Million for Wrongful Termination in Violation of RICO

Two former vice presidents of an oil company raised questions about $46 million in payments by the oil company to foreign sources, including $29 million in payments to an Omani official, in order to obtain access to crude oil in Oman and Abu Dhabi. The vice presidents advised the company that the payments constituted illegal bribes and violated the Foreign Corrupt Practices Act, which bars payments to foreign officials. They charged that the bribes were paid in a surreptitious manner disguised as investments. One vice president was dismissed after expressing his concerns about the Omani deal to the company's board of directors, and the other vice president was terminated when his job was suddenly abolished.

The concerns raised by the two vice presidents came to the attention of the Securities and Exchange Commission (SEC) and Congress. The employer eventually settled civil charges brought against it by the SEC, which alleged that the company had violated the Foreign Corrupt Practices Act by its payment of $29 million to the Omani official.

Each vice president filed a lawsuit against the oil company and its senior executives, alleging that their terminations violated the RICO Act. Their cases were tried together to a jury in Kentucky. After a three-month trial, the jury awarded the vice presidents a total of $69.5 million in damages: $44.6 million for the vice president who was dismissed, and $24.9 million for the vice president whose job was abolished. The awards represented a tripling of their damages by virtue of the treble damages provision in the RICO Act. The cases were reportedly settled for $25 million. *McKay v. Ashland Oil*, No. 84-149 (E.D. Ky. June 13, 1988).

Trust Company Executive Allegedly Terminated to Prevent Disclosure of Fraud May Maintain Action Under RICO

An executive of a trust company wholly owned by a brokerage firm objected to the trust company's practice of charging fees to customers of the brokerage firm for trust services that were never performed. Shortly after receiving a promotion, the executive was abruptly terminated. She claimed that she had been discharged because she refused to participate in the scheme to impose improper charges on customers, and because her employer feared that she was about to disclose these illegal practices to state bank examiners.

The executive filed an action under the RICO Act against the trust company as well as the brokerage firm. In her complaint, she alleged four separate RICO claims. The court dismissed three of her claims, but concluded that the executive could maintain a RICO suit on her fourth claim, where she alleged that the trust company had conspired with the brokerage firm to hire her "as window dressing to perpetuate the fraud, and then fired her to preserve that fraud when she stated that she would not participate in the alleged scheme." *Shearin v. E.F. Hutton Group*, 885 F.2d 1162 (3d Cir. 1989).

Employee Fired After Discovering Stolen Goods Scheme May Maintain RICO Action Against Employer and Supervisor

A purchasing manager for a paper goods manufacturer discovered that her supervisor was engaging in a scheme to steal and distribute goods of the employer. The supervisor used other employees to appropriate the goods and to falsify the employer's records to conceal these activities. Shortly after discovering the scheme, the purchasing manager claimed that her supervisor subjected her to a course of harassment and then caused the company to terminate her employment.

The employee brought an action against her former employer and former supervisor for tortious interference with contractual relations and violation of RICO. On a motion to dismiss, the court held that the employee's loss of her job was a sufficient injury to "business or property." The court also held that the employee's injury was sufficiently related to the "racketeering activities" of theft, inasmuch as she allegedly lost her job as a result of her discovery of the pattern of racketeering activity engaged in by her supervisor. The court therefore permitted the employee to proceed with her RICO claim for treble damages. *Acampora v. Boise Cascade Corp.*, 635 F. Supp. 66 (D.N.J. 1986).

2. Refusal to Participate in an Illegal Scheme

RICO Claim Dismissed Where Loss of Employment Not Proximate Result of Fraudulent Business Practices

A sales representative for a publisher of legal and business publications was responsible for servicing existing subscriptions and promoting new business in an assigned geographic area. After beginning work, he learned of various alleged fraudulent acts committed by two of his superiors as well as the sales representative he had replaced. Specifically, he learned that his superiors and predecessor had allegedly forged customer signatures on orders, billed customers for fabricated or improperly confirmed orders, and disregarded subscription cancellation requests.

The sales representative spoke with his superiors and demanded that these practices be corrected. He was told, however, that he had to either cooperate with the concealment of these practices or lose his job. After he refused to cooperate, the sales representative was terminated for "insubordination."

The sales representative filed a complaint in federal court against his employer and superiors seeking recovery under RICO. He also alleged certain common law theories of recovery, including "prima facie tort" and fraud. The lower court dismissed his RICO claim, concluding that his loss of employment was not proximately caused by any racketeering activity.

On appeal, an appellate court affirmed the dismissal of his RICO claims. It held that while the sales representative's loss of employment may have been a result of his discovery of the RICO violations, it was not "proximately caused" by the RICO violations themselves, since his termination was not a foreseeable and natural consequence of the alleged acts of fraud. *Hecht v. Commerce Clearing House*, 897 F.2d 21, 5 IER Cases 78 (2d Cir. 1990).

Sales Reps Who Refused to Use Commercial Bribery As Sales Technique May Recover for RICO Violation

Several sales representatives of a chemical manufacturer were persuaded by another company to leave their respective jobs and join the other company as sales representatives in a different location. Unknown to the sales reps, their new employer marketed its products exclusively through the use of commercial bribery. Specifically, their new employer required its sales representatives to offer gifts of cash and merchandise to its customers' employees who were responsible for purchasing chemicals.

Each of the new sales reps refused to offer bribes to the purchasing employees. In retaliation for their refusal, they were discharged from their jobs. As a consequence of their discharge, each salesman allegedly suffered loss of income, loss of reputation and standing as a sales rep, mental anguish, and loss of self-esteem.

In their action for treble damages under the RICO Act, the court found that the sales reps had stated a proper claim for a RICO violation. Although the racketeering activities of commercial bribery did not, per se, harm the sales reps, their new employer's adoption of commercial bribery as a mandatory sales technique caused their termination and, hence, could be remedied under RICO. *Callan v. State Chem. Mfg. Co.*, 584 F. Supp. 619 (E.D. Pa. 1984).

3. Physical Coercion of Employees

Female Carpenter May Use RICO Against Union Official for Alleged Physical Coercion and Sexual Harassment

A female carpenter was a member of a union and was employed at a construction site at Harvard Square in Cambridge, Massachusetts. During her employment there, she claimed she was subjected to numerous acts of sex discrimination and sexual harassment. She informed the union business agent about these matters, but he allegedly failed to take any remedial action.

The carpenter also claimed that while working at Harvard Square, she was the victim of an assault by a co-worker. After filing criminal charges against the assailant, the carpenter stated that the union business agent and other union officials demanded that she withdraw her criminal complaint.

In addition, at another job site, the female carpenter was allegedly coerced into purchasing raffle tickets for the local union political action fund. She claimed the union officials made threats of personal injury and loss of employment if she refused to purchase any tickets. These threats were allegedly made in the presence of her employer's general superintendent. Thereafter, the employee did not return to work.

The carpenter filed a RICO action against the local union business agent, other union officials, the employer's general superintendent, and the employer. She also filed a variety of other federal civil rights claims and a state law action for civil conspiracy. On the defendants' motion to dismiss, the court held that a RICO violation had been properly alleged. It noted that an allegation by an employee that he or she had been forced out of work by the actions of union and/or company officials would constitute an injury to "business or property."

Further, according to the appellate court, the employee had satisfied the requirement of alleging two or more acts of "racketeering activity" by claiming that union officials had used the threat of coercion to obtain withdrawal of a criminal charge and the threat of physical injury if she did not purchase raffle tickets. Thus, the employee was allowed to proceed with her RICO claim for treble damages. *Hunt v. Weatherbee*, 626 F. Supp. 1097, 121 LRRM 2408 (D. Mass. 1986).

Notes

1. 18 U.S.C. §§ 1961–1968.
2. *See* Sedima S.P.L.R. v. Imrex Co., 473 U.S. 479 (1985).
3. 18 U.S.C. §§ 1962, 1964.
4. 18 U.S.C. § 1961.
5. 18 U.S.C. § 1961.

Part Two

A Practical Guide to Workplace Torts

Chapter 11

How Different Workplace Torts Arise in Common Employment Contexts

Part One of this book examined each of the workplace torts that have been raised by employees in the employment context. In practice, however, when an employee files a lawsuit against his or her employer based in whole or in part upon the common law of torts, the employee frequently asserts more than one workplace tort when challenging a specific employment action or seeking damages for workplace misconduct.

For example, in one case summarized in Part One, a female employee who alleged she was sexually harassed by her supervisor asserted tort claims for negligent failure to train the offending supervisor not to harass his subordinates, intentional and negligent infliction of emotional distress, invasion of privacy, battery, and false imprisonment.[1] This chapter will examine how different workplace torts arise in common employment contexts.[2]

The employment scenarios addressed in this chapter are:

- Applicant Screening and Hiring of New Employees;
- Workplace Environments, Including:
  - sexual harassment,
  - other forms of workplace harassment,
  - smoking in the workplace, and
  - exposure to toxins and other workplace dangers;
- Employee Disabilities, Including:
  - drug and alcohol abuse,
  - AIDS,

- other illnesses, and
- employee assistance programs;
• Work Assignments, Performance Evaluations, Disciplinary Action, and Demotions;
• Investigating Workplace Misconduct, Including:
  - employee theft,
  - drug and alcohol abuse, and
  - sexual harassment and other forms of employee misconduct;
• Termination and Retention of Employees; and
• Postemployment Matters, Including:
  - postemployment references,
  - criminal and civil proceedings against employees,
  - noncompete agreements, and
  - unemployment and workers' compensation proceedings.

A. Applicant Screening and Hiring of New Employees

A fundamental component of the employment process for all organizations is the process of hiring new employees. This process comprises two principal functions: (1) selecting applicants who are capable of performing the duties of the job and screening out applicants who are unfit; and (2) inducing qualified applicants to accept an offer of employment. While these two functions are closely related and frequently overlap, they are, nonetheless, quite distinct. Indeed, different common law theories of workplace torts are applicable to each function. The tort most likely to arise in the applicant screening and selection process is negligent hiring, whereas the torts most likely to arise in the recruitment and inducement process are fraud and misrepresentation.

1. Negligent Hiring

Actions for negligent hiring arise when the employer is alleged to have hired an unfit or unqualified employee. The focal point for most negligent hiring cases is the extent to which the prospective employer checked the background of the candidate to ensure that, if hired, the applicant would not present a risk of harm to co-workers, customers, or other third parties with whom the employee may come into contact as a result of his or her job.

This background check must ascertain not only whether the applicant has the technical skills or education for the job, but also whether that individual is reliable, trustworthy, honest, or has a propensity to engage in violent, dangerous, criminal, abusive, harassing, or other improper conduct that would disqualify the applicant for the position in question.

The depth and nature of the background check should vary with the type of job being filled. For example, jobs with a higher degree of unsupervised contact with an employer's customers or with other employees require a more stringent check of references, particularly regarding the applicant's violent or dangerous tendencies. Thus, for an employer to minimize liability for negligent hiring, it must be aware of the specific duties and responsibilities of the job in question and then tailor the background inquiry to the position being sought.

The types of conduct that lead to liability for negligent hiring usually involve an employer's *failure* to take certain action. Although it is impossible to catalog each and every action or inaction by an employer that may lead to liability for negligent hiring, examples of such negligent conduct by an employer include:

- failure to check an applicant's driving record for a position requiring driving for the employer;[3]
- failure to determine if an applicant is qualified or competent to perform the job in question;[4]
- failure to contact all prior employers;[5]
- failure to contact all personal references;[6]
- failure to conduct a criminal record search when circumstances warrant such an inquiry;[7]
- failure to determine if an applicant was dangerous;[8]
- failure to ascertain if an employee was trustworthy;[9]
- failure to perform any background check for a temporary worker;[10] and
- sole reliance on a social service agency to conduct applicant screening.[11]

The absence of negative information about an applicant does not insulate an employer from liability for negligent hiring. To the contrary, as the cases vividly demonstrate, the failure to obtain such negative information may actually result in a finding of liability for negligent hiring where such information could have been obtained and, if obtained, may have averted the harm or damages suffered by the plaintiff.[12] Of course, an employer may also become liable for negligent hiring where it actually obtains information showing that an applicant was unfit for hiring, but nonetheless hires or retains the employee despite its awareness of this information. For example, the failure of a city personnel department to reexamine an employee's fitness, after it received a police report showing that the employee had a criminal record, resulted in a $3.5 million jury award against the municipality that employed the worker.[13]

2. Fraud and Misrepresentation

During the course of recruiting and hiring applicants for a particular job, employers typically seek to "sell" the positive aspects of the job in question. In addition, employers frequently make promises regarding compensation, benefits, and other terms and conditions of employment to induce applicants to accept offers of employment. These efforts by employers, first to persuade applicants to consider a particular job, and then to accept a job offer, have led to the filing of numerous lawsuits for fraud and misrepresentation.

Claims of fraud and misrepresentation arising from the recruiting and hiring process can be based on (1) false statements of *existing facts* or (2) false promises of *future events*. Specific examples of the former include:

- misrepresentations that an employer was in good economic condition when in fact it was experiencing serious financial difficulties,[14]
- misleading statements implying that an employer has been profitable over a sustained period of time when in fact it had only been profitable for the past two months after many months of losses,[15] and
- misrepresentations that an employer's relationship with its sole supplier was good when in fact it was troubled.[16]

Examples of the latter include false promises relating to bonuses,[17] future salary,[18] lengthy periods of employment,[19] preferred hours of work,[20] permanency of employment,[21] duties of the job,[22] relocation benefits,[23] profit-sharing plans,[24] and pension benefits.[25]

Misrepresentations made during the recruiting and hiring process may be actionable regardless of whether they were intentionally or negligently uttered.[26] In addition, even if an employee is unable to prove that an employer committed fraud or negligent misrepresentation in connection with a false promise, the employee may still recover damages for breach of contract.[27]

B. Workplace Environments

Employees have become increasingly concerned about the environment in which they work. This concern has transcended the more traditional workplace health and safety issues and embraced broader issues of workplace environment such as sexual harassment, hostile work environments, and smoking in the workplace. Employees have effectively used the law of torts to recover damages for physical injuries and emotional harm caused by these and other forms of workplace ills.

1. Sexual Harassment

Initially, legal actions involving sexual harassment were brought only under Title VII and state antidiscrimination laws. Both male and female employees who feel they have been subjected to sexual harassment have now begun to either append a tort claim to a Title VII or state civil rights lawsuit, or commence an action solely under one or more tort theories of liability. Each of the torts applicable to allegations of sexual harassment is discussed below.

a. Negligent Retention

Employers are susceptible to lawsuits for negligent retention whenever they become aware of complaints of sexual harassment but nonetheless retain the harassing employee or take no other corrective action. For example, in both *Brown v. Burlington Industries*[28] and *Cox v. Brazo*,[29] female employees were subjected to unwelcome physical advances from male supervisors. In both instances, the women complained to management, but the employer failed to take any steps to prevent the harassment from continuing. The female employees in both cases sued their employers for negligent retention, and each recovered damages based on the employer's breach of its duty not to retain a supervisor who had harassed a subordinate.

b. Negligent Failure to Supervise and Train Managers

Even where a female employee fails to advise management that her supervisor is engaging in sexual harassment, an employer may still be liable for damages under a slightly different theory of negligence.

In *Davis v. Utah Power & Light*,[30] a female employee who experienced unwelcome sexual harassment and physical contact by her manager sued her employer for negligently failing to supervise the manager and train him not to violate the laws prohibiting sexual harassment. The court permitted the employee to pursue her negligence claim, concluding that employers have a duty to provide a reasonable amount of training and supervision to supervisory employees to ensure they carry out their duties without endangering their subordinates. According to the court, this duty includes training and supervision as to the prohibited practice of sexual harassment.

c. Defamation

Whenever an employer is presented with a claim of sexual harassment, the employer should be aware that it is not only exposed to potential liability to the harassed employee, but also runs the risk of a lawsuit for defamation by the alleged harasser.

In *Gonzalez v. CNA Insurance Co.*,[31] a court permitted an accused harasser to maintain an action for defamation against his employer where he alleged that his employer falsely accused him of sexual harassment, terminated him for that false reason, and then announced to his fellow employees that he had engaged in sexual harassment. The court concluded that although the employer enjoyed a qualified privilege to utter a defamatory statement about the supervisor's alleged misconduct, the privilege could be lost by widespread publication of the defamatory communication to workers who had no interest in the subject of the communication.

d. Infliction of Emotional Distress

Sexual harassment in the workplace may also lead to claims for intentional infliction of emotional distress. Such claims have usually resulted in liability where repeated acts of sexual harassment create a distressing work environment for the harassed employees.

For example, in *Shrout v. Black Clawson Co.*,[32] a female employee who was subjected to a protracted campaign of sexual harassment by her supervisor after she terminated their voluntary, consensual sexual affair was awarded $125,000 in damages for intentional infliction. Similarly, in *Ford v. Revlon, Inc.*,[33] a female employee who was sexually harassed by her manager was awarded $100,000 in punitive damages for intentional infliction of emotional distress where her employer failed to take any action to halt the harassment after she had complained to management.

e. Invasion of Privacy

Unwelcome inquiries about an employee's sex life may form the basis of a claim for invasion of privacy. In *Phillips v. Smalley Maintenance Services*,[34] a female employee recovered damages from an employer where the company president invaded the employee's interest in her psychological seclusion by constantly asking her "what positions" she used with her husband. And in *Waltman v. International Paper Co.*[35] a court held that a female employee who had been subjected to offensive contact by a male co-worker, including touching her breasts and placing an air hose between her legs, could maintain an action for invasion of privacy based on her "right to be let alone."

f. Assault and Battery

Allegations of sexual harassment in the workplace frequently lead to claims for assault and battery. The tort of battery can be asserted whenever the sexual harassment involves an offensive touching of the harassed employee. Courts have permitted battery claims to be maintained where a bisexual judge kissed his male court reporter on the lips;[36] where a female employee was subjected to a co-worker's touching of her breasts;[37] where a male supervisor made a practice of "rubbing up against" a female employee in the office;[38] where a male supervisor touched a female employee's buttocks;[39] and where a male employee was grabbed between the legs by a male co-worker, who also jumped on top of and tried to mount him.[40]

In each of those cases (except the one involving the bisexual judge), the sexually offensive conduct was reported to management, but no action was taken to abate the harassment. In contrast, where an employer took remedial action promptly after being notified of an allegation of sexual harassment, the employee's tort claim for assault and battery was dismissed.[41]

g. Malicious Prosecution

Claims of sexual harassment in the workplace can even lead to lawsuits by the alleged harasser for malicious prosecution. In *Foley v. Polaroid Corp.*,[42] a male employee who was alleged to have sexually assaulted a female co-worker at work brought a malicious prosecution claim against his employer based on the employer's conduct in initiating the filing of charges against him. The jury returned a $1.5 million verdict against the employer on the malicious prosecution claim, but the verdict was reversed on appeal. The appellate court held that an employer would not be liable for malicious prosecution if it acted in good-faith reliance on the accuser's allegation of sexual assault.

2. Other Forms of Workplace Harassment

Like sexual harassment, employees have filed tort claims seeking damages for a variety of other forms of workplace harassment. The tort most frequently asserted in response to such harassment is intentional infliction of emotional distress. Employees who have been subjected to workplace harassment have also brought claims for invasion of privacy, negligent infliction of emotional distress, battery, and violations of the RICO Act. And, of course, like the plaintiffs in the sexual harassment cases summarized in Part One of this book, employees who have been subjected to other forms of workplace harassment can also seek relief, when the circumstances so dictate, for a number of other torts including negligent retention, negligent failure to supervise and train managers, defamation, and malicious prosecution.

a. Intentional Infliction of Emotional Distress

The tort of intentional infliction of emotional distress is often asserted by employees in response to actions of workplace harassment. As discussed in Chapter 4, to maintain a claim for intentional infliction of emotional distress, an employee must establish that the conduct of the employer was "outrageous."

In *Wilson v. Monarch Paper Co.*,[43] a senior vice president recovered $3.1 million against his employer where he was "totally humiliated" by being demoted from his high-ranking position to a job requiring him to perform janitorial services at work. In addition, he was given the "silent treatment" by the new president, harassed by his new supervisor, and called a "goldbrick" and an "old man." Similarly, in *Dean v. Ford Motor Credit Co.*,[44] a federal appellate court upheld a jury award of $275,000 in damages against an employer based on a supervisor's conduct of planting checks in a female employee's purse to make it appear that she was a thief.

The courts have permitted a number of other tort claims seeking relief for intentional infliction of emotional distress, including a claim that a supervisor purposely assigned a known acrophobic photographer to perform high-rise work.[45] In another case a supervisor tried to "get rid of" an employee by threatening to reduce his hours of work and scheduling him to work on the "graveyard" shift, which interfered with the employee's sabbath observance.[46] The courts have also upheld claims for intentional infliction where an employee was placed in job assignments for which he was not trained and was repeatedly ridiculed and harassed,[47] and where a supervisor intentionally and maliciously used racial slurs and insults because he "did not like Blacks."[48]

b. Negligent Infliction of Emotional Distress

An employee need not prove that an employer's conduct was outrageous in order to recover damages for emotional distress. Rather, in many jurisdictions the employee need only prove that he or she suffered severe emotional distress resulting from the negligence of the employer.

For example, in *Payne v. General Motors Corp.*,[49] the court held that an African-American employee could maintain an action for *negligent* infliction of emotional distress where he allegedly suffered from major depression as a result of the employer's racial harassment and discrimination at work. Such claims for negligent infliction, however, may be vulnerable to the employer's defense that the employee's sole remedy for this type of negligence is under the state workers' compensation law.[50]

c. Invasion of Privacy

Employers are also subject to invasion of privacy claims where, as part of a course of harassment, they place employees, or an employee's spouse, in a highly objectionable false light. In *Keehr v. Consolidated Freightways*,[51] a jury awarded damages to the wife of an employee for invasion of privacy where the employee's supervisor stated in a loud and extremely crude manner that he had "heard that the other night [your] wife was [engaging in oral sex]" with three other workers. The employee had contended that the remark was part of an intended plan by management to harass workers, such as himself, who had challenged work rules and working conditions on the job.

d. Battery

Workplace harassment that results in offensive physical contact may also be actionable under the tort of battery. In *Surrency v. Harbison*,[52] a grievance committee chairperson was harassed at work as part of a scheme instigated by the employer to intimidate him because of his challenge to the employer's new set of work rules. Part of the harassment involved an incident where the grievance committee chairman was struck in the head and back by a piece of heavy machinery. The grievance committee chairman sued his employer for battery and a jury awarded him $120,000 in actual and punitive damages. The award was reduced to $80,000 by the trial court, but was upheld on appeal.

e. RICO

Though not technically a tort, claims of workplace harassment may also subject an employer to liability under the Racketeer Influenced and Corrupt Organizations Act (RICO). In one such case, *Hunt v. Weatherbee*,[53] a court held that a female carpenter could maintain a RICO action against her employer and the union that represented her where agents of the union and the employer assaulted and harassed her and then threatened her with physical injury if she did not withdraw her criminal assault charges against her assailant and "contribute" to the union's political action campaign.

3. Smoking in the Workplace

In response to growing employee concerns about the effects of ambient smoke on the health of nonsmoking employees, many employers have voluntarily promulgated policies to limit smoking in the workplace. In addition, many states, counties, and municipalities have enacted legislation to limit smoking at work. A number of nonsmoking employees have also filed lawsuits against their employers under at least two theories of tort liability.

In *McCarthy v. State*,[54] a court recognized the tort of negligent failure to provide a reasonably smoke-free workplace. The court held that an employer has an affirmative and continuing duty to provide all employees with a reasonably safe place to work, which includes an obligation to provide a working environment reasonably free from tobacco smoke pollution.

In *Carroll v. Tennessee Valley Authority*,[55] a nonsmoking employee filed a lawsuit against her employer for intentional infliction of emotional distress and negligence. The court held that an employer may be liable to an employee for intentional infliction where, after the employee repeatedly complained about the deleterious effect of ambient smoke on her health, her supervisor ignored her requests for a smoke-free environment, told fellow workers about her smoke complaints, gave her poor performance ratings, and verbally harassed her in front of co-workers. The court, however, dismissed her claim for negligent failure to maintain a smoke-free work environment, concluding that such claims of workplace negligence are barred by the exclusive remedy provisions of the state workers' compensation law.

4. Exposure to Toxins and Other Workplace Dangers

Employees have become increasingly concerned about how their health and safety may be at risk by on-the-job exposure to toxins and other workplace dangers. While federal laws, such as the Occupational Safety and Health Act (OSHA), as well as state laws governing toxic substances and workplace dangers, afford a large measure of protection for workers, employees have also resorted to tort actions on occasion to supplement their relief under those safety laws and applicable workers' compensation acts.

a. Assault and Battery

The torts of assault and battery have been used by employees to seek relief from exposure to workplace toxins. In two cases summarized in Chapter 6 of this book, courts permitted employees to maintain lawsuits for assault and battery where there was evidence presented that the employer *intentionally* exposed the employees to toxic substances at work.

In *Gulden v. Crown Zellerbach Corp.*,[56] two temporary employees were directed to clean up a spill that, unknown to them, contained toxic levels of PCBs. The two employees, who were not provided with protective clothing when they cleaned up the spill, filed an action for battery against the employer. The court held that the employees could maintain their action for battery because there was some evidence presented that the employer knew that the level of PCBs in the spilled material far exceeded the levels permitted by EPA standards, but nonetheless assigned the cleanup work to the two temporary employees instead of contracting with a toxic spill cleanup specialist. The court concluded that the employees could recover damages for battery if they could prove at trial that the employer intentionally exposed them to toxic levels of PCBs.

A similar result was reached in *Beauchamp v. Dow Chemical Co.*,[57] where an employee claimed that his employer intentionally assaulted him through exposure to "agent orange." The court held that if the employee could show that the employer knew that workplace injury or damage was substantially certain to result, then the state workers' compensation law would not provide the employee's exclusive remedy. Instead, the employee could maintain a tort claim for battery.

b. Fraud and Misrepresentation

Exposure to workplace toxins can also lead to employee claims for fraudulent concealment. In *Millison v. E.I. du Pont de Nemours & Co.*,[58] an appellate court upheld a $1.3 million jury award for fraud in favor of several employees who claimed that their employer and its company physician concealed from the employees their X-ray results showing the presence of asbestosis-related symptoms, thereby causing the aggravation of their medical conditions.

A comparable holding was reached in *Gulden v. Crown Zellerbach Corp.*,[59] where the appellate court held that two employees could proceed with their fraudulent concealment claims if they could prove that the employer's failure to warn them of the risks involved in cleaning up PCBs constituted a fraudulent omission upon which the employees relied to their detriment by agreeing to perform hazardous work for less than its true value.

c. Negligent Failure to Warn

Two cases summarized in Chapter 1 of this book involve claims that an employer failed to warn employees about known risks of harm posed by other workers. In *Smith v. National Railroad Passenger Corp.*,[60] a federal appellate court upheld a $3.5 million jury verdict based on the employer's negligent failure to warn a supervisor about an employee's known violent propensities. The employee shot the supervisor in the leg with a shotgun after the supervisor reprimanded the employee for lateness. The supervisor asserted that if he had been forewarned of the employee's known violent tendencies, he could have taken actions to avoid injury. The $3.5 million award was affirmed on appeal.

In contrast, in *Paroline v. Unisys Corp.*,[61] a court dismissed a female employee's claim for negligent failure to warn her about her supervisor's allegedly offensive and harassing behavior, holding that such a cause of action does not exist in Virginia.

C. Employee Disabilities

Properly dealing with employee disabilities is one of the most vexing problems in the employee relations field today. Not only must employers comply with federal and state disability discrimination laws, they must also be sensitive to a host of potential tort claims that can be filed by employees who suffer from, or who are regarded as suffering from, drug and alcohol addiction, AIDS, mental illness, and other medical conditions. Even an employee's referral to an employee assistance program has been the subject of tort actions against employers.

Each of the various torts that were the subject of cases summarized in Part One of this book and that pertain in some fashion to employee disabilities are reviewed below.

1. Drug and Alcohol Abuse

Issues relating to the use and abuse of drugs and alcohol and employer efforts to control such workplace ills have led to employee tort claims against employers for negligence, defamation, and invasion of privacy. These three torts, however, are by no means the only ones that may be asserted by employees in the disability context.

For example, it is conceivable that employees who are promised that they would not be discharged if they voluntarily disclosed that they had a drug addiction could assert a claim for fraud or misrepresentation if they were later terminated by their employers. And employers who file criminal charges against employees based on the alleged use of drugs at work face the prospect of malicious prosecution lawsuits if the employees are ultimately acquitted of the charges.

a. Negligent Retention and Other Negligence Theories of Tort Recovery

Alcohol abuse has been the subject of at least one case involving a claim for negligent retention. In *Redd v. Product Development Corp.*,[62] a delivery company that allegedly knew or should have known of a driver's drug and alcohol problem settled a negligent retention suit for $16 million. Although the employee had shown a pattern of drug and alcohol abuse, the employer allowed him to continue to drive one of the company's trucks—until the employee struck a pedestrian one day while driving his vehicle after consuming a pint of vodka.

A negligence claim was also brought against an employer by a motorcyclist who was injured by an employee after the employee became intoxicated at an employer-hosted party and was permitted to drive his own car home. In *Dickinson v. Edwards*,[63] the motorcyclist filed a lawsuit asserting a number of different claims for relief, including the negligent furnishing of alcohol to an intoxicated employee. The court held that where an employer serves alcohol at a company-sponsored party to an employee who the company knows or should have known was intoxicated, a person injured by the employee may recover damages from the employee's employer under the tort of negligence.

b. Defamation

Termination of employees for alleged drug abuse or the alleged sale of drugs has led to several lawsuits for defamation. In *Houston Belt & Terminal Railway v. Wherry*,[64] a jury rendered a $200,000 verdict against an employer for communicating a "false positive" drug test result. Another employer suffered a similar fate in *Loughry v. Lincoln First Bank*,[65] where a jury assessed damages against the employer for making false accusations that an employee had engaged in drug use.

In *LaScala v. D'Angelo*,[66] however, a court ruled in favor of an employer that had made false accusations of drug use against two employees where the employee failed to show that the employer acted with malice or otherwise lost its qualified privilege.[67]

Employees who are terminated for alcohol abuse have also brought claims against their employers for defamation. For example, in *Benassi v. Georgia-Pacific*,[68] a jury rendered a verdict of $350,000 in damages against an employer where the employee's supervisor falsely stated at a meeting of employees that the employee had been fired for drunkenness.

c. Invasion of Privacy

Claims for invasion of privacy have been asserted against employers for making inquiries into an employee's use of drugs. While drug abuse in the workplace is a matter of vital employer interest, certain types of inquiries have been held to be invasions of privacy.

In *O'Brien v. Papa Gino's of America*,[69] an employee brought an invasion of privacy lawsuit against his employer based on the employer's questions, posed during a polygraph exam, about past drug use by the employee as well as other private matters unrelated to his job performance. A jury rendered a verdict of $398,000 in damages against the employer, which was upheld on appeal.

In another case, *Neal v. Corning Glass Works Corp.*,[70] an employee was permitted to maintain a claim for invasion of privacy against his employer where, without the employee's consent, the employer requested and obtained a drug screen from a private physician who examined the employee in the emergency room of a local hospital. The court held that although an employer has a valid and legitimate interest in determining whether an employee is fit for work, it cannot seek to achieve that lawful objective by means involving an unwarranted and unreasonable intrusion into an employee's private affairs.

Invasion of privacy claims have also been asserted against employers who have attempted to secure information about an employee's problem with alcohol. In *Love v. Southern Bell Telephone & Telegraph Co.*,[71] an employer terminated an employee based on information, which was improperly obtained by the employee's co-workers, about the employee's drinking problem. In *Love*, the employee's co-workers had entered his trailer without his consent and discovered an empty whiskey bottle on the floor. The employee filed an invasion of privacy claim and prevailed at trial and on appeal.

In contrast to the above cases, in *Trout v. Umatilla County School District*,[72] an appellate court reversed a $225,000 jury verdict against a school district where school board officials disclosed in interviews with the local news media that three high school teachers had been involved in a drunk-driving accident following a retirement party at which they had been drinking. In that case, the appellate court held that the disclosure of private facts about the teachers' consumption of alcohol during nonworking hours was justified, because the school district was campaigning to stop drinking and driving.

2. AIDS

While most AIDS litigation has involved claims of handicap and disability discrimination under federal, state, and local laws and executive orders, the AIDS epidemic has also produced a number of workplace tort claims in the past few years, including lawsuits for negligent hiring, defamation, and invasion of privacy.

a. Negligent Hiring

One of the most troubling legal issues faced by employers is the hiring and retention of employees with AIDS. In *Doe v. American Airlines*,[73] during an altercation at the departure gate, an airline passenger was bitten by a boarding agent who tested positive for the AIDS virus. The passenger, claiming to be living in fear for her life, sued the airline for $12 million. She contended that the airline had a duty to safeguard its passengers from health and safety risks, yet allowed the boarding agent, who it "knew or should have known ... had been exposed to a deadly virus and [was] a violent person," to remain on the job.

b. Defamation

A false accusation that an employee has AIDS is likely to lead to a claim for defamation. That is exactly what occurred in *Little v. Bryce*,[74] where, after an employee's supervisor was notified by a co-worker that the employee had AIDS, the supervisor gave the employee a choice of voluntarily resigning or being discharged for reasons of health. The appellate court, in a concurring opinion, concluded that the employer had lost its qualified privilege, when, among other things, the co-worker told the employee's supervisor that the *employee had* AIDS, even though the employee had merely stated to the co-worker that one doctor had speculated that his *roommate might* have AIDS.

c. Invasion of Privacy

In *Cronan v. New England Telephone Co.*,[75] an employee was asked by his supervisor why he was requesting permission to be absent for a medical appointment. The employee told his supervisor that he had been diagnosed as having AIDS Related Complex (ARC). The supervisor then disclosed that information to the employee's co-workers at a large group meeting. The employee sued his employer for invasion of privacy, contending that the supervisor's disclosure to his co-workers was not reasonably necessary to safeguard the best interests of the employer. The court denied the employer's motion to dismiss and permitted the employee to proceed further with his claim.

3. Other Illnesses

Although an employee's health may in certain circumstances be of vital interest to an employer, the disclosure of medical information about an employee on occasion may be actionable as an invasion of privacy. Further, an employer may even be held liable for negligent infliction of emotional distress where it disciplines, demotes, or terminates an employee in a manner that it knows will probably cause the employee to suffer physical or emotional distress.

a. Invasion of Privacy

Miller v. Motorola[76] is a case that illustrates the need for tight controls on the dissemination of purely private medical information about employees. In that case, a female employee confided in a company nurse that she had had a mastectomy and needed to undergo reconstructive surgery. The employee later learned from one of her co-workers that her medical condition was known to other employees at work. She then instituted a lawsuit against her employer for invasion of privacy. Although the lower court dismissed the employee's lawsuit, an appellate court reversed. It concluded that the employee was entitled to a jury trial on her claim that the disclosure of her medical condition violated her right to privacy.

Some employers have promulgated elaborate policies addressing the request for and disclosure of medical information about employees. *Bratt v. IBM*[77] demonstrates the need for employers to follow those rules and policies. In that case, an employee was permitted to proceed with his claim for invasion of privacy against his employer and supervisor for seeking, obtaining, and disclosing information from a physician about his mental health. The court held that although the employer had a legitimate interest in the employee's mental condition, its failure to follow its own regulations, which prohibited the request for and release of medical information about an employee without his or her consent, may result in liability for invasion of privacy.

b. Infliction of Emotional Distress

Claims for negligent infliction of emotional distress are particularly troubling for employers because they frequently involve routine employment decisions carried out without any intent to injure or harm the employee. The key to this type of case is recognizing that they are more likely to arise when a supervisor knows, or has reason to know, that the employee is particularly susceptible to physical or emotional distress.

In *Freeman v. Kansas State Network*,[78] a court permitted a television news anchorwoman to maintain a claim for negligent infliction of emotional distress where her employer, on the day she returned from the hospital following the birth of her second child, notified her that she was being terminated. She claimed that, as a result of the emotional distress she suffered from being terminated at that time, she became unable to lactate, which prevented her from breastfeeding her new baby.

In *Payne v. General Motors Corp.*,[79] a court held that an African-American engineer could maintain his claim for negligent infliction of emotional distress where his employer, who was allegedly aware that he was suffering from severe psychological problems, allegedly caused him to suffer "psychological trauma" because of discriminatory treatment he received from his supervisor at work.

Of course, where an employer *intentionally* causes an employee to suffer severe emotional distress as a result of a known medical condition, an employee may recover damages for *intentional* infliction of emotional distress—if the conduct of the employer is regarded as outrageous. Thus, in *Brown v. Ellis*,[80] a court permitted a photographer, who was known to suffer from acrophobia, to maintain an action for intentional infliction of emotional distress when his supervisor purposely assigned him to perform high-rise photography.

4. Employee Assistance Programs

In the past few years, more and more employers have endeavored to provide employees with medical and other types of counseling assistance to help deal with personal, psychological, and other problems. Improper use of an employee assistance program (EAP) has led to the filing of tort claims by employees. Although the only tort claims involving EAPs reported to date involve infliction of emotional distress, invasion of privacy, and false imprisonment, it is likely that in the future employees will file claims seeking relief under other tort theories as well.

a. Infliction of Emotional Distress

In *Wangen v. Knudson*,[81] an employee advised his supervisor that he had recently been hospitalized for depression after he began to drink in order to deal with his depression. The supervisor, following the recommendation of an EAP counselor, insisted that the employee enroll in an alcohol dependency program or be terminated from employment. At the time he tried to force the employee to enroll in the alcohol dependency program, the supervisor knew that the employee was taking medication for depression and was particularly susceptible to emotional distress. The employee, who was never diagnosed by his physician or a consulting psychiatrist as being an alcoholic, refused to enroll in the alcohol dependency program and was fired, resulting in a worsening of his depression. The employee sued the employer, his supervisor, and the company that employed the EAP counselor for intentional infliction of emotional distress. A jury awarded the employee $130,000 against all of the defendants jointly, and the verdict was upheld on appeal.

b. Invasion of Privacy

In *Bratt v. IBM*,[82] also discussed in section C.3.a. above, the physician who released the employee's medical information to his employer was under contract with the employer. The court not only permitted the employee to maintain his invasion of privacy claim against the employer and his supervisor, but also against the physician, who had disclosed the employee's medical information to his employer without his consent. The court held that despite the physician's contractual relationship with the employer, a duty of confidentiality arose where the employee had reason to believe that the physician-patient relationship had been established.

c. False Imprisonment

In perhaps one of the more creative attempts to introduce tort law into the area of employee relations, an employee who was required to attend a 24-hour-a-day drug rehabilitation program for several weeks filed a lawsuit for false imprisonment. In *Pettigrew v. Southern Pacific Transportation Co.*,[83] the employee claimed that his required attendance at the rehab program constituted an intentional act of confinement against his will. The court, however, disagreed with the theory adopted by counsel and granted the employer's motion for summary judgment.

D. Work Assignments, Performance Evaluations, Disciplinary Action, and Demotions

The basic, day-to-day management of an employer's human resources includes assigning work, scheduling shifts, evaluating employees, counseling and disciplining workers, and promoting and demoting them when appropriate. Many employees who believe they have been injured or damaged by improper human resource management have filed lawsuits against their employers. Most often, employees have used federal or state employment discrimination laws to challenge what they perceive as unfair work assignments, evaluations, disciplinary actions, or demotions. Some employees have also brought claims under various tort theories of recovery, including negligence, fraud, defamation, intentional infliction of emotional distress, and interference with contractual relations, as discussed below.

1. Negligent Performance Evaluations

In *Chamberlain v. Bissell, Inc.*,[84] a court held that an employer was liable for negligently performing a job performance evaluation. Chamberlain was a long-term manager who had been terminated for poor attitude, lack of leadership, and lack of cooperation. Although these weaknesses had been discussed with him during his annual evaluation, his superior never disclosed to him that the company was contemplating his discharge if his performance did not dramatically improve. The court concluded that based on language in the employee handbook that annual performance evaluations were intended to benefit employees, the employer had a duty to use ordinary and reasonable care in performing annual evaluations. The court held that the employer breached that duty by failing to warn the manager that he might be terminated if his job performance did not improve dramatically.

In *Loftis v. G.T. Products*,[85] however, a court dismissed a similar claim of negligent performance evaluation, concluding that such a claim can only be maintained if the employee alleges that the employer breached a duty of care distinct from a contractual duty found in an employee handbook. Aside from *Chamberlain* and *Loftis*, there have been few reported cases dealing with the issue of negligent performance evaluations.

2. Fraud and Misrepresentation

There are at least two types of fraud cases that have arisen so far with respect to work assignments: (1) claims of false promises pertaining to job responsibilities, work assignments, and shifts; and (2) claims that an employee was directed to engage in fraudulent business practices.

An example of a fraud claim involving false promises pertaining to work assignments is *Della Croce v. General Electric Co.*[86] In that case, a court permitted an employee to maintain a cause of action for fraud where the employee accepted a transfer based on a promise that her job assignments would include the use of innovative word processing equipment. Likewise, in *Albrant v. Sterling Furniture Co.*,[87] an appellate court reinstated a claim for fraud where an employee accepted a job offer based on the employer's unfulfilled promise that she would not be assigned to work the evening shift.

An example of a claim involving fraudulent business practices is *Russ v. TRW*.[88] In that case, an employee was directed by his superiors to engage in fraudulent pricing practices with respect to federal government contracts. He was told that the pricing practices were permissible because that was the only way that government contractors could ensure a "fair profit." His employer, though, terminated him for engaging in such practices, and then supplied his name to federal law enforcement authorities, who ultimately granted him immunity from prosecution. The employee brought an action against his employer for fraud, and a jury awarded him $600,000 in damages. An appellate court affirmed the verdict, holding that an employee may recover for fraud where he or she engages in conduct, based on the false representations of an employer, that expose the employee to potential criminal liability.

3. Defamation

Employees who have received unfavorable evaluations and disciplinary warnings have brought lawsuits for defamation against their employers. In *Agriss v. Roadway Express*,[89] an employee was permitted to maintain his defamation claim where he alleged that his employer improperly disseminated to his co-workers a warning letter that was placed in his personnel file and that falsely accused him of violating company policy by "opening company mail."

But in *McCone v. New England Telephone & Telegraph Co.*,[90] a court dismissed a defamation claim by an employee who alleged that his employer defamed him by disseminating his subpar performance evaluation to other managers of the employer. The court held that the dissemination of a negative performance evaluation to other company managers served the legitimate interest of the employer in determining the fitness of its employees to perform their jobs.

4. Infliction of Emotional Distress

Supervisors who exercise their authority in an abusive manner when they assign work, schedule shifts, demote employees, and prepare performance evaluations may subject their employers to liability for intentional infliction of emotional distress.

Courts have permitted intentional infliction cases to proceed to trial where:

- an employer intentionally humiliated a senior executive by demoting him to a job requiring him to clean up the cafeteria and perform other janitorial jobs;[91]
- a supervisor threatened to reduce an employee's work hours and intentionally scheduled him for "graveyard" and other shifts that conflicted with his known sabbath observance;[92]
- a union intentionally referred one of its members to undesirable jobs and to jobs for which the employee was not qualified;[93]
- a male supervisor engaged in a persistent campaign of sexual harassment against a female employee, including withholding performance evaluations and salary reviews;[94]
- a supervisor intentionally placed an employee in job assignments for which he was not trained and purposely lowered his performance evaluation;[95] and
- a supervisor purposely assigned an employee to perform a job requiring him to work at heights, where the superior knew that the employee had a medically diagnosed fear of high places.[96]

5. Interference With Contractual Relations

Where supervisors or managers intentionally refuse to assign an employee to perform the type of work the employee was hired or contracted to perform, the supervisor may be subject to liability for interference with contractual relations. In *Trimble v. City of Denver*,[97] a municipal hospital manager was held personally liable in damages for interference where he refused to assign a physician to work in the area of practice for which he had been retained, thereby preventing him from performing his obligations under his agreement with the city.

E. Investigating Workplace Misconduct

Conducting investigations of workplace misconduct is a critical function of management. Typically, employers use traditional investigatory techniques, such as interrogations, to investigate workplace misconduct. Employers have also used polygraph examinations to investigate workplace misconduct.

While is it critical for employers to promptly investigate alleged instances of employee misconduct, a hasty, incomplete, or improperly conducted investigation can substantially increase the potential for employer liability. Employees have come to expect and demand a measure of due process, fairness, and objectivity from their employers during investigations of workplace misconduct. Employees who feel that they have been unjustly accused or abused by the investigative process have shown an increased willingness to sue their employers under one or more theories of tort liability. It is not surprising, given the nature of such investigations, that a broad range of tort theories has been advanced in this area, including negligent hiring and retention, fraud and misrepresentation, defamation, infliction of emotional distress, invasion of privacy, assault and battery, false imprisonment, and malicious prosecution.

This section examines the application of these torts to workplace investigations of the following categories of employee misconduct: employee theft, drug and alcohol abuse, and sexual harassment.

1. Employee Theft

Although workplace theft frequently involves criminal conduct, employers rarely have at their disposal the resources and expertise with which law enforcement authorities are equipped. Instead, employers have frequently used investigative techniques and procedures that are not only wholly inadequate but can also, in certain circumstances, be regarded as abusive. This has led to the filing of employee lawsuits for negligent polygraph administration, defamation, infliction of emotional distress, assault and battery, false imprisonment, and malicious prosecution. In addition, where an employer retaliates against employees who cooperate in workplace investigations despite assurances of nonretaliation, an action for fraud may be asserted. Each of the torts applicable to workplace investigations is addressed below.

a. Negligent Polygraph Administration

Although the use of the polygraph examination has been limited and regulated by the federal Employee Polygraph Protection Act as well as laws in some states (see Appendix B), polygraph examinations are generally permitted in connection with employer investigations of workplace theft. The permissible use of polygraph examinations has, however, led to lawsuits for negligent administration of the test. State courts are currently divided on the validity of this cause of action, but a few states to date have recognized negligent polygraph examination as a valid legal claim.

For example, in *Mechanics Lumber Co. v. Smith*,[98] an employee was permitted to recover damages from his employer when the employer terminated him in reliance on the results of a polygraph exam that was administered despite notification from the employee that he suffered from multiple sclerosis and was taking prescription medication for his illness.

b. Fraud and Misrepresentation

In *Mueller v. Union Pacific Railroad*,[99] four employees of a railroad were asked to provide information to the railroad's internal auditing department in connection with an investigation of the theft of railroad funds and services allegedly stolen by the employees' supervisors. After furnishing the investigators with information about the thefts, each of the employees lost their jobs or were transferred to other positions, despite assurances from the investigators that "no one could lose their jobs" if they cooperated in the investigation. The employees brought an action against the railroad for fraud, and an appellate court upheld their right to proceed to trial on such claims.

c. Defamation

Defamation claims are a genuine concern for employers whenever they conduct investigations of workplace theft and other financial irregularities. For example, in *Howcroft v. Mountain States Telephone & Telegraph Co.*,[100] a court permitted an employee, who was discharged for allegedly using a corporate credit card for personal use, to present his defamation claim to a jury. The court held that the employee's supervisor may have abused the employer's qualified privilege by failing to investigate the credit card incident thoroughly and failing to verify the facts before communicating to senior-level management that the employee had intended to defraud his employer.

Similarly, in *Mechanics Lumber Co. v. Smith*,[101] discussed in section E.1.a. above, the court not only permitted an employee to proceed with his action for negligent polygraph administration but also with his claim for defamation. The court held that defamatory statements based on the questionable results of the polygraph examination could lead to employer liability for defamation.

d. Infliction of Emotional Distress

Abusive and intimidating investigation techniques have led to a number of claims for intentional infliction of emotional distress, many of which have resulted in jury awards against employers.

In *Hall v. May Department Stores Co.*,[102] an employee recovered compensatory damages against her employer where the employer's security director punctuated his investigation of workplace theft with threats of criminal prosecution, unfounded allegations of theft, and references to imprisonment; and then placed the employee under constant surveillance.

In *Moniodis v. Cook*,[103] a jury award of $1.3 million was upheld on appeal where an employer, in connection with its investigation of inventory shortages, first threatened an employee that her hours would be reduced, then tried to force her to resign, and finally fired her after she refused to take an illegal polygraph examination. In addition, the courts have permitted employees to proceed to trial with claims that they suffered severe emotional distress after being required to take polygraph examinations that were prohibited by law.[104]

e. Invasion of Privacy

Searches of employee lockers during the course of an investigation of employee misconduct can subject an employer to an action for invasion of privacy. In *K-Mart Corp. v. Trotti*,[105] the employer searched an employee's locker, on which she had placed her own lock, as part of a general search for goods stolen from the store. A jury awarded the employee over $100,000 in actual and punitive damages. An appellate court upheld the award, concluding that the mere suspicion that an unidentified employee had stolen goods from the employer was insufficient to justify the search of an employee's locker without the employee's consent, particularly where the employee had a reasonable expectation that the locker and its contents would be free from intrusion based on the fact that she had used her own lock on the locker.

f. Assault and Battery

Workplace investigations in which employees are placed in apprehension of physical harm or are actually harmed by employer representatives can lead to claims for assault and battery. In *Singer Shop-Rite, Inc. v. Rangel*,[106] an employee recovered damages for assault and battery where the employee was physically assaulted by two company investigators during an investigation into the disappearance of company funds.

In *Leahy v. Federal Express Corp.*,[107] a jury found that a company investigator placed two employees in apprehension of physical harm by pulling back his jacket to reveal a gun he was carrying and pushing one employee backward when he tried to leave the room where the investigation was being conducted. The jury awarded the employees $50,000 in damages. The trial court, however, overturned the verdict, concluding that the employees had failed to introduce any evidence that their fears were genuine.

g. False Imprisonment

The investigatory process frequently requires some sort of private interview between management and the employee. If, however, an employee is detained without consent or the employee's movement is restrained, the employer may be liable for false imprisonment. This restraint need not be physical, but can be as simple as a loud command to sit down or be the result of mental or physical intimidation, as discussed in more detail in Chapter 8.

In *DeAngelis v. Jamesway Department Store*,[108] an employee was awarded $110,000 for false imprisonment where the employer's loss prevention manager subjected her to an intensive four-hour interrogation and used physical intimidation to detain her. Similarly, in *Redican v. K-Mart Corp.*,[109] two employees were awarded $100,000 for false imprisonment where they were subjected to an abusive detention and then involuntarily escorted to a police station. And in *Tumbarella v. Kroger Co.*,[110] an employee was permitted to present her false imprisonment claim to a jury where company security officers threatened her with prosecution and made menacing gestures to her that gave her the impression that she was in custody.

h. Malicious Prosecution

At the conclusion of an investigation of workplace misconduct, some employers have filed or initiated criminal charges or commenced civil proceedings against employees suspected of theft. Such conduct by an employer, however, can lead to actions by an affected employee for malicious prosecution, especially where the civil or criminal proceedings were initiated without probable cause. The institution of civil proceedings and criminal charges is treated in more detail in section G. below.

2. Drug and Alcohol Abuse

Substance abuse in the workplace has become one of the most urgent problems facing employers in both the public and private sectors. Investigating the sale or use of drugs in the workplace, along with the use of alcohol during working time, has led to a number of employee tort claims against employers, including claims for defamation, infliction of emotional distress, and invasion of privacy.

a. Defamation

Employees have brought a number of defamation claims against employers based on false accusations of drug and alcohol abuse. Many of those claims are based on inadequate or careless investigative procedures.

For example, in *Houston Belt & Terminal Railway v. Wherry*,[111] a personnel manager reported to officers of the employer that an employee had tested positive for methadone, even though the drug test showed only a "trace" of methadone and the testing physician had advised him that a "trace" meant only that it was *possible* that the employee was a methadone or heroin user. After a second test showed that the first was a "false positive," the director of labor relations nonetheless advised third parties that "traces of methadone were present in [the employee's] system." In his action for defamation against the employer, the personnel manager, and the director of industrial relations, the employee was awarded $200,000 in damages. The award was upheld on appeal.

An employer that falsely accused an employee of illegal drug use during an investigative interview was assessed compensatory damages in *Loughry v. Lincoln First Bank*.[112] In that case, the court held that while defamatory statements made at an investigatory meeting are subject to a qualified privilege, the privilege will be lost if the purpose of the defamatory statements was to injure the employee's career.

False accusations of alcohol abuse can also lead to claims for defamation. In *Benassi v. Georgia-Pacific*,[113] an employer was assessed $350,000 in damages for falsely accusing and terminating an employee for drunkenness and misbehavior at a public bar in the presence of other employees who were together on a business trip. The employee's supervisor had relied on an anonymous letter describing the employee as drunk, had never spoken to the accused employee about the alleged incident at the bar, and had disregarded statements by the employee's co-workers that he was not drunk and had not acted improperly.

b. Infliction of Emotional Distress

The use of unreasonable drug testing techniques has led to the filing of tort claims by employees. In *Kelley v. Schlumberger Technology Corp.*,[114] an employee brought a claim for negligent infliction of emotional distress against his employer for requiring him to provide a urine specimen while under the direct observation of a company representative. Even though the employee tested positive for marijuana, he nonetheless recovered $125,000 in damages on his negligent infliction claim.

c. Invasion of Privacy

Investigations regarding the use of drugs in the workplace can also result in liability for invasion of privacy. In *O'Brien v. Papa Gino's of America*,[115] an employer was held liable for $398,000 in damages where it inquired into matters beyond the use of drugs in the workplace, including the employee's past use of drugs and other private matters unrelated to his employment.

3. Sexual Harassment

Every time an employer investigates a charge of sexual harassment, it faces a potential lawsuit not only by the employee who was allegedly harassed but also by the accused harasser in an action for defamation.

In *Gonzalez v. CNA Insurance Co.*,[116] a supervisor brought an action for defamation against his employer after he was accused of sexually harassing a female employee by touching her offensively and making sexual advances. The employer terminated the supervisor and advised his fellow employees that he had been discharged for sexual harassment. A court permitted the employee to present his claim for defamation to a jury, holding that an employer may lose its qualified privilege to defame the employee by publication of the supervisor's alleged sexual harassment to other company workers.

In *Foley v. Polaroid Corp.*,[117] a male employee was accused by investigators of sexually assaulting a female co-worker. Thereafter, the employer initiated the filing of criminal charges against the male employee, who was later acquitted of all charges. The male employee filed an action for defamation and several other tort claims. A jury awarded him $1 million on his defamation claim, but an appellate court reversed, holding that the employer did not abuse its qualified privilege by relying on the female co-worker's allegations.

F. Termination and Retention of Employees

The termination and retention of employees is a breeding ground for workplace torts. Almost all workplace torts are implicated by various management decisions to sever or continue the employment relationship.

1. Termination of Employment

One of the most difficult and unpleasant aspects of employee management is the termination of employees. The process of employee termination is stressful for both the employer and the employee.

While termination decisions are frequently challenged by employees in actions for employment discrimination or wrongful discharge, employees are also using tort theories to seek damages for injury or harm suffered as a result of their terminations. The torts most often encountered by employers with respect to involuntary terminations are fraud and misrepresentation, defamation, infliction of emotional distress, and interference with contractual relations. Claims have also been asserted for invasion of privacy and false imprisonment, as well as under the RICO Act.

In addition to terminations, employees have brought tort claims against employers arising out of voluntary resignations. Such claims are usually brought under the tort of fraud.

a. Fraud and Misrepresentation

Claims of fraud and misrepresentation have been asserted occasionally in connection with an employee's termination from employment. For example, in *Boivin v. Jones & Vining, Inc.*,[118] an employer was held liable for fraud where it terminated a 57-year-old employee after less than a year's employment, where its vice president had promised to employ him until he was at least age 65. An appellate court affirmed a jury award of $110,000 in compensatory damages, holding that the vice president's failure to disclose to the employee that he had no authority to make such a promise constituted actionable fraud.

Employers may also be found liable for fraud in connection with their efforts to retain valued employees. In *Shebar v. Sanyo Business Systems*,[119] a court permitted a manager who was terminated by his employer to present his fraud claim to a jury where he alleged that his employer induced him to forgo another job offer and continue working for the employer by falsely assuring him that it would never fire a manager.

Claims for misrepresentation in connection with employee terminations need not be based on promises that are knowingly false when made; rather, innocent misrepresentations may suffice. In *D'Ulisse-Cupo v. Board of Directors*,[120] a court held that an employer may be liable for *negligent* misrepresentation where a representative of the employer who made unqualified assurances of continued employment *should have known* (and, hence, should have told the employee) that her continued employment was contingent on future need.

In addition, fraud claims have also been asserted by employees who were terminated after being told they had been hired as "permanent" replacements for striking workers. In *Belknap, Inc. v. Hale*[121] and *Verway v. Blincoe Packing Co.*,[122] the courts held that employees who were hired as strike replacements based on assurances that they would become "permanent" employees may recover damages from their employer if they are subsequently laid off or terminated once the strike has ended.

Employees have also asserted claims for fraud and negligent misrepresentation where they have *voluntarily resigned* their employment based on false representations by their employers. In *Sandler v. New York News*,[123] a court permitted an employee to maintain his claim for negligent misrepresentation where he based his acceptance of a "buyout" package on the employer's inflated estimate of his future monthly pension benefits. The court held that the employee may be entitled to damages from his former employer where the employer's pension manager, who miscalculated the benefit, should have known that his calculation was in error.

Similarly, in *Wells v. General Motors Corp.*,[124] 32 employees resigned their employment in exchange for substantial amounts of severance pay. They claimed that their employer fraudulently induced them to accept the severance pay offer by falsely promising that they would be eligible for reemployment. A court held that they could proceed with their fraud claims against their former employer.

b. Defamation

The most frequently asserted tort claim by employees is for defamation resulting from statements regarding the grounds for their terminations. And with the emergence of the doctrine of "compelled self-publication" (see Chapter 3, section C.), literally every termination for cause presents an employer with a potential lawsuit for defamation.

An employer is entitled to a qualified privilege to defame its employees. The ways by which an employer can lose this qualified privilege are addressed at length in Chapter 3.

While the grounds for termination that can be challenged by employees in an action for defamation are virtually endless, the cases summarized in Chapter 3 involve claims of defamation regarding the following reasons for termination:

- use of drugs;[125]
- personal use of a corporate credit card;[126]
- alcohol abuse;[127]
- theft of services;[128]
- theft of company property;[129]
- theft of company funds;[130]
- malicious mischief and destruction of employee property;[131]
- accepting cash gifts from customers;[132]
- falsifying sales records,[133] timesheets,[134] and expense reports;[135]
- sexual harassment[136] and sexual assault;[137]
- "gross misconduct"[138] and "gross insubordination";[139]
- incompetence[140] and lack of capability;[141]

- failure to increase sales;[142]
- decline in sales;[143]
- falsification of employment application;[144]
- "not working" and "not doing a good job";[145]
- fraud and wrongful removal of company files;[146] and
- "cause so serious as to affect the company's integrity."[147]

c. Infliction of Emotional Distress

If an employer terminates an employee in an abusive, reckless, or discriminatory manner, the employer is susceptible to a claim for intentional infliction of emotional distress—even if the employee does not challenge the basis for the discharge. Similarly, an employer may be liable for *negligent* infliction of emotional distress if it *should have known* that the manner in which it terminated an employee would probably result in severe emotional distress.

Claims for intentional infliction have been asserted where an employer:

- fired workers in alphabetical order in order to force the employee responsible for company thefts to come forward and admit his or her wrongdoing;[148]
- created a false performance evaluation for use as a pretext to terminate an employee for his homosexual activities, then falsely advised the unemployment compensation board that the employee resigned (to prevent him from receiving unemployment benefits), and finally notified a headhunter that the employee was a homosexual (to prevent him from obtaining new employment);[149]
- "set up" an employee for discharge by sending her to an out-of-town seminar that only the employer knew had been canceled;[150]
- terminated an African-American employee for failing to disclose her past criminal record on her employment application over ten years earlier while retaining equally deceptive white employees who had lied on company documents about their past criminal records;[151]
- terminated an accountant for engaging in price-gouging of a governmental customer, even though the employee's superiors directed him to do so and told him it was an acceptable practice;[152]

- fired an employee after he took a polygraph examination despite assurances that he would not be terminated;[153] and
- blocked an employee's egress from his work station to prevent him from speaking to a representative from the employee relations department about his termination.[154]

Lawsuits for *negligent* infliction have been commenced by employees where an employer:

- notified a female employee, on the day she arrived home from the hospital after the birth of her second child, that she was being terminated, leading to her inability to breast-feed her child;[155] and
- terminated a long-term employee who suffered anger, depression, embarrassment, and shock as a result of his discharge.[156]

d. Invasion of Privacy

The manner in which an employer terminates an employee may convey an unfavorable impression to his or her co-workers or to others who actually observe the termination process. Where an employer places an employee in a false light in front of his or her co-workers, the employer is susceptible to an invasion of privacy claim for false light publicity.

In *Zechman v. Merrill Lynch, Pierce, Fenner & Smith*,[157] a court held that an employee could proceed with his false light publicity claim where, in plain view of his co-workers, his superiors notified him in his office that he was being fired, refused to allow him to speak to his staff, remained with him while he packed up his personal belongings, interrogated his fellow employees about entries in his travel and entertainment expense reports, and then escorted him out of the building—even though he had engaged in no misconduct or breach of ethics.

e. Interference With Contractual Relations

Employee terminations frequently result from the recommendation by a supervisor that an employee be terminated. When the terminated employee seeks to hold his or her supervisor personally responsible for the employee's discharge, a claim against the supervisor for interference with contractual relations can be asserted.

In *Sorrells v. Garfinkel's*,[158] an employee sued her supervisor for tortious interference. The case was tried to a jury, which returned a verdict against the supervisor personally, awarding the employee $165,000 in compensatory damages and $65,000 in punitive damages. Although the trial court reduced the total amount of damages assessed against the supervisor from $230,000 to $80,000, it refused to overturn the jury's finding of liability, concluding that the supervisor's harassment of the employee and malicious conduct culminating in the employee's termination warranted an award of damages against the supervisor for interference with her subordinate's at-will employment.

Similarly, in *Cronk v. Intermountain Rural Electric Association*,[159] a court permitted three employees to maintain their claim for tortious interference against the company's general manager, who had caused the termination of the three employees for being "disloyal" to him. The court held that where an officer of a corporation is motivated solely by a desire to interfere with an employee's relationship with an employer, the officer can be held personally liable for interference with contractual relations.

Employee terminations caused or initiated by *former* employers may also be the subject of claims for interference with contractual relations. In *In re IBP Confidential Business Documents Litigation*,[160] an executive recovered $1 million in damages for tortious interference where his former employer caused his new employer to fire him, and then effectively blacklisted him from any future employment. Likewise, in *Sterner v. Marathon Oil Co.*,[161] an employer was held liable for over $100,000 in damages for tortious interference where it caused the termination of a former employee who had obtained employment with a contractor that was performing work for the employer.

Finally, in *Yaindl v. Ingersoll-Rand Co.*,[162] a court permitted an employee to proceed to trial on his interference claim where the managers in the division in which he had previously worked caused another division of the same company to rescind its job offer to the employee.

f. False Imprisonment

Employees who are intentionally restrained when they are being terminated have asserted claims for false imprisonment. This can arise by actual physical restraint or by blocking an employee's egress from his or her office or work site.

In *Uebelacker v. Cincom Systems*,[163] a supervisor advised an employee that he was being terminated and directed him to gather his personal effects. When the employee declined to do so and instead asked to speak with a representative from the employee relations department, the supervisor directed another worker to physically block the employee from leaving his work cubicle until he packed up his belongings. The employee brought a false imprisonment lawsuit against his employer, and an appellate court permitted him to present his claim to a jury.

Similarly, in *Dupler v. Seubert*,[164] an employer was found liable for false imprisonment where a supervisor planted himself between an employee and the office door for an hour and a half while the supervisor attempted to coerce the employee into resigning.

g. RICO

Employees have also brought RICO actions against their employers in connection with their termination from employment. In *McKay v. Ashland Oil*,[165] an employer was assessed $69 million in damages under RICO for the wrongful termination of two vice presidents who had objected to illegal bribes given to foreign officials in order to secure Middle East oil. And in *Acampora v. Boise Cascade Corp.*[166] and *Shearin v. E.F. Hutton Group*,[167] courts permitted employees who had refused to participate in illegal schemes and were about to disclose fraud to governmental regulators to proceed with their RICO claims against their employers.

2. Retention of Employees

The failure to terminate an unfit employee can lead to liability for negligent retention, particularly where the employer becomes aware of the employee's lack of fitness yet permits the employee to remain employed.[168] The retention of employees can also lead to liability for fraud, where, for example, an employer falsely promises a valued employee a bonus in order to induce him or her to continue employment with the employer.

a. Negligent Retention

The tort of negligent retention is now widely recognized. Unlike negligent hiring cases, where the focus is usually on information that an employer *should have known about* in advance of the hiring decision, negligent retention cases usually focus on information about an employee's unfitness that an employer *actually knows about* yet fails to act upon.

Claims for negligent retention have been asserted where an employer retained:

- a supervisor who continued to sexually harass a female subordinate after receiving complaints of sexual harassment from the female employee;[169]
- a driver who drove his truck while intoxicated and injured a pedestrian, despite knowledge of his alcohol abuse;[170]
- an employee who sexually assaulted a child he was responsible for overseeing after learning that he had a criminal record for attempted rape;[171]
- an employee who assaulted a customer notwithstanding knowledge of the employee's propensity to "blow up" and use of profane and threatening language when speaking to customers;[172]
- a security guard who stole goods from a facility he was assigned to protect despite its prior belief that he had previously stolen money from a different facility he had been assigned to guard;[173]
- an employee who shot a customer at work where it knew or should have known that the employee had previously discharged his gun at work;[174] and
- a physician who sexually assaulted a patient after receiving complaints about the physician's misconduct from other patients.[175]

b. Fraud and Misrepresentation

Employers who make promises to employees in order to retain them in employment may become liable for fraud or misrepresentation where the employer never intended to fulfill the promises.[176] The promises can involve any number of valuable incentives, such as a future bonus, an increase in future pension benefits, or an assurance that the employee will not be discharged.

For example, in *Spoljaric v. Percival Tours*,[177] an employer was assessed $750,000 in damages for fraud where it made a false promise to pay a bonus worth $30,000 to induce its chief executive officer to continue his employment.

Similarly, in *Greenblatt v. Budd Co.*,[178] an employee agreed to continue his employment based on representations that his employer would provide him with enhanced pension benefits under a corporate pension plan rather than the regular benefits under a subsidiary's pension plan. The employee brought a fraud claim against the corporate parent after he retired and learned that he would only be receiving pension benefits under the subsidiary's pension plan. A court refused to dismiss his claim.

Finally, in *Shebar v. Sanyo Business Systems*,[179] an employer induced a sales manager to forgo a job offer with a competitor by representing to him that it would never fire any of its managers. After the manager was fired four months later, he brought an action against his employer for fraud. An appellate court held that he was entitled to present his fraud claim to a jury.

G. Postemployment Matters

Although the employment relationship formally ends when an employer terminates an employee or when an employee resigns his or her job, there are a number of postemployment matters that can expose an employer to tort liability. Foremost among these matters is postemployment references about former employees. Other postemployment matters that can cause liability include the institution of criminal and civil proceedings against employees, the enforcement of noncompete clauses, and statements made by employers for use in unemployment and workers' compensation proceedings. Each of these postemployment matters is discussed below.

1. Postemployment References

Prospective employers have become increasingly aware of the need to thoroughly assess fitness and competence in light of the potential exposure they face from negligent hiring claims. Thus, prospective employers commonly seek detailed reference information about a candidate for employment. Prospective employers frequently contact past supervisors and managers for this information. Regrettably, such individuals may provide information about former employees that is neither accurate nor complete. Such misinformation may expose the employer to tort liabilities even if the supervisors or managers acted in violation of established company policy by providing references. The type of tort action most likely to arise in this context is defamation. In addition, where the former employer causes a prospective employer to withdraw an offer of future employment, the tort of interference with prospective contractual relations may also arise.

a. Defamation

Inaccurate or misleading information provided to a prospective employer about a former employee can lead to liability for defamation. While a former employer, like a current employer, has a qualified privilege to defame an employee, that qualified privilege can be lost by abuse (see Chapter 3, section B.).

Perhaps the archetype of postemployment reference cases leading to liability for defamation is *Frank B. Hall & Co. v. Buck*.[180] In that case, a salesperson was terminated for insufficient sales. During the course of postemployment inquiries, however, his co-workers referred to him as "untrustworthy," "paranoid," "irrational," "guilty of padding his expense report," and "a zero." More importantly, an official of the company gave a postemployment reference that implied that the employee had been terminated for serious misconduct, telling a prospective employer who inquired about the grounds for termination that "I can't go into it." When the employee was unable to procure new employment, he sued his former employer for defamation. A jury awarded him $1.3 million in damages, and the award was upheld on appeal.

In another case, an employee was awarded $250,000 in damages for a defamatory postemployment reference premised on unsubstantiated office gossip. In *Sigal Construction Corp. v. Stanbury*,[181] an executive of the company who was unfamiliar with the employee's work performance stated in a postemployment reference that the employee was too "detail oriented" and "no longer works for us, and that might say enough." Because the executive failed to advise the prospective employer that he did not have any firsthand knowledge of the employee's work, the employer was held to have lost its qualified privilege.

Other examples of how an employer can expose itself unnecessarily to liability for defamation include providing references that are susceptible to more than one meaning;[182] providing a negative job reference after assuring an employee that he would receive a favorable recommendation;[183] and comparing a former employee to his replacement in such a manner as to imply a negative connotation about the former employee.[184]

b. Interference With Contractual Relations

Negative postemployment references that cause an employee to lose a job opportunity with another employer may also lead to employer liability for interference with contractual or prospective contractual relations.

In *Geyer v. Steinbronn*,[185] a former supervisor falsely advised a prospective employer that an employee had been fired when in fact he had resigned. The prospective employer, which had offered the employee a job subject to employment verification, then rescinded the job offer. In his action for interference with prospective contractual relations and defamation, an appellate court upheld a jury award of $100,000 in compensatory damages against the employer and $50,000 in punitive damages against the supervisor.

Similarly, in *Yaindl v. Ingersoll-Rand Co.*,[186] an employee was permitted to maintain his claim of interference with prospective contractual relations where a manager in one division of a company where the employee previously worked before being terminated caused another division to rescind a new job offer made to the employee.

2. Criminal and Civil Proceedings Against Employees

a. Criminal Charges

In much the same way as employers are free to use the legal process against employers, employers are similarly free to use the legal process against employees. Employers occasionally file or initiate criminal charges against employees who have allegedly committed a crime at work, such as theft or assault. The filing or initiation of such charges, however, can expose an employer to a claim for malicious prosecution and abuse of process.

In *Wainauskis v. Howard Johnson Co.*,[187] an employer filed criminal charges against a terminated employee for theft of funds. The employee was tried before a jury but obtained an acquittal after a first trial resulted in a hung jury. The employee then filed a lawsuit for malicious prosecution against the employer. The jury returned a verdict in favor of the employee and assessed the employer $100,000 in damages. The award was upheld on appeal.

In *Redican v. K-Mart Corp.*,[188] an employer caused two employees to be arrested at work for theft but failed to appear in court to testify against them. The two employees filed a lawsuit for malicious prosecution and were awarded $160,000 in damages against the employer. That award was upheld on appeal.

The jury in *Foley v. Polaroid Corp.*[189] was even more generous, awarding $1.5 million in damages to an employee who filed an action for malicious prosecution. In *Foley,* the employer initiated criminal charges against the employee for his alleged sexual assault against a co-worker at work. The employee was tried but acquitted of all charges. He then filed his lawsuit for malicious prosecution, resulting in the $1.5 million jury award. On appeal, however, an appellate court overturned the verdict in favor of the employer, holding that the employer was not liable for malicious prosecution because it relied in good faith on the accuser's allegation that she had been sexually assaulted.

Employers using the criminal process for retaliatory purposes expose themselves to enormous potential liability. In *Sims v. Kaneb Services,*[190] an employer filed criminal charges against a terminated vice president for allegedly destroying data on a computer disk. He was subsequently indicted but the case was eventually dismissed. In the employee's action for malicious prosecution and abuse of process, a jury found that the employer had commenced the criminal proceedings maliciously, in retaliation for the employee's refusal to sign fraudulent corporate income tax returns and because the employee had filed a lawsuit against the employer for wrongful discharge. The jury awarded him *$34 million* on his malicious prosecution and abuse of process claims. The case was thereafter settled.

b. Civil Proceedings

The institution of civil proceedings by employers against employees not only can lead to claims for malicious prosecution and abuse of process, but also to claims for defamation.

In *Fahnestock & Co. v. Waltman,*[191] an employer filed an arbitration claim against a terminated employee for allegedly removing company documents from work in order to solicit the company's customers in his own competing business. The employee filed a counterclaim for defamation, and the arbitrator assessed the employer $100,000 in damages. The award was upheld on appeal.

3. Noncompete Agreements

Many employers historically have sought to protect their business interests by requiring their employees to sign noncompete agreements. The existence of unreasonable noncompete agreements, however, as well as the unreasonable enforcement of noncompete agreements, can result in liability to the employer for interference with contractual or prospective contractual relations. Further, requiring an employee to execute a noncompete agreement can, in certain circumstances, result in a claim for fraud.

a. Interference With Contractual Relations

In *Torbett v. Wheeling Dollars Savings & Trust Co.*,[192] an employee resigned her employment. Thereafter, she declined to seek new employment for a period of two years because she had signed a noncompete agreement with her former employer barring her for two years from working for any other employer within a 25-mile radius of her old job. On her claim for interference with prospective contractual relations, a jury returned a verdict in her favor, awarding her two years of lost income. An appellate court affirmed, holding that an employer exposes itself to liability if it enters into noncompete agreements that restrict employment of former employees beyond the legitimate and reasonable business interest of the employer.

Even where a noncompete provision may be reasonable, an employer may be liable for tortious interference if it seeks to enforce it under unreasonable circumstances. In *Empiregas, Inc. v. Hardy*,[193] a jury assessed an employer $120,000 in damages for interference with prospective contractual relations where it threatened to sue another employer that was about to offer jobs to two former employees of the first employer. The two employees had previously signed a noncompete agreement, but at the time they did so, a representative of the company told them the agreement was "not worth a damn" and was "just a piece of paper." The award was upheld on appeal.

b. Fraud

When an employer requires an employee to execute an employment agreement containing a noncompete clause, it may also expose itself to liability for fraud if it intends to terminate the employee at the time the employee executes the agreement. In *Freeman v. Kansas State Network*,[194] a court permitted an employee to present her fraud claim to a jury where she alleged that her employer had fraudulently induced her to sign an employment contract containing a provision that prohibited her from working for another employer in the same industry, intending all along to terminate her within a few months.

4. Unemployment and Workers' Compensation Proceedings

Statements made by employers about the circumstances of an employee's termination, when made for use in unemployment compensation proceedings, can lead to a claim for defamation. In *Rogozinski v. Airstream by Angell*,[195] an employer was sued for defamation by two former employees for negative statements made to an unemployment compensation commission in response to the commission's request for separation information. The employer claimed that such statements were subject to an *absolute* privilege, barring the employees' lawsuit altogether. The court disagreed, holding that the statements were only entitled to a *qualified* privilege and could form the basis for liability if the statements were made with malice or for an improper purpose.

And in *Dorr v. C.B. Johnson, Inc.*,[196] a court held that although allegedly defamatory statements made to a state Department of Labor for use in workers' compensation proceedings were subject to an absolute privilege, repetition of these statements to third parties was not even entitled to a qualified privilege.

Notes

Legal citations to all cases summarized in Part One are also included in the Table of Cases at the end of the book.

1. *See* Davis v. Utah Power & Light Co., summarized in Chapter 1, section D.3.c.
2. This chapter incorporates portions of Chapter 3 of a special report entitled *Negligent Hiring, Fraud, Defamation, and Other Emerging Areas of Employer Liability* (BNA, 1988). That chapter of the report was drafted by Victoria J. Smith, and has been substantially expanded and updated in this book.
3. *See* North Houston Pole Line Corp. v. McAllister, summarized in Chapter 1, section D.1.b.
4. *See* Kolator v. State *and* DeLeon v. Hospital of Albert Einstein College of Medicine, summarized in Chapter 1, section D.1.a.
5. *See* Williams v. Feather Sound, summarized in Chapter 1, section D.1.c.
6. *See* R.M. v. McDonald's Corp. *and* Rosen-House v. Sloan's Supermarket, summarized in Chapter 1, section D.1.c., *and* Welsh Manufacturing v. Pinkerton's, Inc., summarized in Chapter 1, section D.2.d.
7. *See* Sallaz v. G-H-I Housing Corp. *and* Ponticas v. K.M.S. Inv., summarized in Chapter 1, section D.1.c.
8. *See* Gaines v. Monsanto Co., Abbott v. Payne, *and* Burch v. A & G Assocs., summarized in Chapter 1, section D.1.c.
9. *See* Weiss v. Furniture in the Raw, summarized in Chapter 1, section D.1.d., *and* Welsh Manufacturing v. Pinkerton's, Inc., summarized in Chapter 1, section D.2.d.
10. *See* Weiss v. Furniture in the Raw, summarized in Chapter 1, section D.1.d.

11. *See* Nigg v. Patterson, summarized in Chapter 1, section D.1.c.
12. *See* Chapter 1, section C.1.
13. *See* Pruitt v. Pavelin, summarized in Chapter 1, section D.1.d., *and* Haddock v. City of N.Y., summarized in Chapter 1, section D.2.c.
14. *See* Berger v. Security Pac. Information Sys., summarized in Chapter 2, section D.1.a.
15. *See* Weisman v. Connors, summarized in Chapter 2, section D.1.a.
16. *See* Harlan v. Intergy, Inc., summarized in Chapter 2, section D.1.a.
17. *See* Dowie v. Exxon Corp. *and* Higgins v. Lawrence, summarized in Chapter 2, section D.1.b.
18. *See* Della Croce v. General Elec. Co., summarized in Chapter 2, section D.1.b.
19. *See* Boivin v. Jones & Vining, Inc., summarized in Chapter 2, section D.1.b.
20. *See* Albrant v. Sterling Furniture Co., summarized in Chapter 2, section D.1.b.
21. *See* Belknap, Inc. v. Hale *and* Verway v. Blincoe Packing Co., summarized in Chapter 2, section D.1.b.
22. *See* Della Croce v. General Elec. Co., summarized in Chapter 2, section D.1.b.
23. *See* Palmer v. Beverly Enters., summarized in Chapter 2, section D.1.b.
24. *See* Dowie v. Exxon Corp., summarized in Chapter 2, section D.1.b.
25. *See* McNamee v. Bethlehem Steel Corp., summarized in Chapter 2, section D.3.
26. *See* Chapter 2, section C.
27. *See* Weisman v. Connors, summarized in Chapter 2, section D.1.a., *and* Higgins v. Lawrence, summarized in Chapter 2, section D.1.b.
28. *See* case summarized in Chapter 1, section D.2.b.
29. *See* case summarized in Chapter 1, section D.2.b.
30. *See* case summarized in Chapter 1, section D.3.c.
31. *See* case summarized in Chapter 3, section D.1.c.
32. *See* case summarized in Chapter 4, section D.2.
33. *See* case summarized in Chapter 4, section D.2.
34. *See* case summarized in Chapter 5, section C.3.
35. *See* case summarized in Chapter 6, section C.1.
36. *See* Johnson v. Ramsey County, summarized in Chapter 6, section C.1.
37. *See* Waltman v. International Paper Co., summarized in Chapter 6, section C.1.
38. *See* Newsome v. Cooper-Wiss, Inc., summarized in Chapter 6, section C.1.
39. *See* Davis v. United States Steel Corp., summarized in Chapter 6, section C.1.
40. *See* Hart v. National Mortgage & Land Co., summarized in Chapter 6, section C.1.
41. *See* Schwartz v. Zippy Mart, summarized in Chapter 6, section C.1.
42. *See* case summarized in Chapter 9, section C.
43. *See* case summarized in Chapter 4, section D.1.
44. *See* case summarized in Chapter 4, section D.3.
45. *See* Brown v. Ellis, summarized in Chapter 4, section D.1.
46. *See* Malone v. Safeway Stores, summarized in Chapter 4, section D.1.
47. *See* Dixon v. Stuart, summarized in Chapter 4, section D.1.
48. *See* Robinson v. Hewlett-Packard Corp., summarized in Chapter 4, section D.3.
49. *See* case summarized in Chapter 4, section D.3.
50. *See* Chapter 13, section E.1..
51. *See* case summarized in Chapter 5, section C.5.
52. *See* case summarized in Chapter 6, section C.6.
53. *See* case summarized in Chapter 10, section C.3.

54. *See* case summarized in Chapter 1, section D.6.
55. *See* case summarized in Chapter 4, section D.8.
56. *See* case summarized in Chapter 6, section C.5.
57. *See* case summarized in Chapter 6, section C.5.
58. *See* case summarized in Chapter 2, section D.7.
59. *See* case summarized in Chapter 6, section C.5.
60. *See* case summarized in Chapter 6, section C.4.
61. *See* case summarized in Chapter 6, section C.4.
62. *See* case summarized in Chapter 1, section D.2.a.
63. *See* case summarized in Chapter 1, section D.8.
64. *See* case summarized in Chapter 3, section D.1.a.
65. *See* case summarized in Chapter 3, section D.1.a.
66. *See* case summarized in Chapter 3, section D.1.a.
67. Qualified privilege is discussed in Chapter 3, section B.
68. *See* case summarized in Chapter 3, section D.4.
69. *See* case summarized in Chapter 5, section D.3.
70. *See* case summarized in Chapter 5, section D.3.
71. *See* case summarized in Chapter 5, section D.4.
72. *See* case summarized in Chapter 5, section D.2.
73. *See* case summarized in Chapter 1, section D.1.b.
74. *See* case summarized in Chapter 3, section D.3.
75. *See* case summarized in Chapter 5, section C.1.
76. *See* case summarized in Chapter 5, section C.1.
77. *See* case summarized in Chapter 5, section C.1.
78. *See* case summarized in Chapter 4, section D.9.
79. *See* case summarized in Chapter 4, section D.3.
80. *See* case summarized in Chapter 4, section D.1.
81. *See* case summarized in Chapter 4, section D.6.
82. *See* case summarized in Chapter 5, section C.1.
83. *See* case summarized in Chapter 8, section C.3.
84. *See* case summarized in Chapter 1, section D.5.
85. *See* case summarized in Chapter 1, section D.5.
86. *See* case summarized in Chapter 2, section D.1.b.
87. *See* case summarized in Chapter 2, section D.1.b.
88. *See* case summarized in Chapter 2, section D.4.
89. *See* case summarized in Chapter 3, section D.2.
90. *See* case summarized in Chapter 3, section D.2.
91. *See* Wilson v. Monarch Paper Co., summarized in Chapter 4, section D.1.
92. *See* Malone v. Safeway Stores, summarized in Chapter 4, section D.1.
93. *See* Farmer v. Brotherhood of Carpenters, Local 25, summarized in Chapter 4, section D.1.
94. *See* Shrout v. Black Clawson Co., summarized in Chapter 4, section D.2.
95. *See* Dixon v. Stuart, summarized in Chapter 4, section D.1.
96. *See* Brown v. Ellis, summarized in Chapter 4, section D.1.
97. *See* case summarized in Chapter 7, section C.3.
98. *See* case summarized in Chapter 1, section D.7.
99. *See* case summarized in Chapter 2, section D.5.
100. *See* case summarized in Chapter 3, section D.1.b.
101. *See* case summarized in Chapter 1, section D.7.

102. *See* case summarized in Chapter 4, section D.4.a.
103. *See* case summarized in Chapter 4, section D.4.b.
104. *See* Kamrath v. Suburban Nat'l Bank *and* Liebowitz v. H.A. Winston Co., summarized in Chapter 4, section D.4.b.
105. *See* case summarized in Chapter 5, section C.4.
106. *See* case summarized in Chapter 6, section C.4.
107. *See* case summarized in Chapter 6, section C.4.
108. *See* case summarized in Chapter 8, section C.1.a.
109. *See* case summarized in Chapter 8, section C.1.a.
110. *See* case summarized in Chapter 8, section C.1.a.
111. *See* case summarized in Chapter 3, section D.1.a.
112. *See* case summarized in Chapter 3, section D.1.a.
113. *See* case summarized in Chapter 3, section D.4.
114. *See* case summarized in Chapter 4, section D.5.
115. *See* case summarized in Chapter 5, section C.3.
116. *See* case summarized in Chapter 3, section D.1.c.
117. *See* case summarized in Chapter 8, section C.1.a.
118. *See* case summarized in Chapter 2, section D.1.b.
119. *See* case summarized in Chapter 2, section D.2.
120. *See* case summarized in Chapter 2, section D.2.
121. *See* case summarized in Chapter 2, section D.1.b.
122. *See* case summarized in Chapter 2, section D.1.b.
123. *See* case summarized in Chapter 2, section D.6.
124. *See* case summarized in Chapter 2, section D.6.
125. *See* Houston Belt & Terminal Ry. Co., summarized in Chapter 3, section D.1.a.; Kelley v. Schlumberger Technology Corp., summarized in Chapter 4, section D.5.; O'Brien v. Papa Gino's of America, summarized in Chapter 5, section C.3.
126. *See* Howcroft v. Mountain States Tel. & Tel. Co., summarized in Chapter 3, section D.1.b.
127. *See* Benassi v. Georgia-Pacific, summarized in Chapter 3, section D.4.
128. *See* Battista v. United Illuminating Co., summarized in Chapter 3, section D.10.
129. *See* Worley v. Oregon Physicians Servs., summarized in Chapter 3, section D.4; Nelson v. Lapeyrouse Grain Corp., summarized in Chapter 3, section D.7.; Turner v. Halliburton Co., summarized in Chapter 7, section C.4.; Young Oil Co. v. Durbin, summarized in Chapter 9.
130. *See* Liebowitz v. H.A. Winston Co., summarized in Chapter 4, section D.4.; Tumbarella v. Kroger Co., summarized in Chapter 8, section C.1.a.; Wainauskis v. Howard Johnson Co., summarized in Chapter 9.
131. *See* Johnson v. Anheuser Busch, Inc., summarized in Chapter 9, section C.
132. *See* Elmore v. Shell Oil Co., summarized in Chapter 3, section D.9.
133. *See* Brannan v. Wyeth Laboratories, summarized in Chapter 3, section D.7.
134. *See* Vinson v. Linn-Mar Community School Dist., summarized in Chapter 3, section D.8.
135. *See* Lewis v. Equitable Life Assurance Soc'y, summarized in Chapter 3, section D.9.
136. *See* Gonzalez v. CNA Ins. Co., summarized in Chapter 3, section D.1.c.
137. *See* Foley v. Polaroid Corp., summarized in Chapter 8, section C.1.a.

242 *Employer's Guide to Workplace Torts*

138. *See* Bradley v. Hubbard Broadcasting, summarized in Chapter 3, section D.5.
139. *See* Lewis v. Equitable Life Assurance Soc'y, summarized in Chapter 3, section D.9.
140. *See* Holland v. Kennedy, summarized in Chapter 3, section D.5.
141. *See* Rogozinski v. Airstream by Angell, summarized in Chapter 3, section D.10.
142. *See* Frankson v. Design Space Int'l, summarized in Chapter 3, section D.5.
143. *See* Rogozinski v. Airstream by Angell, summarized in Chapter 3, section D.10.
144. *See* Zinda v. Louisiana Pac. Corp., summarized in Chapter 3, section D.6.
145. *See* Brannan v. Wyeth Laboratories, summarized in Chapter 3, section D.7.
146. *See* Fahnestock & Co. v. Waltman, summarized in Chapter 3, section D.10.
147. *See* Rogozinski v. Airstream by Angell, summarized in Chapter 3, section D.10.
148. *See* Agis v. Howard Johnson Co., summarized in Chapter 4, section D.9.
149. *See* Collins v. Shell Oil Co., summarized in Chapter 4, section D.9.
150. *See* McCool v. Hillhaven Corp., summarized in Chapter 4, section D.9.
151. *See* Walker v. South Cent. Bell Tel. Co., summarized in Chapter 4, section D.9.
152. *See* Russ v. TRW, summarized in Chapter 2, section D.4.
153. *See* Jeffers v. Convoy Co., summarized in Chapter 2, section D.5.
154. *See* Uebelacker v. Cincom Sys., summarized in Chapter 8, section C.1.b.
155. *See* Freeman v. Kansas State Network, summarized in Chapter 4, section D.9.
156. *See* Abston v. Levi Strauss & Co., summarized in Chapter 4, section D.9.
157. *See* case summarized in Chapter 5, section C.5.
158. *See* case summarized in Chapter 7, section C.1.a.
159. *See* case summarized in Chapter 7, section C.1.a.
160. *See* case summarized in Chapter 7, section C.1.b.
161. *See* case summarized in Chapter 7, section C.1.b.
162. *See* case summarized in Chapter 7, section C.4.
163. *See* case summarized in Chapter 8, section C.1.b.
164. *See* case summarized in Chapter 8, section C.1.b.
165. *See* case summarized in Chapter 10, section C.1.
166. *See* case summarized in Chapter 10, section C.1.
167. *See* case summarized in Chapter 10, section C.1.
168. *See* Chapter 1, section C.
169. *See* Brown v. Burlington Indus. *and* Cox v. Brazo, summarized in Chapter 1, section D.2.b.
170. *See* Redd v. Product Dev. Corp., summarized in Chapter 1, section D.2.a.
171. *See* Haddock v. City of N.Y., summarized in Chapter 1, section D.2.c.
172. *See* Greenfield v. Spectrum Inv. Corp., summarized in Chapter 1, section D.2.c.
173. *See* Welsh Manufacturing v. Pinkerton's, Inc., summarized in Chapter 1, section D.2.d.
174. *See* Giles v. Shell Oil Corp., summarized in Chapter 1, section D.3.a.
175. *See* Mercer v. State, summarized in Chapter 1, section D.3.b.
176. *See* Chapter 2, section B.
177. *See* case summarized in Chapter 2, section D.2.
178. *See* case summarized in Chapter 2, section D.3.
179. *See* case summarized in Chapter 2, section D.2.
180. *See* case summarized in Chapter 3, section D.8.
181. *See* case summarized in Chapter 3, section D.8.
182. *See* Vinson v. Linn-Mar Community School Dist., summarized in Chapter 3, section D.8.

183. *See* Stuempges v. Parke, Davis & Co., summarized in Chapter 3, section D.8.
184. *See* Falls v. Sporting News Publishing Co., summarized in Chapter 3, section D.8.
185. *See* case summarized in Chapter 7, section C.4.
186. *See* case summarized in Chapter 7, section C.4.
187. *See* case summarized in Chapter 9, section C.
188. *See* case summarized in Chapter 9, section C.
189. *See* case summarized in Chapter 9, section C.
190. *See* case summarized in Chapter 9, section C.
191. *See* case summarized in Chapter 3, section D.10.
192. *See* case summarized in Chapter 7, section C.5.
193. *See* case summarized in Chapter 7, section C.5.
194. *See* case summarized in Chapter 2, section D.9.
195. *See* case summarized in Chapter 3, section D.10.
196. *See* case summarized in Chapter 3, section D.10.

Chapter 12

Avoiding Exposure to Workplace Tort Liability: Practical Suggestions

Lawsuits based on workplace torts are usually costly to defend and involve potentially crippling damage awards. It is therefore imperative for employers to undertake preventive measures to minimize exposure to such liability. While the specific outcome of a tort action is dependent, in large measure, on the particular facts of the case and the sense of a jury, the cases summarized in Part One of this book provide some practical approaches that employers can use to lessen the chance that they will face extraordinary liability from employee tort claims. Described below are more than 200 practical suggestions that employers can follow to minimize exposure to the emerging theories of employer tort liability. These practical suggestions fall into the following general categories of recommendations:

- Properly Screening for Unfit Applicants;
- Counseling, Supervising, and Terminating Unfit Employees;
- Using Disclaimers in Recruitment and Hiring;
- Avoiding Employee Detrimental Reliance;
- Properly Conducting Drug and Alcohol Testing;
- Properly Investigating Employee Misconduct;
- Minimizing Defamatory and Other Actionable Statements About Employees;
- Avoiding Unnecessary Inquiries About and Disclosure of Personal Employee Matters;
- Minimizing Abusive and Harassing Treatment of Employees by Supervisors and Co-Workers;
- Converting Terminations Into Resignations;
- Obtaining Releases From Employees;

- Qualifying Postemployment References; and
- Avoiding Other Post-Termination Tortious Conduct.

The suggestions that follow are not exhaustive or all-inclusive; rather, they are illustrative of the steps that employers can take to address a large number of common employee relations matters that ultimately may lead to the filing of a tort claim against an employer by an employee or third party.[1] Many of the suggestions included in this chapter are derived from the cases summarized in Part I of this book. Others emanate from the experience of the authors. And some are based on the contributions of other practitioners, including lawyers who represent employees in employment tort cases.[2]

A. Properly Screening for Unfit Applicants

Now more than ever before employers must properly and uniformly screen out unfit applicants for employment, doing so in a manner that is consistent with federal, state, and local laws. This requires a well-prepared, comprehensive program that enables the employer's representatives to carefully assess and verify the information on a candidate's application (and résumé where provided), and to contact previous employers and individuals listed as personal references. Such a program will substantially minimize the likelihood of negligent hiring lawsuits by employees, customers, and other third parties who come into contact with an employer's employees.

A request for criminal conviction information may also be necessary in certain circumstances. Most courts agree that, as a *general* proposition, an inquiry into the possible criminal record of an applicant is not required, provided the employer makes an adequate inquiry into the employee's general and job-specific fitness.[3] There are certain types of positions, however, such as those involving safety or protection of property, or those exposing co-workers or customers to a significant risk of harm, where a criminal record search may be regarded as essential. Further, whenever "suspicious" factors, such as abbreviated periods of different residences or gaps in employment, are revealed on an employment application or in interviews with the applicant, a reasonable employer would be well-advised to inquire further into an applicant's background, including a search for a criminal record.[4]

Given the sensitive nature of criminal record inquiries and the need to conduct them in a responsible, appropriate, and thorough manner, it is advisable to use one of the several prominent and experienced vendors specializing in background checks. A number of major corporations today employ such vendors to provide a complete "applicant profile."

Federal, state, and local laws govern the use of criminal conviction information in the applicant screening process. A review of pertinent state laws in selected jurisdictions, as well as the policy of the EEOC regarding the use of arrest and conviction information, is included in Appendix A.

Some employers also use consumer credit reports in verifying an applicant's employment and personal information and assessing an applicant's candidacy for employment. Federal and state laws govern the use of this type of information as well. A review of federal law and selected state laws regarding the use of consumer credit reports is included in Appendix C.

Employers should recognize that there is no prescribed or approved manner of screening applicants. Many factors will ultimately be taken into account by a court or jury in making the determination of whether the employer acted reasonably under the circumstances to safeguard its employees and customers from foreseeable harm. Those factors include the nature of the position being filled, the capability and resources of the employer to conduct a thorough job search, the cost of obtaining information (including criminal record data), as well as the capability of the employer to afford such cost. With those considerations in mind, three dozen practical suggestions for properly screening applicants for employment are set forth below.

• Review applicable federal, state, and local laws regarding the information that may be sought on an employment application or during the interview process. Confer with counsel to ensure that the application form itself conforms to all such laws.

• Inspect the information provided by the applicant, and look for gaps in employment and other suspicious or unusual entries or omissions.

• Whenever a significant gap of time between jobs is apparent from the information provided on an employment application or résumé, ask the applicant to explain the reason for the gap. Document the reason provided by the employee and, if possible, determine the validity of the explanation.

• Before hiring an applicant with a sizable gap of time between jobs, independently verify the reason provided by the applicant for the gap. If the reason for the gap cannot be independently verified,

conduct a comprehensive criminal record search before hiring the applicant.
- Contact each previous employer and personal reference listed on the application. If the information provided by the applicant is insufficient, obtain further information from the applicant, such as forwarding addresses for references.
- Ask all former employers, preferably the applicant's prior immediate supervisors:
  - if they have any reason to believe the applicant may not be:
    - competent for the position being sought,
    - reliable,
    - trustworthy,
    - honest, and
    - safe.
- Also ask all former employers if they have any reason to believe the applicant may be:
  - dangerous,
  - violent, or
  - abusive.
- In addition, ask all former employers if they have any knowledge the employee has ever engaged in any:
  - violent,
  - dangerous,
  - criminal,
  - improper,
  - discriminatory,
  - abusive, or
  - harassing conduct at work.
- Tailor additional questions to the job in question. A position with customer contact requires different inquiries from one involving the handling of money.
- Obtain the applicant's consent to procure information from former employers, personal references, past and present landlords, credit bureaus, and other sources, and secure a valid waiver and release from liability in connection with the reference check.
- Advise prospective employers that you have obtained the applicant's consent and a release in connection with the reference check.
- Ask the same questions of applicants that are asked of prior employers; that is, "Have you ever engaged in any violent, dangerous, improper, abusive, or harassing conduct at work?"

- Comply with all federal, state, and local fair credit reporting laws when obtaining credit, employment, and other information about applicants. Where required, advise applicants of their rights under such laws.
- Obtain a release from the applicant to seek verification of educational degrees, high-school or trade-school diplomas, undergraduate coursework, and so forth.
- Document efforts to obtain information from each previous employer, personal reference, and other source—even if information could *not* be obtained from such sources.
- Document *all* information received from previous employers, personal references, and all other sources.
- Determine whether it is appropriate to conduct a criminal record search in view of the job to be filled.
- Perform a criminal record search before hiring any applicants for jobs that require either entry into customers' homes or businesses (such as service technicians, moving company employees, and delivery persons), or entrustment of customers into the custody of employees (such as taxi drivers, child-care workers, teachers, or camp counselors).
- Undertake a full background verification, including a criminal record search, before hiring any applicant referred by a state or local vocational rehabilitation bureau.
- Decide whether any information provided by the applicant on the application form or obtained from previous employers or personal references or through an interview suggests that a criminal record search is essential.
- If an applicant fails to certify unequivocally on his employment application that he has never been convicted of a crime other than minor traffic violations, conduct a comprehensive criminal record search before hiring the applicant.
- Whenever an applicant lists a criminal conviction on an employment application, follow up with the employee to determine the nature and dates of the conviction and then conduct a comprehensive criminal record search to confirm this information.
- If an employer learns that an applicant has been convicted of a crime, consult with legal counsel to determine whether a federal, state, or local statute governs the use of that information in hiring decisions, and, if so, how the statute should be applied in the circumstances presented.

- Before hiring an applicant with a criminal record, consult with others in the organization as well as legal counsel to determine the employee's fitness for the job in question. Do not keep such information to yourself. Such consultation should be documented.
- Check thoroughly the expertise and background of drivers and others whose jobs involve public safety or the safety of co-workers.
- Conduct a complete driving record search *before* allowing a new employee to drive a company vehicle or his or her own vehicle on company business.
- When considering applicants from state or local social services or treatment centers, conduct an independent interview of applicants. Do not rely on a governmental agency to screen applicants for trustworthiness, safety, or propensity for violence.
- Use as many of the same applicant screening procedures for temporary workers as you do for regular employees. Although usually time is of the essence when hiring temporary workers, applicants for temporary positions should, whenever possible, be required to complete application forms and be interviewed to determine whether there is any reason to believe that they may be unsafe, untrustworthy, or violent.
- If a temporary worker's assignment is other than short-term, verify all employment and personal references as well as the other information on the completed employment application form as you would when hiring an employee for a regular position.
- Applicants for seasonal employment should be screened in the same comprehensive manner and to the same extent as applicants for regular full-time employment. Applicants for regular part-time positions should also be screened in this manner.
- Never rely on an employment agency to screen out unfit applicants for regular full-time or regular part-time positions. Unlike the situation involving employment of temporary workers, where there is frequently little or no time to screen employees, there is usually adequate time to thoroughly screen applicants for regular employment.
- Before deciding whether to retain a predecessor employer's employees, a successor employer should not merely determine whether the employees are competent; rather, where feasible, it should also determine for itself that each of the predecessor's employees is trustworthy, safe, and nonviolent.
- In addition, when a successor employer is considering whether to hire a supervisory employee of a predecessor employer, it should

also assure itself that the supervisor has not previously shown a propensity for sexual or other types of employee harassment.
- Do not offer employment to an applicant until all preemployment screening has been completed.
- Reevaluate hiring decisions if negative information about an employee is received subsequent to his or her employment. Never just file the information away.
- Where special circumstances require an employer to hire an applicant before the entire screening process has been completed, the process should nonetheless be completed as soon as reasonably feasible.
- Advise employees who commence employment before the screening process has been completed that their employment is subject to the satisfactory completion of reference checking.
- Consistent with federal and state laws, obtain the consent of all applicants to a post-offer, preemployment physical examination as well as all tests necessary to determine fitness for the position in question.
- Perform a post-offer, preemployment physical examination of all applicants where appropriate for the job in question, consistent with and subject to all federal, state, and local laws.

B. Counseling, Supervising, and Terminating Unfit Employees

Screening unfit persons from an employer's work force or applicant pool is not merely a function of the application process. Rather, the unsuitability of an employee frequently is not apparent or does not arise until after the employee has been hired and has sometimes worked for the employer for several months or even years. Where an employer *retains* an unfit employee that it knows or should have known presents an unreasonable risk of foreseeable harm to the employee's co-workers, customers, or other third parties with whom the employee may come into contact, the employer can become liable for *negligent retention*. Similarly, where an employer learns or should have learned that an employee is unfit for the job in question, yet fails to properly supervise the unsuitable employee or provide him or her with adequate training, the employer may become liable for *negligent supervision or training* if the unfit employee causes damage or injury to others.

Employees may become unfit for continued employment or for certain jobs by virtue of illegal drug use, alcohol abuse or communicable disease, or by demonstrating a propensity for violent, dangerous, unsafe, harassing, unreliable or untrustworthy behavior. The following practical suggestions should assist employers in minimizing their potential exposure for negligently retaining or supervising unfit employees.

• Immediately investigate employee complaints of workplace harassment or misconduct allegedly engaged in by supervisors or co-workers. Complaints about an employee's physical or emotional mistreatment of customers, clients, patients or others, as well as employee misconduct or carelessness, should likewise be immediately investigated.

• Following a thorough and prompt investigation of workplace misconduct or harassment, the employer should not only decide whether disciplinary action may be appropriate, but also whether the employee is unfit to remain in his or her job.

• After an employee is suspected of wrongdoing, he or she should be supervised carefully to ensure that the employee will not engage in another act of wrongdoing.

• After an employee is counseled, disciplined, or warned about abusive, offensive, or harassing conduct toward a subordinate or co-worker, the employer should periodically monitor the employee's activities at work to ensure that the employee who was the victim of the misconduct, as well as similarly situated co-workers, are free from repeated acts of abuse or harassment.

• Provide training to supervisors and managers, as well as rank-and-file employees, about legal prohibitions on sexual and other forms of harassment.

• Promptly investigate complaints and reports of sexual harassment as required by federal and state laws and regulations. Discipline, demote, or discharge the offending supervisor, manager, or employee where appropriate.

• Take affirmative steps to limit alcoholic beverages to employees at employer-hosted social activities, and insist that no alcoholic beverages be furnished to any intoxicated employee.

• Provide alternative transportation home for employees who have been impaired at employer-sponsored social activities, as well as for employees who have been required to work an extensive amount of overtime in any one day or over a prolonged period of time.

• Reassign employees who display irascible behavior or difficulty in controlling their tempers (especially with patrons) to positions with little or no customer or client contact.

- Be aware of the signs of employee drug use and alcohol abuse. Subject to and consistent with federal, state, and local disability discrimination laws, do not allow any employee known or reasonably believed to be using illegal drugs or abusing alcohol to continue to work in any safety-sensitive position without first determining whether the employee is a safety risk to himself or others.
- After an employee engages in a physical assault upon a customer or client, promptly remove the employee from all positions involving customer contact and take disciplinary action, up to and including discharge where appropriate, if the employee was not acting in self-defense.
- If an employee brings a weapon to work, he or she should not only be promptly disciplined but subjected to increased supervision as well—or discharged from employment.
- Conduct a complete driving record search on existing employees who regularly—or even occasionally—drive company vehicles or their own vehicles for company use. Federal and state laws may require driving record searches for interstate transportation, hauling of dangerous cargo, etc.
- Require all employees who drive company vehicles or their own vehicles for company use to notify their employer whenever they receive any points on their license.
- Require all employees who drive company vehicles or their own vehicles for company use to certify in writing, at least once per year, whether they have received any points on their driver's license, and, if so, for what driving offense.
- Reevaluate an employee's fitness if he or she is changing jobs within the organization where the nature of the new job is different from the old one.

C. Using Disclaimers in Recruitment and Hiring

As noted in the preceding chapter, the recruitment and hiring process is the most fertile area for employee claims of fraud and misrepresentation. To recruit applicants effectively yet minimize claims of fraud and misrepresentation, employers should routinely use disclaimers and consider the other practical suggestions set forth below.

- If any job-related promises or representations are made, they should be accompanied by disclaimers such as "*unless* our plans change," "*assuming* we continue to operate in the same fashion," "*if* we continue to do as well as we have in the past," or "subject to change."

• Use words such as "possible," "potential," and "maybe" when describing career opportunities.

• If promises or representations are made, they should be accompanied by disclaimers explaining that the representations are only statements of possible future events, not promises or guarantees.

• Emphasize that bonuses are "discretionary."

• Do not predict future pay raises or bonuses, and refer to past increases or bonuses as "purely a guide."

• Use words such as "currently," "at present," or "now" when describing benefits, and expressly state that all employee benefit plans are "subject to change."

• If an applicant asks whether he or she will be afforded certain job opportunities, refer to the career development achievements of other unnamed employees. For example, instead of making commitments to applicants, state that "a number of our clerical employees have gone on to administrative (or management) positions."

• Advise applicants that statements made to them during the interview process may be subject to change based on unforeseen business conditions.

• When offering an employee a job for certain hours per week or a special shift, advise the employee in writing that the terms and conditions of employment on which the employee is being hired may be modified by the employer at any time and that the employer cannot guarantee that such terms and conditions of employment will continue for any particular length of time.

• When making offers of employment to strike replacements, advise the replacements that their continued employment is subject to the terms of a strike settlement agreement and an NLRB or court order providing that the strikers be reinstated.

• Advise employees that your description of employee benefit plans should not be relied upon; rather, they should check with the plan administrator, review the plan documents, or both.

• Never use phrases such as "no problem" or "things look good" or "not to worry" to current employees, unless such statements are qualified by the phrase "while nothing is guaranteed" or words to that effect.

• Toward the conclusion of the interview, emphasize that you "cannot, of course, promise any particular raise [or future promotion, etc.]."

- Avoid promises. If promises are made, the promisor should advise the employee that he or she has no authority to make any such representations.
- Include in the personnel manual or employee handbook such statements as employment is "at will"; that the employee or employer can terminate the employment relationship at any time; and that no oral or written promises regarding any terms or conditions of employment can be made, *or should be relied upon,* except for those made in writing by the company president or other designated officer of the organization.
- Never make promises you know the employer will not be able to keep or you have no authority to make. Disclaimers will not necessarily afford protection if, at the time a promise is made, the company representative making the promise knows that the employer cannot or has no expectation to fulfill the promise.

D. Avoiding Employee Detrimental Reliance

Two essential elements of an employee claim for fraud or misrepresentation are (1) *reliance* upon an employer's false representation, and (2) damage, loss, or *detriment* suffered by the employee as a result of the reliance.[5] Especially in the area of hiring and recruitment, employers can minimize their potential liability for fraud and misrepresentation by taking steps to avoid detrimental reliance on their statements.

- Avoid making promises regarding an employee's future economic terms of employment, including future compensation, benefits, profit plan participation, and so forth.
- When an applicant inquires into the financial status or profitability of the employer, respond accurately to the inquiry.
- Avoid half-truths during the recruitment process, particularly where partial revelation of the truth would be misleading to a job applicant.
- Avoid false promises to *current employees* when seeking to persuade them to remain with the employer.
- When an employer offers a job to an applicant requiring him or her to relocate, specify in writing all relocation benefits as well as all expenses, costs, and obligations *not* being undertaken by the employer, such as the cost of selling an old house, buying a new house, and purchasing an old house if the employee is unable to sell it.

- Refrain from making statements that may not be accurate. If such statements are unwittingly made, the statement should be checked afterward, and the applicant should be immediately advised of any corrections to the statement.
- Never make representations known to be untrue.
- Avoid unnecessary "puffery" about the job, the prospects for advancement, or job security.
- Refrain from promising indefinite, lifetime, or continued employment.
- Do not make any promises or representations about the level or availability of any benefits or the terms of any pension, health, or other employee benefit plans. Refer employees and applicants for employment to the plan administrator. At the very least, qualify all such representations by stating that while you "think" the employee may be entitled to certain benefits, the employee should not rely on such statements but rather should check with the plan administrator and review the plan documents, or do both.
- Ask applicants if anyone who interviewed them made any promises. If they answer in the affirmative, ask them to advise you of all promises made. Document their response so they cannot subsequently claim a promise was made when in fact it was not.
- Advise the applicant, if he or she states that a promise was made, not to forgo any other job opportunities or resign his or her current job until the promise has been verified and it is clear that the employer will be able to fulfill it.
- Do not assure employees that their complaints or any other statements will be treated as "confidential," since some disclosure is often necessary in order for the employer to take further action. If a pledge of confidentiality must be made, however, the pledge should be honored. If there is a need to communicate the information to others, prior consent should be obtained from the employee as to each person to whom the confidential statement is to be repeated.
- If assurances of nonretaliation are given to an employee for disclosing information about a superior's misconduct, such assurances, like any other similar promises, should be honored.
- Where the employer is contemplating termination of an employee based on shortcomings in a particular area of performance, the employer should advise the employee that continued employment depends on improvement in that area.
- Do not intentionally conceal dangerous working conditions or require employees to perform dangerous work without disclosing to them the nature and risks involved in the work.

E. Properly Conducting Drug and Alcohol Testing

Drug and alcohol testing has been a fertile source of workplace tort litigation. Set forth below are a number of practical suggestions for limiting exposure to employee tort actions in this vital area of employee relations.

- Before engaging in drug or alcohol testing, review current federal, state, and local laws regarding drug and alcohol testing of applicants and employees. Also check to see whether any new legislative developments govern, restrict, or forbid any type of applicant or employee testing.
- Ensure that the particular tests to be administered are not prohibited by an applicable collective bargaining agreement.
- Early in the interview process, advise applicants that they may be subject to a drug or alcohol test before commencing employment for the employer.
- Establish an employer-wide policy providing for drug and alcohol testing (after conferring with inside or outside counsel regarding the applicability of any federal or state constitutional or other legal restrictions on such testing), and announce the policy to all employees in writing.
- Although not necessarily required by law, obtain a written consent, waiver, and release from the employee before conducting a drug or alcohol test.
- Subject to any applicable federal, state, or local law or constitutional provision, advise employees who decline to give consent that their refusal to cooperate *may* lead to discharge or discipline.
- Retain only highly qualified, well-regarded companies and professionals to conduct drug and alcohol tests.
- Advise applicants and employees of their test results. If the results are positive, allow the applicant or employee an opportunity to explain the results.
- Protect the confidentiality of test results, consistent with any applicable federal, state, or local laws.
- Do not communicate the results of any test to anyone except persons with a demonstrable need to know.
- Refrain from using inconclusive test results.
- Consider the appropriateness of conducting a second screen of the initial specimen where the results are positive.
- Where drug testing results reveal a positive screen for controlled substances in an employee's system, care should be taken not

to accuse the employee of illegal use of drugs. Rather, to the maximum extent possible, an employer should carefully limit all communications, both oral and written, to reporting the "cold facts" only (*i.e.,* the results of the drug test), and not draw conclusions from those facts.

• Do not require employees to provide urine samples under direct observation of a company representative—absent special circumstances.

F. Properly Investigating Employee Misconduct

Investigations of employee misconduct can lead to employee lawsuits for a variety of torts, including defamation, invasion of privacy, intentional infliction of emotional distress, false imprisonment, assault and battery, and malicious prosecution. Employers, however, can limit their exposure to such employee suits by following the practical suggestions below.

• Determine whether in-house or outside counsel should be involved in a workplace investigation, especially if circumstances indicate that termination might be appropriate and that the employee involved might seek to contest the termination in an administrative, arbitral, or judicial forum.

• Conduct a *complete and thorough* investigation.

• When conducting an investigation into allegations of misconduct, obtain signed, written statements from all witnesses.

• Obtain corroborating statements from other employees.

• Whether questioning an employee suspected of wrongdoing or a possible witness, never make accusations of wrongdoing about any employee who may be the subject of an investigation. Always state that the purpose of the questioning is to obtain information, that no conclusions have yet been reached, and that the questions should not be regarded as implying any accusations of wrongdoing.

• Witnesses should also be advised not to discuss the subject of the inquiry with any other persons at work or outside the workplace.

• Verify facts before concluding an investigation of workplace misconduct and prior to reaching a determination and communicating it to other persons at the employer or to third parties.

• Review the employee's personnel records during the investigation to ascertain if that employee has been involved in other similar incidents.

- Do not assume a supervisor's accusations are true. Test the veracity of all supervisors' statements the same way that statements of nonsupervisory employees are scrutinized.
- Avoid reliance on anonymous letters implicating employees in criminal wrongdoing. Results of investigations should be based on statements by firsthand witnesses. While "circumstantial" evidence of wrongdoing may supplement firsthand witness statements, allegations of wrongdoing should not usually be based solely on "circumstantial" evidence.
- Always allow an employee suspected of wrongdoing an opportunity to provide an explanation of events. Interview or reinterview witnesses to determine if the employee's explanation remains valid.
- Do not conduct a lengthy interrogation. Get the facts quickly.
- Do not threaten employees with prosecution, loss of their jobs, or other adverse consequences for their wrongdoing.
- Do not touch or make threatening gestures toward employees who are being questioned.
- Do not try to frighten employees or lead them to fear for their safety during an investigation.
- Do not restrain employees or forbid them from leaving the room where the questioning is being conducted.
- Never lock the door to the room where an employee is being questioned or stand in front of or block the exit or means of egress.
- Private-sector employers should establish a written policy notifying employees that all areas of the workplace, including employee lockers, desks, and files, are subject to inspection at any time, with or without cause. Such a policy should also provide that the use of an employee's own lock at work is prohibited.
- Do not inspect lockers, drawers, or files on which employees have placed their own locks unless (1) there is a demonstrable need to search the locker; and (2) employees previously have been notified in writing that (a) such areas are subject to inspection or (b) use of an employee's own lock is prohibited.
- Searches of employee lockers, files, and drawers without employee locks should either be conducted in the presence of the employee or be limited to those occasions where there is (1) a demonstrable need to conduct the search; and (2) reasonable suspicion that the matter being searched for may be located in the employee locker, file, or drawer.
- Refrain from asking employees about private matters unrelated to the allegations of misconduct.

- Obtain a signed admission, if possible, from the employee suspected of wrongdoing.
- Information obtained in an investigation of workplace misconduct should not be disclosed to others within or outside the workplace except to those with a demonstrable need to know. Those who are informed of such information should be advised to avoid all disclosures except to others with a need to know.
- Promptly investigate all allegations of sexual or other forms of workplace harassment by supervisors, managers, and co-workers—as otherwise required by federal, state, and local discrimination laws.
- Before requesting any employee to undergo a polygraph examination, ascertain whether the federal Employee Polygraph Protection Act or any state or local polygraph law *prohibits* the request for or use of such a test. If a polygraph examination is permitted under applicable laws, confer with inside or outside counsel to ensure that all legal requirements regarding the manner of conducting and using the results of a polygraph examination are observed.
- If, as permitted by the Employee Polygraph Protection Act, an employee refuses to submit to a lawful request by an employer that the employee take a polygraph exam, be sure that no retaliation against the employee occurs.
- If an employee raises questions about the validity of polygraph exam results (where, for example, he or she is on a form of medication that can affect the results of the exam), do not disclose the test results to others until the validity of the test has been firmly established.

G. Minimizing Defamatory and Other Actionable Statements About Employees

As the cases summarized in Part One make clear, virtually any uncomplimentary statement about an employee can form the basis of an action for defamation. Further, virtually any statement regarding a termination based on an employee's inadequate performance or misconduct can be found to be defamatory. And because the law of defamation permits recovery for even the *negligent* publication of a defamatory statement, the tort of defamation represents the most difficult of all workplace torts for an employer to avoid.

While employers theoretically are insulated from liability for defamation of employees by virtue of the qualified privilege, as a practical matter the qualified privilege is frequently lost through abuse. But that need not be the case if an employer carefully and assiduously protects its qualified privilege. The practical suggestions detailed below are designed to afford employers the basic guidance to maintain their qualified privilege and to avoid making statements that are unprivileged.

- Before making any potentially defamatory statement about an employee, the person making the communication should possess a good faith belief in the truth of the statement. Because a good faith belief is frequently based on whether there has been a thorough investigation of the facts underlying the allegedly defamatory statement, employers should follow the suggestions in the preceding section involving investigations to assist in establishing their good faith beliefs.
- Do not publicize any potentially defamatory statement about an employee to any co-workers, supervisors, or officials of the employer unless the communication serves a genuine business purpose.
- Avoid potentially defamatory communications about an employee to persons outside the employer unless there is a legitimate business purpose to be served by the disclosure or a duty to disclose the information.
- When considering the termination of an employee for several grounds of misconduct, rely solely on those grounds that are most "solid." And, if possible, base the discharges on facts that the employee admits or are essentially undisputed.
- Avoid stating to anyone that the employee engaged in misconduct or wrongdoing, unless otherwise required by law.
- Avoid unnecessary statements containing comparisons between a terminated employee and his or her replacement.
- Do not place in writing any statement that could be misconstrued or that you would otherwise regret being discovered.
- Avoid references to employees as "incompetent" when a less objectionable phrase would be sufficient.
- Never knowingly use a false or inaccurate reason as a ground for termination of employment.
- If an employee disputes the grounds for termination or the validity of the facts underlying his or her discharge, avoid all unnecessary communications regarding the matter in dispute, and qualify all such communications by acknowledging that the employee has challenged or contested the termination.
- If asked by co-workers about an employee who has been disciplined or discharged, advise them that company policy prohibits

discussing or disclosing the reasons for the employee's discipline or separation from employment.

• If the reason for an employee's discipline or termination is announced or discussed at an employee meeting, provide a short, concise, and accurate statement, not a lengthy discourse about the conduct of the disciplined or terminated employee.

• Unless essential and justified by a valid business purpose, avoid widespread dissemination of the reasons for an employee's termination, particularly where the employee disputes the factual predicate for his or her termination.

H. Avoiding Unnecessary Inquiries About and Disclosure of Personal Employee Matters

Invasion of privacy claims are on the increase, in large part as a result of an increased awareness that employees in many states have a "right to be let alone."

The following suggestions are designed to assist employers in avoiding invasion of privacy suits by minimizing unnecessary inquiries about personal employee matters and limiting the disclosure of private information about an employee that is unrelated to his or her job.

• Under no circumstances should any supervisor or manager inquire into an employee's sexual affairs.

• Instruct supervisors and managers to refrain from calling employees at home absent pressing business needs.

• Do not open mail addressed to an employee at work that is marked "personal."

• Do not enter an employee's residence without permission.

• Ensure compliance with all federal, state, and local laws regarding the request for, retention, and disclosure of medical and mental information about employees.

• Maintain separate personnel and medical files and ensure that both are secure.

• Personal, private information in an employee's personnel or medical file should be regarded as confidential. Disclosures should be limited to circumstances where the personal and private information bears directly upon a work-related matter, and such disclosures should be consistent with all federal, state, and local laws governing the confidentiality of such information.

- Where a private or personal matter regarding an employee, if disclosed, might be highly offensive or objectionable to the employee, any disclosures should be limited solely to those persons who have a demonstrable need to know the information. Further, the person who makes the disclosure should advise the individual to whom the information is being communicated not to further disclose the information except to others with a demonstrable need to know.
- When a supervisor or manager learns of an employee's private or personal matters, such information should never be communicated to the employee's co-workers, or to anyone else without a demonstrable need to know—no matter how interesting the information may be. The urge to gossip and to divulge confidential information should be addressed by a firm company policy that supervisors or managers who do so will be subject to discipline, demotion, or even discharge.
- Employers should rarely pledge or promise to keep information confidential unless otherwise required by federal, state, or local law. If necessary, an employer could state that the information will be provided only to those with a demonstrable need to know.
- If a pledge or promise of confidentiality *is* given to an employee, it should be honored except in truly exceptional circumstances. Where disclosure would be in the best interests of the employer, the person pledging confidentiality should obtain the employee's agreement to release the information on terms satisfactory to the employee.
- Medical information disclosed by an employee to a company physician, nurse, or counselor, or to a physician or counselor retained by the employer, should be disclosed only where the employer's interest in disseminating the information clearly outweighs the employee's interest in the privacy of the information, and then only in accordance with all applicable federal, state, and local laws.
- All company policies regarding confidentiality of medical records and information should be followed, except in extraordinary circumstances.
- Where personal or private information in the possession of the employer is requested by an outside source, including a governmental agency or law enforcement bureau, notify the employee of the request and, if disclosure is to be made, provide the employee with an opportunity to seek a court order barring the disclosure. Exceptions to this suggestion should only be made in extraordinary circumstances after consultation with in-house or outside counsel.
- Do not disclose the terms of confidential agreements between an employer and employee to anyone without a genuine need to know.

I. Minimizing Abusive and Harassing Treatment of Employees by Supervisors and Co-Workers

Abusive and harassing treatment of employees by supervisors and co-workers remains a problem in the workplace. Although respect for the well-being of other employees appears to be increasing, the number of lawsuits against employers based on offensive or outrageous conduct is increasing dramatically.

The torts most often used by employees who have been subjected to abusive and harassing conduct are intentional and negligent infliction of emotional distress, assault and battery, negligent retention, and negligent failure to supervise and train managers. The following practical suggestions are designed to assist employers in minimizing the likelihood that they will be sued for one or more of these torts.

• Issue guidelines to supervisors not to use their authority to assign work, schedule shifts, evaluate employees, issue warnings, recommend demotions, or take similar action as a means to harass employees. Provide employees with an effective means to complain about supervisory harassment.

• Ensure that supervisors refrain from using undesirable assignments or shifts as means to "get rid of" employees.

• Provide employees with proper protective work clothing when their work would expose them to workplace hazards, and disclose the existence of such hazards to employees before they undertake the work assignment.

• Never assign work to employees, including work involving exposure to toxins, that is certain to cause injuries to them.

• Prohibit supervisors from lowering performance evaluations or placing employees on assignments for which they are not trained as a means to harass employees.

• Avoid using humiliating demotions and job assignments as a means to induce employees to resign their employment.

• Consider implementation of a no-dating rule between supervisors and subordinates to avoid personal "friendliness" that can be abused by supervisors and can lead to sexual harassment.

• Conduct training of supervisors and managers to ensure that they are aware of the legal prohibitions against sexual harassment, and instruct them that sexual harassment is grounds for termination of the harasser.

• As required by federal and state laws prohibiting sexual harassment, respond to an employee's complaint of sexual harassment or hostile work environment in a manner that ensures that if the complainant was harassed, he or she is no longer victimized by a superior or co-workers and is not retaliated against for bringing the complaint to the attention of management.

- Discipline or discharge employees who engage in offensive horseplay or physical or mental abuse of co-workers. Investigate such claims promptly after receiving notice of such abuse.
- Discipline, demote, or discharge supervisors and managers who violate the law prohibiting sexual harassment.
- Issue and enforce work rules prohibiting offensive contacts and assaults upon employees.
- Where an employee shows that he or she is unstable or particularly susceptible to emotional harm, ensure that his or her supervisors do not cause emotional distress by abusing or harassing the employee. Monitor such supervisor-employee relationships regularly to identify potential areas where the supervisor's actions or inaction might result in emotional distress to the employee.
- Counsel and train supervisors and co-workers to avoid making racial, ethnic, religious, or other insults toward employees, and take immediate action—including discipline, demotion, or discharge of the harassing supervisors or co-workers—to remedy such harassment.
- Require and encourage lower-level managers to report sexual and other forms of harassment to the human resources department, even where complaints are made against more senior managers of the organization.
- Where an employee requests a brief and reasonable postponement of the time to make a decision or sign a document, provide the employee with the additional time and specify, preferably in writing, when the decision must be made or paper signed.
- Where an employee complains about smoking in the workplace or some other condition affecting the workplace environment, the matter should be promptly examined by the employee's supervisor, who should refrain from taking any reprisals against the employee or harassing the employee who filed the complaint.
- Absent special circumstances, do not advise employees on disability leave that they are being or will be terminated for cause. Wait until they return to work or until the disability leave is coming to a close.
- Do not fire an employee for a false reason.
- Do not "set up" employees for termination.
- Do not use termination methods that implicate an entire department's work force, *i.e.*, terminating all employees in a department

or office who had access to company property. Use individualized methods of inquiry.

• Supervisors and managers should not terminate or recommend the termination of employees for malicious or illegitimate reasons.

J. Converting Terminations Into Resignations

Employee lawsuits for defamation tend to arise most frequently in connection with terminations from employment. After being terminated, employees sometimes tend to view their employers and supervisors with a sense of hostility, an emotion that can lead them to file a lawsuit. There are, however, several practical suggestions that allow employers to minimize the likelihood of employee lawsuits.

One of the most effective suggestions is to offer employees who are about to be terminated the option of tendering their resignations instead. This option allows employees to truthfully advise prospective employers that they resigned from their last job, thereby assisting them in obtaining new employment. This has the effect of mitigating any potential damages that may be claimed by an employee and substantially lessens the likelihood of a claim for defamation by compelled self-publication (see Chapter 3, section C.). Ideally, the conversion of a termination into a resignation can lead the employee and employer to enter into a valid separation agreement, including a proper waiver and release of all potential claims by the employee against the employer (see Chapter 13, section H.).

Conversion of terminations into resignations is not necessarily appropriate or desirable in every instance, nor is a separation agreement warranted in certain circumstances. Each situation should be examined separately and the facts should be evaluated carefully to ensure that the best interests of the employer are being served.

If an employer decides to afford an employee the option of resigning from employment in lieu of termination, there are a few other practical suggestions to consider.

• Advise employees that a voluntary resignation may assist them in their attempt to obtain new employment.

• Determine whether outplacement assistance will help induce the employee into resigning. If so, consider the appropriateness of offering such assistance to employees, especially to those who would otherwise be terminated for unsatisfactory work performance.

• Notify employees that, where consistent with state unemployment insurance laws, a voluntary resignation in the face of certain discharge will not preclude them from receiving unemployment benefits.

• Document all the circumstances surrounding an employee's separation from employment, including the opportunity given the employee to resign in lieu of being terminated.

K. Obtaining Releases From Employees

In connection with or apart from the preceding step, employers can attempt to insulate themselves from lawsuits by obtaining a written release from an employee who is being terminated or who resigns. Releases from employees are regulated in part by federal and state law, including the Older Workers Benefit Protection Act (OWBPA), 29 U.S.C. section 626(f), which dictates the contents of releases for age discrimination claims. Because of the significant legal implications of releases, they should be drafted in consultation with an employer's inside or outside counsel.

Further, the enforceability of releases frequently depends on the circumstances under which they were obtained. For example, a release procured by fraud, duress, or coercion is unenforceable. Set forth below are a few practical recommendations to enhance the enforceability of releases.

• Provide the employee with legal "consideration," such as a modest amount of severance pay to which the employee otherwise would not have been entitled. Absent this or some other type of consideration, the release may not be enforceable as a matter of law.

• Make sure the release is in plain English or in the employee's native language where appropriate. Provide a translator if necessary.

• Where the employer seeks a valid release for claims of age discrimination, the provisions of the OWBPA should be followed.

• Afford the employee an opportunity to review the proposed release with anyone of his or her choice, including an attorney.

• Give the employee ample time to consider his or her decision to sign a release.

• Do not coerce or force employees to sign a release.

L. Qualifying Postemployment References

Although prospective employers generally seek complete reference information to minimize their own potential liabilities for negligent hiring, more and more former employers are seeking ways to avoid liability for defamatory postemployment references. Employers should continue to exercise caution in providing postemployment references. The following practical suggestions can be used to qualify postemployment references.

• Develop a written postemployment reference policy, and direct those in the organization who are responsible for such references to follow the policy. Disseminate the policy to all supervisors and managers as well.

• Avoid responding to oral requests for information about former employees. Verify that the party requesting this information has a bona fide need to know.

• Where possible, limit the information provided to a prospective employer to verification of dates of employment and positions held by the former employee.

• Do not advise prospective employers of the reasons for an employee's separation from employment.

• Do not volunteer any information. Respond only to the questions asked by the prospective employer.

• Obtain the employee's consent to disclose employment data.

• Obtain a release from the employee waiving all claims against the employer in connection with the disclosure of employment data.

• Document all requests for references, including who made the request, how the request was made, and what information was provided.

• Limit postemployment references to objective facts; do not provide opinions.

• Never give a postemployment reference about an employee based on any information based on unverifiable "office gossip."

• Refer a prospective employer seeking a reference about a former employee to persons with firsthand knowledge of the former employee's employment. Do not provide secondhand information unless it is based on reliable information documented in writing. And, if any information provided is based on secondhand "facts," advise the prospective employer that your information is not based on personal knowledge.

• Consider implementing a policy requiring all postemployment references to be furnished by the human resources or employee relations department.

• If a favorable employment reference is promised to an employee, an unfavorable reference should not be given.

- Follow the same suggestions for independent contractors as you do for employees with respect to references.

M. Avoiding Other Post-Termination Tortious Conduct

Even though an employee is no longer employed by an employer, the employer can become liable to the employee for a workplace tort based on post-termination conduct by the former employer or his agents. For example, post-termination tort actions may arise as a result of the commencement of civil or criminal proceedings against employees, enforcement of restrictive covenants, and inducing current employers to terminate a former employee's present employment. A few practical suggestions to avoid these types of post-termination tort claims are set forth below.

- Carefully evaluate demands by managers and officials to institute criminal proceedings against employees who have filed lawsuits against the employer.
- Do not file any civil or criminal proceedings against any employee without probable cause to believe that the employee engaged in the alleged misconduct (see Chapter 9, note 7, defining the term "probable cause").
- Do not file or assist in the filing of criminal charges against employees unless the employer has first conducted a thorough investigation and obtained sworn statements supporting the charges and verified the facts underlying the allegations.
- Confer with in-house or outside counsel before filing or assisting in the filing of criminal charges against an employee.
- If criminal charges are filed against an employee by an employer, one or more suitable representatives of the employer should appear in court if required for the prosecution of the employee.
- Do not file professional misconduct charges against an employee with a state licensing agency before fully investigating and verifying the facts supporting the allegations.
- If criminal charges against an employee for theft are discussed, do not file civil proceedings against the employee without first considering the likelihood that the employee will file a counterclaim for malicious prosecution.
- Do not seek or threaten to enforce covenants not to compete that are overbroad or otherwise unreasonable. Confer with in-house or outside counsel before enforcing any such clauses.

- Refrain from recommending or inducing another employer to fire an employee.
- Refrain from interfering with the selection of employees by other employers.
- Supervisors and managers should not use a postemployment reference as an opportunity for retaliation against an employee who caused problems at work for the supervisor or manager.
- Postemployment references should be objective and factual. Opinions and speculation should be avoided, even if requested by a prospective employer.

N. Other Practical Suggestions

- Forewarn an employee's supervisor as well as the human resources or employee relations department of all incidents of employee violence.
- Use the negligent retention theory, where applicable, as an additional ground for termination of unfit or incompetent employees.
- Provide alternative means of transportation for employees who attend parties or gatherings where alcoholic beverages are served.
- Advise employees of company policy against excessive consumption of alcoholic beverages at employer-sponsored parties or outings; instruct servers to limit employees' consumption; and serve only nonalcoholic beverages during the final hour of any such gatherings.

Notes

Legal citations to all cases summarized in Part One are also included in the Table of Cases at the end of the book.

1. The suggestions in this chapter are mere guidelines—they do not address specific factual situations. Before following any recommendation, carefully evaluate the facts and determine whether the suggestion applies or should be followed. Consultation with legal counsel may even be called for in certain situations, especially where competing interests of the employer and employee are involved. Further, before implementing any employment practice, especially one dealing with applicant screening, ascertain if it may cause a disparate impact on the basis of race, color, religion, sex, national origin, or any other protected category. If so, be sure the employment practice is job-related for the position in question, consistent with business necessity, and is otherwise lawful under § 105 of the Civil Rights Act of 1991 as well as comparable state and local fair employment practices laws.

2. Special appreciation is extended to Anne C. Vladeck, Esq. of Vladeck, Waldman, Elias & Engelhard of New York City, whose firm has represented employees in hundreds of lawsuits against employers, many of which have involved state law tort claims similar to those summarized in Part One of this book. Ms. Vladeck provided valuable ideas for various practical suggestions.
3. *See* Evans v. Morsell, summarized in Chapter 1, section D.1.c.
4. *See* Ponticas v. K.M.S. Invs., summarized in Chapter 1, section D.1.c.
5. *See* Chapter 2, section B., dealing with fraud and misrepresentation.

Chapter 13

Litigating Workplace Tort Actions

A. Overview

Until recently, workplace tort claims were usually added to complaints alleging employment discrimination and were generally regarded as peripheral causes of action. Now, they are often the principal claims asserted against an employer, and sometimes even the only claims in an employee lawsuit. The reason for this legal development may well be that six-figure jury awards for workplace torts have become commonplace, and million-dollar jury verdicts are no longer unusual.

This chapter provides employers with guidance in defending against workplace torts. It includes a discussion of multiple tort claims, selection of defendants, jurisdiction, employer defenses, pretrial discovery, motions to dismiss and for summary judgment, jury trials, punitive damage awards, and attorneys' fees. In addition, this chapter includes a discussion of out-of-court settlements—one of the most practical but frequently ignored areas of the law—and concludes with a detailed examination of the terms of settlement agreements.

B. Multiple Tort and Other Employment Claims

An employee or other injured party who commences a tort action against an employer usually asserts more than one workplace tort claim in his or her complaint. By suing an employer for a number of tort claims, an employee maximizes the likelihood that at least one claim will survive a pretrial motion to dismiss or a motion for summary judgment and be presented to a jury. And, where more than one tort claim reaches the jury, employees have, on occasion, recovered compensatory and punitive damages for each of several different torts.

Similarly, it is not at all unusual for an employee to accompany his or her tort claim with another type of employment claim, such as an action for breach of contract, wrongful discharge, or violation of a federal or state discrimination statute. Employees who prevail on both their tort and other employment claims have likewise been awarded damages for more than one type of claim.

Several of the cases summarized in Part One of this book illustrate the challenges faced by employers in defending against multiple legal claims. In *Davis v. Utah Power & Light Co.*,[1] a female employee who claimed that she was sexually harassed and unjustly terminated by her superior filed a lawsuit against her employer asserting ten different claims: negligent failure to adequately supervise the offending superior and train him not to sexually harass his subordinates, intentional infliction of emotional distress, negligent infliction of emotional distress, invasion of privacy, battery, false imprisonment, fraud, violation of Title VII, breach of employment contract, and breach of implied covenant of good faith and fair dealing. The employer filed a motion to dismiss all of the tort and contract claims on the ground of preemption, arguing that the state antidiscrimination statute was the employee's exclusive remedy. The court agreed with the employer, but only to a limited extent: while it dismissed the two state law contract claims for breach of employment agreement and breach of an implied covenant, it refused to dismiss any of the seven tort claims asserted against the employer.

Similarly, a salesman of a consumer electronics company brought an action for fraud, defamation, intentional infliction, tortious interference, and breach of contract in *Shebar v. Sanyo Business Systems*.[2] He claimed that he decided to forgo a job opportunity with one of his employer's competitors after being assured by senior executives of the company that he would not be terminated. Shortly after rescinding his acceptance of the other job offer, he was discharged. The lower court granted the employer's motion for summary judgment and dismissed all of the employee's claims. But, on appeal, the appellate court reinstated his fraud, breach of contract, and tortious interference claims, remanding them to the lower court for trial.

In *Howcroft v. Mountain States Telephone & Telegraph Co.*,[3] a company terminated an employee for allegedly using a corporate credit card for personal use. The employee filed a lawsuit alleging 13 claims for relief, including defamation, intentional infliction, tortious interference, breach of contract, and sex discrimination. The employer filed a motion for summary judgment. The court granted the motion as to 12 of the 13 claims, but permitted the employee to proceed to trial with his defamation claim.

A terminated employee who was blocked from leaving his work cubicle when he asked to speak with representatives of the employee relations department commenced a lawsuit in *Uebelacker v. Cincom Systems*,[4] alleging six separate claims for relief: false imprisonment, assault and battery, defamation, intentional infliction, breach of contract, and wrongful discharge. Although the lower court granted the employer's motion for summary judgment as to all six claims, an appellate court reversed as to the claims for false imprisonment and intentional infliction of emotional distress, remanding those two claims to the lower court for trial.

When multiple tort claims are tried, an employee's recovery is not necessarily limited to a single tort. For example, in *Foley v. Polaroid Corp.*,[5] an employee was interrogated for several hours by his employer and later tried (but acquitted) on criminal charges of sexual abuse of a co-worker. He then filed a lawsuit against his employer for false imprisonment, intentional infliction, defamation, malicious prosecution, and violation of his civil rights. His spouse also sued the employer for loss of consortium. At trial, a jury awarded the employee $1.5 million for his malicious prosecution claim, $1 million on his defamation claim, and $500,000 on his false imprisonment claim. His wife also was awarded $2 million for loss of consortium. On appeal, however, all of the judgments were reversed, except for the false imprisonment claim, which was remanded for a new trial.

In *Sims v. Kaneb Services*,[6] an employer fired a vice president who refused to sign fraudulent corporate tax returns. After the vice president filed a wrongful discharge claim against the employer, the company filed a criminal complaint against him for theft of corporate property. Following the dismissal of the criminal case, the vice president added tort claims for malicious prosecution and abuse of process. At trial, a jury awarded the vice president compensatory and punitive damages of $17 million on his malicious prosecution claim, $17 million on his abuse of process claim, and $14 million on his wrongful discharge claim.

In *Wilson v. Monarch Paper Co.*,[7] a vice president who was humiliated by his employer's action of demoting him to a job requiring him to perform janitorial duties filed an action for intentional infliction of emotional distress and age discrimination. A jury not only awarded him $3.1 million in compensatory and punitive damages for intentional infliction, but also added $300,000 in damages on his age discrimination claim.

C. Selection of Defendants

1. Suing the Individual Wrongdoer

The selection of one or more defendants is a critical strategic consideration in any workplace tort action.

Where the alleged wrongdoer acted within the scope of employment or in furtherance of the employer's interest, the employer can be sued under the well-known doctrine of *respondeat superior*.[8] As a general rule, there is no legal prohibition in a workplace tort action against suing both the employer *and* the individual who is the alleged wrongdoer.

Many of the cases summarized in Part One include claims by employees against individual defendants. The individual defendants most often sued are the employee's direct superiors. Employees, however, have also sued co-workers;[9] human resource professionals;[10] company presidents, vice presidents, and other executives;[11] loss prevention officers;[12] physicians who were employed by or rendered services under contract with an employer;[13] and even employee assistance counselors employed by other companies that provide counseling and employee assistance.[14]

An employee may sue an individual wrongdoer to vindicate a principle, or may do so based on pure vindictiveness. Other times, the naming of a high-level corporate officer may be part of a strategic attempt on the part of a plaintiff's lawyer to procure a quicker or larger settlement—although it can have the opposite effect and actually protract the litigation. Some plaintiffs' lawyers, in fact, purposely choose *not* to name an individual wrongdoer as a defendant out of concern that a jury will sympathize or identify with an individual defendant.

These are tactical litigation decisions that depend on the circumstances of each case and the judgment of counsel for the plaintiff/employee.

2. Suing the Corporate Parent: Deeper Pockets

In addition to the individual wrongdoer and his or her employer, employees sometimes seek to sue the employer's corporate parent.

This tactic is employed for many reasons, but is most commonly used to reach the "deeper pockets" of a more substantial corporate entity. Indeed, punitive damage awards are usually higher where the defendant has greater assets.

For example, where a visitor to a housing complex was fatally assaulted by an employee of the housing corporation, the victim's estate sued the housing company *and* its parent corporation.[15] Similarly, if an employer is a franchisee or distributor of a larger company's products, an injured employee or customer of the smaller employer may sue the smaller company *and* the larger firm.[16]

A plaintiff's attorney may also name a corporate parent as a defendant in the belief that the defendants will settle more quickly or offer more money to settle a case. Most corporate parents, however, vigorously resist such tactics.

D. Jurisdiction

Another tactical decision by plaintiffs' lawyers involves where the lawsuit is brought: state or federal court.

Because common law actions for torts are generally governed by state law, the state courts have jurisdiction over such actions. Where, however, the plaintiff/employee is a citizen of a different state than his or her employer, the action may be brought in federal court under the court's "diversity of citizenship" jurisdiction, provided that the amount in controversy exceeds $50,000 (which is usually the case in employee tort actions).[17] A corporation is regarded as a citizen of any state where it is incorporated and where it has its principal place of business.[18] Hence, many corporations, especially those with facilities in many different states, are subject to being sued in federal court.

Where there is a choice of forums, more often than not the employee chooses to bring his or her action in state court. This, again, is a strategic decision by the plaintiff's attorney. Some plaintiffs' counsel are more familiar with state than federal court procedures; sometimes the state courthouse is far closer than the federal courthouse; and some plaintiffs' attorneys feel that state courts are more sympathetic to local plaintiffs or are more unsympathetic to out-of-state corporations than are federal courts.

Employers are not necessarily required to accept the state court forum chosen by the employee. Instead, if the corporation is a citizen of a different state than the plaintiff, it may generally "remove" the case from state to federal court.[19] Removal is a strategic decision that must be decided on a case-by-case basis. Where an employer, however, anticipates raising the affirmative defense of federal preemption (see section E.2. of this chapter), removal of the case from state to federal court is usually advisable.[20]

Conversely, an employee may bring his or her state law tort action in federal court—even if there is no diversity of citizenship—if the employee appends to the action a claim under a federal law, such as Title VII, the Age Discrimination in Employment Act (ADEA), the Americans With Disabilities Act (ADA), or some other federal statute. This is called *supplemental jurisdiction*.[21] An employer may, however, oppose the plaintiff's attempt to litigate a state law tort claim in federal court, and may, in certain circumstances, ask the federal court to decline to exercise supplemental jurisdiction over the state law claim.[22]

In sum, employers should not willingly accept an employee's selection of a forum to litigate his or her state law tort claims. Rather, an employer should first decide in which forum *it* would prefer to try an employee's tort claims, and then determine whether removal or opposition to supplemental jurisdiction is appropriate and in its best interests.

E. Employer Defenses

One of the principal defenses that most employers assert in workplace tort actions by their employees or injured third parties is that the allegations are untrue (or, more precisely, are not supported by any admissible evidence). In addition, employers have available to them an array of affirmative defenses to workplace tort actions. These affirmative defenses, which are discussed below, bar recovery by plaintiffs even if they are otherwise able to prove their allegations.

1. Workers' Compensation

State workers' compensation laws generally provide that an employee's *exclusive* remedy for most injuries arising out of employment consists of the benefits provided in the workers' compensation act. This means that when an employee is injured by a supervisor or co-worker, he or she may be barred from commencing a common law tort action against the employer and/or the supervisor. This is one of the principal affirmative defenses asserted by employers in workplace tort actions.

There are, however, exceptions to the exclusive remedy provisions. Some state workers' compensation laws exclude injuries resulting from *intentional* acts by co-workers and superiors, while other workers' compensation laws include them. Some exclude intentional injuries committed by supervisors; others do not. Because each state's workers' compensation laws are different, it is necessary to check the scope of the exclusive remedy provision and each of its exceptions.

For example, in *Cole v. Fair Oaks Fire Protection District*,[23] a captain of a fire department suffered a stroke after his supervisor demoted him, publicly stripped him of his captain's badge, and assigned him to menial tasks—all in retribution for his union activities. The California Supreme Court ruled that the captain's claim for intentional infliction of emotional distress was barred by the exclusive remedy provisions of the state workers' compensation law. It concluded that demotions, criticisms of work, and frictions in negotiations over grievances are a "normal part of the employment relationship," and, as such, are to be compensated solely under the state workers' compensation law.

In contrast, in *Hart v. National Mortgage and Land Co.*,[24] a California appellate court held that sexual harassment of a male employee, including being grabbed and pinched by a male co-worker, was not "a normal part of the employment relationship." The employee's claims for assault and battery and intentional infliction of emotional distress were not, therefore, barred by the exclusive remedy provisions of the California workers' compensation law.

Other courts, however, have barred tort claims arising out of intentional misconduct in the workplace. In *Schwartz v. Zippy Mart*,[25] two female employees who were grabbed and pinched by their supervisor commenced an action for assault and battery. Because the two employees had not previously made any complaints about the supervisor's conduct, an appellate court held that the employer "could be guilty of only simple negligence," for which the Florida workers' compensation law provided the exclusive remedy.

The workers' compensation defense should be considered in virtually every workplace tort action filed by an employee against an employer. This defense, however, is not available to an employer in negligent hiring and retention lawsuits brought by customers, clients, or visitors of an employer, as it is generally applicable solely to actions brought by employees.[26]

2. Preemption

A state law tort claim may be "preempted"—and therefore barred—if it is also covered by a federal or state statute that precludes all other causes of action for the same wrong. The federal labor laws are the primary source for the preemption defense in workplace tort actions.[27]

a. NLRA Preemption

An employee's tort claim against his or her employer may be preempted if the alleged wrong is arguably prohibited or protected under the National Labor Relations Act (NLRA).[28] In *Belknap, Inc. v. Hale*,[29] the employer asserted this defense in response to a fraud claim by "permanent" strike replacements who were terminated at the end of a strike when the employer entered into a strike settlement agreement with its employees' union requiring the reinstatement of some of the striking employees. The United States Supreme Court rejected the employer's preemption defense, concluding that while the employer's conduct of hiring "permanent" replacements was permitted by the NLRA, that law did not nullify an employer's valid promise of permanent employment.

The defense of NLRA preemption should be evaluated in every tort action. Employers frequently overlook the fact that the NLRA not only covers unionized employees, but also nonunion employees who engage in concerted activities for mutual aid or protection.[30]

b. LMRA Preemption

Another source of federal preemption is section 301 of the Labor Management Relations Act (LMRA), which governs suits for violations of collective bargaining agreements.[31] Under this source of federal preemption, if the employer's conduct, upon which the employee bases a tort claim, requires the interpretation of a collective bargaining agreement, the tort claim is preempted by the LMRA.[32]

For example, in *Strachan v. Union Oil Co.*,[33] two union employees suspected of drug use were required, during the course of a medical examination, to provide blood and urine samples for use in drug tests. The employees sued their employer for assault and battery. An appellate court held that inasmuch as the governing collective bargaining agreement permitted the employer to conduct medical examinations in certain circumstances, the validity of the employees' claim depended on whether the employer had the right under the collective bargaining agreement to conduct such tests. The court therefore held that the employees' claims must be resolved by an arbitrator, pursuant to the arbitration provisions of the collective bargaining agreement, and not by a court.

Similarly, in *Jeffers v. Convoy Co.*,[34] an employee suspected of theft was terminated by his employer. After the employee filed a grievance with his union, the employer offered to reinstate him if he took a polygraph exam and the results showed that he had not been involved in the theft. The employee agreed to take the test even though the governing collective bargaining agreement prohibited the use of polygraph exams as a condition of employment. The test proved inconclusive, but the employee was not reinstated. He then filed suit against his employer for fraud, defamation, negligent and intentional infliction of emotional distress, breach of contract, and breach of implied covenant of good faith and fair dealing. The court held, however, that the entire lawsuit was preempted by the LMRA because the use of polygraphs was a matter dealt with in the collective bargaining agreement. Thus, the court ruled, all of the employee's claims were subject to resolution through the grievance and arbitration provisions of the labor contract.

However, many tort claims filed by employees who are covered by a collective bargaining agreement are *not* preempted. For example, in *Surrency v. Harbison*,[35] a grievance committee chairman who was harassed and then intentionally struck with a piece of heavy machinery at the instigation of the employer filed a lawsuit for battery. The employee alleged that he was harassed because of his refusal to approve certain work rules. The employer contended that the tort claim was preempted by the LMRA, but an appellate court disagreed, holding that the battery claim could be maintained by the employee because it did not require an interpretation of the terms of the collective bargaining agreement.

In *Johnson v. Anheuser Busch, Inc.*,[36] a union employee was arrested at work at the instigation of his employer and charged with destruction of property. He was also terminated for violating a company policy prohibiting malicious mischief. After he was acquitted, he filed a lawsuit against the employer for malicious prosecution, false arrest, intentional infliction of emotional distress, tortious interference with contractual relations, slander, and wrongful discharge. The employer made a motion to dismiss all of the claims, arguing that each was preempted by the LMRA because the events related to events surrounding an alleged violation of the governing collective bargaining agreement. An appellate court held that all of the employee's tort and contract claims were preempted *except for* the malicious prosecution and false arrest claims. It concluded that, unlike the other causes of action, those two tort claims did not require interpretation of the collective bargaining agreement.

The preemption defense under the LMRA should always be considered whenever an employee who commences a lawsuit alleging a state law tort or contract claim is covered by a collective bargaining agreement. The defense should also be considered when defending a loss of consortium claim by the spouse of a union-represented employee. If this defense, like any other affirmative defense, is not raised at the appropriate time in the litigation, it can be waived, possibly resulting in unnecessary liability.

For example, in *Sweeney v. Westvaco Co.*,[37] the wife of a disabled employee covered by a collective bargaining agreement filed a loss of consortium claim against her husband's employer, based on the severe and debilitating emotional distress he suffered as the result of a prolonged course of malicious harassment at work, which included an unwarranted warning and demotion. A jury awarded the wife $1.5 million in damages. On appeal, the employer raised the defense of preemption by the LMRA, claiming that the validity of the warning and demotion was governed by a collective bargaining agreement. The appeals court refused to consider the preemption defense, holding that the employer's failure to raise the preemption issue until after the jury verdict was rendered constituted a waiver of the defense.

c. ERISA Preemption

Another source of preemption frequently raised in state law tort (and contract) claims involving pensions and employee benefits is the federal Employee Retirement Income Security Act (ERISA). ERISA contains a broad preemption provision, which states that the employee protection provisions of ERISA "shall supersede any and all State laws insofar as they may now or hereafter relate to an employee benefit plan."[38]

In *Powell v. Chesapeake & Potomac Telephone Co.*,[39] an employee beneficiary under a self-funded disability benefits plan claimed that she and her son suffered severe emotional distress as a result of an unjustifiable delay in benefit payments and being required to furnish unnecessary medical reports. She filed an action for intentional infliction of emotional distress against her employer and the insurance company that administered the plan. An appellate court held that the employee's tort claim was preempted by the broad preemption provision contained in ERISA.

In contrast, courts have rejected the ERISA preemption defense in a series of fraud cases summarized in Chapter 2 of this book. In *McNamee v. Bethlehem Steel Corp.*,[40] a court held that ERISA did *not* preempt an employee's fraud, negligent misrepresentation, and breach of contract claims, based on the employer's alleged misrepresentation that it would credit him with his prior years of service for pension benefits purposes. The court reasoned that ERISA does not preempt an employee's lawsuit for damages against his or her employer where the employee is seeking neither benefits nor damages for refusal to provide benefits *under a plan.*

A similar result was reached in *Greenblatt v. Budd Co.*,[41] where an employee was permitted to maintain a fraud claim against his employer and the company's personnel manager based on an alleged misrepresentation that the benefits he would be receiving under a subsidiary's pension plan would be equal to the superior benefits available under the corporate pension plan.

Likewise, the preemption defense was rejected in *Sandler v. New York News*,[42] where an employee brought a negligent misrepresentation claim against his employer based on an innocent miscalculation of future early retirement benefits by the employer's pension manager.[43]

The defense of ERISA preemption should be considered whenever an employee's state law tort claim involves an employee benefit, including severance pay and other types of benefits that are governed by ERISA.[44]

d. Other Sources of Preemption

Other federal laws, such as the Railway Labor Act and various state laws governing labor and employment matters, preempt state common law tort actions against employers or provide for an exclusive remedy for certain alleged wrongs. As soon as a workplace tort action is commenced against an employer, its counsel should determine whether any federal or state statutes might arguably bar the employee's tort claim in court.[45] Preemption defenses sometimes are not readily apparent to labor practitioners. This is also an area where creative legal reasoning can possibly free an employer from potential tort liability.

3. No *Respondeat Superior* or Employer Ratification

An employer is not generally liable for the torts of its employees unless the plaintiff can show that the employee causing the injury or harm was acting *within the scope of his or her employment*. This is the doctrine of *respondeat superior*, which is the cornerstone of employer liability for workplace torts.[46] Further, even if the employee who engaged in tortious conduct was acting *outside* the scope of his or her employment, an employer may still be liable if it subsequently ratified or condoned the misconduct of the employee.[47]

Conversely, if the plaintiff fails to show that the employee's tortious conduct was either within the scope of employment or ratified or condoned by the employer, there is generally no recovery against the employer.

Even though the plaintiff has the burden of proving these factual issues, many employers assert as a "defense" that the conduct of the offending employee was outside the scope of his or her employment and was neither ratified nor condoned by the employer.

This defense is most frequently asserted in assault and battery claims. In *Waltman v. International Paper Co.*,[48] the employer asserted that the conduct of a male co-worker who lifted a female employee in and out of a hopper, touched her breasts, and placed an air hose between her legs, was outside the scope of his employment. An appellate court held that this was an issue to be decided by a jury. Similarly, in *Hester v. Church's Fried Chicken*,[49] the employer contended that its supervisor, who sought to reprimand one of his subordinates for unsatisfactory job performance, was acting outside the scope of his employment when he lost control and grabbed the employee by the shirt collar, threw her to the ground, and kicked her in the back. The appellate court affirmed the lower court's holding that the supervisor's conduct fell outside the scope of his employment.

Even when the evidence establishes that the offending employee was acting *outside* the scope of his or her employment, an employer must still rebut any evidence submitted by the plaintiff that it ratified or condoned the tortious conduct. In *Hester*, the appellate court affirmed the lower court's entry of summary judgment in favor of the employer where the plaintiff had failed to introduce any evidence that the employer had ratified or condoned the conduct of the supervisor. Other employers, however, have not been as fortunate. In *Newsome v. Cooper-Wiss, Inc.*,[50] the plaintiff presented evidence that the employer had failed to take prompt action after she complained about her supervisor's sexual harassment, and thereafter discharged her and retained the alleged harasser. In *Davis v. United States Steel Corp.*,[51] the employee introduced evidence that her supervisor's boss had seen her supervisor touch her buttocks but did nothing about it. And in *Hart v. National Mortgage & Land Co.*,[52] the plaintiff introduced evidence that his employer was aware that a co-worker had been engaging in sexual horseplay but took no action to put an end to the offensive conduct. In each of those three cases, appellate courts held that there was sufficient evidence of employer ratification to preclude entry of summary judgment in favor of the employer and to require that the issue be presented to a jury.

4. Arbitration

As discussed in section 2 above, arbitration clauses contained in collective bargaining agreements can support a preemption defense under the LMRA. An arbitration provision contained in an individual employment contract may also bar an employee from maintaining a workplace tort claim in court.

Employers in the securities industry have traditionally entered into arbitration agreements to resolve disputes with certain employees. In *Gilmer v. Interstate/Johnson Lane Corp.*,[53] the United States Supreme Court endorsed the use of arbitration clauses in resolving age discrimination claims brought by employees in the securities industry. In *Gilmer*, the Court held that the employee's lawsuit for age discrimination should be dismissed and referred to arbitration under the provisions of the Federal Arbitration Act (FAA),[54] because the employee had entered into a compulsory agreement to arbitrate all disputes with his employer.

Depending on how the federal courts construe the *Gilmer* decision and the provisions of the FAA, employers in other industries may begin to enter into compulsory arbitration agreements with their employees as well.

Where an employee who has agreed to arbitrate disputes with his or her employer commences a workplace tort claim in court, it may be advantageous to assert the arbitration agreement as an affirmative defense to the action. The principal advantages to arbitration include the fact that decisions are rendered by arbitrators, not juries; and the costs of cases referred to arbitration are frequently less than the costs of judicial litigation. Further, punitive damage awards in arbitration are sometimes prohibited by applicable law. For example, in *Fahnestock & Co. v. Waltman*,[55] a court vacated an arbitrator's award of punitive damages in a securities dealer's claim for defamation and wrongful discharge. The court held that New York state law prohibited the award of punitive damages by an arbitrator.

Whether an employer asserts an arbitration agreement as an affirmative defense to a tort claim is a tactical decision to be decided on a case-by-case basis. Although arbitration may be preferable to jury trials in some cases, there may well be advantages to litigating the tort claims in court. Thus, before asserting this defense, employers should carefully evaluate the post-*Gilmer* decisions and applicable court decisions regarding the preclusive effect of arbitration awards on subsequent court litigation.

5. Consent and Release

Consent is a valid defense to many workplace torts. For example, consent to the publishing of a defamatory statement is a complete defense in an action for defamation.[56] Consent is also a defense to battery[57] and false imprisonment.[58]

Written consents are sometimes used by employers before engaging in conduct that may become the basis for an employee's tort claim. These written consents, which sometimes provide that the employee releases the employer from liability for all claims arising out of the employer's conduct, are often used by employers before providing postemployment references and prior to conducting a drug test or investigation. These consent and release forms, however, have not always met with judicial approval.

In *Kellums v. Freight Sales Centers*,[59] a Florida appellate court examined a release contained in an employment application signed by an employee. The application form authorized the prospective employer to obtain information from previous employers and released all parties from liability for any damage that might result from the dissemination of the information. The court held that a release absolving a party from liability for its tortious conduct violates the public policy of that state and is therefore unenforceable. Thus, the release provided no defense to the employee's defamation action against his former employer for allegedly making a defamatory postemployment reference to the prospective employer.

In contrast, in *Columbia Sussex Corp. v. Hay*,[60] a Kentucky appellate court upheld a consent form signed by an employee who commenced a false imprisonment action against her employer for allegedly coercing her to submit to a polygraph examination that restrained her movement. The form signed by the employee acknowledged that she was neither coerced nor under duress when she agreed to take the examination.[61]

In *Crowe v. J.C. Penney, Inc.*,[62] a Georgia appellate court likewise upheld a consent form signed by an employee consenting to be questioned regarding matters of company business. The employee commenced an action against the employer for false imprisonment, but the court held that the employer's interrogation was lawful since the employee had signed a written form consenting to the interrogation and had not requested that the questioning be discontinued.

Consent need not be written to be effective. In *Hardy v. La-Belle's Distributing Co.*,[63] the Montana Supreme Court affirmed a jury verdict in favor of the employer in an action for false imprisonment, holding that an employee consented to being restrained in a store manager's office. The court ruled that the employee's testimony that she willingly remained in the store manager's office to prove her innocence established that she consented to the restraint.

Employee releases have also become the subject of statutory regulation. For example, under the Older Worker Benefit Protection Act (OWBPA),[64] Congress has set forth minimum requirements for employee releases of age discrimination claims. Increased worker protection in the area of releases is likely, either in the form of additional legislation or court decisions striking down releases as involuntary, unknowing, or in violation of state public policy.

6. Contributory and Comparative Negligence

In any negligence action, including actions for negligent hiring and retention, the defenses of contributory or comparative negligence may bar the lawsuit altogether or limit the plaintiff's recovery. The doctrines of "contributory negligence" and "comparative negligence" refer to the conduct of the injured party and may limit his or her damages.[65]

Two cases summarized in Chapter 1 illustrate the application of this defense. In *Brown v. Burlington Industries*,[66] a female employee who was sexually harassed by one of her superiors brought a negligent retention claim against her employer after the company failed to take prompt action to remove the harassing manager. A jury returned a verdict in favor of the female employee but limited her award to $60,000, based on its additional finding that she was contributorily negligent, presumably in not bringing her complaints to the attention of management at the earliest possible time. Similarly, in *Chamberlain v. Bissell, Inc.*,[67] a court held that an employee was entitled to damages in his action for negligent performance evaluation but reduced the award by 83 percent based on its finding that the employee was contributorily negligent by engaging in conduct that precipitated his own discharge.

7. Other Defenses

Workplace tort claims are also subject to the same affirmative defenses that apply to other causes of action. Among the affirmative defenses that may be applicable in workplace tort actions, besides those discussed earlier in this section, are collateral estoppel, *res judicata*, statute of limitations, tavern owner laws, sovereign or governmental immunity, charitable immunity, failure to mitigate damages, estoppel, laches (delay), release, waiver, choice of law, election of remedies, independent contractor, merchant detention laws, and unclean hands.

F. Pretrial Discovery

Pretrial discovery can serve a number of useful objectives in defending against a workplace tort suit. For example, evidence obtained from the plaintiff during pretrial discovery can be used to support a motion for summary judgment, thereby avoiding trial on all or part of a plaintiff's case if the motion is successful. Discovery can also provide an employer with a meaningful assessment of the strengths and weaknesses of a plaintiff's claim, and its own defenses, in deciding whether to proceed to trial or settle the case. And, of course, pretrial discovery can assist an employer in preparing for trial.

Discovery can, however, serve to educate a plaintiff's attorney about an employer's defenses and proof. And discovery is rarely inexpensive. Thus, employers should carefully assess their objectives before embarking upon the discovery stage of litigation and should devise a discovery plan that will best serve those objectives.

Discovery can generally be obtained from either party by any of the following means: deposition upon oral or written questions, requests for production of documents, interrogatories, requests for admission, and medical or psychiatric examinations. As part of its discovery plan, an employer should decide which forms of discovery it will need to use, and for what purpose.

Although discovery tactics in workplace tort actions vary from case to case, the following practical suggestions are offered.

- The employer should serve a comprehensive document request upon the plaintiff's attorney at a very early stage of the proceedings. As a general rule, a plaintiff's document response should be substantially complete before an employer takes the plaintiff's deposition.
- The employer should attempt to secure "priority" in depositions, that is, the plaintiff's deposition should be conducted first whenever possible. This will assist the employer's witnesses in preparing for their own depositions.
- One or more knowledgeable representatives of the employer should attend the plaintiff's deposition or be available for telephone consultation during a break in the deposition or an overnight adjournment. This can assist counsel in formulating follow-up questions to unexpected answers or responses that raise factual issues about which the employer's counsel is unfamiliar.
- An employer's inside counsel should, if available, attend the deposition. This will provide the employer with a meaningful opportunity to observe firsthand how well or poorly the plaintiff may testify if the case ever reaches trial. In addition, attendance at the plaintiff's deposition may further assist inside counsel in formulating his or her assessment of the strengths and weaknesses of the plaintiff's case.
- An employer may wish to avoid serving interrogatories upon a plaintiff until after the plaintiff's deposition has been taken. Interrogatory answers are prepared by attorneys, so the likelihood of obtaining a meaningful admission as to a factual dispute or substantive legal issue is remote. Interrogatories are often helpful, though, in following up on details of factual matters that were raised at the deposition but may not have been completely responded to by the plaintiff. Interrogatories can also require the plaintiff to provide the employer with the names and addresses of all persons with personal knowledge of the factual allegations of the complaint (and sometimes a brief statement by the plaintiff of what the witnesses supposedly know). So-called "contention" interrogatories may also be helpful, especially if the plaintiff's attorney refuses to allow the plaintiff during the course of the deposition to state the basis for an unclear allegation or cause of action.
- When an employer responds to a plaintiff's interrogatories or request for production of documents, all legal privileges should be considered, including the attorney-client privilege and the attorney work product doctrine.

- Employers should not disclose trade secrets, confidential commercial information, or personal or private information about other employees. As a general rule, employers should only make such disclosures, if at all, in redacted form or pursuant to a comprehensive confidentiality stipulation and court order. All other applicable objections, including lack of relevance, should be considered by the employer before responding.
- Employers may wish to conduct a medical or psychiatric examination of the plaintiff in accordance with the applicable rules of procedure, especially if the plaintiff seeks damages for physical or emotional injury. A deposition of the treating physician and a subpoena for production of the physician's records pertaining to the plaintiff may also be appropriate.
- Requests for admissions may be helpful in preparing for trial. However, because attorneys prepare the responses to such requests, their value in workplace tort actions may be limited.

Pretrial discovery disputes can arise during the course of litigating a workplace tort action, including disputes over a party's response or failure to respond. In order to keep the cost of discovery reasonable, as many of these disputes as possible should be resolved informally.

G. Pretrial Motions to Dismiss and Motions for Summary Judgment

In the proper circumstances, it may be advisable for an employer to file a pretrial motion to dismiss all or part of an employee's workplace tort suit or a motion for full or partial summary judgment. Many of the affirmative defenses discussed in section E. of this chapter can be adjudicated by the judge in a motion to dismiss or for summary judgment.[68] Indeed, in a number of the cases summarized in Part One of this book, motions to dismiss and motions for summary judgment successfully eliminated some or all of the plaintiff's claims for relief.

These pretrial motions may not only serve to eliminate the need for trial or trim down the number of claims that might otherwise proceed to trial, but also may facilitate the settlement of a workplace tort suit. A case can sometimes be settled for a reasonable sum after a court grants an employer's pretrial motion for partial dismissal or partial summary judgment. The costs of a potential settlement can be significantly increased, however, if a plaintiff is able to successfully defend against such a motion. Thus, as a general rule, such pretrial motions should only be made where there is a reasonable probability of full or partial dismissal or summary judgment in favor of the employer.[69]

H. Jury Trials

Parties have a right under the United States and state constitutions to a trial by jury on common law claims.[70] Inasmuch as most juries are composed primarily of nonsupervisory employees or former workers, plaintiffs in workplace tort actions tend to regard juries as sympathetic to their causes. Thus, employees who sue their employers almost always exercise their right to a jury trial.

I. Compensatory and Punitive Damage Awards

Employees who prevail in workplace tort suits are entitled to damages. There are two types of damages that can be awarded: compensatory and punitive damages. Compensatory damages may include, but are not limited to, lost earnings; lost benefits; reimbursement of medical expenses; reimbursement of expenses for finding a new job; damage to reputation; payments for pain, suffering, humiliation, mental anguish, and other forms of emotional distress; lost future wages and benefits; future medical expenses; and even future emotional distress.

While employers are justifiably concerned about juries awarding millions of dollars in *punitive* damages in workplace tort actions, the amount of *compensatory* damages that can be awarded in such cases may also be substantial—especially when the plaintiff is a high-income executive. For example, a jury in Texas awarded a vice president $12 million in compensatory damages in his malicious prosecution and abuse of process lawsuit against his employer.[71] A Connecticut jury in a fraud claim awarded another vice president $1.1 million in compensatory damages,[72] and an executive vice president was awarded $2.7 million in compensatory damages by a Maryland jury in his negligent misrepresentation claim.[73] A judge in California awarded $3.3 million in compensatory damages to an executive on his intentional infliction of emotional distress and other tort claims,[74] and a jury in a federal court action in Texas awarded a former vice president $850,000 in compensatory damages for his intentional infliction claim.[75]

Substantial compensatory damages have also been awarded in workplace tort actions to middle-management and nonsupervisory employees. For example, a jury in a federal court action in Oregon awarded two public relations managers for a railroad $850,000 in compensatory damages on their tortious interference claims.[76] And a jury in Texas awarded an insurance salesman $600,000 in compensatory damages in a tort action against his employer based on a defamatory postemployment reference.[77]

Punitive damages, of course, can add substantially to the total amount of a jury award in a workplace tort action. For example, the two public relations managers referred to above, who were awarded $850,000 in compensatory damages for tortious interference, were also awarded $2 million in punitive damages; and the insurance salesman who was awarded $600,000 in compensatory damages for defamation collected another $1.3 million in punitive damages for his defamation action.

The amounts of punitive damages awarded to the executives in the cases above were likewise astounding, ranging from $2 million and $2.25 million in the intentional infliction cases to $22 million in the malicious prosecution and abuse of process case. Plainly, the $1 million threshold for punitive damage awards has long since been crossed by juries in workplace tort actions, and multimillion-dollar jury awards are becoming more and more commonplace.

It is therefore not surprising that virtually every employee who sues his or her employer for one or more workplace torts seeks an award of punitive damages. An award of punitive damages, however, is not automatic whenever a plaintiff prevails in a workplace tort suit. Courts usually require something more than the mere commission of a tort to support a punitive damage award. Aggravated conduct, such as actions motivated by spite, malice, improper motive, or a conscious disregard of the interests or safety of others is generally required as a precondition to an award of punitive damages.[78] As a practical matter, though, punitive damages are awarded in the overwhelming number of tort cases where liability is imposed on an employer.

Most courts have held that punitive damages may be assessed against an employer for an agent's tortious act performed within the scope of the agent's employment—even in the absence of approval or ratification by the employer.[79] Punitive damages may be awarded where the employee who caused the injury or harm was unfit and the employer was reckless in employing the unfit employee, where the tortious conduct was performed by a managerial employee, or where the tortious conduct was authorized by the employer or later ratified or approved by a managerial agent of the employer.[80]

While most courts have held that an award of punitive damages should generally be in reasonable proportion to the amount of compensatory damages awarded, some punitive damage awards have been upheld despite having little relationship to the amount of compensatory damages awarded. For example, in an action for intention infliction of emotional distress and battery by a female employee who was sexually harassed by her manager, an appellate court upheld a jury award of $100,000 in punitive damages, even though the amount of compensatory damages was only $10,000.[81] And in a case where an employer defrauded an employee with a false promise to pay a year-end bonus, a jury awarded the employee punitive damages of $750,000, even though the award of compensatory damages only amounted to $30,000.[82] Although the trial court in that case lowered the punitive damage award, the Supreme Court of Texas remanded the issue of punitive damages to an intermediate appellate court to determine whether the trial court erroneously reduced the $750,000 punitive damage award.

Finally, *non*employee victims in negligent hiring and retention lawsuits have also obtained seven-figure jury awards against employers. In two illustrative cases involving assaults on youngsters by employees who had criminal records, juries in Texas and New York imposed $5 million and $2.5 million damage awards on the responsible employers.[83]

In sum, the amounts of compensatory and punitive damage awards in workplace tort actions are virtually limitless. The prospect of a million-dollar jury verdict appears to be one of the principal reasons why more and more employees and injured parties are bringing workplace tort actions against employers—and one of the principal reasons why employers settle such cases before they are submitted to a jury.

J. Attorneys' Fees

Under the so-called "American Rule," attorneys' fees are generally *not* recoverable by a prevailing party in a common law action; rather, each party must bear its own attorneys' fees.[84] Usually, the only means for an employer to obtain an award of attorneys' fees is if the court "sanctions" a plaintiff or his or her attorney for bringing or maintaining a frivolous claim for relief.[85] Such sanctions, however, are usually imposed only in exceptional circumstances, and the amounts awarded rarely approach the actual attorneys' fees incurred by an employer.

Attorneys' fees may, however, be awarded to prevailing plaintiffs under discrimination and whistleblower statutes.[86] This is one reason why plaintiffs frequently add federal and state statutory claims to their common law workplace tort actions.

K. Out-of-Court Settlements

Although there are no statistics available regarding the percentage of workplace tort claims that are resolved by out-of-court settlements, it is believed that well over 90 percent of such claims never reach trial. Further, the overwhelming bulk of cases that are settled before trial are never reported in legal journals or newspapers and are the subject of confidential settlement agreements that never become known to the public.

A number of the cases summarized in Part One of this book were settled before trial. For example, in *Rosen-House v. Sloan's Supermarket*,[87] an employer reportedly settled a negligent hiring case for a six-figure sum before trial, following a lower court decision denying the employer's motion for summary judgment. In *Redd v. Product Development Corp.*,[88] a delivery company settled a negligent retention lawsuit for $16 million only days before trial in a case involving an injured pedestrian's claim that the employer knew or should have known that the company's driver was an alcohol and drug abuser. And in *Freeman v. Kansas State Network*,[89] a television station settled an infliction of emotional distress and fraud claim before trial, following the lower court's grant of partial summary judgment to the employer.

Many cases are also settled after trial or during the appellate stage of litigation. For example, in *Sallaz v. G-H-I Housing Corp.*,[90] a nonprofit organization and its parent corporation settled a negligent hiring case for $3.7 million after a jury returned a $5 million verdict in favor of the parents of a nine-year-old girl who was fatally assaulted by a paroled ex-convict hired by the nonprofit corporation. And in *Dowie v. Exxon Corp.*,[91] the employer settled a fraud case for an undisclosed seven-figure sum after appealing a jury's $10.1 million verdict in favor of the employee.

Of course, not all workplace tort suits are settled for six- and seven-figure sums. Many are settled for five-figure amounts, and some are even settled for very modest sums of money.

Various factors influence the amount of a settlement, but the most significant one is frequently the amount of economic damages, such as lost wages, suffered by the employee. Another important factor is whether the employee or injured party has suffered physical or emotional injury requiring hospitalization and treatment. Naturally, the workplace tort action's validity is also a key factor in settlement negotiations. For example, an employee fraud claim based on nothing other than unsupported allegations can sometimes be settled for nuisance value, whereas a similar claim supported by competent or credible testimony or documents may require the expenditure of a more substantial amount of money in order to induce a plaintiff to settle.

Another important settlement factor for employers is the cost of defending a workplace tort action, both in terms of the legal fees likely to be incurred and the management time needed to be expended. Indeed, the cost of litigation is often a significant factor to employers when considering when and whether to settle a workplace tort case.

L. Settlement Agreements

Whenever a lawsuit is settled out of court, the terms of settlement are invariably reduced to writing in a settlement agreement. Settlements should also be reduced to writing whenever an employer settles a claim with an employee who has not filed a lawsuit. While some out-of-court settlement agreements of nonlitigated claims are negotiated and drafted by human resource managers or other managerial personnel, the need for attorney supervision in the settlement process has been heightened by the enactment of laws such as the Older Worker Benefit Protection Act (OWBPA),[92] which governs the validity of waivers and releases of asserted and unasserted claims of age discrimination.

Besides the very basic terms of an out-of-court settlement agreement, such as the amount of money, if any, being paid to the employee, there are a number of other matters that should be considered when negotiating and drafting an effective settlement agreement. These include:

- legal consideration,
- valid waivers and releases,
- confidentiality,
- employment references,
- tax considerations,

- loss-of-consortium concerns, and
- "choice of law," "nonadmission," and "complete agreement" clauses.

1. Legal Consideration

As a basic principle of contract law, a settlement agreement between an employee and employer will not be enforceable unless it is supported by "legal consideration" from both parties. Legal consideration usually consists of a payment of money or another exchange of value, including performance or a promise to perform an act or to forgo a valuable right.[93]

From the standpoint of an employee who has already commenced a lawsuit against an employer, consideration will usually consist of his or her withdrawal or dismissal of the lawsuit, together with a waiver and release of all legal claims against the employer as of the date of the agreement. Where no lawsuit has yet been commenced, consideration usually consists of a waiver and release of all claims, perhaps together with an agreement not to commence a lawsuit or other legal proceeding based on any conduct of the employer as of the date of the agreement.

An employer likewise must provide legal consideration to the employee. Consideration by employers usually, but not necessarily, takes the form of money. Not all exchanges of money, however, will constitute valid consideration. Payment of an employee's accrued vacation time and earned commissions, for example, would usually be inadequate as legal consideration because those are amounts of money that the employer already owes to the employee. As a basic rule, an employer must provide an employee with something of value that it does not already owe to the employee in order to satisfy the requirement of legal consideration.[94]

2. Valid Waivers and Releases

As a general rule, a waiver of rights or a release of claims by an employee must be knowing and voluntary.[95] It cannot be coerced, procured by duress, or be the product of unawareness or lack of knowledge on the part of the employee. Use of "plain English" is therefore highly recommended in drafting a waiver or release, especially when the employee is not represented by counsel.

Under the OWBPA, which covers workers who are protected by the federal Age Discrimination in Employment Act (ADEA), a waiver of an employee's rights under the ADEA will not be regarded as knowing and voluntary unless it is written in clear terms that are calculated to be understood by the employee; contains an express reference to the ADEA; does not waive claims or rights that may arise after the date it is signed; provides the employee with something of value in addition to anything to which the employee is already entitled; contains a provision permitting the employee a prescribed period of time to consider the terms of the proposed agreement; includes a provision permitting the employee a prescribed period of time to "back out" of the agreement after it has been signed; and advises the employee to consult with an attorney.[96] The OWBPA also requires disclosures of certain information whenever the employee is part of a group or class of employees being offered something in exchange for a waiver or release.[97]

Waivers and releases should be comprehensive in scope and tailored to the particular circumstances of each case. Waivers should cover a broad array of employee rights, and releases should cover all potential claims and forms of employer liability. Waivers and releases should also cover all rights and all claims not only against the employer, but also against the employer's subsidiaries, affiliates, and parent corporation as well as all officers, agents, and employees of the employer.

3. Confidentiality

As a condition of settlement, employers frequently require that the employee agree to a provision requiring confidentiality and nondisclosure of the terms of the settlement. This type of provision is designed to ensure, to the maximum extent possible, that other employees of the employer do not view a settlement agreement with one employee as an invitation for them to commence their own lawsuits against the employer.

As a practical matter, though, confidentiality cannot be assured, and a breach of the confidentiality provision is difficult to prove and even more difficult to remedy. For that reason, an employer may seek to insert into the settlement agreement a provision whereby the employee must return or forgo all or part of the consideration provided by the employer. Employees and their counsel, however, usually regard such provisions as unduly harsh and vigorously resist inclusion of them in the settlement agreement.

4. Employment References

In cases where employees have been terminated or have resigned, it may be advisable for an employer to include in the settlement agreement a provision regarding an agreeable postemployment reference. The most compelling reason to do so is because a settlement agreement can only settle past and present claims—and may not validly foreclose an employee from filing a *future* claim against the employer based on an allegedly defamatory postemployment reference provided after the settlement agreement is executed. By agreeing to the terms of a postemployment reference in the settlement agreement, this type of future claim can be minimized or avoided.

5. Additional Settlement Provisions

An employer may also wish to include in a settlement agreement a provision addressing the issues of reinstatement or reemployment, loss of consortium by the employee's spouse, and tax considerations of funds paid to the employee. The agreement may also need to state whether the employee is resigning from employment and whether ERISA or other claims are excluded from a waiver or release. In addition, it may be advisable to include a clause stating that the settlement agreement constitutes the full agreement of the parties and supersedes all other agreements between the employee and employer, except for any trade secret agreements previously signed by the employee.

If the employee has consulted an attorney, an employer may wish to include in the agreement a provision noting that the employee was represented by counsel, and may require the employee's attorney to witness the employee's signature. In addition, a statement should be included in the settlement agreement that the employee understands all the terms and conditions and enters into the agreement voluntarily.

An employer may also wish to add a provision dealing with the resolution of any future disputes that may arise under the terms of the agreement, as well as a clause expressly stating that the terms of the agreement shall be governed by the laws of a particular state.

Finally, it is advisable to include a "nonadmission" clause in a settlement agreement, stating that neither the execution of the settlement agreement nor the payment of any money to the employee under the terms of the settlement agreement constitute an admission by the employer that it has violated any law or breached any duty or contract.

The settlement provisions discussed above are not intended to be an exclusive list of terms to be considered in negotiating and drafting out-of-court settlement agreements. Rather, this discussion is intended to be a general guide for employers. Each case to be settled requires an independent evaluation by counsel to determine what provisions are necessary, desirable, and appropriate to include in a settlement agreement. Thus, boilerplate agreements should be avoided unless they are reevaluated and given a "fresh look" before being used.

Notes

Legal citations to all cases summarized in Part One are also included in the Table of Cases at the end of the book.

1. *See* case summarized in Chapter 1, section D.3.C.
2. *See* case summarized in Chapter 2, section D.2.
3. *See* case summarized in Chapter 3, section D.1.b.
4. *See* case summarized in Chapter 8, section C.1.b.
5. *See* case summarized in Chapter 8, section C.1.a.
6. *See* case summarized in Chapter 9.
7. *See* case summarized in Chapter 4, section D.1.
8. *See* Restatement (Second) of Agency §§ 219(1), 228.
9. *See* Love v. Southern Bell Tel. & Tel. Co., summarized in Chapter 5, section C.4; Surrency v. Harbison, summarized in Chapter 6, section C.6; Johnson v. Anheuser Busch, Inc., summarized in Chapter 9.
10. *See* Greenblatt v. Budd Co., summarized in Chapter 2, section D.3.; Benassi v. Georgia-Pacific, summarized in Chapter 3, section D.4.; Kobeck v. Nabisco, Inc., summarized in Chapter 5, section C.2.; Sorrells v. Garfinkel's, summarized in Chapter 7, section C.1.a.
11. *See* Loughry v. Lincoln First Bank, summarized in Chapter 3, section D.1.a.; Worley v. Oregon Physicians Servs., summarized in Chapter 3, section D.4.; Falls v. Sporting News Publishing Co., summarized in Chapter 3, section D.8.; Nelson v. Lapeyrouse Grain Corp., summarized in Chapter 3, section D.7.; Phillips v. Smalley Maintenance Servs., summarized in Chapter 5, section C.3.; McKay v. Ashland Oil, summarized in Chapter 10, section C.1.
12. *See* Elmore v. Shell Oil Co., summarized in Chapter 3, section D.9; Hall v. May Dep't Stores Co., summarized in Chapter 4, section D.4.a.
13. *See* Millison v. E.I. du Pont de Nemours & Co., summarized in Chapter 2, section D.7.; Bratt v. IBM, summarized in Chapter 5, section C.1.
14. *See* Wangen v. Knudson, summarized in Chapter 4, section D.6.
15. *See* Sallaz v. G-H-I Housing Corp., summarized in Chapter 1, section D.1.c.
16. *See* Giles v. Shell Oil Corp., summarized in Chapter 1, section D.3.a.
17. *See* 28 U.S.C. § 1332(a)(1).
18. *See* 28 U.S.C. § 1332(c)(1).
19. *See* 28 U.S.C. § 1441(a). If, however, the employer or a co-defendant is a citizen of the state in which the action is brought, removal is not permissible. *See* 28 U.S.C. § 1441(b).
20. *See* Jeffers v. Convoy Co., summarized in Chapter 2, section D.5. (case removed to federal court by employer; federal court dismissed state law tort claims, holding that they were preempted by federal labor law); Johnson v. Anheuser Busch, Inc., summarized in Chapter 9 (case removed to federal court by employer; federal court dismissed four of six tort claims on the basis of

federal preemption). A lawsuit filed in state court may also be removed to federal court where one of the claims asserted arises under federal law. *See* 28 U.S.C. § 1441(c).
21. *See* 28 U.S.C. § 1367(a). The state law tort claims must, however, relate to the federal claims. *See* 28 U.S.C. § 1367(a).
22. There are four circumstances set forth in 28 U.S.C. § 1367(c).
23. *See* case summarized in Chapter 4, section D.1.
24. *See* case summarized in Chapter 6, section C.1.
25. *See* case summarized in Chapter 6, section C.1.
26. The workers' compensation defense may also be available to employers in actions brought against them by the spouses, parents, or children of their employees. *See generally* 2 LARSEN'S WORKERS' COMPENSATION § 66.20 (desk ed.).
27. The discussion of preemption in this book is not intended to be an exhaustive review of this frequently litigated issue, but rather an illustrative discussion of the topic.
28. *See* International Longshoremen's Ass'n v. Davis, 476 U.S. 380, 122 LRRM 2369 (1986); San Diego Bldg. Trades Council v. Garmon, 359 U.S. 236 (1959). This "preemption" defense is frequently referred to as an "exclusive jurisdiction" or "exclusive remedy" defense. See the actual court opinion in *Wells v. General Motors Corp.*, summarized in Chapter 2, section D.6.
29. *See* case summarized in Chapter 2, section D.1.b.
30. *See* NLRA § 7, 25 U.S.C. § 157.
31. *See* 29 U.S.C. § 185(a).
32. *See* Lingle v. Norge Div., 486 U.S. 399, 3 IER Cases 481 (1988); Allis-Chalmers Corp. v. Lueck, 471 U.S. 202, 1 IER Cases 541 (1985); Farmer v. United Bhd. of Carpenters Local 25, summarized in Chapter 4, section D.1.; Linn v. United Plant Guard Workers, 383 U.S. 53 (1966). *See also* United Steelworkers of Am. v. Rawson, 495 U.S. 362, 5 IER Cases 493 (1990).
33. *See* case summarized in Chapter 6, section C.2.
34. *See* case summarized in Chapter 2, section D.5.
35. *See* case summarized in Chapter 6, section C.6.
36. *See* case summarized in Chapter 9, Section C.
37. *See* case summarized in Chapter 4, section D.1.
38. *See* 29 U.S.C. § 1144(a). *See generally* Ingersoll-Rand Co. v. McClendon, 111 S. Ct. 478, 5 IER Cases 1601 (1990); Fort Halifax Packing Co. v. Coyne, 482 U.S. 1, 2 IER Cases 134 (1987); Metropolitan Life Ins. Co. v. Taylor, 481 U.S. 58 (1987); Pilot Life Ins. Co. v. Dedeaux, 481 U.S. 41 (1987); Shaw v. Delta Air Lines, 463 U.S. 85 (1983).
39. *See* case summarized in Chapter 4, section D.3.
40. *See* case summarized in Chapter 2, section D.3.
41. *See* case summarized in Chapter 2, section D.3.
42. *See* case summarized in Chapter 2, section D.6.
43. *See also* Cory v. Binkley Co., summarized in Chapter 2, section D.3.
44. *See, e.g.*, Blau v. Del Monte Corp., 748 F.2d 1348 (9th Cir. 1984), *cert. denied*, 474 U.S. 865 (1985).
45. Other preemption-type cases summarized in Part One of this book include *Davis v. Utah Power & Light Co.*, summarized in Chapter 1, section D.3.c. (state antidiscrimination statute as source of preemption/exclusive remedy); and

Glass Molders Int'l Union v. Wickes Cos., summarized in Chapter 7, section C.1.d.
46. *See* Introduction, section B.
47. *See* Introduction, section B.
48. *See* case summarized in Chapter 6, section C.1.
49. *See* case summarized in Chapter 6, section C.6.
50. *See* case summarized in Chapter 6, section C.1.
51. *See* case summarized in Chapter 6, section C.1.
52. *See* case summarized in Chapter 6, section C.1.
53. 111 S. Ct. 1647 (1991).
54. *See* 9 U.S.C. §§ 1 *et seq.*
55. *See* case summarized in Chapter 3, section D.10.
56. *See* text at note 8 in Chapter 2, section B.
57. Part of an employee's "prima facie" case in a claim for battery is that the offensive contact was "unpermitted." *See* text at note 7 in Chapter 6, section B.
58. *See* text at note 10 in Chapter 8, section B.
59. *See* case summarized in Chapter 3, section D.8.
60. *See* case summarized in Chapter 8, section C.2.
61. The Federal Employee Polygraph Protection Act, 29 U.S.C. §§ 2001–09, now limits an employer's use of polygraph examinations and requires an employer to obtain the written consent of an employee to take a polygraph examination. *See* 29 U.S.C. § 2007(a), (b).
62. *See* case summarized in Chapter 8, section C.1.a.
63. *See* case summarized in Chapter 8, section C.1.a.
64. *See* 29 U.S.C. § 626(f). See also this chapter, section L.2., regarding settlements.
65. *See* Restatement (Second) of Torts § 467; W. KEETON, PROSSER AND KEETON ON THE LAW OF TORTS §§ 65, 67 (5th ed. 1984). Some states also recognize "assumption of the risk" as another defense to a cause of action for negligence. *See* W. KEETON at § 68.
66. *See* case summarized in Chapter 1, section D.2.b.
67. *See* case summarized in Chapter 1, section D.5.
68. Summary judgment is only appropriate, though, when there is no genuine issue as to any facts that are material to any of the claims or defenses. *See generally* Celotex Corp. v. Catrett, 477 U.S. 317 (1986); Anderson v. Liberty Lobby, 477 U.S. 242 (1986).
69. Legal costs should also be taken into account. While a pretrial motion may be costly to prepare and argue before the court, the costs of preparing for and conducting a defense at trial are usually far greater than the cost of a pretrial motion and can require an enormous amount of management time and effort.
70. *See* United States Constitution, Seventh Amendment; New York Constitution, art. 1, § 2; art. 6, § 18.
71. *See* Sims v. Kaneb Servs., summarized in Chapter 9, section C.
72. *See* Dowie v. Exxon Corp., summarized in Chapter 2, section D.1.b.
73. *See* Weisman v. Connors, summarized in Chapter 2, section D.1.a.
74. *See* Collins v. Shell Oil Co., summarized in Chapter 4, section D.9.
75. *See* Wilson v. Monarch Paper Co., summarized in Chapter 4, section D.1.
76. *See* Kraus v. Santa Fe S. Pac. Corp., summarized in Chapter 7, section C.1.c.
77. *See* Frank B. Hall & Co. v. Buck, summarized in Chapter 3, section D.8.

78. *See* W. KEETON, PROSSER AND KEETON ON THE LAW OF TORTS § 2 (5th ed. 1984).
79. *See* W. KEETON, PROSSER AND KEETON ON THE LAW OF TORTS § 2 (5th ed. 1984). *See also* Pacific Mut. Life Ins. Co. v. Haslip, 111 S. Ct. 1032 (1991).
80. *See* Restatement (Second) of Agency § 217C.
81. *See* Ford v. Revlon, Inc., summarized in Chapter 4, section D.2.
82. *See* Spoljaric v. Percival Tours, summarized in Chapter 2, section D.2.
83. *See* Sallaz v. G-H-I Housing Corp., summarized in Chapter 1, section D.1.c.; Haddock v. City of N.Y., summarized in Chapter 1, section D.2.c.
84. *See* Alyeska Pipeline Serv. Co. v. Wilderness Soc'y, 421 U.S. 240 (1975).
85. *See* FED. R. CIV. P. 11; 28 U.S.C. § 1927; Roadway Express v. Piper, 447 U.S. 752 (1980); Christiansburg Garment Co. v. EEOC, 434 U.S. 412 (1978). State rules of procedure may also provide for sanctions.
86. *See* 42 U.S.C. § 1988; 42 U.S.C. § 2000e-5(k); 42 U.S.C. § 12205. Many state discrimination and whistleblower statutes also provide for attorneys' fees as a form of damages or costs. *See, e.g.*, N.J. STAT. ANN. 34:19-5(e).
87. *See* case summarized in Chapter 1, section D.1.c.
88. *See* case summarized in Chapter 1, section D.2.a.
89. *See* case summarized in Chapter 4, section D.9.
90. *See* case summarized in Chapter 1, section D.1.c.
91. *See* case summarized in Chapter 2, section D.1.b.
92. *See* 29 U.S.C. § 626(f).
93. *See* Restatement (Second) of Contracts §§ 71, 72, 74, 75.
94. *See* Restatement (Second) of Contracts § 73.
95. *See, e.g.*, Stroman v. West Coast Grocery Co., 884 F.2d 458 (9th Cir. 1989), *cert. denied*, 111 S. Ct. 151 (1990).
96. 29 U.S.C. § 626(f).
97. 29 U.S.C. § 626(f)(1)(F)(ii).

Chapter 14

Other Significant Legal Issues

A. Personal Liability of Managers

As discussed in Chapter 13, employees who have been injured or harmed by the tortious conduct of their superiors can sue the individual wrongdoer in addition to their employer. When named as a defendant, the individual is subject to *personal liability* to the injured employee.

For example, in *Wangen v. Knudson*,[1] a jury rendered a $130,000 verdict in favor of an employee against his employer, his supervisor, and an employee assistance program (EAP) counselor for intentional infliction of emotional distress. The employee claimed that the EAP counselor had improperly told him that he would have to decide whether to enroll in an alcohol treatment program or be terminated—despite the fact that the employee was *not* an alcoholic. He also claimed that his supervisor improperly terminated him when he requested additional time to decide what to do. The jury assessed damages against the supervisor and EAP counselor for their reckless conduct, which caused the employee's psychological condition to worsen and require medical treatment.

In *Sorrells v. Garfinkel's*,[2] a jury assessed $230,000 in compensatory and punitive damage for tortious interference against a supervisor for maliciously recommending the termination of a beauty sales consultant at a department store. Although the court reduced the jury award to $80,000, it upheld the jury's verdict of personal liability against the supervisor.

In *Geyer v. Steinbronn*,[3] a jury awarded an employee compensatory damages of $100,000 against both his employer and supervisor based on the supervisor's conduct of providing a knowingly false postemployment reference, which caused the employee to lose a job offer from another employer. The jury also assessed the supervisor $50,000 in punitive damages for his malicious conduct.

Perhaps the most costly personal liability verdict in a workplace tort action was rendered in *Sims v. Kaneb Services*.[4] In that case, a jury assessed punitive damages of $1 million against the chief executive officer and $1 million against the chief financial officer of a company where the two maliciously caused the company to file a criminal complaint against an employee in retaliation for his filing of a wrongful discharge lawsuit against the employer.

Even judges are subject to personal liability when they engage in tortious conduct with respect to their employees. In *Johnson v. Ramsey County*,[5] a jury assessed punitive damages of $300,000 for battery against a bisexual judge who made repeated propositions and sexual advances toward his male court reporter and then kissed him on the lips. The trial court reduced the punitive damage award to $50,000 based on the judge's inability to pay the full amount of the jury verdict.

B. Defendant Conflicts of Interest

As noted in Chapter 1, under the doctrine of *respondeat superior* an employer is liable for the tortious acts of its agents where the agents act *within* the scope of their employment.[6] Conversely, where an agent of the employer acts *outside* the scope of employment or in a manner that does not further the employer's interests, an employer may escape liability altogether—unless the employer was negligent in hiring or retaining the employee.

As a result, an employer's interest and the interest of its agent often differ dramatically where the agent, such as a supervisor, acts *outside* the scope of employment. In that event, the agent may be left as the only viable defendant in a workplace tort action by an employee or injured party.

Immediately after a workplace tort action is commenced, the employer must determine whether the agent who allegedly committed the wrongful conduct acted within or outside the scope of employment. If it is determined that the agent acted outside the scope of employment, an attorney representing the employer may be ethically precluded not only from representing the agent, but also from conferring with the agent any further, inasmuch as the agent's interests may conflict with those of the employer.[7] In such circumstances, the employer's counsel may need to advise the agent of the possible conflict of interest and to recommend that he or she retain independent counsel.

In contrast, where it is evident that an agent acted *within* the scope of employment, counsel may wish to advise the agent that company attorneys will represent him or her as an agent of the employer.[8] Where the agent is a potential defendant and potentially may be liable to the injured employee, the employer and its counsel should determine whether it wishes to offer the agent the services of company counsel or an independent attorney.

Moreover, where the agent has acted within the scope of employment, the employer should determine whether it wishes to indemnify the agent if the injured employee obtains a damage award against the agent. In making this determination, employers must examine the relevant state laws regarding indemnification of officers and employees, because some states prohibit employers from indemnifying individual employees where an injured employee obtains an award of punitive damages against an individual. Employers also must review their corporate bylaws, resolutions, personnel policies, and insurance policies regarding indemnification.

The determination as to whether the employee acted within or outside the scope of employment may not be feasible at an early stage of the litigation. A common technique under such circumstances is to offer the employee a common defense with the employer but to advise the employee that he or she may wish to retain separate counsel to oversee and protect the employee's interests.

C. Insurance Considerations

Many states have statutes or public policies that prohibit insurance for *intentional* torts. In states that allow such coverage, many insurance policies exclude some or all intentional torts from coverage, absent a special rider.

Where an insurance policy *excludes* intentional torts, the insurance carrier may only pay for or provide a defense to a workplace tort action and not agree to indemnify the employer for any damage award. Where an insurance policy *includes* coverage for intentional torts, however, the insurer generally has an obligation both to pay for or provide a defense to the workplace tort action *and* to indemnify the employer in the event it is found to be liable.

Whether a workplace tort claim is covered by a general liability policy of insurance is not always clear. For example, in *NPS Corp. v. Insurance Co. of North America*,[9] an insurance carrier declined to defend or indemnify an employer in a lawsuit for battery arising out of allegations of sexual harassment. The employee who commenced the lawsuit claimed that a male co-worker repeatedly touched her in an offensive manner, causing her to suffer serious emotional distress and mental anguish. The general liability policy only covered "bodily harm," and the carrier concluded that emotional distress and mental anguish did not comprise "bodily harm." Thereafter, the employer entered into a settlement agreement with the employee without the participation, consent, or approval of the insurance company. The employer then filed a lawsuit against the insurance carrier seeking to recover its costs of settlement and legal fees. An appellate court held that because emotional distress can and often does have a direct effect on other bodily functions, the term "bodily harm" included emotional distress caused by sexual harassment.

When an insurance carrier acknowledges at the outset that it has a duty to indemnify an employer in a workplace tort action, it may advise the employer that it will provide counsel selected by the carrier. Before agreeing to any such an arrangement, an employer should determine whether any possible conflicts of interest exist between the carrier and employer. For example, in one of the negligent hiring cases summarized in Chapter 1, the employers involved agreed to settle the case for the limit of their liability insurance policy—$500,000. The insurance company, however, chose not to settle the case at that time. A jury subsequently rendered a verdict against the employers for $5 million.[10]

Even where no conflicts exist, though, employers usually select counsel of their choice to maintain maximum control over the litigation. In that event, most insurance companies will pay at least part of the legal fees incurred by the employer.

Notes

1. *See* case summarized in Chapter 4, section D.6.
2. *See* case summarized in Chapter 7, section C.1.a.
3. *See* case summarized in Chapter 7, section C.4.
4. *See* case summarized in Chapter 9, section C.
5. *See* case summarized in Chapter 6, section C.1.
6. See Introduction, section B.
7. *See* ABA Model Rules of Professional Conduct, Rule 1.7 and comment.
8. *See* ABA Model Rules of Professional Conduct, Rule 4.2 comment.
9. *See* case summarized in Chapter 6, section C.1.
10. *See* Sallaz v. G-H-I Housing Corp., summarized in Chapter 1, section D.1.c.

Appendices

Many of the workplace tort cases summarized in Part One of this book involve drugs and drug testing, AIDS, smoking in the workplace, failure to conduct criminal record searches or adequate background searches on applicants, polygraph examinations, and interference with an employee's ability to obtain new employment. The appendices summarize selected state and federal statutes as they apply to employers regarding the above topics. They cover

- criminal record inquiries (Appendix A),
- polygraph examinations (Appendix B),
- consumer credit reports (Appendix C),
- drug testing (Appendix D),
- AIDS testing (Appendix E),
- smoking in the workplace (Appendix F),
- employee access to personnel records (Appendix G), and
- blacklisting of employees (Appendix H).

All appendices were prepared by Peter S. Gray, Esq., and are current as of January 1992. Practitioners should review their latest statutory materials to check for new or amended laws regarding the covered topics.[1]

Note

1. The appendices in this book focus primarily on statutes regulating private, nongovernmental employers. Some states have extensive statutory provisions governing public employees that should be reviewed by governmental employers. In addition, state constitutional provisions should be reviewed, as well as judicial opinions recognizing a cause of action for violation of public policy. Finally, the federal constitution should be reviewed, particularly as it applies to drug testing and testing for AIDS.

Appendix A

Criminal Record Inquiries

Selected State Statutes

California

The California Labor Code prohibits public and private employers from asking applicants to disclose information concerning arrests or detention that do not result in convictions. Cal. Lab. Code § 432.7. The Labor Code provides that no employer may ask an applicant for information, either directly or indirectly, about arrests that did not lead to convictions or whether the applicant has ever participated in any pre- or posttrial diversion program. Moreover, the statute expressly prohibits employers from seeking this information "from any source whatsoever," or, where the employer has such information, from using it in connection with a hiring decision. The Labor Code permits employers to ask applicants to disclose arrest records if the applicant is seeking a position in a criminal justice agency, as a peace officer, or as a health worker with access to drugs or patients. Cal. Lab. Code § 432.7(e), (f).

Significantly, the statute permits employers to ask applicants about pending criminal actions: an applicant may be asked whether he or she currently "is out on bail or on his or her own recognizance pending trial." Employers also may ask applicants whether they have been indicted but not yet tried.

The California Penal Code limits employer access and use of criminal record history. In particular, the Penal Code prohibits an employer from requiring that applicants provide a copy of their criminal records. Cal. Penal Code § 13326. Demanding such information in itself constitutes a misdemeanor. The Penal Code describes pre- or posttrial diversion, and notes that successful completion of the program permits an applicant to treat an arrest and, where applicable, a conviction, as though they never occurred. Absent the applicant's consent, a "divertee's" record may not be used in any way that would result in the denial of employment. Cal. Penal Code § 1000.5. The Penal Code also permits persons convicted and sentenced to probation to petition a court to set aside the conviction. When the petition is granted, the petitioner need not admit to the conviction or plea in response to employment-related inquiries. Cal. Penal Code § 1203.4a. Persons convicted of a misdemeanor or otherwise entering a plea and not sentenced to probation also may petition for a set-aside. Cal. Penal Code §§ 1000, 1001.

The California Fair Employment Practice Rules are consistent with the labor and penal code provisions governing use of criminal records. The Rules provide generally that it is unlawful for an employer to inquire or seek information concerning any arrest or detention that did not result in conviction. The Rules also prohibit employers from asking employees about information contained in records sealed by court order, expunged, or statutorily erased (such as juvenile convictions). That section also prohibits inquiries concerning misdemeanors following successful completion of probation and misdemeanors otherwise discharged where the individual petitions the court to dismiss the original accusation against him or her pursuant to § 1203.4 of the Penal Code. The Rules also disallow inquiries concerning matters closed following completion of a pretrial diversion program.

The California Pre-employment Inquiries Guide similarly requires that inquiries about convictions be accompanied by a statement that conviction will not necessarily disqualify the applicant.

Connecticut

Under Connecticut law, employers are not prohibited from inquiring into an applicant's arrest record. Rather, state law provides that the portion of a job application form that contains information concerning the arrest record of an applicant shall not be available to any employee or member of the company, firm, or corporation interviewing the applicant except the members of the personnel department or, if such company, firm, or corporation has no personnel department, the person in charge of employment. Conn. Gen. Stat. § 31-511.

A separate statute provides that Connecticut "encourage[s] all employers to give favorable consideration to provide jobs to qualified individuals, including those who may have criminal conviction records." Conn. Gen. Stat. § 46a-79. The section further prohibits the state or any of its agencies from disqualifying an individual for employment or from the practice of any occupation for which a license is required "solely because of a prior conviction of a crime." Conn. Gen. Stat. § 46a-80. If conviction of a crime is one factor used to reject an application for employment, the statute provides that such rejection shall be in writing and shall set forth the evidence on which the decision was based. Conn. Gen. Stat. § 46a-80(c).

Connecticut law provides that public employers must give due consideration to an ex-offender's rehabilitation and the job-relatedness of the crime for which he or she was convicted before making employment decisions. Conn. Gen. Stat. § 46a-80(b). No comparable section of the law, however, addresses a private employer's obligation in this regard.

Florida

No Florida statute or regulation prohibits an employer's collection and use of arrest, indictment, or conviction information. Public employers cannot disqualify a person for employment as the result of a prior conviction unless "the crime was a felony or first degree misdemeanor and directly related to the position of employment sought." Fla. Stat. § 112.011. Florida does not have a comparable statute governing private employers.

Illinois

The Illinois Human Rights Act expressly prohibits preemployment inquiries concerning arrest records. Ill. Rev. Stat. Ann. ch. 68, § 2-103. The section exempts from its coverage local government units and school districts and permits them to use conviction records attained from the Department of State Police under § 55(a), (b), and (e) of the Civil Administrative Code in evaluating the qualifications and character of an employee or a prospective employee. This provision has been interpreted by the Illinois Human Rights Commission in its Guidelines on Discrimination in Employment, which states that the use by an employer of an application form seeking arrest or similar (nonconviction) information about an applicant violates state law regardless of the purpose for which such information is sought or the use to be made of it. Guidelines § 4.2. The Guidelines further state that an applicant may not waive his or her rights under this section. The Guidelines note that the Illinois Human Rights Act "also prohibits oral inquiries directed to applicants about their arrest records."

The Illinois Human Rights Act does not address employer collection and use of indictment or conviction information. The Illinois Human Rights Commission has taken the position that conviction records are not within the prohibition attendant to arrest record information. Guidelines § 4.4. Nonetheless, the Commission has concluded that inasmuch as the use of arrest or conviction records impacts significantly on minority group members and causes their exclusion from employment at a higher rate than job applicants from other groups, such criteria are "unlawfully discriminatory unless the user can demonstrate in each instance that the applicant's record renders him unfit for the particular job in question." Guidelines § 4.5.

A separate Illinois statute provides for the expungement of arrest record information. Ill. Rev. Stat. ch. 38, § 206-5.

Massachusetts

Under Massachusetts law, an employer seeking conviction information must provide the following statement to applicants:

> An applicant for employment with a sealed record on file with the commissioner of probation may answer "no record" with respect to an inquiry herein relative to prior arrests, criminal court appearances or convictions. An applicant for employment with a sealed record on file with the commissioner of probation may answer "no record" to an inquiry herein relative to prior arrests or criminal court appearances. In addition, any applicant for employment may answer "no record" with respect to any inquiry relative to prior arrests, court appearances and all adjudications in all cases of delinquency or as a child in need of services which did not result in a complaint transferred to the superior court for criminal prosecution.

Mass. Gen. Laws ch. 276, § 100A(4). The statute sets forth the rules governing who may seek to have a criminal conviction sealed. In particular, persons convicted of a misdemeanor may seek to have the record sealed ten years following conviction or the completion of a period of incarceration or probation. Persons convicted of a felony must wait 15 years before petitioning the Commonwealth to seal the record. Persons convicted of a crime within ten years of the request are not eligible. The statute designates the Commonwealth's Attorney General as the party responsible for its enforcement.

A provision in the Commonwealth's Fair Employment Practices Law, Mass. Gen. Laws ch. 151B, provides that an employer may not ask applicants about arrests that did not result in convictions; first convictions of misdemeanors involving drunkenness, simple assault, speeding, minor traffic violations, affray, or disturbance of the peace; and convictions of misdemeanors generally where the conviction or release from incarceration following such conviction occurred more than five years prior to the date of the application, unless the applicant subsequently was convicted of any offense within that five-year period. Mass. Gen. Laws. ch. 151B, § 4(9).

Michigan

The Elliot-Larsen Civil Rights Act specifically states that employers other than public law enforcement agencies shall not "request, make, or maintain a record of information regarding an arrest, detention, or disposition of a violation of law in which a conviction did not result." Mich. Comp. Laws Ann. § 377.205a. The statute's bar on arrest record inquiries does not extend to information concerning pending felony charges that have not yet resulted in dismissal or conviction. Mich. Comp. Laws Ann. § 37.2205a.

No provision in the Michigan statute or the Interpretative Guidelines promulgated by the Michigan Civil Rights Commission prohibits an inquiry concerning convictions. Moreover, no provision distinguishes between felony and misdemeanor convictions or places a time limit on the permissible inquiries. Indeed, the Michigan Guidelines denoted as a lawful inquiry: "Have you ever been convicted of a crime? If so, when, where, and nature of offense?"

Michigan has adopted by reference the federal Uniform Guidelines in Employee Selection Procedures. *See* Michigan Interpretative Guidelines § 5. Under the Uniform Guidelines, the use of criminal history information could be deemed a test, as it may constitute a "selection procedure used as a basis for making employment decisions." Uniform Guidelines § 2B. If an employer's use of criminal history information constitutes a discrete qualifying or disqualifying step in the employment process and adversely affects a group protected by the Michigan statute, such use would be deemed violative of state law absent the employer's demonstration that the selection criterion was related to job performance.

Finally, a separate Michigan statute permits ex-offenders to request a court to set aside a criminal conviction that would permit the individual to treat the conviction as though it never occurred. Mich.

Comp. Laws Ann. § 780.621. The conviction set-aside law is limited, however, to a first conviction, and only for convictions involving crimes more serious than minor traffic infractions but less serious than crimes for which the maximum penalty is life imprisonment. Mich. Comp. Laws Ann. § 780.621(2). Employers and others are forbidden from demanding information concerning convictions that have been set aside. Mich. Comp. Laws Ann. § 780.623(4). The release or use of such information itself constitutes a misdemeanor. Mich. Comp. Laws Ann. § 780.623(5).

New Jersey

No provision in the New Jersey Law Against Discrimination addresses preemployment inquiries concerning arrest, indictment, or conviction records. In a separate publication, the New Jersey Division of Civil Rights has deemed questions pertaining to arrest records as "impermissible" but does allow employers to inquire about prior convictions if reasonably related to the job.

Another New Jersey statute prohibits employer use of expunged arrest or conviction records. N.J. Stat. Ann. § 3C:52-1. Under the expungement statute, individuals who have been convicted of certain indictable offenses, disorderly-persons offenses, or municipal-ordinance violations may, under certain conditions, petition for expungement. N.J. Stat. Ann. §§ 2C: 52-2–4. Applicants for employment in New Jersey who have petitioned successfully for the expungement of criminal records need not respond to requests for information about criminal history. Under the statute, expungement effectively renders the criminal conviction a "non-event" for employment purposes. N.J. Stat. Ann. § 2C:52-27.

New York

In New York, the Human Rights Law prohibits employers from asking applicants about arrests that did not result in conviction or other adverse adjudication. N.Y. Exec. Law. § 296(16).

The use of conviction information is addressed in both the New York Human Rights Law and the New York Correction Law. Section 296(15) of the New York Human Rights Law prohibits an employer from denying employment based on a criminal conviction not related to the requirements of the job at issue. The New York Human Rights Law incorporates by reference the provisions of article 23-a of the correction law, which permits employers to make limited use of conviction information in making employment decisions, provided such use relates in some fashion to the job at issue. Section 752 of the New York Correction Law allows use of criminal conviction information where: "(1) there is a direct relationship between one or more of the previous criminal offenses and the specific ... employment sought; or (2) ... the granting of the employment would involve an unreasonable risk to property or to the safety or welfare of specific individuals or the general public." N.Y. Correct. Law § 752.

Section 753 of the Correction Law further provides that, in making a determination under section 752, the employer must consider the following eight factors:

(a) The public policy of this state ... to encourage the ... employment of persons previously convicted of one or more criminal offenses.

(b) The specific duties and responsibilities necessarily related to the ... employment sought.

(c) The bearing, if any, the criminal offense or offenses for which the person was previously convicted will have on his fitness or ability to perform one or more such duties or responsibilities.

(d) The time which has elapsed since occurrence of the criminal offense or offenses.

(e) The age of the person at the time of occurrence of the criminal offense or offenses.

(f) The seriousness of the offense or offenses.

(g) Any information produced by the person, or produced on his behalf, in regard to his rehabilitation and good conduct.

(h) The legitimate interest of the ... private employer in protecting property, and the safety and welfare of specific individuals or the general public.

N.Y. Correct. Law. § 753(1). The statute further provides that in making a determination the employer shall also give consideration to a certificate of relief from disabilities or a certificate shall create a presumption of rehabilitation in regard to the offense or offenses specified therein. N.Y. Correct. Law § 753.

Finally, the statute provides that when an applicant is refused employment because of reliance on a criminal record, the applicant has a right to request from the employer and receive within 30 days a written statement of the reasons for denial of employment. N.Y. Correct. Law. § 754.

Texas

There is no provision under Texas law that expressly prohibits employer inquiries into arrests, indictments, or convictions.

Federal Law Under Title VII

Even if a state law permits consideration of criminal arrests and/or convictions in hiring decisions, employers also must consider the impact of Title VII of the Civil Rights Act of 1964, as amended, 42 U.S.C. § 2000e *et seq.* The courts and the Equal Employment Opportunity Commission (EEOC) have long held that employer use of *arrest* record information adversely affects the employment of persons protected under Title VII. See *Gregory v. Litton Systems*, 472 F.2d 631 (9th Cir. 1972).

The EEOC also issued a Policy Statement on September 7, 1990, dealing with arrest records. In the policy statement, the EEOC has opened the door slightly to permit employer use of arrest record information where the employer predicates its action on the person's conduct causing his or her arrest, and the conduct is job-related and relatively recent. In evaluating the basis for such use of arrest record information, the EEOC will look for evidence that:

(1) the employer took significant steps to investigate the conduct, including providing the employee with an opportunity to explain;
(2) accurate and current statistics support the existence of an adverse impact; and
(3) the exclusion was based on the relationship of the criminal charges to the position at issue.

On February 27, 1987, the EEOC issued a revised Policy Statement on the Issue of Conviction Records under Title VII. The policy statement provides that where an employer fails to hire or terminates an individual as a result of a conviction policy or practice that has an adverse impact on a protected class to which the charging party belongs (for example, blacks or Hispanics), the employer must show that it considered three factors to demonstrate that its decision was justified by business necessity:

(1) the nature and gravity of the offense or offenses;
(2) the time that has passed since the conviction and/or completion of the sentence; and
(3) the nature of the job held or sought.

The EEOC policy statement essentially follows the thrust of several long-standing federal court decisions on this subject. See, e.g., *Green v. Missouri Pacific Railroad Co.*, 523 F.2d 1290 (8th Cir. 1975).

Appendix B

Polygraph Examinations

Selected State Statutes

California

Under California law, an employer, other than the federal or state government and their agencies and subdivisions, cannot require an applicant or employee to submit to a polygraph, lie detector, or similar test as a condition of employment or continued employment. Cal. Lab. Code. § 432.2(a). While an employer may request that an employee or applicant take such a test, the employer must first advise the person in writing, at the time of the test, that it does not have the right to demand or require such testing. Cal. Lab. Code § 432.2(b).

An employer further cannot use any device that examines or records a person's voiceprints or other voice stress patterns to determine the truth or falsity of statements made, without that person's express written consent. Cal. Penal Code § 637.3(a).

Connecticut

The Connecticut Labor Code provides that an employer, including the state or any of its political subdivisions but excluding a police department with regard to its noncivilian employees, cannot request or require any employee or prospective employee to take a polygraph examination as a condition of obtaining or continuing employment, or dismiss or discipline an employee for failing to take such an examination. Conn. Gen. Stat. § 31-51g. Connecticut law defines "polygraph" as any mechanical or electrical instrument or device used to examine, test or question individuals for the purpose of determining truthfulness. Conn. Gen. Stat. § 31-51g. An employer who violates this law is subject to a fine of between $250 and $1,000 for each violation. Conn. Gen. Stat. § 31-51g.

Florida

No specific statute has been enacted in Florida limiting or otherwise prohibiting the testing of employees or prospective employees by polygraph. Florida does, however, have specific licensing requirements for polygraph examiners, none of which relates to the conduct of the test itself.

Illinois

The regulation of polygraphs in Illinois concerns the licensing of those who administer lie detector tests. Although Illinois law addresses when and how testing is to be conducted and further requires that test results be made available to the person tested, none of the provisions addresses employer obligations or liability for use or misuse of such testing in an employment context. Under state law, a licensed examiner must use an instrument that meets state standards and must make the test results known to the examinee within five days of his or her receipt of a written request. Ill. Ann. Stat. ch. 111. Moreover, a polygraph examiner may lose his or her license if he or she inquires into subjects that are not directly related to employment, such as religious beliefs or affiliations, racial beliefs or opinions, political beliefs or affiliations, matters concerning labor organizations, and sexual preference or activity. Violation of this law is a misdemeanor.

Massachusetts

Under Massachusetts law, an employer may not require that applicants or employees take lie detector tests for employment-related purposes. Mass. Gen. Laws ch. 149, § 19B. The statute bars use of such tests within the Commonwealth and outside the Commonwealth for use within it. Further, applications used in Massachusetts must include the following statement: "It is unlawful in Massachusetts to require or administer a lie detector test as a condition of employment or continued employment. An employer who violates this law shall be subject to criminal penalties and civil liability." Persons violating the statute face fines of between $300 and $1,000 for a first offense and up to $1,500 plus up to 90 days in jail for subsequent violations. A person claiming adverse employment action based on the impermissible use of a lie detector may file a civil action seeking injunctive relief plus damages, which may include three times his or her lost wages and benefits, costs, and attorneys' fees.

Michigan

Michigan's Polygraph Protection Act of 1981, Mich. Comp. Laws Ann. § 37.201 *et seq.*, prohibits employers and employment agencies from requiring polygraph examinations of employees and applicants for employment, and prohibits discrimination against employees or applicants who refuse to take such examinations. The Act, however, does not prohibit an employee or applicant for employment from voluntarily requesting a polygraph examination. Before doing so, an employer or employment agency is required to provide the employee or applicant with a copy of the Act.

If an employee or applicant voluntarily requests a polygraph examination, the employer or employment agency must use the services of an examiner licensed under Michigan law to administer a polygraph examination. Before the examination, the examiner must inform the employee or applicant (1) of all specific question areas to be explored, (2) or his or her right to accept or refuse the examination, (3) of his or her right to stop any examination in progress at any time, (4) that he or she need not answer any questions or give any information, and (5) that any information volunteered could be used against the employee or applicant or be made available to the employer unless otherwise specified and agreed to in writing by the employee or applicant. The examiner also must provide the employee or applicant with a copy of the examination results and all reports and analyses prepared by the examiner that are shared with the employer.

Just as an employer or employment agency cannot lawfully decline to hire an applicant because the applicant has refused to take a polygraph examination, an employer or employment agency cannot take any action against an employee or applicant based on an opinion that the employee or applicant did not tell the truth during a polygraph examination.

Michigan law also prohibits an employer or employment agency from communicating the results or analysis of an employee's or applicant's polygraph examination or disclosing that an employee or applicant refused to submit to a polygraph examination. The law also prohibits any information obtained from an employee or applicant during a polygraph examination from being admissible in a criminal proceeding.

An employer or employment agency that violates Michigan's polygraph law faces liability to a discharged employee for double the wages lost and damages for injury or loss caused by each violation of the law, as well as reasonable attorneys' fees. The violation of this law also constitutes a misdemeanor, punishable by a fine of not more than $1,000, imprisonment for not more than 90 days, or both.

Michigan's statute broadly defines the term "polygraph examination" to mean a psychological stress evaluator examination or any other procedure that involves the use of instrumentation or mechanical device to enable or assist in the detection of deception, the verification of truthfulness, or the rendering of a diagnostic opinion regarding either of these, including a lie detector or similar test.

New Jersey

Chapter 40A of New Jersey's Code of Criminal Justice prohibits employers from influencing, requesting, or requiring an employee or prospective employee to take or submit to a lie detector test as a condition of employment or continued employment.

Chapter 40A does not apply to an employee or prospective employee of an employer authorized to manufacture, distribute or dispense controlled dangerous substances who is or will be directly involved in the manufacture, distribution, or dispensing of, or has or will have access to, legally distributed controlled dangerous substances. In these circumstances, the scope of a lie detector test must be limited to the work of the employee or prospective employee and that individual's improper handling, use, or illegal sale of legally distributed controlled dangerous substances. Any employee or prospective employee who is required to take a lie detector test as a condition of employment or continued employment has the right to be represented by counsel.

An individual who has taken a lie detector test must be provided, on request, a written copy of the report containing the results of the test. The law prohibits the dissemination of the information obtained from the test to anyone other than the employer. The employee or prospective employee has the right to present to his or her employer the results of an independently administered second lie detector test before the employer makes any personnel decision concerning the individual.

The New Jersey statute provides for a $1,000 fine and/or a maximum term of imprisonment of six months for violation of this law.

New York

New York law prohibits employers and agents of employers from requiring, requesting, suggesting or knowingly permitting any employee or prospective employee to submit to a psychological stress evaluator examination. New York Lab. Law §§ 733–39.

The law defines psychological stress evaluator examination as: (1) the questioning or interviewing of an employee or applicant for the purpose of subjecting the statements of such employee or applicant to analysis by a psychological stress evaluator; (2) the recording of statements made by an employee or applicant for the purpose of subjecting such statements to analysis by a psychological stress evaluator; or (3) analyzing, with a psychological stress evaluator, statements made by an employee or applicant for the purpose of determining the truth or falsity of such statements.

A psychological stress evaluator means any mechanical device or instrument that purports to detect deception as shown by changes in the subject's voice. *It does not include polygraph devices.*

The statute bars employer administration of the test or use of test results within or outside the state for any reason whatsoever. The law protects employees from retaliation, including discharge, discipline, or discrimination, for filing a complaint or testifying in any proceeding or action involving a violation of this law.

Any employee discriminated against in violation of the New York statute must be compensated by his or her employer for double the amount of any loss of wages and benefits arising out of such discrimination, and must be restored to his or her previous position of employment. An employee or prospective employee who is damaged as the result of a violation of this law may file an action for damages in New York Supreme Court. Any individual or employer who is found to have violated this law shall be guilty of a Class B Misdemeanor, punishable by a $500 fine and/or three months' imprisonment upon the first conviction; and, upon any subsequent convictions, a Class A Misdemeanor, punishable by a maximum $1,000 fine and one year of imprisonment.

Texas

Texas Polygraph legislation neither expressly prohibits nor permits polygraph examinations of employees. Texas law on this issue is limited to a licensing statute that governs the qualifications and regulates the conduct of polygraph examiners. Tex. Rev. Civ. Stat. Ann. art. 4413, § 29cc. The statute provides that a polygraph license can be revoked if an examiner fails to inform a subject that his or her participation in the examination is voluntary.

Federal Law

Under the federal Employee Polygraph Protection Act of 1988, 29 U.S.C. § 2001-09, most private employers are prohibited from using lie detector tests to screen applicants or test current employees unless they reasonably suspect that the employee was involved in a workplace theft or other incident causing economic loss to the employer. Federal, state, and local government employers are exempted from the Act and therefore may, to the extent permitted under state law, conduct polygraph tests of their employees. Before testing any employee, an employer is required to provide the employee with a written statement of the reasons for testing that employee.

The law permits private armored car, security alarm, and security guard firms to administer polygraph tests to certain prospective employees and permits companies authorized to manufacture, distribute, or dispense controlled dangerous substances to administer polygraph tests to certain current and prospective employees.

The federal law prohibits employers from disciplining, discharging, discriminating against, or denying employment or promotions to prospective or current workers based solely on polygraph test results.

Under the United States Department of Labor's regulations implementing the Act, 29 C.F.R. § 801 *et seq.*, employers may not use polygraph testing instruments as a means of threatening employees. Those who threaten to use a test but do not actually do so will still be deemed in violation of the law. The regulations further provide that while the use of voice stress analyzers to determine whether an employee is being truthful is prohibited, an employer may use handwriting analysis as a means of evaluating job applicants. According to the regulations, employers are not responsible for any polygraph tests administered to their employees by police authorities in the course of an investigation of workplace theft.

The federal act authorizes the Secretary of Labor to commence civil suits against employers and gives federal courts the power to award legal and equitable relief. The Department of Labor may seek civil fines up to $10,000 against employers who violate the law.

The Act does not preempt any state or local law or collective bargaining agreement that prohibits lie detector tests or that is more restrictive with respect to the regulation of lie detector tests than the federal law. Employers in states that do not have polygraph legislation or have more permissive legislation must comply with the requirements of the federal Act.

Appendix C

Consumer Credit Reports

Selected State Statutes

California

An employer may obtain consumer credit reports for employment purposes, provided the employer discloses in writing to the applicant the nature and scope of its investigation. Cal. Civ. Code Ann. § 1785. A consumer report is one that contains information about an individual's credit worthiness, credit standing, character, general reputation, personal characteristics, and mode of living that is limited to factual, record information. Cal. Civ. Code Ann. § 1785.3(c). An *investigative* consumer report is one that contains information about an individual's character, general reputation, personal characteristics, or mode of living that is obtained through personal interviews with the individual's friends, colleagues, and other acquaintances. Cal. Civ. Code Ann. § 1786.2(c). An employer may not obtain an investigative consumer report for employment purposes unless it first informs the individual that such report is being sought. Cal. Civ. Code Ann. § 1786.16(a)(2). The law further provides, however, that such report may be obtained without notice for promotion or reassignment purposes, Cal. Civ. Code Ann. § 1786.16(a)(2), or to determine whether to retain the employee, Cal. Civ. Code Ann. § 1786.16(b)(1).

When an individual is denied employment as a result of information provided in a consumer credit report, the employer must disclose the name and address of the credit agency that supplied the report. Cal. Civ. Code Ann. § 1785.20. If an employer violates state law, an individual may recover actual damages, attorneys' fees, and costs.

Cal. Civ. Code Ann. § 1785.31. If the employer's actions were willful, the individual may recover up to $5,000 per violation. Cal. Civ. Code Ann. § 1785.31.

Connecticut

The Connecticut statute addressing the use of consumer credit reports is silent with respect to their use for employment purposes. See Conn. Gen. Stat. § 36-432 *et seq.*

Florida

Florida law permits disclosure of consumer credit reports only to persons with a legitimate business need, which arguably would permit disclosure for employment purposes. Fla. Stat. § 599.72. The law otherwise is silent with regard to obligations of employers who properly use such reports.

Illinois

There is no state statute addressing employer use of consumer reports.

Massachusetts

An employer may obtain consumer credit reports for employment purposes, provided the employer discloses in writing to the applicant the nature and scope of its investigation. Mass. Gen. Laws Ann. ch. 93, § 50 *et seq.* When an individual is denied employment or terminated from employment as a result of information provided in a consumer credit report, the employer must disclose the name and address of the credit agency that supplied the report. Mass. Gen. Laws Ann. ch. 93, § 50. Massachusetts law mirrors the California statute discussed above with respect to the distinction between consumer reports and *investigative* consumer reports. Mass. Gen. Laws Ann. ch. 93, § 50.

If an employer violates state law, an individual may recover actual damages, attorneys' fees, and costs. If the employer's actions were willful, the individual may recover punitive damages. Mass. Gen. Laws Ann. ch. 93, § 50-68.

Michigan

There is no state statute addressing employer use of consumer reports.

New Jersey

There is no state statute addressing employer use of consumer reports.

New York

An employer may request the consumer credit report of an individual for employment purposes if the employer informs the individual in writing that a request *may* be made. N.Y. Gen. Bus. Law § 380-b. In addition, an employer must advise the employee that, upon request by the individual, the employer will inform him or her if a consumer report actually was used and the name and address of the credit reporting agency that furnished the report. N.Y. Gen. Bus. Law § 380-b. When denial of employment or any related benefit is based on a consumer report, the employer cannot disclose the basis for the unfavorable report to a third party unless the third party has a "legitimate need" for the information. N.Y. Gen. Bus. Law § 380-i(c).

As with California and Massachusetts, New York law provides for the distinction between consumer reports and *investigative* consumer reports. An employer must inform and seek consent from an individual before it may seek an investigative consumer report. *See* N.Y. Gen. Bus. Law § 380-c.

The statute provides that persons injured by a violation of the statute may seek to recover actual as well as punitive damages, plus attorneys' fees and costs. N.Y. Gen. Bus. Law § 380-l.

Texas

There is no state statute addressing employer use of consumer reports.

Federal Law

The Fair Credit Reporting Act (FCRA), 15 U.S.C. § 1681 *et seq.*, regulates the use of consumer credit reports. It does not, however, alter, affect, or exempt any provision of a state law, except to the extent that the state law is inconsistent with any provision of the FCRA, and then only to the extent of the inconsistency. The FCRA permits covered consumer credit agencies to provide either consumer reports or *investigative* consumer reports to employers for use in determining an individual's suitability for employment. The FCRA defines "consumer report" as a report that bears on, among other things, an individual's character, general reputation, personal characteristics, or mode of living, and is prepared from factually verifiable information. 15 U.S.C. § 1681a(d). By contrast, an *investigative* consumer report means a consumer report compiled in part with information from the subject's neighbors, friends, associates, and acquaintances. 15 U.S.C. § 1681a(e).

The FCRA permits disclosure of a consumer report to a person who intends to use it for employment purposes. 15 U.S.C. § 1681b(3)(b). The reporting agency is required either to (1) inform the individual that a report is being made if the report contains public-record information and is likely to have an adverse impact on the individual's ability to obtain employment, or (2) "maintain strict procedures to insure that [such] public record information ... is complete and up to date." 15 U.S.C. § 1681k. An employer must inform the applicant of the name and address of the agency making the report if it denies employment based in whole or in part on the information contained in the consumer report. 15 U.S.C. § 1681m. Private investigators may be regarded as a consumer credit agency if they regularly obtain information on job applicants from their former employers or personal references and furnish the information to prospective employers.

A person willfully violating the FCRA may be liable for actual damages, punitive damages, attorneys' fees, and costs. 15 U.S.C. § 1681n. Negligent noncompliance may similarly result in an award of actual damages, attorneys' fees, and costs. 15 U.S.C. § 1681o. A person who obtains information under false pretenses may be fined up to $5,000 and imprisoned for up to a year, or both. 15 U.S.C. § 1681q.

Appendix D

Drug Testing

Selected State Statutes

California

There is no California statute that regulates employee drug testing. California has enacted the Drug-Free Workplace Act of 1990, Cal. Gov't Code §§ 8350–57, which is similar to the federal Drug Free Workplace Act of 1988, 41 U.S.C. §§ 701–07. Under the Act, entities engaged in performing a state contract or receiving a grant from a state agency must certify that they operate a drug-free workplace. They also must notify employees that the unlawful use of drugs is prohibited in the employer's workplace; establish a drug-free awareness program; and provide a copy of the policy concerning the unlawful use of drugs in the workplace to employees engaged in the performance of the contract or grant. The Act does not address drug testing.

On the local level, several municipalities have enacted ordinances affecting workplace drug testing. For example, San Francisco has a drug-testing ordinance that permits an employer to conduct blood, urine, or encephalographic testing of employees only when there are "reasonable grounds" to believe that an employee's faculties are impaired by drug use *and* where such impairment "presents a clear and present danger to the safety of the employee, another employee, or to a member of the general public." San Francisco Ordinance 572-85. The ordinance applies to employers in the public and private sector but excludes uniformed public safety workers and city emergency service vehicle operators. The ordinance does not permit random or company-wide testing. Employers are required by the ordinance to give employees an opportunity to rebut any positive finding and to have the samples tested at state-licensed laboratories. Employers may, however, override the ordinance through negotiation of a collective bargaining agreement that provides otherwise.

Connecticut

Connecticut's drug-testing statute prohibits a private employer from using a urinalysis to test an employee for drug use unless it has "reasonable suspicion" that the employee is under the influence of drugs or alcohol that affects or could affect his or her job performance. Conn. Gen. Stat. Ann. § 31-51t *et seq*. (The Connecticut law applies to urinalysis only. An employer thus may be free to test employees using other methods without regard to the requirements set forth in the statute.) According to the legislative history, whether "reasonable suspicion" exists to test is an employer's judgment call. A good faith belief that an employee may be drug-involved thus may be sufficient to perform a test.

The Connecticut law permits random drug testing only when authorized by federal law; when an employee serves in a "high risk" or "safety-sensitive" occupation, as very narrowly defined by the state labor department; or when the employee has been voluntarily participating in an employer-sponsored employee assistance program of which the test is a part.

The Connecticut statute prohibits an employer from conducting a witnessed test. Further, an employer may not refuse to hire an applicant or discipline, terminate, or deny an employee a raise or promotion except on a confirmed positive test. That is, the statute requires that a specimen that tests positive following a broad-range screen be retested a second time using the gas chromatography/mass spectrometry or other method determined by the state to be equally reliable. The law also forbids an employer from requiring that an applicant submit to a drug test unless it gives written disclosure of its intent to test applicants at the time of application. Applicants must be given a copy of a positive test result.

Employers are required to keep test results with an employee's medical records and to observe state laws that govern such records. Current state law prohibits disclosure of medical records to third parties without the employee's express written consent, except in certain situations.

A separate state law, enacted in 1991, applies to employers of drivers of commercial motor vehicles. It requires the drivers to submit to drug testing as provided in federal Department of Transportation regulations. 1991 Conn. Pub. Act. 91-316.

Florida

Florida's workers' compensation law addresses testing of employees injured in accidents that they cause. Fla. Stat. Ann. § 440.07. Under this section, "if the employer has reason to suspect that the injury was occasioned primarily by the intoxication of the employee or by the use of any drug, which affected the employee to the extent that the employee's normal faculties were impaired, the employer may require the employee to submit to a test for the presence of drugs or alcohol in his system."

The workers' compensation law provides that employers may conduct drug tests of applicants and current employees. Fla. Stat. Ann. § 440.102. Prior to testing, however, all employees and job applicants must be given a written policy statement from the employer that must contain certain elements as set forth in the statute.

Additionally, Florida has enacted a comprehensive statute governing applicant and employee drug testing by state agencies. Fla. Stat. Ann. § 112.0455.

Illinois

No statutory provision under Illinois law generally regulates the use of employee drug tests.

Effective January 1, 1992, state agencies may not contract with or award grants to those entities employing at least 25 persons unless the contractor or grantee provides a drug-free workplace by establishing and communicating to employees a policy regarding drugs in the workplace. Ill. Ann. Stat. ch. 127, § 132.011 *et seq.* The Illinois law is similar to the federal Drug-Free Workplace Act of 1988, 41 U.S.C. §§ 701–07. The policy must inform applicants and employees of the employer's prohibition on the use, sale, manufacture, transfer, and so forth, of controlled substances. It further must inform employees of the consequences for violating the policy and require that employees agree to notify their employer within five days of a conviction of a drug statute where the violation occurred in the workplace. Employers also are required to establish a drug-free awareness program to inform employees of the dangers of drug abuse, the employer's policy, any rehabilitation or counseling that the employer offers, and the penalties that will be imposed for policy violations. Nothing in the Act addresses drug testing.

The Act further requires an employer to take disciplinary action against an employee convicted of a drug statute violation involving the workplace and requires the employee to engage in rehabilitation or other drug abuse treatment program. The statute does not set forth a minimum disciplinary action that an employer must take, but notes only that such discipline may include termination for a first offense. An employer that fails to comply with the Act faces suspension, debarment, or both.

Massachusetts

There is no statutory provision under Massachusetts law that regulates the use of employee drug tests.

Michigan

There is no statutory provision under Michigan law that regulates the use of employee drug tests.

New Jersey

There is no statutory provision under New Jersey law that regulates the use of employee drug tests.

New York

There is no statutory provision under New York law that regulates the use of employee drug tests.

Texas

If an employer is currently carrying workers' compensation insurance, a regulation implemented by the Commission is particularly worth noting. Effective April 15, 1991, employers with 15 or more employees were required to adopt a policy to eliminate drug abuse or face an administrative penalty not to exceed $500 if such policy was not adopted. 16 Tex. Reg. 646-647, 28 Tex. Admin. Code §§ 169.1–169.2. The regulation requires employers to provide a copy of the drug abuse policy to each employee on or before the first day of employment or within 30 days after the date the policy is adopted by the employer. The Workers' Compensation Commission may also request a copy of the employer's policy.

The regulation provides that compliance with the federal Drug-Free Workplace Act of 1988, 41 U.S.C. §§ 701–07 (which applies to federal contractors and grantees), allows for automatic compliance with the new state regulation. Thus, an employer's drug policy that complies with the federal law allows the employer to do nothing further. Alcohol is not required to be addressed in a Drug-Free Workplace policy.

Selected Federal Laws

Drug-Free Workplace Act

The Drug-Free Workplace Act of 1988, 41 U.S.C. §§ 701–07, requires covered government contractors and recipients of federal financial assistance to certify to the government that they have developed and distributed policies and programs that address the issue of drugs in the workplace.

The law provides that an employer covered by the Act must establish a drug-free awareness program to inform employees about (1) the dangers of drug abuse in the workplace; (2) the employer's policy of maintaining a drug-free workplace; (3) any available drug counseling, rehabilitation, and employee assistance programs; and (4) the penalties that may be imposed on employees for drug abuse violations.

The Act's coverage is limited to persons, other than an individual, that seek and enter into contracts to provide goods or services with a value of $25,000 or more to the federal government or who obtain grants of federal financial assistance, regardless of value, from the government.

Department of Defense Regulations

The Department of Defense (DOD) has issued a regulation setting forth a policy for use by defense contractors. In particular, the regulation applies to all defense contractors that involve access to classified information. The regulation further gives defense contracting officers the discretion to apply the requirements to contracts that may involve national security issues or the health and safety of employees engaged in the performance of the contract.

The DOD regulation defines "illegal drugs" to include those on Schedules I and II of 21 U.S.C. § 802(6). See 48 C.F.R. § 223.7502. Although the DOD policy thus encompasses most of the principal drugs of abuse, it is not as comprehensive as the Drug-Free Workplace Act. For example, amphetamines are a Schedule III drug. Nonetheless, employees of DOD contractors are covered under the broader Act governing government contractors.

Of particular importance is the requirement that certain DOD contractors develop and implement drug testing programs that test covered employees on a random basis. Specifically, the regulation adds a clause to all defense contracts that states that contractors are to "provide for the random drug testing of Contractor employees working in sensitive positions." 48 C.F.R. § 252.223-7004(b). Such employees are those who have been granted access to classified information; possess or use firearms; are involved in the design, manufacture, testing, and evaluation of, or control, operate, or use, *inter alia*, airplanes, vessels, vehicles, weapons and weapon systems, toxic materials, potentially dangerous equipment, or medical equipment with potentially life-threatening consequences; are involved in the transport, storage, or protection of toxic or nuclear materials; direct the treatment of persons undergoing substance abuse rehabilitation; or are employed as air traffic controllers. 48 C.F.R. § 252.223-7004(a).

The regulation leaves it to the determination of the defense contractor as to what type of random testing program it will establish. It states, however, that contractors may not permit the continued employment of a person in a sensitive position who tests positive. 48 C.F.R. § 252.223-7004(c). Similarly, a contractor must remove an employee convicted of violating a drug statute from a sensitive position. Such employee may be returned to the position only with the approval of the Contracting Officer and on completion of a rehabilitation program. 48 C.F.R. § 252.223-7004(d). Similarly, employers are free to decide whether they test applicants for employment. 48 C.F.R. § 252.223-7500(c)(4)(iii).

Department of Transportation Regulations

The Department of Transportation (DOT) and various agencies within DOT have issued regulations concerning drug testing applicable to employers in businesses regulated by DOT and its constituent agencies. 49 C.F.R. Part 40. For covered employers and employees, the regulations require applicant drug testing and periodic, reasonable suspicion, and random drug testing of employees; describe how the tests are to be conducted; establish laboratory quality assurance standards; set forth how test results should be communicated; and indicate the type of access employees should have to test results. The DOT regulations can also require the establishment of employee assistance programs (EAPs) to train supervisors in the determination of whether an employee is impaired. (The EAP does not have to involve employee counseling or drug rehabilitation.)

The DOT regulations apply to all employers subject to the jurisdiction of the DOT. The DOT regulations identify the drugs for which employers should test, establish procedures that an employer must follow, and identify the employees subject to testing.

The Omnibus Transportation Employees Testing Act of 1991

The Omnibus Transportation Employees Testing Act of 1991, signed into law on October 28, 1991, mandates random drug and alcohol testing of transportation workers in "safety-sensitive" positions. The Act requires the DOT to issue final regulations by October 28, 1992.

As described above, the DOT currently has a program requiring drug testing of transportation workers. That program does not apply, however, to transit workers, and it does not require any alcohol testing. Under this new law, workers in safety-sensitive positions in air, rail, trucking, and mass-transit industries will be subject to both drug and alcohol testing. The Act also incorporated Department of Health and Human Services guidelines on laboratory accuracy and other safeguarding measures for test results.

The Americans With Disabilities Act of 1990

The Americans With Disabilities Act of 1990 (ADA), 42 U.S.C. § 12101 *et seq.*, which is effective on July 26, 1992, for employers with 25 or more employees and on July 26, 1994, for employers with 15 or more employees, prohibits discrimination against "qualified individuals with disabilities." Under the ADA, current drug users are expressly excluded from protection. The Act does, however, protect a person who has completed a drug rehabilitation program and is not a current user of drugs. It also protects a person who currently is participating in a drug rehabilitation program and is no longer a user of drugs or who erroneously is perceived as a drug user but in fact is not engaging in drug use. Further, a person who currently engages in the use of illegal drugs may not be denied health services or services provided in connection with drug rehabilitation on the basis of current use if the individual otherwise is entitled to such services.

Under the ADA, an employer may ban the use of alcohol or illegal drugs in the workplace by all employees; require that employees not be under the influence of alcohol or illegal drugs in the workplace; require that employees conform to the requirements of the Drug-Free Workplace Act, 41 U.S.C. §§ 701–07 *et seq.*; and hold alcohol or drug addicted employees to the same standards as all other employees, even if their unsatisfactory job performance is caused by their drug addiction or alcoholism.

Moreover, nothing in the ADA prohibits an employer from testing employees for drug use. The Act further states that a drug test is not considered a medical examination.

Persons addicted to alcohol are protected under the ADA to the extent that they are otherwise qualified to perform. As noted above, however, their employment may be adversely affected if they violate work rules prohibiting use of alcohol at the workplace. The ADA also states that, where applicable, employers may require that their employees comply with Department of Defense, Nuclear Regulatory Commission, and Department of Transportation drug policy and testing regulations.

The ADA amends the Rehabilitation Act of 1973 to make its provisions addressing drug use consistent with the ADA. Unlike the ADA employment provisions (which became effective on July 26, 1992 for larger companies), the amendments to the Rehabilitation Act became effective on the signing of the ADA.

Appendix E

AIDS Testing

Selected State Statutes

California

The California Health & Safety Code limits serological testing to detect antibodies to the human immunodeficiency virus (HIV) as a condition of hire or continued employment. The statute provides that blood tests to detect antibodies to the HIV virus shall not be performed on a person without first obtaining that person's written consent, Cal. Health & Safety Code § 199.22(a), and further states that the results of such blood tests "shall not be used in any instance for the determination of ... suitability for employment." Cal. Health & Safety Code § 199.21(f).

Subject to limited exceptions, the disclosure of HIV-related test results "in a manner which identifies or provides identifying characteristics of the person to whom the test results apply," can result in civil penalties of $1,000 for negligent disclosure and $5,000 for willful disclosure as well as an award of "actual damages including damages for economic, bodily, or psychological harm which is the proximate cause of the act." Cal. Health & Safety Code § 199.21(a), (b), (d). Section 199.21(h) of the Code provides that nothing in this statute "limits or expands the right of the injured subject to recover damages under any other applicable law."

Several California cities, including San Francisco and West Hollywood, have adopted ordinances that bar, among other things, employment-related HIV testing or use of HIV information to make an employment decision.

Connecticut

There is no employment-specific state law in Connecticut that expressly prohibits testing employees or job applicants for the presence of antibodies to the HIV virus. The Connecticut AIDS Testing and Confidentiality Law provides, however, that no person shall order the performance of an HIV-related test without first receiving the written or oral informed consent of the subject of the test or person authorized to consent for the individual to be tested. Conn. Gen. Stat. § 19a-582. Written consent is preferred; oral consent must be noted in the person's medical record. Conn. Gen. Stat. § 19a-582. Such consent must include a statement that explains the test, its purpose, meaning of results, benefits of early diagnosis and treatment; an acknowledgment that consent to a test does not constitute a condition for receiving medical treatment; a description of test procedures; a statement that testing is voluntary and may be done anonymously; and an explanation that test results are confidential. Conn. Gen. Stat. § 19a-582(b).

Any person who willfully violates the Act "shall be liable for injuries suffered as a result of such violation." Conn. Gen. Stat. § 19a-590.

Florida

The Florida AIDS Act prohibits an employer from requiring an individual to undergo an HIV-related test as a condition of hiring, promotion, or continued employment, unless the absence of HIV infection is a bona-fide occupational qualification (BFOQ) for the job in question. Fla. Stat. Ann. § 760.50(3)(a). Employers asserting the BFOQ exception for HIV-related testing bear the burden of proving that such testing is necessary to determine whether employees currently are able to perform particular jobs without presenting a significant risk of transmitting the infection to others in the course of normal work activities, and that there exists no reasonable means of accommodation short of requiring the test. Fla. Stat. Ann. § 760.50(3)(c).

Any person aggrieved by a violation of the Florida AIDS Act may recover, for each violation, liquidated damages of $1,000 or actual damages, whichever is greater. Fla. Stat. Ann. § 760.50(6)(a)(2). If the violation is deemed intentional or reckless, the statute permits recovery of liquidated damages of $5,000 or actual damages, whichever is greater. Fla. Stat. Ann. § 760.50(6)(a)(3). The statute also permits recovery of reasonable attorneys' fees and other costs.

The Florida Public Health Law also provides that before testing an individual for antigens or antibodies to the HIV virus, the party seeking the test must obtain the informed consent of the person to be tested. Fla. Stat. Ann. § 381.609(3)(a). By statute, informed consent includes an explanation of the test, including its purpose, potential uses, and limitations; the meaning of its results; and an explanation of the procedures to be followed. The statute further requires that the person to be tested be told that the test is voluntary; that he or she has the right to withdraw consent to the testing process at any time prior to the HIV test; and that he or she has the right to confidential treatment of information identifying the subject of the test and the results of the test to the extent provided by law.

Except under limited circumstances, "no person who has obtained knowledge of a test result ... may disclose or be compelled to disclose the identity of any person upon whom a test is performed, or the results of such a test in a manner which permits identification of the subject of the test ...." Fla. Stat. Ann. § 301.609(3)(f). The exceptions include informing the tested party, or his or her legal representative, of the test results; disclosing the test results to another person designated by the tested individual pursuant to a legally effective release; reporting the test results to a health facility or health-care provider for the purpose of diagnosis or treatment; and reporting test results to the State Department of Health and Rehabilitative Services. Fla. Stat. Ann. § 301.609(3)(f).

Illinois

There is no state law in Illinois that expressly prohibits testing employees or job applicants for the presence of antibodies to the HIV virus. Under the Illinois AIDS Confidentiality Act, however, no person may be tested for antibodies to the HIV virus without his or her written consent, and no person may disclose the identity of a person who has been tested or the test results. Ill. Ann. Stat. ch. $111^{1}/_{2}$, § 7301. Written consent includes providing the person to be tested with a statement that explains the test, its purpose, meaning of results, and benefits of early diagnosis and treatment; an acknowledgment that consent to a test does not constitute a condition for receiving medical treatment; a description of test procedures; a statement that testing is voluntary and may be done anonymously; and an explanation that test results are confidential. Violation of the AIDS Confidentiality Act permits recovery of liquidated damages of $1,000 or actual damages, whichever is greater. If the violation is deemed intentional or reckless, a party may recover liquidated damages of $5,000 or actual damages, whichever is greater.

Massachusetts

Under Massachusetts law, employers are prohibited from requiring an HIV test as a condition of employment. Mass. Gen. Laws. ch. 111, § 70F. Where a test otherwise is performed, the person conducting the test must obtain the written informed consent of the person to be tested. Mass. Gen. Laws ch. 111, § 70F. Disclosure of test results also requires written informed consent for each such disclosure that states the reason for the disclosure. Mass. Gen. Laws ch. 111, § 70F. The statute states that a general release of medical records would not suffice for the disclosure of HIV test information. Mass. Gen. Laws ch. 111, § 70F.

Michigan

There is no state law in Michigan that expressly prohibits testing employees or job applicants for the presence of antibodies to the HIV virus. Under the Michigan AIDS Testing and Confidentiality Act, however, no HIV-related testing may be conducted without the written informed consent of the person to be tested. Mich. Consol. Laws Ann. § 5131. In addition, the Act provides for the confidentiality of test results. Mich. Consol. Laws Ann. § 5131. Penalties under the Act include liquidated damages of $1,000 or actual damages, whichever is greater, and costs and reasonable attorneys' fees. Mich. Consol. Laws Ann. § 5131(8).

New Jersey

There is no state law in New Jersey that expressly prohibits testing to detect antibodies to the AIDS virus or inquiring about the result of any such test.

New York

There is no state law in New York that expressly prohibits testing of employees or job applicants for the presence of antibodies to the HIV virus. The New York AIDS Testing Confidentiality Act, however, prohibits testing for antibodies to the HIV virus without the informed consent of the individual to be tested. N.Y. Public Health

Law art. 27-f, § 2781(1). Informed consent to an HIV-related test shall consist of a signed statement that includes an explanation of the test, including its purpose; an explanation of the procedures to be followed, including a statement that the test is voluntary and that consent may be withdrawn at any time; and an explanation of the confidentiality protections afforded confidential HIV-related information under the statute. N.Y. Pub. Health Law § 2782.

Furthermore, except under limited circumstances, no person who obtains confidential HIV-related information pursuant to a lawful release may disclose or be compelled to disclose such information. N.Y. Pub. Health Law § 2782. The statute permits disclosure to the subject of the test and any person to whom disclosure is authorized pursuant to a release of confidential HIV-related information. N.Y. Pub. Health Law § 2782.

Violation of the law permits recovery of a civil penalty not to exceed $5,000 for each occurrence. N.Y. Pub. Health Law § 2783. If violation is deemed willful, a criminal penalty may be assessed. N.Y. Pub. Health Law § 2783.

Texas

Under the Texas Communicable Disease Prevention and Control Act, an employer may not require an employee to undergo any medical procedure or test "designed to determine or help determine if a person has AIDS or HIV infection, antibodies to HIV, or infection with any other probable causative agent of AIDS" unless the test is necessary as a bona-fide occupational qualification (BFOQ) and there exists no less discriminatory means of satisfying the occupational qualification. Tex. Health & Safety Code Ann. § 81.102(a)(1) & (3)(A). An employer who alleges that a test is necessary as a BFOQ has the burden of proving the allegation. Tex. Health & Safety Code Ann. § 81.102(b).

The statute provides that all test results are confidential. Tex. Health & Safety Code Ann. § 81.103(a). Any employer that possesses or has knowledge of a test result may not release or disclose a test result or allow a test result to become known. Tex. Health & Safety Code Ann. § 81.103(a). The test may be disclosed to, among others, the person tested, a person legally authorized to receive the results on behalf of the person tested, and to such other persons with the written consent of the person tested or another person authorized to consent for the person tested. Tex. Health & Safety Code Ann. § 81.103(b)(6) & (d).

Any person injured by a violation of the Act may bring a civil action for damages. Tex. Health & Safety Code Ann. § 81.104. If a court finds that the person or entity has negligently or willfully released or disclosed a test result, the person or entity is liable for actual damages; a civil penalty up to $1,000 if negligent, and up to $5,000 if willful; and court costs and reasonable attorneys' fees incurred by the person bringing the action. Tex. Health & Safety Code Ann. § 81.104.

Federal Law

The recently enacted American With Disabilities Act of 1990 (ADA), 42 U.S.C. § 12101 *et seq.*, which takes effect on July 26, 1992, for employers with 25 or more employees and on July 26, 1994, for employers with 15 or more employees, prohibits discrimination against "qualified individuals with disabilities." Infection with a contagious disease, including HIV, can bring a person within the scope of ADA protection. According to the ADA's legislative history, a person with HIV meets the statutory definition of "qualified individual with disabilities" and is protected by the Act. Moreover, employers often make assumptions about persons with HIV regarding their abilities to work; those assumptions, unless based on fact about the specific individual, also will result in extending the protection of the ADA to the person.

The ADA further prohibits preemployment medical examinations and inquiries of an applicant regarding the individual's physical or mental condition or regarding the nature or severity of a disability. 42 U.S.C. § 12112(c)(2)(A). An employer may make preemployment inquiries as to an individual's ability to perform "job-related functions." 42 U.S.C. § 12112(c)(2)(B). The ADA permits an employer to extend an offer of employment that is conditioned on completion of a physical examination. The offer may be withdrawn if the physical examination reveals a condition that would prevent the individual from performing the essential functions of the job either with or without reasonable accommodation. Because the physical examination occurs after the offer of employment, the applicant likely would deduce that the basis of the withdrawal of the job offer related to the examination. Thus, the employer may have to justify its reasons for withdrawing the offer.

With respect to current employees, employers are prohibited from requiring medical examinations or from inquiring of an employee whether he or she is disabled or as to the nature or severity of his or her disability, unless such examination is shown to be "job-related and consistent with business necessity." 42 U.S.C. § 12112(c)(4)(A).

Appendix F

Smoking in the Workplace

Selected State Statutes

California

California does not regulate smoking in the private workplace. By statute, the state permits municipalities or local governments to ban or regulate smoking as long as they do not violate any other provision of state law. Cal. Health & Safety Code § 25946.

Consequently, by 1990 at least 140 municipalities or counties had ordinances regulating smoking in the private workplace. For example, Los Angeles, Palo Alto, and San Francisco have enacted ordinances regulating smoking in the workplace that are much more specific than comparable legislation from other states. The Palo Alto law provides that nonsmokers should be granted "precedence" over smokers in the event a conflict should arise. San Francisco authorizes the city attorney to obtain a court order requiring the employer to make corrections in its smoking regulation policy and civil penalties for violations to the ordinance can be as high as $500 per day for as long as the violation continues.

In Anaheim and Fremont, every employer must adopt, implement, and maintain a written smoking policy that prohibits smoking in employer conference and meeting rooms, classrooms, auditoriums, rest rooms, medical facilities, hallways, and elevators. The smoking policy also must provide for a contiguous no-smoking area of not less than one-half of the seating capacity and floor space in cafeterias, lunchrooms, and employee lounges. In addition, each employee has the right to designate and post signs identifying his or her immediate work space as a nonsmoking area. Employers must also give preferential consideration to nonsmokers in any dispute. If the workplace is occupied exclusively by smokers, however, the ordinance does not apply, unless smoking is otherwise prohibited. The ordinance specifies the size and style of the no-smoking signs wherever they must be posted. The employer is not required, however, to incur any expense to make structural or other physical modifications in providing smoke-free areas. A violation of the ordinance is punishable by a fine not exceeding $50 for the first violation, not exceeding $150 for the second violation ($200 in Fremont), and not exceeding $500 for the third violation.

The San Diego ordinance mandates that employers provide smoke-free areas for nonsmokers, but employers are not obligated to incur any expense to make physical modifications to provide these areas.

Connecticut

Under Connecticut law, every employer with fifty or more employees must establish one or more clearly designated nonsmoking work areas. Conn. Gen. Stat. Ann. § 31-40q. In areas where smoking is permitted, employers must use existing physical barriers and ventilation systems to minimize the impact of smoking on the nonsmoking areas. Nothing in the Act prohibits an employer from designating an entire business facility as a nonsmoking area.

An employer can be exempted from the requirements of the law if the employer made a good faith effort to comply with the provisions of the law and any further requirement to so comply would constitute an unreasonable financial burden on the employer.

A separate Connecticut statute bars employers from refusing to hire applicants or from adversely affecting current employees because of their use of tobacco products outside the workplace. The statute exempts employers whose primary purpose is to discourage use of tobacco. It also exempts from coverage the hiring practices of municipal employers of paid fire fighters and police officers, and the provisions of collective bargaining agreements between municipalities and paid fire fighters or police officers.

Florida

Under the Florida Clean Indoor Air Act, Fla. Stat. Ann. §§ 386.201–09, an employer in a private workplace must develop, implement, and post a policy regarding designation of smoking and nonsmoking areas, taking into consideration the proportion of smokers and nonsmokers. An employer can designate an entire area as a smoking area if all the employees who routinely work in that area at the same time agree. An employer is considered in compliance with this act if it makes reasonable efforts to develop a policy. A smoking area must not contain common facilities that are expected to be used by the public, and a smoking area cannot be declared in an elevator, rest room, hospital emergency room, doctor's or dentist's waiting room, or any other area prohibited by law.

The Act expressly preempts any municipal or county ordinance on the same matter.

Illinois

The Illinois Clean Indoor Air Act, Ill. Rev. St. ch. 111½, prohibits smoking generally in public places except those not usually frequented by the public, such as "factories, warehouses, and other similar places ...." The Act covers employers that operate public places (defined to include hospitals, restaurants, retail stores, offices, commercial establishments, theaters, museums, educational facilities, and the like). The statute allows smoking areas to be designated within the public place, but such areas must be located so as to minimize the intrusion of smoke into areas where smoking is not permitted.

Fourteen Illinois municipalities or counties, including Chicago, have some sort of restriction of smoking in the private workplace. The Chicago Clean Indoor Air Ordinance applies to employers with one or more employees. Chicago Mun. Code § 192-20 *et seq.* It requires the development of written policies, which must be communicated to all employees. The ordinance bars smoking in public places except in designated areas, and further requires that employers designate nonsmoking areas in places of employment. The ordinance does not require that employers undertake any modifications of the areas designated as nonsmoking, but does require the posting of notices indicating whether smoking is permitted. Individual employees also may designate their personal work space as nonsmoking. If this designation does not prevent the employee from being affected by smoke from other employees, the employer is required to take steps to improve the ventilation, expand the employee's personal work space, or relocate the employee to a comparable work area where he or she would be less likely to be affected by smoke. The ordinance also contains a priority in favor of the nonsmoker where disputes arise with smokers. Employers found in violation of the ordinance may be fined not less than $25 or more than $100.

Massachusetts

Massachusetts has not enacted a statute that addresses smoking in the workplace.

Michigan

Michigan has no state laws regulating smoking in the private workplace. There is, however, a state law that limits smoking to designated areas in public places. Mich. Comp. Laws Ann. § 333.12601 *et seq.* The statute defines "public place" as an enclosed indoor area used by the general public that is an educational facility, a health facility, an auditorium, an arena, a theater, a museum, a concert hall, or other facility used for performance or art exhibition. It excludes private offices or rooms used exclusively by smokers. The statute prohibits smoking in public places except in designated smoking areas. A facility's existing physical barriers and ventilation system should be used to minimize the "toxic effect" of smoke on nonsmokers, and the nonsmoking area should be located closest to the source of fresh air. In a public place consisting of one room, the owner or operator complies with the statute if at least half of the room is designated as nonsmoking. The statute also requires the posting of notices indicating where smoking is and is not permitted.

Persons violating the statute may be fined up to $100 for a first violation of the statute and up to $500 for subsequent violations. The statute may be enforced by the state and by private action for injunctive relief by an individual who has used the public place within 60 days of filing suit.

Separate statutes regulate smoking in hospitals, nursing homes, and in food service establishments.

A few Michigan municipalities or counties have enacted laws restricting smoking in the private sector.

New Jersey

A New Jersey statute requires covered employers to establish written rules governing smoking within the employer's facility. N.J. Rev. Stat. §§ 26:3D-23 *et seq.* The statute, which applies to employers with 50 or more employees within an enclosed structure not generally open to the public, requires that the rules designate nonsmoking areas. The rules also may identify areas where employees and others may smoke, except with respect to areas where smoking may be otherwise restricted by safety or health ordinances. The statute states that designated smoking and nonsmoking areas must be marked by signs using universally recognized symbols.

Under the statute, where the State Department of Health believes that an employer is violating the statute, it first will provide written notice to the employer identifying the alleged violation and set fort recommendations for complying with the statute. The employer may request a meeting with a representative of the Department to discuss the allegations, at which time the employer may present its position. The Health Department will provide assistance, if necessary, to enable the employer to comply. If the Commissioner of Health determines that the employer is not in compliance, he or she may file a civil action in state court. The Commissioner may not file suit before ninety days after the Health Department has provided written notice of the alleged violation. The statute expressly bars a private right of action by parties other than the Health Commissioner.

A separate state law prohibits employers from refusing to hire applicants or from adversely affecting or discharging employees who smoke or use tobacco products, "unless the employer has a rational basis for doing so which is reasonably related to the employment, including the responsibilities of the employee or prospective employee." N.J. Stat. Ann. § 2A:58-1. Notwithstanding this statute, an employer may implement a workplace smoking policy and discipline any employee who violates it.

New York

A New York statute limits smoking in the workplace and requires employers to implement and post written workplace smoking policies that prohibit smoking in common areas. N.Y. Pub. Health Law § 1399-o. The statute covers employers with one or more employees and further requires that nonsmokers be provided with smoke-free work areas and smoke-free sections in cafeterias and lounges. Although employers are not required to make any expenditures or structural changes to create a smoke-free work area, if the employer is unable to make an employee's area smoke-free without restricting the use of tobacco products, it will be required to designate the area as smoke-free. Thus, the statute contains a preference favoring nonsmokers. Further, the statute prohibits smoking in conference and meeting rooms unless all persons using the room agree to allow smoking. In addition, any provision in a smoking policy that is "more restrictive than the minimum requirements set forth in this subdivision shall, if a collective bargaining unit exists, be subject to applicable law governing collective bargaining." Employers must post notices indicating where smoking is and is not permitted.

The statute provides additional rules applicable to different types of public accommodations, such as hospitals, stores, food service establishments, banks, theaters, and so forth. These rules would apply to both patrons of the entity as well as employees.

The New York City Clean Indoor Air Act requires all employers in the city with 15 or more employees to adopt, implement, and disseminate a written smoking policy. Each employer's smoking policy must include certain provisions. For example, an employer's policy must indicate that each employee can designate his or her working area as a nonsmoking area, and that nonsmoking areas must be, "to the extent reasonably practicable in the employer's discretion, no less than eight feet from an area where smoking is permitted." The Act also provides that an employer may be required to make additional "reasonable accommodations" to minimize the effects of smoke on nonsmoking employees, including rearranging employee work areas or expanding the size of the smoke-free work area. Each employer's smoking policy also must include a procedure to resolve disputes arising under the policy.

Under the Act, smoking is permitted in private offices and enclosed areas occupied exclusively by employees who do not object to smoking. Smoking is prohibited in auditoriums, classrooms, elevators, hallways, rest rooms, and photocopy areas. In addition, smoking is prohibited in conference and meeting rooms unless each person present in the room consents. Nonsmoking areas in employee lounges and cafeterias must be at least 50 percent of seating capacity or floor space.

The law is enforced by the New York City Department of Health, with which any person can register a complaint. The Department of Health attempts to obtain voluntary compliance with the law through publicity, education programs, and the issuance of warnings, where appropriate. The law also provides for civil penalties varying in amount from $50 to $500. Employers can apply for waivers from application of a specific provision of the law if strict compliance would cause undue financial hardship or otherwise be unreasonable.

Several counties and municipalities in New York State, including Suffolk, Nassau, Orange, and Westchester, have ordinances restricting smoking in the private workplace. Generally, these no-smoking ordinances are much more specific than comparable state legislation and impose harsher penalties.

Texas

Although Texas has no state legislation regulating smoking in the private workplace, 28 municipalities or counties have ordinances restricting such smoking in some manner.

Appendix G

Employee Access to Personnel Records

Selected State Statutes

California

The California Labor Code provides that "[e]very employer shall at reasonable times, and at reasonable intervals as determined by the Labor Commissioner, upon the request of an employee," permit the employee to inspect his or her personnel files that are or have been used to determine the employee's qualifications for employment, promotion, additional compensation, termination, or other disciplinary action. Cal. Lab. Code § 1198.5(a). The statute excludes reference letters and employee records relating to the investigation of a possible criminal offense from this broad grant of access. The statutory right of access applies to private and public employers except the state or any of its agencies.

The statute requires the employer to keep a copy of the employee's personnel records where the employee reports to work. In the alternative, the employer must make the records available at the employee's work location within a reasonable time after the employee requests them.

The Labor Code also provides that where a local agency has established an "independent employee relations board or commission," that board or commission has jurisdiction over matters or disputes arising under the Code. The existence of a board or commission does not prohibit an employee from pursuing an available judicial remedy whether the employee seeks relief from the board or commission or sues directly in court. Cal. Lab. Code § 1198.5(d).

Connecticut

Under Connecticut law, a private employer must allow current or former employees to inspect their personnel files upon the employee's written request. Conn. Gen. Stat. § 31-128b. Records or documents subject to inspection are those that the employer uses to make employment-related decisions affecting the employee. It does not include certain management information, reference letters from third parties, medical records,[1] information concerning future plans, test-related information that would undermine the integrity of the test, or information related to a criminal investigation. The statute provides for inspection during regular business hours and at a location at or "reasonably near" the employee's place of employment. An employee may request to review his or her records no more than twice a year. Conn. Gen. Stat. § 31-12h.

The statute contains a mechanism for correcting or removing information. Conn. Gen. Stat. § 31-128e. If the employee disagrees with information contained in the file, the information may be removed by the employer if it agrees with the employee. If the employer chooses not to remove the information, the employee may submit a statement to be included in the file.[2]

The statute also imposes a record retention requirement on the employer by providing that the personnel files of terminated employees be kept for at least one year after the employee is terminated.

A separate state law addresses the access rights of professional employees certified by the state board of education and employed by any local or regional board of education. Conn. Gen. Stat. § 10-151a. The statute limits access to records or reports of competence, personal character, and efficiency regarding an evaluation of the employee's performance as a professional employee.

Florida

The Florida statute on employee access to personnel files applies exclusively to public education institutions. Fla. Stat. § 231.291.

Illinois

Under the Illinois Personnel Record Review Act, Ill. Ann. Stat. ch. 48, §§ 2001 *et seq.*, employers with five or more employees must permit their employees to inspect and obtain copies of their personnel records on request. Ill. Ann. Stat. ch. 48, § 2002.[3] Records encompassed within the statute are those that "are, have been, or are intended to be used in determining that employee's qualifications for employment, promotion, additional compensation, discharge or other disciplinary action . . . ." The employer may require that such request be in writing. The section further requires that records be made available within seven days of the request, unless the employer demonstrates a need for more time, and that employees may make up to two requests per year unless otherwise provided by a collective bargaining agreement.

The statute excludes from disclosure reference letters; portions of test documents; materials relating to employer's staff planning, business development plans, and similar documents where they relate to more than one employee, unless the documents have been or will be used to assess the individual employee's qualifications for promotion, transfer, compensation, discipline or discharge; personal information about other persons that may be in the requesting employee's file; records relevant to a pending claim where the employee may gain access through discovery; and investigatory records involving possible criminal conduct unless the employer uses the records to take adverse action against the employee. Ill. Ann. Stat. ch. 48, § 2012. An employer may not use documents not included in the personnel file in a judicial proceeding unless the employer's failure to include the information was not intentional and the employee has been given reasonable time to review the documents. Ill. Ann. Stat. ch. 48, § 2004.

The statute provides a mechanism for employees who contend that the file contains incorrect information. Ill. Ann. Stat. ch. 48, § 2006. The parties may agree to correct or remove information. If they fail to agree, the employee may submit a written statement for insertion into the file. If either the employer or employee knowingly inserts false information into the file, the other party may seek judicial intervention to have the information removed.

The statute provides that an employer may be fined up to $200 for willfully violating its provisions. Ill. Ann. Stat. ch 48, § 2012. Furthermore, employees denied access to their files or seeking other relief as permitted under the statute may file a complaint with the state's Department of Labor, which has the power to investigate the allegations and file an action in the Illinois Circuit Court for enforcement.

Massachusetts

In Massachusetts, current and former employees (not including current or former tenured or tenure-tracked instructors of private higher educational institutions) may seek access to their personnel records by providing a written request. Mass. Gen. Laws ch. 149, § 52c. A personnel record is that file containing information that has been or will be used to affect the employee's employment, including continued employment, promotion, compensation, or discipline. Excluded is personal information about persons other than the employee, the disclosure of which would constitute an unwarranted invasion of privacy. If the employee disagrees with any of the information in the file, the information may be removed by the employer if it agrees with the employee. If the employer chooses not to remove the information, the employee may submit a statement to be included in the file.

Michigan

In Michigan, the Bullard-Plawecki Employee Right to Know Act, Mich. Comp. Laws Ann. § 423.501 *et seq.*, provides for current and former employee right of access to personnel files. The Act covers employers with four or more employees and states that an employer must provide employees with the opportunity to review personnel records up to twice a year, on the employee's written request. The Act encompasses records that are, have been, or are intended to be used in connection with decisions affecting employment, promotion, additional compensation, and discharge or other disciplinary action. It excludes from disclosure references; staff planning information involving more than one employee; medical information available from the physician or facility that provided it to the employer; personal information about someone other than the employee seeking disclosure; investigative information kept separate from the personnel file; records relating to grievance investigations kept separate from other information; and records kept by administrative, managerial, or executive employees in their sole possession that are not shared with others.

The Act also provides that the employee's review must take place at a location reasonably near the place of employment and during regular office hours. If the review requires the employee to take time off from work, then the employer must provide the employee with some other reasonable time to conduct the inspection. The employee may have the employer duplicate the contents of his or her personnel file and the employer may charge a fee equal to the actual cost of duplicating the information. Mich. Comp. Laws Ann. § 423.504.

The Act allows an employee to remove or correct information contained in the file that the employee contends is incorrect on the mutual agreement of the employer. Mich. Comp. Laws Ann. § 423.505. If the employer refuses to remove or correct the information at issue, the Act allows the employee to insert a statement into the file stating the employee's position. The statement may be no longer than five letter-size pages. If either the employer or employee knowingly includes false information in the file, the other party may pursue legal action to remove it.

The Act bars employers from divulging a disciplinary report, reprimand letter, or other disciplinary action to a third party, even after the employee has been terminated, without mailing notice to the employee that the information will be divulged. Mich. Comp. Laws Ann. § 423.506. The notice must be sent on or before the day that the employer plans to divulge the information. This provision does not apply, however, where the employee waives notice as part of a written employment application with another employer; where the disclosure is ordered in a legal action or arbitration to a party in such a proceeding; or if the information is requested by a government agency as a result of an action filed by an employee. The Act also states that an employer may not use information improperly excluded from the personnel file in a judicial or quasi-judicial proceeding unless the exclusion was inadvertent and the employee has a reasonable time to review the information prior to its use. Mich. Comp. Laws Ann. § 423.502.

The Act requires employers to review personnel files prior to any release of the file to third parties and remove disciplinary reports, letters of reprimand, or other disciplinary records that are more than four years old. Mich. Comp. Laws Ann. § 423.507. This section does not apply to the release of records sought by legal process or for use in arbitration.

Where an employer has "reasonable cause" to believe that an employee is engaged in criminal activity that may result in loss or damage to the employer's property or disrupt its business operation, and the employer investigates the matter, the Act requires the employer to maintain a separate file relating to that investigation. Mich. Comp. Laws Ann. § 423.509. At the earlier of either the conclusion of the investigation or two years after its commencement, the employee must be given notice of the investigation and the criminal activity suspected. If no disciplinary action has been taken after the employer completes the investigation, the employer must destroy the file.

If the employer fails to comply with the statute's provisions, the employee may commence an action in the circuit court against the employer and may be awarded actual damages plus costs. A fine and attorneys' fees will be assessed in addition to this award where the violation is proved to be willful. Mich. Comp. Laws Ann. § 423.511.

New Jersey

There is no statutory provision in New Jersey that provides for an employee's access to his or her personnel records.

New York

There is no specific provision in New York requiring employers to provide their employees with access to their personnel records. In *Bigelow v. Board of Trustees,* 63 N.Y.2d 473 (1984), the New York Court of Appeals recognized the right for *public* employees, in certain situations, to have access to their personnel files. In *Bigelow,* the court held that a civil service employee found guilty of misconduct must be given notice of the information contained in his or her personnel file and an opportunity to submit a written response to the information before the employer considers such information in determining appropriate discipline. In its decision, the court noted that "[f]undamental fairness to [the employee] ... as well as regard for the integrity of the [employer's] consideration of his employment record, ... required that examination of the documents in ... his file not be ex parte." 63 N.Y.2d at 474. The court expressed its concern that public employees be given the opportunity to rebut "unestablished allegations of misconduct in [the employee's] personnel file" before a public employer uses the information to determine the discipline of the employee for an infraction or violation of the employer's rules or policies.

Texas

There is no statutory provision under Texas law requiring an employer to grant an employee access to his or her personnel file.

Notes

1. A separate statutory provision addresses employee access to medical records. Conn. Gen. Stat. § 31-128c. It permits access, but requires that disclosure of the record occur under the supervision of a physician selected either by the employee or employer.

2. An employee further may request that the employer provide a copy of his or her medical file to a physician selected by the employee.
3. The term "employee" includes current employees as well as former employees seeking access within one year of their separation from employment.

Appendix H

Blacklisting of Employees

Selected State Statutes

California

No business establishment shall discriminate against, boycott, or blacklist any person in the state of California because of race, creed, religion, color, national origin, sex, blindness, or physical disability of the person or of the person's partners, agents, employees, or customers. Cal. Civ. Code § 51.5.

The California Labor Code makes it a misdemeanor to misrepresent information about a former employee with the intent to prevent that employee from obtaining employment. Cal. Lab. Code § 1050. Employers similarly may not require an applicant or employee, as a condition of obtaining or retaining employment, to be photographed or fingerprinted for the purpose of furnishing these photographs, fingerprints, or information to any other employer or third person to the detriment of the employee or applicant. Cal. Lab. Code § 1051. An employer may also be found liable for knowingly permitting, or failing to take reasonable steps to prevent, an agent or employee from disclosing information in violation of either § 1050 or 1051. Cal. Lab. Code § 1052. Nothing in the statute shall prevent an employer from furnishing, on request, a truthful statement concerning the reasons an employee voluntarily left or was discharged from employment. Cal. Lab. Code § 1053.

Connecticut

Connecticut law prohibits any person, agent, or officer of a company from blacklisting any employee, publishing or causing to be published the name of any employee, or conspiring or contriving, with the intent and purpose of preventing the employee from securing employment with any other person or company. Conn. Gen. Stat. § 31-51. The statute does not prohibit a company from giving a truthful statement of facts concerning a present or former employee. Conn. Gen. Stat. § 31-51.

A second state law prohibits an employer from belonging or subscribing to or maintaining any organization that provides information about the character, skill, acts, or affiliations of any person that may affect the reputation, standing, or employability of the person unless the complete record of information is available for inspection by and comment from the person. Conn. Gen. Stat. § 31-134.

Florida

Under Florida law, persons are permitted to provide employment information to a financial institution, or to a third-party supplying such information to a financial institution, if the information concerns an employee's or former employee's known or suspected involvement in any unlawful undertaking reported to a state or federal authority. Fla. Stat. § 655.51. Persons providing such information pursuant to this statute are not protected from civil liability if the information is false or it is supplied with reckless disregard for the truth. Fla. Stat. § 655.51.

Florida law provides that where two or more persons agree, conspire, or combine to prevent an individual from obtaining employment or to cause an individual's discharge, such persons shall be guilty of a misdemeanor. Fla. Stat. § 448.045.

Illinois

No Illinois statute or regulation addresses the issue of blacklisting in the employment context.

Massachusetts

No Massachusetts statute or regulation addresses the issue of blacklisting in the employment context.

Michigan

No Michigan statute or regulation addresses the issue of blacklisting in the employment context.

New Jersey

No New Jersey statute or regulation addresses the issue of blacklisting in the employment context.

New York

The New York Human Rights Law prohibits the boycotting or blacklisting of any person, including a present or former employee, because of the race, creed, color, national origin or sex of such person, or of such person's partners, employees, customers, etc. This law does not apply to boycotts connected with labor disputes or boycotts to protest unlawful discriminatory practices. N.Y. Exec. Law. § 296(13).

Texas

Texas law defines "discrimination" to include the blacklisting, preventing, or attempting to prevent employees who were discharged or voluntarily left employment of the employer from obtaining other employment. The law does not prohibit the employer from truthfully stating, *in writing,* on request from the employee or prospective employer, the reason(s) why the employee was discharged or voluntarily left employment. Tex. Civ. Stat. Ann. art. 5196. If such writing is provided, the former employee is entitled to a copy of the written statement or communication. Tex. Civ. Stat. Ann. art. 5196.2. If the employer fails to provide such statement or communication within ten days after written demand, the employer may not provide such communique to any third party thereafter. Tex. Civ. Stat. Ann. art. 5196.5.

Under a separate section of the code specifically addressing "blacklisting," employers are prohibited from blacklisting any discharged employee with the intent of preventing that person from obtaining employment. Tex. Civ. Stat. Ann. art. 5196d. Blacklisting is defined as placing or causing to be placed the name of a discharged employee or employee who voluntarily left employment in any publication or list with the intent of preventing the employee from obtaining employment. Tex. Civ. Stat. Ann. art. 5196c.

Table of Cases

A

Abbott v. Payne, 457 So. 2d 1156 (Fla. Dist. Ct. App. 1984)   17, 238

Abston v. Levi Strauss & Co., 684 F. Supp. 152, 3 IER Cases 1329 (E.D. Tex. 1987)   116, 242

Acampora v. Boise Cascade Corp., 635 F. Supp. 66 (D.N.J. 1986)   190, 231

Adams v. Alderson, 723 F. Supp. 1531 (D.D.C. 1989), *aff'd*, No. 89-5265 (D.C. Cir. Apr. 10, 1990)   23

Agis v. Howard Johnson Co., 371 Mass. 140, 355 N.E.2d 315 (1976)   117, 242

Agriss v. Roadway Express, 334 Pa. Super. 295, 483 A.2d 456 (1984)   72, 217

Albrant v. Sterling Furniture Co., 85 Or. App. 272, 736 P.2d 201, *review denied*, 304 Or. 55, 742 P.2d 1186 (1987)   49, 217, 239

Alyeska Pipeline Serv. Co. v. Wilderness Soc'y, 421 U.S. 240 (1975)   300

Anderson v. Liberty Lobby, 477 U.S. 242 (1986)   299

B

Battista v. United Illuminating Co., 10 Conn. App. 486, 523 A.2d 1356, *cert. denied*, 204 Conn. 802, 525 A.2d 1352 (1987)   64, 241

Beauchamp v. Dow Chem. Co., 427 Mich. 1, 398 N.W.2d 882 (1986)   146, 208

Belknap, Inc. v. Hale, 463 U.S. 491, 113 LRRM 3057 (1983)   50, 226, 239, 278

Benassi v. Georgia-Pacific, 62 Or. App. 698, 662 P.2d 760, *modified on other grounds*, 63 Or. App. 672, 667 P.2d 532, *review denied*, 295 Or. 730, 670 P.2d 1035 (1983)   74, 91, 210, 224, 241, 297

Berger v. Security Pac. Information Sys., 795 P.2d 1380, 5 IER Cases 951 (Colo. Ct. App. 1990)   43, 62, 239

Bigelow v. Board of Trustees, 63 N.Y.2d 473 (1984)   352

Blau v. Del Monte Corp., 748 F.2d 1348 (9th Cir. 1984), *cert. denied*, 474 U.S. 865 (1985)   298

Boivin v. Jones & Vining, Inc., 578 A.2d 187, 6 IER Cases 48 (Me. 1990)   46, 226, 239

Bradley v. Hubbard Broadcasting, 471 N.W.2d 670 (Minn. Ct. App. 1991)   65, 76, 242

Brannan v. Wyeth Laboratories, Inc., 516 So. 2d 157, 3 IER Cases 61 (La. Ct. App. 1987), *rev'd in relevant part*, 526 So. 2d 1101, 3 IER Cases 609 (La. 1988)   81, 241, 242

Bratt v. IBM, 785 F.2d 352 (1st Cir. 1986)   124, 213, 215, 297

Brown v. Burlington Indus., 93 N.C.

Brown—cont'd
App. 431, 378 S.E.2d 232 (1989), *review dismissed*, 326 N.C. 356, 388 S.E.2d 769 (1990)   20, 201, 242, 285
Brown v. Ellis, 40 Conn. Supp. 165, 484 A.2d 944 (1984)   97, 214, 239, 240
Burch v. A&G Assocs., 122 Mich. App. 798, 333 N.W.2d 140 (1983)   17, 238

C

Callan v. State Chem. Mfg. Co., 584 F. Supp. 619 (E.D. Pa. 1984)   191
Carroll v. Tennessee Valley Auth., 697 F. Supp. 508, 3 IER Cases 149 (D.D.C. 1988)   32, 112, 207
Celotex Corp. v. Catrett, 477 U.S. 317 (1986)   299
Chamberlain v. Bissell, Inc., 547 F. Supp. 1067 (W.D. Mich. 1982)   30, 37, 216, 285
Chastain v. Litton Sys., 694 F.2d 957 (4th Cir. 1982), *cert. denied*, 462 U.S. 1106 (1983)   35
Christiansburg Garment Co. v. EEOC, 434 U.S. 412 (1978)   300
Chuy v. Philadelphia Eagles Football Club, 595 F.2d 1265 (3d Cir. 1979)   111
Cole v. Fair Oaks Fire Protection Dist., 43 Cal. 3d 148, 729 P.2d 743, 233 Cal. Rptr. 308, 1 IER Cases 1644 (1987)   100, 277
Collins v. Shell Oil Co., 56 FEP Cases 440 (Cal. Super. Ct. Alameda County 1991)   113, 117, 242, 299
Columbia Sussex Corp. v. Hay, 627 S.W.2d 270 (Ky. Ct. App. 1981)   175, 284
Cory v. Binkley Co., 235 Kan. 906, 684 P.2d 1019 (1984)   56, 61, 298
Cox v. Brazo, 165 Ga. App. 888, 303 S.E.2d 71, *aff'd*, 251 Ga. 491, 307 S.E.2d 474 (1983)   21, 201, 242
Cronan v. New England Tel. Co., 41 FEP Cases 1273 (Mass. Super. Ct. Suffolk County 1986)   121, 212
Cronk v. Intermountain Rural Elec. Ass'n, 765 P.2d 619, 3 IER Cases 1049 (Colo. Ct. App. 1988)   154, 230
Crowe v. J.C. Penney, Inc., 177 Ga. App. 586, 340 S.E.2d 192 (1986)   173, 285

D

D'Ulisse-Cupo v. Board of Directors, 202 Conn. 206, 520 A.2d 217, 2 IER Cases 948 (1987)   52, 62, 226
Davis v. United States Steel Corp., 779 F.2d 209, 39 FEP Cases 955 (4th Cir. 1985)   140, 239, 283
Davis v. Utah Power & Light Co., 5 IER Cases 1713 (D. Utah 1988)   28, 202, 238, 272, 298
Dean v. Ford Motor Credit Co., 885 F.2d 300, 4 IER Cases 1623 (5th Cir. 1989)   103, 204
DeAngelis v. Jamesway Dep't Store, 205 N.J. Super. 519, 501 A.2d 561 (App. Div. 1985)   171, 177, 222
DeLeon v. Hospital of Albert Einstein College of Medicine, 164 A.D.2d 743, 566 N.Y.S.2d 213 (1st Dep't 1991)   9, 238
Della Croce v. General Elec. Co., 2 IER Cases 1548 (D. Mass. 1988)   47, 217, 239
Dickinson v. Edwards, 105 Wash. 2d 457, 716 P.2d 814 (1986)   34, 210
DiCosala v. Kay, 91 N.J. 159, 450 A.2d 508 (1982)   36, 11
Dixon v. Stuart, 85 N.C. App. 338, 354 S.E.2d 757 (1987)   97, 239, 240
Doe v. American Airlines, No. 86 C 7801 (Cook County, Ill. 1986),

Table of Cases 361

reported in 173 Daily Lab. Rep. A-5 (1986)   10, 212
Dorr v. C.B. Johnson, Inc., 660 P.2d 517 (Colo. Ct. App. 1983)   90, 238
Dowie v. Exxon Corp., 12 Conn. L. Trib. No. 29 (July 28, 1986), at 1   xxiv, 45, 62, 239, 292, 299
Dupler v. Seubert, 69 Wis. 2d 373, 230 N.W.2d 626 (1975)   174, 177, 231

E

Eddy v. Brown, 715 P.2d 74 (Okla. 1986)   120, 129, 134
Elmore v. Shell Oil Co., 733 F. Supp. 544, 5 IER Cases 185 (E.D.N.Y. 1988)   87–88, 241, 297
Empiregas, Inc. v. Hardy, 487 So. 2d 244 (Ala. 1985), *cert. denied*, 476 U.S. 1116 (1986)   166, 237
Evans v. Morsell, 284 Md. 160, 395 A.2d 480 (1978)   15, 270

F

Fahnestock & Co. v. Waltman, No. 90 Civ. 1792 (S.D.N.Y. Aug. 23, 1990), *aff'd*, 935 F.2d 512 (2d Cir.), *cert. denied*, 112 S. Ct. 380 (1991)   89, 236, 242, 283
Falls v. Sporting News Publishing Co., 834 F.2d 611, 2 IER Cases 1239 (6th Cir. 1987), *on remand*, 714 F. Supp. 843 (E.D. Mich. 1989), *aff'd mem.*, 899 F.2d 1221 (6th Cir. 1990)   85, 243, 297
Faniel v. Chesapeake & Potomac Tel. Co., 404 A.2d 147 (D.C. 1979)   176
Farmer v. United Bhd. of Carpenters, Local 25, 430 U.S. 290, 94 LRRM 2759 (1977)   98, 240, 298
Foley v. Polaroid Corp., 400 Mass. 82, 508 N.E.2d 72, 2 IER Cases 328 (1987)   171, 177, 185, 186, 203, 225, 236, 241, 273
Ford v. Revlon, Inc., 153 Ariz. 38, 734 P.2d 580, 1 IER Cases 1571 (1987)   102, 202, 300
Fort Halifax Packing Co. v. Coyne, 482 U.S. 1, 2 IER Cases 134 (1987)   298
Frank B. Hall & Co. v. Buck, 678 S.W.2d 612 (Tex. Ct. App. 1984), *cert. denied*, 472 U.S. 1009 (1985)   82, 91, 234, 299
Frankson v. Design Space Int'l, 380 N.W.2d 560 (Minn. Ct. App.), *rev'd on other grounds*, 394 N.W.2d 140 (Minn. 1986)   77, 91, 242
Freeman v. Kansas State Network, 719 F. Supp. 995, 5 IER Cases 155 (D. Kan. 1989)   114, 117, 214, 237, 242, 292

G

Gaines v. Monsanto Co., 655 S.W.2d 568 (Mo. Ct. App. 1983)   36, 238
Geyer v. Steinbronn, 351 Pa. Super. 536, 506 A.2d 901 (1986)   162, 166, 235, 301
Giles v. Shell Oil Corp., 487 A.2d 610 (D.C. 1985)   25, 242, 297
Gilmer v. Interstate/Johnson Lane Corp., 111 S. Ct. 1647 (1991)   283
Glass Molders Int'l Union v. Wickes Cos., 707 F. Supp. 174, 4 IER Cases 1718 (D.N.J. 1989), *on remand*, 243 N.J. Super. 44, 578 A.2d 402, 5 IER Cases 1060 (Law Div. 1990)   160, 299
Gonzalez v. CNA Ins. Co., 717 F. Supp. 1087 (E.D. Pa. 1989)   71, 202, 225, 241
Green v. Missouri Pac. R.R., 523 F.2d 1290 (8th Cir. 1975)   313
Greenblatt v. Budd Co., 666 F. Supp. 735 (E.D. Pa. 1987)   55, 232, 281, 297

Greenfield v. Spectrum Inv. Corp., 174 Cal. App. 3d 111, 219 Cal. Rptr. 805 (1985)   23, 37, 242

Gregory v. Litton Sys., 472 F.2d 631 (9th Cir. 1972)   313

Grell v. Poulsen, 389 N.W.2d 661 (Iowa 1986)   186

Gulden v. Crown Zellerbach Corp., 890 F.2d 195, 4 IER Cases 1761 (9th Cir. 1989)   146, 207, 208

H

Haddock v. City of New York, 75 N.Y.2d 478, 553 N.E.2d 987, 554 N.Y.S.2d 439, 5 IER Cases 358 (1990)   22, 37, 239, 242, 300

Hall v. May Dep't Stores Co., 292 Or. 131, 637 P.2d 126 (1981)   106, 221, 297

Hardy v. LaBelle's Distrib. Co., 203 Mont. 263, 661 P.2d 35 (1983)   172, 177, 285

Harlan v. Intergy, Inc., 721 F. Supp. 148, 4 IER Cases 497 (N.D. Ohio 1989)   44, 62, 239

Hart v. National Mortgage & Land Co., 189 Cal. App. 3d 1420, 235 Cal. Rptr. 68 (1987)   140, 239, 277, 283

Hecht v. Commerce Clearing House, 897 F.2d 21, 5 IER Cases 78 (2d Cir. 1990)   191

Henley v. Prince George's County, 305 Md. 320, 503 A.2d 1333 (1986)   26, 36

Hester v. Church's Fried Chicken, 27 Ohio App. 3d 74, 499 N.E.2d 923 (1986)   282

Hickman v. Winston County Hosp. Bd., 508 So. 2d 237 (Ala. 1987)   161

Higgins v. Lawrence, 107 Mich. App. 178, 309 N.W.2d 194 (1981)   49, 61, 239

Holland v. Kennedy, 548 So. 2d 982 (Miss. 1989)   76, 242

Houston Belt & Terminal Ry. v. Wherry, 548 S.W.2d 743 (Tex. 1976), *appeal dismissed*, 434 U.S. 962 (1977)   67, 210, 223, 241

Howcroft v. Mountain States Tel. & Tel. Co., 712 F. Supp. 1514, 4 IER Cases 1225 (D. Utah 1989)   70, 91, 221, 241, 272

Hunt v. Weatherbee, 626 F. Supp. 1097, 121 LRRM 2408 (D. Mass. 1986)   192, 206

I

In re IBP Confidential Business Documents Litigation, 797 F.2d 632, 1 IER Cases 871 (8th Cir. 1986), *cert. denied*, 479 U.S. 1088 (1987)   156, 166, 230

Ingersoll-Rand Co. v. McClendon, 111 S. Ct. 478, 5 IER Cases 1601 (1990)   298

International Longshoremen's Ass'n v. Davis, 476 U.S. 380, 122 LRRM 2369 (1986)   298

Iverson v. Atlas Pac. Eng'g, 143 Cal. App. 3d 219, 191 Cal. Rptr. 696 (1983)   176

J

Jeffers v. Convoy Co., 636 F. Supp. 1337, 1 IER Cases 919 (D. Minn. 1986)   58, 61, 242, 279, 297

Johnson v. Anheuser Busch, Inc., 876 F.2d 620, 4 IER Cases 709 (8th Cir. 1989)   183, 241, 279, 297

Johnson v. Ramsey County, 424 N.W.2d 800, 3 IER Cases 629 (Minn. Ct. App. 1988)   137, 239, 302

K

K-Mart Corp. v. Trotti, 677 S.W.2d 632 (Tex. Ct. App. 1984), *writ*

denied, 686 S.W.2d 593 (Tex. 1985)   130, 134, 221
Kamrath v. Suburban Nat'l Bank, 363 N.W.2d 108 (Minn. Ct. App. 1985)   107, 241
Keehr v. Consolidated Freightways, 825 F.2d 133, 2 IER Cases 565 (7th Cir. 1987)   134, 205
Kelley v. Schlumberger Technology Corp., 849 F.2d 41, 3 IER Cases 696 (1st Cir. 1988)   109, 117, 224, 241
Kellums v. Freight Sales Centers, 467 So. 2d 816 (Fla. Dist. Ct. App. 1985)   86, 284
Kobeck v. Nabisco, Inc., 166 Ga. App. 652, 305 S.E.2d 183, 1 IER Cases 200 (1983)   125, 297
Kolator v. State, No. 71232 (N.Y. Ct. Cl. Apr. 8, 1988)   9, 238
Kraus v. Santa Fe S. Pac. Corp., 878 F.2d 1193 (9th Cir. 1989), *cert. dismissed*, 493 U.S. 1051 (1990)   158, 166, 299

L

LaScala v. D'Angelo, 104 A.D.2d 930, 480 N.Y.S.2d 546 (2d Dep't 1984)   69, 210
Leahy v. Federal Express Corp., 613 F. Supp. 906 (E.D.N.Y. 1985)   144, 222
Leibowitz v. H.A. Winston Co., 342 Pa. Super. 456, 493 A.2d 111 (1985)   108, 241
Lewis v. Equitable Life Assurance Soc'y, 389 N.W.2d 876, 1 IER Cases 1269 (Minn. 1986)   87, 91, 241, 242
Lingle v. Norge Div., 486 U.S. 399, 3 IER Cases 481 (1988)   298
Linn v. United Plant Guard Workers, 383 U.S. 53 (1966)   298
Little v. Bryce, 733 S.W.2d 937 (Tex. Ct. App. 1987)   73, 212

Loftis v. G.T. Prods., 167 Mich. App. 787, 423 N.W.2d 358, 3 IER Cases 641 (1988)   31, 37, 216
Loughry v. Lincoln First Bank, N.A., 67 N.Y.2d 369, 494 N.E.2d 70, 502 N.Y.S.2d 965 (1986)   68, 210, 224, 297
Love v. Southern Bell Tel. & Tel. Co., 263 So. 2d 460 (La. Ct. App.), *writ denied*, 262 La. 1117, 266 So. 2d 429 (1972)   131, 211, 297

M

McCarthy v. State, 110 Wash. 2d 812, 759 P.2d 351, 3 IER Cases 710 (1988)   32, 206
McCone v. New England Tel. & Tel. Co., 393 Mass. 231, 471 N.E.2d 47 (1984)   71, 218
McCool v. Hillhaven Corp., 97 Or. App. 536, 777 P.2d 1013, 4 IER Cases 1026, *review denied*, 308 Or. 593, 784 P.2d 1100 (1989)   115, 242
McKay v. Ashland Oil, No. 84-149 (E.D. Ky. June 13, 1988)   189, 231, 297
McNamee v. Bethlehem Steel Corp., 692 F. Supp. 1477 (E.D.N.Y. 1988)   54, 62, 239, 281
Malone v. Safeway Stores, 698 F. Supp. 207, 2 IER Cases 1470 (D. Or. 1987)   98, 239, 240
Meany v. Newell, 367 N.W.2d 472 (Minn. 1985)   35
Mechanics Lumber Co. v. Smith, 296 Ark. 285, 752 S.W.2d 763, 3 IER Cases 891 (1988)   33, 220, 221
Mercer v. State, 125 A.D.2d 376, 509 N.Y.S.2d 103 (2d Dep't 1986)   26, 242
Metropolitan Life Ins. Co. v. Taylor, 481 U.S. 58 (1987)   298
Milkovich v. Lorain Journal Co., 497 U.S. 1 (1990)   91, 132

Miller v. Motorola, 202 Ill. App. 3d 976, 560 N.E.2d 900, 5 IER Cases 885 (1990)   122, 134, 213

Millison v. E.I. du Pont de Nemours & Co., 226 N.J. Super. 572, 545 A.2d 213 (App. Div. 1988), *aff'd*, 115 N.J. 252, 558 A.2d 461 (1989)   61, 62, 208, 297

Millross v. Plum Hollow Gulf, 429 Mich. 178, 413 N.W.2d 17 (1987)   35

Moniodis v. Cook, 64 Md. App. 1, 494 A.2d 212, 1 IER Cases 441, *cert. denied*, 304 Md. 631, 500 A.2d 649 (1985)   106, 117, 221

Mueller v. Union Pac. R.R., 220 Neb. 742, 371 N.W.2d 732 (1985)   58, 220

N

National Treasury Employees Union v. Von Raab, 489 U.S. 656, 4 IER Cases 246 (1989)   134

Neal v. Corning Glass Works Corp., 745 F. Supp. 1294, 5 IER Cases 1636 (S.D. Ohio 1989)   128, 211

Nelson v. Lapeyrouse Grain Corp., 534 So. 2d 1085, 5 IER Cases 1812 (Ala. 1988)   80, 241, 297

New York Times v. Sullivan, 376 U.S. 254 (1964)   64

Newsome v. Cooper-Wiss, Inc., 179 Ga. App. 670, 347 S.E.2d 619 (1986)   139, 239, 282

Nigg v. Patterson, 226 Cal. App. 3d 551, 276 Cal. Rptr. 587, 6 IER Cases 65 (1990), *superseded*, 279 Cal. Rptr. 99, 806 P.2d 841 (1991)   14, 239

North Houston Pole Line Corp. v. McAllister, 667 S.W.2d 829 (Tex. Ct. App. 1983)   11, 238

NPS Corp. v. Insurance Co. of N. Am., 213 N.J. Super. 547, 517 A.2d 1211, 2 IER Cases 471 (App. Div. 1986)   142, 304

O

O'Brien v. Papa Gino's of Am., 780 F.2d 1067, 1 IER Cases 458 (1st Cir. 1986)   127, 134, 211, 241

O'Connor v. Ortega, 480 U.S. 709, 1 IER Cases 1617 (1987)   134

Otis Eng'g Corp. v. Clark, 668 S.W.2d 307 (Tex. 1983)   35

P

Pacific Mut. Life Ins. Co. v. Haslip, 111 S. Ct. 1032 (1991)   300

Palmer v. Beverly Enters., 823 F.2d 1105, 3 IER Cases 218 (7th Cir. 1987)   48, 239

Paroline v. Unisys Corp., 900 F.2d 27 (4th Cir. 1990) (*en banc*), *vacating in part* 879 F.2d 100 (4th Cir. 1989), *on remand*, No. 88-0063-A (E.D. Va. July 13, 1990)   29, 37, 209

Payne v. General Motors Corp., 5 IER Cases 1081, 53 FEP Cases 471 (D. Kan. 1990), *aff'd mem.*, 943 F.2d 57 (10th Cir. 1991)   104, 117, 205, 214

Pettigrew v. Southern Pac. Transp. Co., No. 849343 (Super. Ct. San Francisco County Nov. 25, 1985)   176, 215

Phillips v. Smalley Maintenance Servs., 711 F.2d 1524, 1 IER Cases 221 (11th Cir. 1983)   128, 134, 203, 297

Pilot Life Ins. Co. v. Dedeaux, 481 U.S. 41 (1987)   298

Ponticas v. K.M.S. Invs., 331 N.W.2d 907 (Minn. 1983)   16, 36, 37, 238, 270

Powell v. Chesapeake & Potomac Tel. Co., 780 F.2d 419 (4th Cir.

Table of Cases 365

1985), *cert. denied*, 476 U.S. 1170 (1986)   105, 280
Pruitt v. Pavelin, 141 Ariz. 195, 685 P.2d 1347 (1984)   19, 239

R

R.M. v. McDonald's Corp., No. 89-CV-17012 (Colo. Dist. Ct. Mar. 8, 1991), reported in 53 Daily Lab. Rep. A-6 (1991)   12, 238
Redd v. Product Dev. Corp., No. 89-1119 (D.C. Super. Ct. 1990)   19, 37, 209, 242, 292
Redican v. K-Mart Corp., 734 S.W.2d 864 (Mo. Ct. App. 1987)   170, 177, 184, 222, 235
Roadway Express v. Piper, 447 U.S. 752 (1980)   300
Robertson v. LeMaster, 171 W. Va. 607, 301 S.E.2d 563 (1983)   36
Robinson v. Hewlett-Packard Corp., 183 Cal. App. 3d 1108, 228 Cal. Rptr. 591 (1986)   104, 239
Rogozinski v. Airstream by Angell, 152 N.J. Super. 133, 377 A.2d 807 (Law Div. 1977), *modified on other grounds*, 164 N.J. Super. 465, 397 A.2d 334 (App. Div. 1979)   89, 238, 242
Rosen-House v. Sloan's Supermkt., N.Y.L.J., Sept. 27, 1988, at 18, col. 4 (Sup. Ct. New York County), *aff'd mem.*, 148 A.D.2d 1020, 540 N.Y.S.2d 120 (1st Dep't 1989)   13, 36, 238, 292
Russ v. TRW, 59 Ohio St. 3d 42, 570 N.E.2d 1076, 6 IER Cases 769 (1991)   57, 62, 217, 242

S

Sallaz v. G-H-I Hous. Corp., No. 85-66859 (Tex. Dist. Ct. Harris County 1986)   xxvii, 12, 37, 238, 292, 297, 300, 304

San Diego Bldg. Trades Council v. Garmon, 359 U.S. 236 (1959)   298
Sandler v. New York News, 721 F. Supp. 506 (S.D.N.Y. 1989)   59, 62, 227, 281
Schwartz v. Zippy Mart, 470 So. 2d 720 (Fla. Dist. Ct. App. 1985)   141, 239, 277
Sedima S.P.L.R. v. Imrex Co., 473 U.S. 479 (1985)   193
Shaw v. Delta Air Lines, 463 U.S. 85 (1983)   298
Shearin v. E.F. Hutton Group, 885 F.2d 1162 (3d Cir. 1989)   190, 231
Shebar v. Sanyo Bus. Sys., 111 N.J. 276, 544 A.2d 377, 3 IER Cases 1385 (1988)   53, 61, 226, 233, 272
Shrout v. Black Clawson Co., 689 F. Supp. 774, 3 IER Cases 492 (S.D. Ohio 1988)   101, 202, 240
Sigal Constr. Corp. v. Stanbury, 586 A.2d 1204, 6 IER Cases 201 (D.C. App. 1991)   83, 91, 234
Simmons v. Baltimore Orioles, 712 F. Supp. 79, 4 IER Cases 572 (W.D. Va. 1989)   25
Sims v. Kaneb Servs., No. 86-2474 (Tex. Dist. Ct. Harris County Dec. 1, 1989), reported in 4 IER No. 23 (1989)   181, 186, 236, 273, 299, 302
Singer Shop-Rite v. Rangel, 174 N.J. Super. 442, 416 A.2d 965 (App. Div.), *cert. denied*, 85 N.J. 148, 425 A.2d 299 (1980)   144, 222
Skinner v. Railway Labor Executives' Ass'n, 489 U.S. 602, 4 IER Cases 224 (1989)   134
Smith v. Greyhound Lines, 614 F. Supp. 558 (W.D. Pa. 1984), *aff'd mem.*, 800 F.2d 1139 (3d Cir. 1986)   143
Smith v. National R.R. Passenger

Smith—cont'd

Corp., 856 F.2d 467 (2d Cir. 1988)   28, 37, 208
Sorrells v. Garfinkel's, 2 IER Cases 618 (D.C. Super. Ct. 1987)   153, 166, 230, 297, 301
Spoljaric v. Percival Tours, 708 S.W.2d 432 (Tex. 1986)   52, 62, 232, 300
Sterner v. Marathon Oil Co., 767 S.W.2d 686, 4 IER Cases 592 (Tex. 1989)   157, 230
Strachan v. Union Oil Co., 768 F.2d 703, 1 IER Cases 1844 (5th Cir. 1985)   142, 278
Stroman v. West Coast Grocery Co., 884 F.2d 458 (9th Cir. 1989), *cert. denied*, 111 S. Ct. 151 (1990)   300
Stuempges v. Parke, Davis & Co., 297 N.W.2d 252 (Minn. 1980)   84, 243
Surrency v. Harbison, 489 So. 2d 1097 (Ala. 1986)   147, 206, 279, 297
Sweeney v. Westvaco Co., 926 F.2d 29, 6 IER Cases 289 (1st Cir.), *cert. denied*, 112 S. Ct. 274 (1991)   100, 117, 280

T

Tomson v. Stephan, 696 F. Supp. 1407, 4 IER Cases 1648 (D. Kan. 1988)   132, 134
Torbett v. Wheeling Dollar Savs. & Trust Co., 173 W. Va. 210, 314 S.E.2d 166 (1983)   165, 237
Trimble v. City of Denver, 697 P.2d 716 (Colo. 1985)   161, 166, 219
Trout v. Umatilla County School Dist., 77 Or. App. 95, 712 P.2d 814 (1985), *review denied*, 300 Or. 704, 716 P.2d 758 (1986)   125, 211
Tumbarella v. Kroger Co., 85 Mich. App. 482, 271 N.W.2d 284 (1978)   172, 177, 223, 241

Turner v. Halliburton Co., 240 Kan. 1, 722 P.2d 1106 (1986)   163, 241

U

Uebelacker v. Cincom Sys., 48 Ohio App. 3d 268, 549 N.E.2d 1210, 3 IER Cases 1853 (1988)   174, 177, 231, 242, 273
United Steelworkers of Am. v. Rawson, 495 U.S. 362, 5 IER Cases 493 (1990)   298
University of Pa. v. EEOC, 493 U.S. 182 (1990)   xxvii

V

Vernars v. Young, 539 F.2d 966 (3d Cir. 1976)   130
Verway v. Blincoe Packing Co., 108 Idaho 315, 698 P.2d 377 (1985)   51, 226, 239
Vinson v. Linn-Mar Community School Dist., 360 N.W.2d 108 (Iowa 1984)   84, 241, 242

W

Wainauskis v. Howard Johnson Co., 339 Pa. Super. 266, 488 A.2d 1117 (1985)   182, 185, 235, 241
Walden v. General Mills Restaurant Group, 31 Ohio App. 3d 11, 508 N.E.2d 168 (1986)   143
Walker v. South Central Bell Tel. Co., 904 F.2d 275, 5 IER Cases 1373 (5th Cir. 1990)   116, 242
Waltman v. International Paper Co., 3 IER Cases 1336 (W.D. La. 1988), *rev'd in part on other grounds*, 875 F.2d 468 (5th Cir. 1989)   138, 203, 239, 282
Wangen v. Knudson, 428 N.W.2d 242 (S.D. 1988)   110, 117, 215, 297, 301

Weintraub v. Phillips, Nizer, Benjamin, et al., 172 A.D.2d 254, 568 N.Y.S.2d 84 (1st Dep't 1991)   91

Weisman v. Connors, 312 Md. 428, 540 A.2d 783, *rev'd and remanded on remand*, 76 Md. App. 488, 547 A.2d 636 (Ct. Spec. App. 1988), *cert. denied*, 314 Md. 497, 551 A.2d 868 (1989)   61, 62, 239, 299

Weiss v. Furniture in the Raw, 62 Misc. 2d 283, 306 N.Y.S.2d 253 (Civ. Ct. Queens County 1969)   18, 37, 238

Wells v. General Motors Corp., 881 F.2d 166, 4 IER Cases 1392 (5th Cir. 1989)   60, 227, 298

Wells v. Premier Indus. Corp., 691 P.2d 765 (Colo. Ct. App. 1984)   126

Wells v. Thomas, 569 F. Supp. 426 (E.D. Pa. 1983)   126

Welsh Mfg. v. Pinkerton's, Inc., 474 A.2d 436 (R.I. 1984)   24, 37, 238, 242

Williams v. Feather Sound, 386 So. 2d 1238 (Fla. Dist. Ct. App. 1980), *review denied*, 392 So. 2d 1374 (Fla. 1981)   18, 37, 238

Wilson v. Monarch Paper Co., 939 F.2d 1138, 6 IER Cases 1344 (5th Cir. 1991)   96, 117, 204, 240, 273, 299

Worley v. Oregon Physicians Servs., 69 Or. App. 241, 686 P.2d 404, *review denied*, 298 Or. 334, 691 P.2d 483 (1984)   74–75, 241, 297

Y

Yaindl v. Ingersoll-Rand Co., 281 Pa. Super. 560, 422 A.2d 611, 115 LRRM 4738 (1980)   164, 230, 235

Young Oil Co. v. Durbin, 412 So. 2d 620 (La. Ct. App. 1982)   184, 241

Z

Zechman v. Merrill Lynch, Pierce, Fenner & Smith, 742 F. Supp. 1359, 5 IER Cases 1665 (N.D. Ill. 1990)   133, 134, 229

Zinda v. Louisiana Pac. Corp., 149 Wis. 2d 913, 440 N.W.2d 548, 4 IER Cases 703 (1989)   79, 242

Index

This index is alphabetized letter-by-letter (i.e., Postemployment references precedes Post-termination proceedings).

A

Abuse of process (*see* Malicious prosecution and abuse of process)
Access to personnel records, state laws (Appendix G) 348–54
Age Discrimination in Employment Act (ADEA) 276, 294–95
AIDS 211–13
    Americans with Disabilities Act testing provisions, Appendix E summary 339–40
    defamation suits arising from employer's false statements about employee 63, 72–73, 212
    federal law on testing (Appendix E) 339–40
    invasion of privacy 118–19, 121, 212–13
    negligent hiring suits 9–10, 212
    state laws on testing (Appendix E) 334–39
Alcohol abuse 209–11, 223–24
    alcohol furnished to intoxicated person, employer's negligence 4, 6, 34–35
    preventive measures to avoid tort liability at work functions where alcoholic beverages are served 269

defamation 223
testing, preventive measures to avoid tort liability 256–57
Americans with Disabilities Act (ADA) 124, 276
    AIDS testing provisions, Appendix E summary 339–40
    drug testing provisions, Appendix D summary 332–33
Applicants (*see* Hiring)
Arbitration clauses in collective bargaining agreements 283–84
Arrests
    false arrests 182–84 (*see also* False imprisonment)
    record inquiries (*see* Criminal record inquiries)
Assault and battery 135–48
    "backup" claims to intentional infliction of emotional distress 136
    drug testing, action arising from contact with equipment 135–36, 142
    elements of proof 135–36
    exposure to toxic substances 135–36, 145–46, 207–9
    harassment 206
    investigations of employee misconduct giving rise to 144, 222
    threats 136

Assignments, work (*see* Work assignment)
Attorneys
  conflicts of interest 302–3
  fees xxv, 291–92, 300 n.86
Avoiding exposure to tort liability (*see* Preventive measures)

B

Background checks for hiring purposes 198–200
Battery (*see* Assault and battery)
Benefits (*see also* Health insurance; Pension benefits)
  misrepresentations 53–56
Blacklisting 154–56
  state laws (Appendix H) 355–57
Blocking employee's exit from workplace (*see* False imprisonment)
Bonuses, false promises to pay (*see* Fraud and misrepresentation)
Breach of contract actions (*see also* Interference with contractual relations)
  fraud claims accompanying 40, 49, 200

C

Choice of forums for workplace tort actions 275–76
Civil Rights Act of 1964 (*see* Title VII)
Civil Rights Act of 1991 269 n.1
Civil suits, unwarranted (*see* Malicious prosecution and abuse of process)
COBRA compliance 56
Coercion, RICO civil action against employer 192
Collective bargaining agreements, arbitration clauses 283–84
Common law xix
Company newsletters, defamation suits arising from 77–79
Compelled defamation (*See* Defamation)
Compensatory damages (*see* Damages)
Concealment of material information 40, 60–61
Conditions of employment, fraud and misrepresentation 45–51
Confidentiality of settlement agreements 295
Confinement of employee (*see* False imprisonment)
Conflicts of interest for defendants' attorney 302–3
Consent and release
  defense 172–73, 284–85
  preventive measure to avoid tort liability 266
  settlement agreements 294–95
Consumer credit reports, federal and state laws (Appendix C) 322–25
Contributory and comparative negligence 285–86
Costs of litigation xxv (*see also* Attorneys)
Credit reports (*see* Consumer credit reports)
Criminal prosecution
  threats of, constituting infliction of emotional distress 105–6
  unwarranted defense against (*see* Malicious prosecution and abuse of process)
Criminal record inquiries 15–16, 21–22
  federal law under Title VII 16
    Appendix A summary 314
  state laws 16
    Appendix A summary 307–13

D

Damages 289–91 (*see also* Punitive damages)
  breach of contract 40

fraud and misrepresentation 40
infliction of emotional distress 93–95
RICO suits 187–88
Dangerous employees (*see also* Unsafe and untrustworthy employees)
  negligent failure to warn 4, 6, 28, 208–9
  negligent hiring 11–18
  negligent retention 21–23, 232
  negligent supervision 25–26
  preventive measures to avoid tort liability 269
Defamation 63–91
  AIDS, employer's false statements about employee having 63, 72–73, 212
  company newsletters 77–79
  compelled self-publication xxii, 65, 86–88
  defenses 64–65 (*see also* Privilege as defense to defamation)
  discharge cases (*see* Termination of employment)
  drug abuse, employer investigations 67–69, 210, 223–24
  elements of proof 63–65
  evaluation of employees 71, 217–18
  gossip in office, references including 82–83
  internal memos 75–77
  investigations of employee misconduct 67–72, 220–21
  malice shown in defamation suit 64–65
  opinion vs. fact 84–85
  post-termination proceedings, suits arising from statements made during 88–91, 236, 238
  preventive measures to minimize tort liability 259–61
  reference check information provided by former employer xxii, 81–86, 233–34

sexual harassment investigations 70–71, 202, 224–25
theft investigations 69–70
unprivileged statements 79–81
warnings 71–72, 217–18
Defendants, selection for employee tort action 274–75
Defending against workplace tort actions (*see* Litigation of workplace tort actions)
Defense Department regulations on drug testing for contractors (Appendix D) 330–31
Defenses of employers xxiv–xxv, 276–86
  affirmative defenses 286
  arbitration clause in collective bargaining agreement 283–84
  consent and release 284–85
  contributory and comparative negligence 285–86
  defamation 64–65 (*see also* Privilege as defense to defamation)
  false imprisonment 168, 172–73
  no *respondeat superior* or employer ratification 282–83
  preemption 276–81
  workers' compensation (*see* Workers' compensation)
Demotions, infliction of emotional distress 95–96, 100
Depositions 286–88
Detention and questioning of employees (*see* False imprisonment; Investigations of employee misconduct)
Detrimental reliance, preventive measures to avoid tort liability 254–55
Disabilities discrimination law 209 (*see also* Americans with Disabilities Act)
Discharge (*see* Termination of employment; Wrongful discharge)

Discipline (*see also* Termination of employment)
  demotions, infliction of emotional distress 95–96, 100
  warnings, defamation suits arising from 71–72, 217–18
Disclosure
  illegal activities (*see also* Whistleblowers)
    RICO 188–90
  private facts, of (*see* Invasion of privacy)
Discovery, pretrial 286–88
Discrimination (*see also* Disabilities discrimination law)
  ADEA (*see* Age Discrimination in Employment Act)
  attorneys' fees 292
  infliction of emotional distress 104, 116
Dismissal, pretrial motions 288–89
Driving (*see* Transportation)
Drug abuse
  defamation suits arising from employer investigations 67–69, 210, 223–24
  employees' tort claims arising from 209–11
  invasion of privacy 210–11, 224
  negligent retention of employees 209–10
Drug-Free Workplace Act (Appendix D) 330, 333
Drug rehabilitation program, false imprisonment suit 167, 176
Drug testing
  Americans with Disabilities Act (ADA) provisions (Appendix D) 332–33
  battery action arising from contact with equipment 135–36, 142
  Defense Department regulations for contractors (Appendix D) 330–31
  federal laws (Appendix D) 330–33
  infliction of emotional distress 108–9, 224
  invasion of privacy 127–28, 210–11, 224
  Omnibus Transportation Employees Testing Act (Appendix D) 332
  preventive measures to avoid tort liability 256–57
  state laws (Appendix D) 326–30
  Transportation Department regulations (Appendix D) 330–33
Drunk employees (*see* Alcohol abuse)

E

EAPs (*see* Employee assistance programs)
Elements of proof
  assault and battery 135–36
  defamation 63–65
  false imprisonment 167–68
  fraud and misrepresentation 39–40
  infliction of emotional distress 92–93
  interference with contractual relations 149–51
  invasion of privacy 118–20
  malicious prosecution and abuse of process 178–79
  negligent hiring 5–6
  RICO civil action 188
Emotional distress (*see* Infliction of emotional distress)
Employee assistance programs (EAPs) 214–16
  false imprisonment 215–16
  infliction of emotional distress for improper referral 109–10, 215, 301
  invasion of privacy 215

Employee benefits (*see* Benefits)
Employee Polygraph Protection Act 34, 58, 107
  Appendix B summary 320–21
Employee Retirement Income Security Act (ERISA) 54, 59, 280, 296
Entry into employee's home, invasion of privacy 130–31
Environment of workplace giving rise to tort actions 201–9
  (*see also* Hazardous substances, exposure to; Sexual harassment; Smoke-free workplace)
ERISA (*see* Employee Retirement Income Security Act)
Evaluation of employees
  defamation suits arising from 71, 217–18
  infliction of emotional distress 97, 112–13, 218
  negligence 4, 6, 29–31, 216–17
Evidence (*see* Elements of proof)
Exhausted employees, employer's negligent failure to provide transportation home 4, 6, 35–36
Exposure to hazardous substances (*see* Hazardous substances, exposure to)

F

Failure to warn of workplace dangers 4, 6, 28, 208–9
Fair Credit Reporting Act (FCRA) 324–25
False arrest 182–84 (*see also* False imprisonment)
False imprisonment 167–77, 222–23, 230–31
  defenses 168, 172–73
  elements of proof 167–68
  employee assistance programs 215–16

"False light publicity" (*see* Invasion of privacy)
False statements (*see* Fraud and misrepresentation)
Federal Arbitration Act (FAA) 283
Financial status or profitability of business, misrepresentation 42–44, 200
Firing employees (*see* Termination of employment)
Foreign Corrupt Practices Act 189
Fourth Amendment 119, 130
Fraud and misrepresentation 38–67
  benefits 53–56
  concealment of material information 40
  hazardous substances, exposure to 39, 60–61, 208
  defamation suits arising from employer investigations 69–70
  discharge giving rise to actions for fraud 39, 226–27
  elements of proof 39–40
  employee as part of job told to engage in fraudulent practice 56–57
  financial status or profitability of business 42–44, 200
  health insurance coverage 55–56
  inducing employees' actions by 38–67, 200
  material information, defined 40
  noncompetition agreements 237
  nonretaliation promises for assisting in investigations 57–58, 220
  pension benefits 53–55, 227, 233
  recruiting and hiring process (*see* Hiring)
  resignations of employees, fraudulently induced 59–60, 226–27

Fraud and misrepresentation—cont'd
  retention of employees 51–53, 232–33
  terms or conditions of employment 45–51

G

Gossip in office, references including, basis for defamation suit 82–83

H

Harassment 204–6 (*see also* Sexual harassment)
  battery actions arising from 206
  infliction of emotional distress 100–107, 111–12, 204–5
  interference with contractual relations 160–61
  invasion of privacy 205–6
  preventive measures to avoid tort liability 263–65
  RICO actions 206
Hazardous substances, exposure to
  battery action arising from contact with 135–36, 145–46, 207–9
  fraudulent concealment of information 39, 60–61, 208
Health insurance
  COBRA compliance 56
  misrepresentation of coverage 55–56
Hiring (*see also* Negligent hiring, retention, and supervision)
  background checks 198–200
  detrimental reliance, preventive measures 254–55
  financial status or profitability of business showing misrepresentation 42–44, 200
  fraud and misrepresentation 38, 42–51, 200
    detrimental reliance, preventive measures 254–55
  disclaimers to avoid tort liability 252–54
  preventive measures to avoid tort liability 245–50
  screening applicants
    preventive measures to avoid tort liability 245–50
    tort actions arising from 198–200
  terms or conditions of employment, fraud and misrepresentation 45–51
HIV virus (*see* AIDS)
Hostile takeovers 159–60
Humiliation (*see* Infliction of emotional distress)

I

Illegal activities by employer
  RICO
    disclosure 188–90
    opposition 188–90
    refusal to participate 190–91
  whistleblowing by employees (*see* Whistleblowers)
Illnesses (*see* AIDS; Injuries and illnesses, workplace; Medical or mental condition of employee; Workers' compensation)
Imprisonment, false (*see* False imprisonment)
Incompetent employees
  negligent hiring 8–9
  preventive measures
    counseling, supervising, or terminating 250–52
    screening for unfit applicants 245–50
Inducing employees' actions by fraud or misrepresentation 38–67, 200
Infliction of emotional distress 92–117, 214
  demotions 95–96, 100, 218

Index   375

discharge methods   112–17, 228–29
discrimination   104, 116
drug testing   108–9, 224
elements of proof   92–93
evaluation   97, 112–13, 218
harassment   100–107, 111–12, 204–5 (*see also* Sexual harassment)
illness incorrectly reported   110–11
investigations into employee misconduct   105–8, 221
negligent   93–94, 103–4, 113–16, 214, 228–29
punitive damages   93–94
racial insults   104
reckless misconduct   93
sexual harassment   101–2, 202–3, 218
smoking at work   111–12, 207
threats   97–98, 105–6
work assignment   96–97, 218
Injuries and illnesses, workplace (*see also* Medical or mental condition of employee; Workers' compensation)
infliction of emotional distress in connection with   110–11, 214
Insults (*see* Infliction of emotional distress)
Insurance
liability, coverage   303–4
medical (*see* Health insurance)
Intentional conduct, liability   xx–xxi
Intentional infliction of emotional distress (*see* Infliction of emotional distress)
Interference with contractual relations   149–66, 229–30, 235–37
elements of proof   149–51
noncompetition agreements   149, 164–66, 236–37
Internal memos, defamation suits arising from   75–77
Interrogations (*see* Investigations of employee misconduct)
Interrogatories   286–88
Intoxication (*see* Alcohol abuse)
Invasion of privacy   118–34
AIDS   118–19, 121, 212–13
alcohol or drug use of employees, investigation   127–28, 210–11, 224
elements of proof   118–20
"false light publicity"   119, 131–34, 229
harassment   205–6
investigations of employee misconduct   221–22
mail, personal   130
medical or mental condition of employee, disclosure   121–24, 213
personal matters about employees
disclosure   124–26
investigation into   126–29
preventive measures to avoid tort liability   261–62
sex life of employees   118–20, 128
Investigations of employee misconduct   219–25
assault and battery actions arising from   144, 222
defamation of employee   67–72, 220–21
false imprisonment   167–73, 222–23
fraud   57–58
infliction of emotional distress   105–8, 221
invasion of privacy   221–22
preventive measures to avoid tort liability   257–59
theft   219–20

J

Job evaluations (*see* Evaluation of employees)

Jokes, battery actions resulting from 137–38
Jurisdiction 275–76
Jury trials xxiii, 289

L

Labor Management Relations Act (LMRA) 142, 145–47, 159, 182, 278–80, 283
Libel (*see* Defamation)
Lie detector testing (*see* Polygraph testing)
Litigation of workplace tort actions 271–300
  attorneys' fees 291–92
  conflicts of interest for defendants' attorney 302–3
  corporation as defendant 274–75
  damages 289–91
  defendants, selection of 274–75
  defenses of employers 276–86
    affirmative defenses 286
    arbitration clause in collective bargaining agreement 283–84
    consent and release 284–85
    contributory and comparative negligence 285–86
    no *respondeat superior* or employer ratification 282–83
    preemption 276–81
    workers' compensation 276–77
  jurisdiction 275–76
  jury trials 289
  multiple tort claims 271–74
  pretrial discovery 286–88
  pretrial motions to dismiss and motions for summary judgment 288–89
  punitive damages 289–91
  settlements 292–97
    agreements 293–97
LMRA (*see* Labor Management Relations Act)
Local laws (*see* State and local laws)
Locker searches (*see* Searches)

M

Mail, invasion of privacy action 130
Malice shown in defamation suit 64–65
Malicious prosecution and abuse of process 178–86, 223, 235–36, 302
  elements of proof 178–79
  preventive measure to avoid tort liability 268–69
Managers
  personal liability xxiv, 301–2
    interference with contractual relations 151
Material information, defined 40
Medical insurance (*see* Health insurance)
Medical or mental condition of employee (*see also* Infliction of emotional distress; Injuries and illnesses, workplace)
  disclosure constituting invasion of privacy 121–24, 128–29
Memos, defamation suits arising from 75–77
Mental condition of employee (*see* Infliction of emotional distress; Medical or mental condition of employee)
Misconduct (*see* Investigations of employee misconduct; Theft)
Misrepresentation (*see* Fraud and misrepresentation; Negligent misrepresentation)
Motions to dismiss and motions for summary judgment 288–89
Multiple tort claims 271–74

N

National Labor Relations Act (NLRA) 50, 147, 278
Negligence xxi–xxii, 3–37
  contributory and comparative negligence 285–86
  defined 6
  proximate cause 7
Negligent failure to warn of workplace dangers (*see* Warnings)
Negligent hiring, retention, and supervision 3–28, 198–200, 231–32
  AIDS exposure risks 9–10, 212
  drug and alcohol abuse by employee 209–10
  elements of proof 5–6
  preventive measures to avoid tort liability 245–52, 269
Negligent infliction of emotional distress 93–94, 103–4, 113–16, 214, 228–29
Negligent misrepresentation 40–41
  pension benefits 41, 53–54, 59
Newsletters, defamation suits arising from 77–79
NLRA (*see* National Labor Relations Act)
Noncompetition agreements
  fraud 237
  interference with contractual relations 149, 164–66, 236–37

O

Occupational Safety and Health Act (OSHA) 207
Offers of employment, interference with contractual relations 163–64
Older Workers Benefit Protection Act (OWBPA) 266, 293–95
Omnibus Transportation Employees Testing Act (Appendix D) 332
Opinion vs. fact
  defamation suits 84–85
  invasion of privacy "false light publicity" suits 131–32
Out-of-court settlements (*see* Settlement of lawsuits)
Outrage (*see* Infliction of emotional distress)
OWBPA (*see* Older Workers Benefit Protection Act)

P

Pension benefits
  fraud 53–55, 227, 233
  negligent misrepresentation 41, 53–54, 59
Performance evaluation (*see* Evaluation of employees)
Personal liability of managers xxiv, 301–2
Personnel records, employee access; state laws (Appendix G) 348–54
Polygraph testing (*see also* Employee Polygraph Protection Act)
  battery arising from contact with equipment 135–36, 142–43
  false imprisonment 167, 174–75
  fraudulent representation to induce employee to take 39, 58
  infliction of emotional distress 106–8, 221
  invasion of privacy 120, 126–27
  negligent administration 4, 6, 32–34, 220
  state laws (Appendix B) 315–20
Postemployment references (*see* References, postemployment)

Post-termination proceedings (*see also* Unemployment compensation; Workers' compensation)
   defamation suits arising from statements made during 88–91, 236, 238
Practical jokes, battery actions resulting 137–38
Practical suggestions to avoid exposure to tort liability (*see* Preventive measures)
Preemption defense xxiv, 278–81 (*see also* name of specific act)
Pretrial discovery 286–88
Pretrial motions to dismiss and motions for summary judgment 288–89
Preventive measures xxv, 244–70
   avoiding employee detrimental reliance 254–55
   counseling unfit employees 250–52
   defamation 259–61
   disclaimers in recruiting and hiring process 252–54
   harassment of employees 263–65
   invasion of privacy 261–62
   investigations of employee misconduct 257–59
   malicious prosecution and abuse of process 268–69
   references, postemployment 266–68
   releases from employees 266
   screening for unfit applicants 245–50
   supervision of unfit employees 250–52
   termination of unfit employees 250–52
      defamation action arising from 265–66
Privacy (*see* Invasion of privacy)

Privilege as defense to defamation 64–65, 79–81, 227
   preventive measures to minimize tort liability 259–61
Promises by employer (*see* Breach of contract actions; Fraud and misrepresentation)
Proof (*see* Elements of proof)
Psychological problems (*see* Infliction of emotional distress; Medical or mental condition of employee)
Public disclosure of private facts (*see* Invasion of privacy)
Punitive damages xxiii–xxiv, 289–91
   fraud and misrepresentation 40
   infliction of emotional distress 93–94
Purse searches (*see* Searches)

R

Racial insults, infliction of emotional distress 104
Racketeer Influenced and Corrupt Organizations Act (RICO) 187–93, 231
   elements of proof 188
   harassment 206
Railway Labor Act 281
Ratification of employee misconduct 282–83
Recklessness
   defined 93
   liability xx–xxi
Records and reports
   consumer credit reports, state and federal laws (Appendix C) 322–25
   criminal record inquiries, state and federal law (Appendix A) 307–14
   personnel records, employee access; state laws (Appendix G) 348–54

Recruiting (*see* Hiring)
References, postemployment 233–35
   defamation suits arising from xxii, 81–86, 233–34
   interference with contractual relations 149, 151, 162–64, 235
   preventive measures to avoid tort liability 266–68
   settlement agreements 295–96
Rehabilitation Act amendments (*see* Americans with Disabilities Act)
Releases (*see* Consent and release)
Reliance by employees
   detrimental reliance, preventive measures to avoid tort liability 254–55
   false representations, upon 38–67
Reports (*see* Records and reports)
Requests for production of documents 286–88
Resignations of employees
   fraudulent inducement 59–60, 226–27
   terminations converted into 265–66
Respondeat superior doctrine xx, 5, 148, 274, 282–83, 302
Retaliation
   false promises of no retaliation for whistleblowing on supervisors' fraudulent practices 57–58, 220
   malicious prosecution by employer (*see* Malicious prosecution and abuse of process)
Retention of employees
   employee tort actions arising from 231–33
   fraudulent 51–53, 232–33
   negligent (*see* Negligent hiring, retention, and supervision)

RICO (*see* Racketeer Influenced and Corrupt Organizations Act)
Right-to-know laws 146

S

Safety, workplace (*see also* Hazardous substances, exposure to)
   Occupational Safety and Health Act (OSHA) 207
Scope of workplace torts xxii–xxiii
Screening applicants (*see* Hiring)
Searches 118, 120, 129–31, 221–22
Securities filings, defamation suits arising from statements made on forms 88–89
Self-defamation (*see* Defamation)
Settlement of lawsuits 292–97
   agreements 293–97
      confidentiality 295
      legal consideration requirement 294
      nonadmission clause 296
      references, postemployment 295–96
      releases and waivers 294–95
Sex life of employees, invasion of privacy 118–20, 128
Sexual harassment 201–4, 224–25
   assault and battery suits 135, 137–42, 203
   defamation suits arising from employer investigations 70–71, 202, 224–25
   infliction of emotional distress 101–2, 202–3, 218
   invasion of privacy 131–32, 203
   malicious prosecution 203–4
   negligent failure to warn 28–29
   negligent retention of harasser 19–21, 201, 232
   negligent supervision 26–28, 201–2
   RICO civil action against employer 192

Slander (*see* Defamation)
Smoke-free workplace
  infliction of emotional distress 111–12, 207
  negligent failure of employer to provide 4, 6, 31–32, 206
  state and local laws 112, 206
    Appendix F summary 341–47
State and local laws
  AIDS testing (Appendix E) 334–39
  blacklisting (Appendix H) 355–57
  consumer credit reports (Appendix C) 322–24
  criminal record inquiries 16
    Appendix A summary 307–13
  disability laws 209
  drug testing (Appendix D) 326–30
  exposure to toxic substances 207
  invasion of privacy 118–19
  personnel records, employee access (Appendix G) 348–54
  polygraph testing (Appendix B) 315–20
  preemption 281
  right-to-know laws 146
  smoke-free workplace 112, 206
    Appendix F summary 341–47
Strike replacements 38, 49–51
Substance abuse (*see* Alcohol abuse; Drug abuse)
Summary judgment motions 288–89

T

Takeovers 159–60
Termination of employment (*see also* Wrongful discharge)
  converting into resignation 265–66
  defamation cases related to xxii, 65–66, 73–74, 86–88, 227–28
  preventive measures to avoid 265–66
  employees' tort claims arising from 225–31
  false imprisonment actions arising from 230–31
  fraud and misrepresentation 39, 226–27
  infliction of emotional distress 112–17, 228–29
  interference with contractual relations 149, 151–54, 229–30
  invasion of privacy "false light publicity" 229
  RICO actions 231
Terms or conditions of employment showing fraud and misrepresentation 45–51
Testing (*see also* Drug testing; Polygraph testing)
  AIDS testing, state and federal laws (Appendix E) 334–40
  alcohol abuse testing, preventive measures to avoid tort liability 256–57
Theft
  defamation suits arising from employer investigations 69–70
  infliction of emotional distress when employee set up to look like thief 102–3
  investigations giving rise to tort actions 219–20
  malicious prosecution and abuse of process 178–86
  RICO action against employer 190
Threats
  assault and battery 136
  false imprisonment 168, 170–72
  infliction of emotional distress 97–98, 105–6
Title VII xxiii, 114, 128, 276
  criminal record inquiries (Appendix A) 314
Tort, defined xix

Tort law, duty for liability under 6–7
Toxic substances (*see* Hazardous substances)
Transportation
  employer's negligent failure to provide 4, 6, 35–36
    Omnibus Transportation Employees Testing Act (Appendix D) 332
    preventive measures to avoid tort liability at work, functions where alcoholic beverages are served 269
  Transportation Department regulations on drug testing (Appendix D) 331–32
Trials, jury xxiii, 289
Truth as defense to defamation 64

U

Unemployment compensation, defamation suits arising from statements made during proceedings 89, 238
Unintentional torts xxi–xxii (*see also* Negligence)
Unsafe and untrustworthy employees (*see also* Dangerous employees)
  negligent hiring 9–11, 18–19
  negligent retention 19, 23–24, 232
  negligent supervision 24–25

V

Violent employees (*see* Dangerous employees)

W

Waivers, settlement agreements 294–95
Warnings (disciplinary), defamation suits arising from 71–72, 217–18
Warnings (safety), negligent failure to warn of workplace dangers 4, 6, 28, 208–9
Whistleblowers
  attorneys' fees 292, 300 n.86
  false promises of no retaliation 57–58
"Within scope of employment" (*see Respondeat superior* doctrine)
Work assignment 216–19
  fraudulent practice as part of 56–57, 217
  infliction of emotional distress 96–97, 218
  interference with contractual relations 149, 151, 161, 218–19
  threat of assignment giving rise to infliction of emotional distress 97–98
Workers' compensation
  defamation suits arising from statements made during proceedings 90, 238
  exclusive remedy
    assault and battery claims 140–41, 145, 208
    defense for employer 276–77
    false imprisonment claims not barred by 175–76
Workplace environment giving rise to tort actions 201–9 (*see also* specific type of tort action)
Wrongful discharge xxiii, 23 (*see also* Termination of employment)
  defamation cases related to 66
  infliction of emotional distress (*see* Infliction of emotional distress)
Wrongful use of civil proceedings (*see* Malicious prosecution and abuse of process)

About the Authors

Ronald M. Green is a partner in the New York office of Epstein Becker & Green, P.C., with offices in New York; Washington, D.C.; San Francisco; Los Angeles; Dallas; Stamford; Newark; Miami; Tallahassee; Boston; and Alexandria, Virginia.

Richard J. Reibstein is a partner in the New York office of McDermott, Will & Emery, with offices in Boston; Chicago; Los Angeles; Miami; Newport Beach; New York; and Washington, D.C.